Jolyon Laycock

A CHANGING ROLE FOR THE COMPOSER IN SOCIETY

A Study of the Historical Background and Current Methodologies of Creative Music-Making

PETER LANG

Oxford · Bern · Berlin · Bruxelles · Frankfurt am Main · New York · Wien

Bibliographic information published by Die Deutsche Bibliothek
Die Deutsche Bibliothek lists this publication in the Deutsche Nationalbibliografie;
detailed bibliographic data is available on the Internet at ‹http://dnb.ddb.de›.

British Library and Library of Congress Cataloguing-in-Publication Data:
A catalogue record for this book is available from The British Library, Great
Britain, and from The Library of Congress, USA

ISBN 3-03910-277-X
US-ISBN 0-8204-7204-2

© Peter Lang AG, European Academic Publishers, Bern 2005
Hochfeldstrasse 32, Postfach 746, CH-3000 Bern 9, Switzerland
info@peterlang.com, www.peterlang.com, www.peterlang.net

Printed in Germany

To Katherine Anna

Contents

Geographical journey in music; Myth or legend associated with a particular place.

The project timetable; Phase one; Phase two; Mid-project meeting; Phase three; Phase four; The four-phase model in projects of long duration.

The nature of emotional catharsis; The importance of emotional engagement; Barry Russell and the Cardew Ensemble – *Rituals for Orpheus.*

Continuity and project legacy; Musical scores; Project reports and evaluations; Three types of evaluation; Anonymity and confidentiality; Childrens' Music Workshop; Spitalfields Festival education programme; The Association of British Orchestras.

Framing, action and creativity; Classification; The community of learners; Age and ability; Places and people; The four-phase model; Final concerts; The holistic model; Evaluation.

Reconciliation of opposites: The five dichotomies; Examples and case studies; The value of creative music-making: a struggle for recognition; Why is there so much scepticism? What is so special about composers? Defining a new role; Can all this be learned? The need for training; Who will be the advocate? The need for specialised agencies; Where will the money come from? Cultural contact and collaboration through creative music-making.

Preface

When, back in 1963, together with George Self, I started persuading an unruly class of year 9 boys to compose their own music, using, among other things, sawn up chair legs, I never thought that, within forty years this concept, born partly out of desperation, would become standard practice in all areas of education. It was, of course, the introduction of GCSE with its requirement for pupils to compose, that initiated what one might call the 'big bang' of composers going into schools to help students and teachers with this new idea. A good composer is not necessarily a good workshop leader – other social and, indeed, disciplinary skills are needed, and Jolyon Laycock points out firmly the need for training.

I welcome Laycock's book both as an excellent history of this whole process and an examination of its social and philosophical background. It's probably the only major historical and theoretical study of creative music making and composers in education currently available.

I have been involved in creative work with children and grown-ups for over forty years and it is fascinating to read this book and to see the development of the various strands of this area from its very beginnings up to the present. Nowadays there is hardly an orchestra or ensemble which does not work have an education programme. Indeed it is often used as a way to fund concerts.

I have known the author since the mid 1960s. One of the strands in his book is the result of a meeting in a London café where, during a discussion of the various types of projects involving composers working with participants in a project, we devised a way of describing the amount of creativity allowed to the children in my own work. These are the Bedford Categories (page 51). There is no implicit value judgement in the categories – each workshop leader will have his or her preferred way of working based on their own skills and/or philosophy. Britten's *Noyes Fludde*, for example, would come under

Category 1 – interpretation of a fully written score. My *Frameworks*, which is for four school instrumental groups, would be Category 3 – the orchestra plays fully notated music but, on four occasions, is provided with the equivalent of a backing track. A CD of this is taken into four schools and the pupils work out their own music to go above the orchestra. This therefore is an early example of a 'windows' piece.

Creative music making is a rapidly developing field. In the two years since the book was written there have been many new initiatives. Youth Music has initiated a number of new programmes such as Remix and the Song for Youth programme. The PRS Foundation, of which I was the first Chairman and am still one of the Trustees, has taken over and greatly enlarged the work of the PRS Donations Committee's Composer in Education Scheme, and, together with the Society for the Promotion of New Music and Youth Music, has embarked on a huge countrywide 'Sound Inventors' project.

If there is one thing that is certain in the world of music, it is that the concept that everyone is potentially creative has now become widespread. Starting with children and young people in schools where composition is a requirement of the GCSE, the idea has now extended itself into hospitals, prisons, the workplace and even hostels for ex-alcoholics.

Jolyon Laycock's book is a welcome and timely summary of the current situation and its historical origins, and his final part – 'Conclusions, proposals and recommendations' should become required reading for any of us involved in this field.

David Bedford

Acknowledgements

I am grateful to the following for help and support in many different ways: Pauline Allen, Lorenç Barber, Matthew Barley, David Bedford, Robin Benton, Gerard le Berre, Prof. David Blake, Karen Broadbent, Gill Brooke-Taylor, Tabitha Bowers-Broadbent, Ruth Burchmore, Ian Burton, Michel and Elizabeth Camatte, Ian Chance, Bruce Cole, John Cooney, Sue Clifford, Philip Craig, Hywel Davies, Tansy Davies, Vic Ecclestone, Philip Flood, David Francis, Dag Franzen, Jo Glover, Gill Graham, Evelyn Grant, Marilyn Groves, Kimmo Hakola, Christine Harrington, Barbara Hasselbach, Henk Heuvelmans, Ruth Hill, Lindsay Hughes, Brian Humpherson, Dr. John Irving, Nicholas Keyworth, Vesselin Koytchev, Joscelin Laycock, Katherine Laycock, Rachel Leach, Prof. Nicola LeFanu, Karen Lundstrom, Ian McQueen, Alex Manessen, Bob Martens, Philip Meikle, Richard McNicol, Ian Mitchell, Catherine Monk, Dr. Stephen Montague, Clare Nichols, Rachel Pantin, Michel and Maxine Pascal, Prof. John Paynter, Prof. Margarida Pinto do Amaral, Gillian Perkins, Dr. John Pickard, Andrew Potter, Jane Pountney, Barry Russell, Jonathan Scott, Maria van de Sluis, Ivo Stoykov, Prof. Nikolay Stoykov, Kate Stridwick, László Tihanyi, Carole Timms, Fraser Trainer, Kees van Unen, Heidi Vaughan, Prof. Peter Wiegold, Karen Wimhurst, Dr. Julia Winterson, Dr. Trevor Wishart, Jackie Wishart, John Woolrich.

Rainbow over Bath

'Rainbow over Bath' was founded in 1989. The Rainbow was seen as a symbol of unity. At first it stood for unity between the two stakeholder institutions, the University of Bath, and Bath Spa University College, and the seven colours stood for seven strands of music: contemporary, jazz, world, electronic, early, classical and folk. In 1995, I formulated the idea of building musical bridges towards towns twinned with Bath, and later with other cities in several countries in Europe, including Aix en Provence (France), Alkmaar and Zwolle (The Netherlands), Salzburg (Austria), Kaposvár (Hungary), and Plovdiv (Bulgaria).

'Rainbow over Bath', and its successor the Rainbow Foundation, acknowledge the financial support of The Arts Council of England Arts for Everyone Lottery Fund, the European Union Kaleidoscope Fund, the Esmée Fairbairn Foundation, South West Arts, Southern Arts, Bath and North East Somerset District Council, the Paul Hamlyn Foundation, the Joyce Fletcher Charitable Trust, the Holst Foundation, the Hinrichsen Foundation, the Britten-Pears Foundation, the Michael Tippett Foundation, the Performing Right Society Foundation, Green Park Station, Arts Council England South West and the Musicians Union.

Citations and cross references:

All citations use the author-date-page system e.g. (Kodály, 1974: 185). The formula: (page 100) denotes a cross reference within this book. The formula: (rainbow: Track 01) refers to sound recordings on the Rainbow Foundation website: www.rainbowtrack.co.uk.

Introduction

In his address 'Who is a good Musician' to the Budapest Academy in 1953, Zoltàn Kodály challenged his audience of new graduates:

> And what is the aim of all this long and tiring work? To win competitions? To out-shine one's fellow-musicians, to obtain fame and renown? – No. It is the bounden duty of the talented to cultivate their talent to the highest degree, to be of as much use as possible to their fellow men. For every person's worth is measured by how much he can help his fellow men and serve his country. Real art is one of the most powerful forces in the rise of mankind and he who renders it accessible to as many people as possible is a benefactor of humanity (Kodály, 1974: 185).

There are many examples in Britain today of composers working in schools, community centres, hospitals, and other situations which are not 'traditional' contexts for music. Such activities have been identified by many titles such as 'Educational Outreach', 'Community Music', 'Composing in Education', 'Composing in the Community' or 'Performance and Communication Skills', and the movement is supported on a sound basis of academic research. For the purposes of discussion I group these activities together under the generic title of 'creative music-making'.

Music is unique amongst the arts in its ability to bring together large numbers of people in a communal creative process which transcends linguistic barriers. In creative music projects at both school and community level, it is the personality, commitment and leadership qualities of the project-director which are the true keys to success, rather than the adherence to any particular methodology. It is only under such leadership that the individual participants in a creative music project can themselves achieve the level of commitment, teamwork and emotional engagement, leading to final cathartic experience, which are the hallmarks of a successful project, and without which its full educational and social value cannot be truly realised.

The European Commission has stated its belief that: 'Culture is able to strengthen social cohesion, especially in vulnerable areas or marginalised groups of the population. Culture, through cultural exchange and dialogue, consolidates peace – one of the primary goals of European integration'. It concludes that 'cultural creation should therefore be made a priority' (European Commission, 1998b: 10).

The phrase 'Creative music-making' is very general in its meaning, referring not to any particular kind of musical activity but, rather, to an approach applicable to a great many or, perhaps, to all forms of musical activity. There is a body of British expertise established by theory and practice over several decades which is distinct from any wider European tradition. This can form the basis of models applicable in other countries in Europe.

Composers and musicians possessing the right kind of leadership qualities, as well as experience and knowledge of the tradition of creative music-making developed in Britain, have a particular role to play in this process of European cultural integration. The achievement of such integration, though ambitious, must be seen as only one step towards a much wider aim of international cultural understanding.

Frames of reference

This book sets out to answer a number of questions. What are the origins of creative music-making? What are its essential features? How can the various methodologies be categorised? Are there features which link them as a unified movement? Are there demonstrable and long-lasting cultural and social benefits in the development of musical creativity? How important are personal qualities of leadership among workshop leaders, and how can they be defined?

Do similar activities take place in other European countries, and if so, do they derive from the same origins? What possibilities exist for their introduction and propagation within Europe? Is the model especially applicable in Europe? What long-lasting value can be derived from a sharing of expertise? How can Creative Music programmes support the process of European cultural integration? Is such integration a desirable goal in itself, or should it be seen as part of a move towards greater understanding and sharing of culture in a world-wide context? Is it possible to define what is meant by European culture, or is the concept of European cultural integration meaningless?

Objectives

The book has the following four principal objectives:

1. To trace the historical origins of creative music-making.
2. To formulate a theoretical model to support the categorisation and evaluation of projects.
3. To examine critically some present-day manifestations and to assess their potential as models for creative activity in music which can play a part in the development of European cultural identity.
4. To create a compilation of philosophies, methodologies and case-studies which can be used as a resource to help composers, musicians, arts organisers, teachers and others to develop their own creative music projects.

Research sources

It is based on the following areas of research:

1. Historical: Study of the origins of creative music making through books, reports and other documentation.
2. Personal: My own experience as composer, leader or co-ordinator of creative music projects.
3. Action-based: My observations of the work of composers leading or participating in projects in the UK and Europe which I organised as Programme Director of 'Rainbow over

Bath'. All projects were fully documented with written evaluations, sound recordings and photographs.
4. Consultative: The views of composers and project organisers, collected in interviews or conversations, or in response to printed questionnaires. A record of all conversations was kept in the form of journal entries.
5. Observational: My own personal visits to observe projects undertaken by a wide variety of other arts organisations in the UK and Europe. Records of all visits were kept in the form of journal entries, sound recordings and photographs.
6. Documentary: Study of reports, printed documentation and web-sites of a wide range of organisations and projects in the UK, Europe and other parts of the world.

The list of composers and projects which I studied is long, but not exhaustive. It was compiled from the following sources:

1. My own personal knowledge of the field, based on twenty-five years of experience.
2. Project reports and evaluations from organisations such as the Performing Right Society, the Arts Council of England, the Association of British Orchestras and the European Commission.
3. Responses from composers and project organisers to articles and announcements in the following music periodicals: Classical Music, NewNotes (The newsletter of the Society for the Promotion of New Music), Sounding Board (The journal of 'Sound Sense', community music organisation) and Agenda (The newsletter of the Gaudeamus Foundation, Amsterdam).

Exceptions

I have said that 'creative music-making', is not widely practised in other parts of Europe. My conversations with composers and promoters from outside the UK indicate that, with certain exceptions, 'creative music-making' is regarded as a British specialism. But lack of evidence is not evidence of a lack. It is possible, and even probable, that there are a vast number of significant examples of creative music projects taking place in other countries, but if there are, I have not yet discovered them. Their discussion must await a more exhaustive and wide-ranging study. However the exceptions are notable ones, and they make significant contributions to my argument.

In studying manifestations of creative music-making outside the UK, my research was limited to the following:

1. Critical assessments of how specific organisations in different countries responded to music projects organised by 'Rainbow over Bath'.
2. Examination of the direct impact of British methodologies on organisations outside the UK.
3. Studies of a small number of composers and organisations outside the UK whose work seems to represent parallel developments.

The methodologies of creative music-making overlap significantly with those of music therapy. Some of the composers discussed in my book regard the application of their creative and leadership skills to music therapy as a legitimate and important extension of their social roles. I acknowledge that creative music-making and music therapy share some aspects of methodology, but discussion of specific clinical applications is beyond the scope of my book.

The value of creative music-making

The notion that there is intrinsic value in human artistic creativity is compellingly valid. Most of the composers and theorists cited in my book agree that the musical urge is potentially present in all of us and that, whatever other forms of artistic self-expression we may use, music is a common language for all of us. I put forward three arguments during the course of my book: firstly, that artistic self-expression is an essential element of human behaviour, secondly, that artistic self-expression through music, as distinct from other art forms, has a special social role and, thirdly, that self-expression through music which involves individual creativity in the form of original composition is of greater value than musical activity which is essentially re-creative.

Some commentators have drawn attention to the dwindling audiences for certain types of contemporary and classical music (Small, 1977: 168). They conclude that we are witnessing the dying throes of a musical culture. They see the vigorous efforts to educate new young audiences as nothing more than the desperate attempts of a dwindling community of devotees to keep it alive. Justifications such as 'educational projects help to create new audiences for the future' no longer carry any conviction, if indeed they ever did. Such views engender a mood of deep pessimism, but they are an expression – albeit an extreme one – of well-founded fears about the future of cultural and artistic values in contemporary society.

The priorities of the European Union Agenda 2000 include cultural diversity, creativity, and the importance of regional and folklore cultures. These are presumed to be threatened by the alienation and marginalisation of minority groups, and by growing conformity as a result of unification and the influence of global mass-media (European Commission, 1998b: 3–4). All these pre-occupations find pre-echoes in the ideological thinking of Zoltan Kodály, but are re-echoed in the more recent 'Culture 2000' proposals from the European Commission. Kodály thought in terms of the benefits to the culture of his own country. Now there is a wider geographical imperative for Europe as a whole.

The Communication from the European Commission to the European Parliament, the Council of Ministers and Committee of Regions entitled *First European Community Framework Programme in Support of Culture* sets out the aims and objectives of 'Culture 2000'. It talks of 'the need to assert and respect cultural identity' and declares that 'The EC [...] is determined to ensure respect for cultural diversity'. It finds that 'In the community there is too little awareness of the cultures which make up Europe [...]', but that 'Culture is increasingly emerging as a driving force in society, a source of vitality, dynamism and social development. Cultural creation should therefore be made a priority' (European Commission, 1998b: 10).

My study proposes models for collaboration between organisations in European cities. Some of these have been tested and subjected to practical application by 'Rainbow over Bath'. These models conform to the 'holistic principle' defined in the Arts Council of England consultative document *Creating New Notes* (Gowrie, 1996) which in turn influenced the drafting of the New Lottery Guidelines for the 'Arts for Everyone Scheme' in 1997.

The 'holistic principle' advocates that, when public funds are used to support the work of living composers, the works produced should form part of a wider project in which creative involvement of musicians in rehearsals, performances and recordings, and the organisation of related educational and community activities play an integral part. The over-riding aim of such projects should be to inspire and develop musical knowledge, understanding and creativity amongst a wide range of people.

Arts organisations throughout Europe, therefore have the opportunity of becoming a key players in a process of European cultural development of extraordinary importance. Social and cultural contact between people of different nationalities is imperative. If we apply the 'holistic principle' to international touring by contemporary music ensembles, it becomes clear why it is not enough to fly in, give a concert, then fly out again. Projects organised as part of 'Rainbow across Europe' were an example of music's power to cross national and linguistic boundaries and to bring people together in a communal aesthetic experience which celebrates a common humanity and can help to bring about a European cultural identity.

Part 1
Background

Chapter 1
Historical background

The twentieth century witnessed a development from the nineteenth century Romantic view of the 'heroic' composer, creating music as an expression of his own inner emotional life, towards a more socially conscious and less self-obsessed idea of an inspirational catalyst whose role is to stimulate musical creativity in others.

Several philosophical and political strands run throughout the period. Socialist-inspired philosophies, engendering a belief in the rights of all people to have access to creative artistic experience, and a fascination with eastern forms of religion have both helped to shape the movement. Some composers have allied themselves to particular political movements. Others have adopted a more personal philosophical stance, or combined elements of the two. Above all, the importance of inspirational leadership is a recurrent theme.

The origins of creative music-making in Britain

Gustav Holst

No discussion of the development of creative music-making can begin without mention of Gustav Holst. Socialism was central to his personal philosophy. It was the inspiration for his commitment to educational and community music since he first heard lectures by George Bernard Shaw and William Morris soon after he joined the Royal College of Music in May 1893.

Holst's career as a teacher began in 1904 when he was appointed music master at James Allen's Girls' School, West Dulwich. By 1907 we find him teaching evening classes at Morley College for Working

Men and Women (founded September 1889 by Emma Cons 'to help the poorer classes by providing entertainment dissociated from the customary evils of alcohol'). With Holst as Director, the College acquired a reputation as a centre for adult music-making. Imogen Holst called it 'A sort of heaven we go to on Mondays and Wednesdays' (Holst, 1938; cited in Short, 1990: 69).

In 1917, Holst was appointed YMCA Music Organiser for the internment camps 'to develop musical activities in YMCA huts throughout the field of war' (Short, 1990: 168). His work in Salonica, Bulgaria and Constantinople pre-figures that of Nigel Osborne's team in Bosnia, and of American Laura Hassler's 'Musicians Without Borders' project in Kosovo eighty years later.

Holst later retreated from a thorough-going socialist viewpoint. In a letter to Vaughan Williams in 1926 about the General Strike he wrote: 'I find I am a hopeless half-hogger and am prepared to sit on the fence for as long as possible'. Prefiguring later composers' interest in eastern forms of religion he went on to say that he believed in the Hindu doctrine of Dharma, 'which is one's path in life' (Holst, 1959; cited in Short, 1990: 30). 'Holst therefore concentrated on musical work, leaving politics to the more militant members of the Hammersmith Socialist Society' (Short, 1990: 30).

Diane Lucas pays tribute to Holst's qualities of inspirational leadership in her 1921 biography: 'He was so kind and full of deep feeling that he improved everyone who knew him' (Lucas, 1921; cited in Short, 1990: 59). Holst himself likened the role of a composition teacher to that of a medieval craftsman:

> In the middle ages a great painter had several pupils working in close comradeship with him in his studio. This is one of the best ways of fostering the artistic impulse and the power of artistic expression. And one of its best features is the continual comradeship with the master. This ensures education in the deeper sense: the unfolding of the pupil's mind – largely unconsciously (Lucas, 1921; cited in Short, 1990: 179).

Holst followed no rigid methods, but insisted that his pupils' compositions should be practical, an approach which anticipates the similar views of John Paynter. They should write for amateurs as well as professionals, organising ad hoc ensembles to give performances, developing musical technique through direct practical experience. He emphasised the importance of the pupils' inner resources, telling W. Probert-Jones 'If you have no ideas, I can't do anything for you; I can only bring out what is already inside, I cannot put music into you' (Probert-Jones, 1935; cited in Short, 1990: 189).

As Music Director of Morley College in 1907, Holst became one of the first in a long line of 'composers-in-education'. Harold Nicolson pays tribute to Holst's influence in his introduction to Denis Richards' book about the College's history, writing of '[…] the good fortune that, in Gustav Holst, the College obtained the guidance and inspiration of a teacher of genius who encouraged the passion for music which has always been one of its most distinctive and admirable characteristics' (Nicolson; quoted in Richards, 1958: xviii).

A list of music directors and composers associated with Morley College reads like a role call of the most revered British composers. Michael Tippett, Ralph Vaughan Williams, Peter Racine Fricker, Benjamin Britten, Matyas Seiber, Ian Hamilton, John Gardner, Anthony Milner, Michael Graubart, Cornelius Cardew, Nicola LeFanu, and Barry Anderson have all passed through its doors at some time in their careers.

Michael Tippett

Michael Tippett took over from Arnold Foster as Music Director at the outbreak of war. It is well known that his pacifist views led to a period of imprisonment. His report on the International Workers' Music Olympiad in Strasbourg, printed in the *Comradeship and Wheatsheaf* (the journal of the Royal Arsenal Co-operative Society, 1935), reveals his early involvement with the Communist Party and the origins of his humanitarian ideals. He refers to the workers' choirs which appeared at the congress, of which 'very many consisted of unemployed people from mass unemployment regions' (Tippett, 1980: 34).

As a choral conductor associated with this 'working class movement', he encouraged choirs to sing 'political songs' of the type pioneered by Hans Eisler. The oratorio *A Child of our Time* (Tippett, 1941) celebrates humanitarian ideals and was written for amateur choirs, using so-called Negro Spirituals as a more contemporary musical vernacular to substitute for the Lutheran Chorales of the Bach cantatas. In his writings on the aesthetics and philosophy of music, Tippett probed deeply into the question of the composer's role in society.

Benjamin Britten

It was through the influence of Tippett that Britten found an early platform at Morley College. Britten's role as a composer-in-education is well documented, but it is important to be clear about his longer-lasting influence. Britten's works for young people fall into a category, which I will discuss later, of works written for young people and amateurs to perform. They are part of a tradition still carried on today by organisations such as 'Contemporary Music-Making for Amateurs' (COMA), the 'Composing for Kids' (C4K) project of the Society for the Promotion of New Music (SPNM), and Chamber Music 2000. *The Little Sweep* (1949) and *Noyes Flood* (1958), with their audience participation (congregational hymns) and incorporation of parts for a wide range of musical ability, became the model for many later works, although there is no suggestion that anyone but Britten should do the composing.

The European contribution

Zoltán Kodály

As well as producing an enormous body of fine music, Kodály dedicated himself tirelessly to his efforts to ensure the future of musical culture in his own country, chiefly through the establishment of a teaching method for schools. He wanted to 'make the masterpieces of world (musical) literature public property, to convey them to people of every kind and rank' (Kodály, 1974: 160).

It is well known how much emphasis Kodály placed on the heritage of Hungarian folk music as a means of developing musical awareness. The widespread adoption of Kodály's method in Hungary and other neighbouring former-communist countries has led to an impressively high level of musical literacy among ordinary people. His ideas exercised a profound influence also on British music education: 'All my activity, musical or other, was devoted entirely to my country. It was for me an unexpected pleasure and satisfaction that my work found so many friends abroad, especially in English speaking countries' (Kodály; cited in Tippett, 1980: 110).

The words of Kodály's address 'Who is a Good Musician' to the Budapest Academy (p.15) resonate down the years as a challenge to all musicians and composers but, writing later in 'Music of the Angels', Michael Tippett points to what he sees as the dilemma of Kodály's position and, by inference, the dilemma of all composers who believe it is their duty to devote a large proportion of their energies to educational and community work:

> Kodály, far more absorbed in educational work than either Bartok or Vaughan Williams, dissipated too much of his creative vitality. By the end, he was indeed beloved of his countrymen for giving such genuine attention to their musical well-being. But he paid the price for all this as a composer (Tippett, 1980: 110).

Kodály stands as the model of a composer who is prepared to suppress his own egotistical desires for fame and fortune as a 'great composer' to direct his energies towards the greater good of his fellow man and the culture to which all belong. His ideas carry, for all countries and continents, a universal message which is as relevant now within Europe, as it grows towards political and economic union, as it was in Hungary during the early part of the twentieth century.

Carl Orff

Carl Orff was strongly influenced by the teachings of Jacques Dalcroze whose theory of 'Eurhythmics' formed the basis of music education in many countries in Europe during the early years of the twentieth century. By developing a regimen of physical movement in time with music, he sought to internalise musical feelings and emotions by giving them a direct physical expression. He believed that musical expression could be available to all children and that the primary aim of musical education should be the production of musically developed people, not just of instrumentalists and singers.

The starting point for Orff's work with Dorothée Gunther, beginning with the formation of the Gunther School in August 1923, is summed up by Orff's resonant sound-byte credo: 'In the beginning was the drum.' Orff's message was simple: 'The drum induces dance. Dance has the closest relationship to music. My idea and the task I had set myself was a regeneration of music through movement, through dance' (Orff, 1976: 17).

He too emphasised the importance of inspirational leadership, a quality which he admitted was not to be found in all teachers:

> Spontaneous teaching that comes from improvisation is, and remains, an excellent starting point. Experience has nevertheless shown that not everyone is capable of teaching in this way; it can therefore not be expected from everyone (Orff, 1976: 131).

His method has frequently been criticised as over-prescriptive. However, his autobiography expresses frustration, following the publication of 'Orff-Schulwerk – Elementare Musikubung' from 1930 to 1934 which contained over two hundred and fifty written-out musical examples. Orff complained that people tended to rehearse and play them as written, instead of using them as inspirational guides to improvisation: 'It is not the playing from notation but the free making of music in improvisation that is meant and demanded, for which the printed examples give information and stimulus' (Orff, 1976: 131).

Socialism was a significant influence on Orff during his earlier years, in spite of his subsequent, and not unfounded reputation as a Nazi sympathiser. In 1932, Orff met Eberhard Preussner, Director of the Music Department of Central Institute for Education and Training in Berlin. In turn Preussner introduced Orff's work to the highly influential Leo Kestenberg, Principal of the Central Institute for Education and Training in Berlin. In his autobiography, Orff quotes Preussner's eulogy of Kestenberg on the occasion of his 70th birthday:

> Through his Socialist Party he had an influential position in the Ministry of Culture. The way he administered his office was not for the good of the party, but for the general good. Even his political opponents had then to recognise, and must do so even more today, that Kestenberg conceived his post as a real mission. He instigated a reform of music education that outlasted the times and the political parties. Never has there been a minister in charge of music that had such significance (Preussner, 1952; cited in Orff, 1978: 202).

Kestenberg immediately invited Orff to give courses to music teachers from selected Berlin schools, but the rise of Hitler had a decisive, and, for a time, destructive effect on the work. In 1933 the political climate changed. Kerstenberg was relieved of his post, and left Germany. Preussner remained in Berlin till 1939 when he was appointed director of the Mozarteum in Salzburg.

The accusations against Orff as a Nazi collaborator date from 1934 when, although some of his work was banned or subjected to ideological 'correction', he was asked to compose music for the Berlin Olympics, to form part of the opening celebrations, with dance inspired by the style of the Dorothée Gunther School. The result was *Einzug und Reigen der Kinder und Mädchen*. Orff protests that his collaboration with this festival did not represent a capitulation to Nazism and the Third Reich:

> Only when Diem (Carl Diem, General Secretary of the 1936 Olympic Games in Berlin) assured me that the festival was an international Olympic occasion that allowed no kind of political bias did I agree to his request and only then if the contract came directly from the Olympic committee (Orff, 1978: 207).

Orff's reputation at least survived after the war, and the influence of Preussner, still in position as Director of the Mozarteum in Salzburg, led to the establishment in October 1963 of the Orff Institute at Schloss Frohnburg, Salzburg, where it is still situated today. Orff's ideas have not been immune to the ravages of progress, and although the name 'Orff Institute' is still emblazoned above the main entrance to the building, his influence is relegated almost to an after-thought in

31

the department's present title of 'Universität Mozarteum Salzburg, Department XI Music and Dance Pedagogy (Orff Institute)'.

The department is currently undergoing a radical re-think. However, the curriculum still adheres to the central principle of the teaching of Orff and Gunther, that music, dance and stage presentation should develop together in equal creative partnership. Graduates of the School achieve a remarkable all-round facility as composers, instrumentalists, choreographers, dancers and stage designers.

The influence of Carl Orff is still alive in the many Orff Societies which have sprung up all over the world. This movement propagates the orthodox interpretation of his ideas, not the radicalised versions developed by the Mozarteum. John Paynter's collaborative book with his wife Elizabeth *The Dance and the Drum* (1974) hints at some influence of Gunther and Orff. No primary school in the UK is immune to their legacy, expressed not through musical ideas but through the collection of classroom percussion instruments based on the simple designs developed by Orff for his 'Instrumentarium'.

One small aspect of the Orff method which still forms part of creative music making grew out of the realisation that conducting was a form of dance:

> The conducting exercises that arose [...] had little to do with the usual conducting of music that is written down and supplied to both players and conductor [...]. It was the forming of an improvisation through gesture (Orff, 1978: 74).

Such techniques have been re-invented many times since, by the 'Instant Composers Pool' of Dutch improvising musician, Mischa Mengelberg, and by composers and workshop leaders in Britain such as Peter Wiegold and Sean Gregory.

In his autobiography, Orff describes the collaborative process which took place during the creation of performances by the group of dancers and musicians formed in the early 1930s and based on the principles of his work with Dorothée Gunther:

> Group dances with their own rules of form and their inherent dynamics usually came before the music, according to the ideas of the choreographer; the music grew stepwise as the dance composition unfolded, forming a unity together. The sustaining melody and characteristic accompanying parts, as well as purely

rhythmic dance accompaniments with all possible gradations of colour, formed the foundation in sound of the dance. To this individual members of the group often contributed ideas that were tried out and evaluated by everyone together (Orff, 1978: 150).

Example 1: Keetman, G. (1930) Extract from *Bolero* bars 141–148.

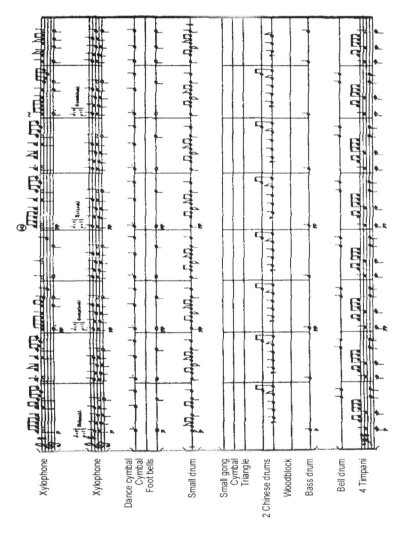

The closing bars of Keetman's *Bolero* typify the group's use of ostinato, an approach which has influenced the riff-building techniques of Peter Wiegold and Sean Gregory (Example 1). The collaborative and improvisational nature of this process revolutionised the traditional relationship between composer and choreographer. Orff's biography lists press quotations as evidence of performances by the Gunther Dance Group in Berlin, Dresden, Vienna, Paris, Köln and Hamburg. Intriguingly, one of them, dated 20 July 1930, is from the New York *Herald*: '[...] Gunild Keetman's attractive music – here is an actual example that shows that percussion music can mean something other than deafening noise [...]' (Orff, 1978: 198). Does this imply that, like many other artistic and cultural influences which crossed the Atlantic from Germany at this time, the group's influence spread to the USA? The combination of percussion and dance developed by Orff and Gunther anticipates, by some seven years, John Cage's first percussion scores for the Modern Dance Group at UCLA in 1937.

The influence of American Experimental music

John Cage

Many who have worked alongside John Cage have paid tribute to his qualities of inspirational leadership. Peter Wiegold who took part in the Gulbenkian Music and Dance Summer School with Cage and Cunningham in 1986, has described Cage's ability to give unspoken permission for a particular creative solution, or silently to indicate disapproval of another. In *The community education work of orchestras and opera companies – principles, practice and problems*, Julia Winterson comments on Cage's involvement in an educational project during the 1998 Huddersfield Contemporary Music Festival: 'Cage's charismatic presence on the final day was inspirational. He was very generous with his time and the comments he made on their work were incisive, encouraging and critical in equal measure' (Winterson, 1998: 11).

It is my subjective view, based on personal experience, that, in spite of Cage's philosophy of non-involvement, there was a marked difference between performances of his music on which the composer's influence was evident, and those in which it was not. Performances of *Variations V* (Cage, 1968) which I attended at the Saville Theatre in London in 1968 seemed to carry a kind of authenticity, an apparent contradiction of Cage's own philosophy, although it was undoubtedly the excruciatingly high volume level of the sound system which provoked Christopher Small's remarks that:

> [...] the simple refusal to make a value judgement, the unquestioning acceptance of any sound that happens along (which obliges us, it must be said, to accept at times some pretty excruciating sounds), is based on perhaps too facile an interpretation of Zen doctrines in art (Small, 1977: 149).

Views differ about the inspirational qualities of Cage's teaching approach. The silences in which Wiegold thought he detected 'permission' or 'disapproval' suggest the influence of Zen Bhuddism. The Zen use of the 'koan' or anecdotal riddle, the contemplation of which can lead to enlightenment, brought Cage to the invention of his own anecdotes which often have the effect of obscuring rather than clarifying any message which may lie behind them. At the centre of the Zen philosophy there is a contradiction which must be faced, or rather not faced, by all students of Zen. You cannot achieve enlightenment by the exercise of your will, but rather by denying it – like trying deliberately not to think about something or other.

In his book *Experimental Music – Cage and Beyond* Michael Nyman describes how Cage, Earle Brown, Morton Feldman, and Christian Wolf found different routes towards a common goal of 'will-less-ness'. Cage emphasised the importance of disengaging music from any kind of associative meaning: 'one may give up the desire to control sound, clear his mind of music, and set about discovering means to let sounds be themselves rather than vehicles for man-made theories or expressions of human sentiments' (Cage, 1957; cited in Cage, 1967: 10). Nyman refers to: 'The self-effacing unwillingness of experimental music to draw attention to itself' (Nyman, 1999: 36). In retrospect we can see that Cage's pursuit of 'will-less-ness', and his abdication of responsibility for the musical result, was a necessary step in the direction of a changed role for the composer which is implied in Cardew's wish to emphasise the collective nature of creativity.

As Cage said: 'when silence, generally speaking, is not in evidence, the will of the composer is' (Cage; cited in Nyman, 1999: 60). This makes the silent piece *4'33"* the supreme example of abdication of the composer's will. In this case, the composer has written nothing at all, but defined a time frame during which this 'nothing' takes place. The division of *4'33"* into three movements invites comparison with the classical sonata. As well as being a philosophical statement about the 'will-less-ness' of the composer, or about the idea that there is no such thing as silence, it is also designed to shock and perplex by deliberately parodying what Chris Small calls 'the small rituals of the concert hall' (Small, 1977: 25).

Fluxus

Cage's ideas had a profound influence on the group of young New York composers who enrolled in his New School of Social Research (1960), later dubbing themselves the 'Fluxus' Group. Fluxus became a byword for absurdist events using, or deliberately flouting, those 'small rituals' of the concert hall. 'Bring a bale of hay and a bucket of water onto the stage for the piano to eat and drink' (*Piano Piece for David Tudor no.1*), 'Build a fire in front of the audience' (*Composition 1960 no.2*) and 'The performers (any number) sit on the stage watching and listening to the audience in the same way the audience usually looks at and listens to performers' (*Composition 1960 no.6*), are all instructions to be found in text pieces from La Monte Young's 'Fluxus' period.

An important feature of Young's text pieces is that they require no musical ability in either composition or performance. They are important forerunners of the idea that 'anyone can write music'. An advert for a Fluxus concert in the Village Voice of 23 September 1965 declares:

The minimalism of La Monte *Young's Composition 1960 no.7*, in
which the notes B and F# are 'to be held for a long time' initiated a
genre which retains its influence on creative music making to the
present day. Terry Riley's *In C*, which seemed so shockingly radical
to hard-line avant-gardists and twelve-tone serialists in 1964, now
appears on the COMA data-base amongst 'Works with flexible
scoring'. The simplicity of conception of Steve Reich's *Clapping
Music* (1971) and *Music for Pieces of Wood* (1973), requiring no
specific instrumental skill, just an ability to count accurately, keep in
time, and keep up with the intricacies of an arithmetical process, has
ensured that these pieces continue to be used in music workshops.

Creative music-making in Britain after 1960

Cornelius Cardew

Cornelius Cardew was the crucial link by which the ideas of American
experimental music, in particular of Cage, Christian Wolff, and La
Monte Young, found their way into Britain. Morton Feldman predicted Cardew's impact in a famous pronouncement:

> Any direction modern music will take in England will come about only through
> Cardew, because of him, by way of him. If the new ideas in music are felt today
> as a movement in England, it's because he acts as a moral force, a moral centre
> (Feldman; cited in Nyman, 1999: 115).

The phrase 'unskilled instrumentalists' is crucial to the influence
of Fluxus on Cardew. According to Nyman, Cardew always conceived
of notation not as an end in itself or a means of unlocking sounds 'but
as a way of engaging the most valuable resource of any music –

people' (Nyman, 1999: 115). Cardew's works from 1960 follow in a logical progression towards a certain goal. *Autumn 60* and *Octet 61* require an act of composition on the part of performers who have to acquaint themselves with the musical principles underlying the work, investigate the range of possibilities opened up by the score, and finally accept the responsibility for their musical contribution to the piece.

Treatise (1963–1967) is totally graphic, and thus a further step away from notations which are only available to trained musicians. Graphic notation has become a much tried method of unlocking musical creativity and allowing people who have no knowledge of written notation to experience some of the excitement of musical creation without having to spend time and effort mastering the complexities of staff notation. John Paynter explored its potential in *Sound and Silence*: 'In recent years composers have been finding the traditional notation inadequate: they are evolving new systems, many of which use graphic symbols'. He argued that by using these new graphic techniques, children could write down the sounds they imagined in their heads in a more direct way:

> If children want to write their music down that may be the moment to teach some of the conventions; but guard against the danger of killing the music's spontaneity. It might be better to let children invent their own notation or to adapt the conventions in some way (Paynter/Aston, 1970: 14).

However, Cardew seems to have rejected *Treatise* as a means of involving musical innocents. The classic early recorded performances of *Treatise* were made by the group AMM who could hardly be described as 'musical innocents'. Eddie Prevost, Lou Gare, Keith Rowe, and Cardew himself brought to these performances their own musical experience and sophistication as improvisers, composers or jazz musicians.

Schooltime Compositions (1968) – also called 'an Opera Book' – came closer to the ideal of integrating, in the same project, musically skilled and unskilled people. Cardew redefines 'opera' as 'many people working'. The work belongs to the same music-theatre genre as Cage's *Musicircus*. The title hints at the possibility of an educational application for the piece. Cardew made the cover page of the published score look like a school exercise book with his own name scrawled in red ink. Was it ever performed by school children? Probably not. Did Cardew intend it to be used in that way? Did he imply that it required child-like qualities of playfulness and lack of inhibitions of a child, or that it was like something which had been made in school? My questions to him on this point at the time elicited an evasive response: '*Schooltime Compositions* is the sort of thing where what you get out of it depends on what you put in'. The use of cryptic remarks of this kind was, in my experience, an affectation adopted by many who, at this time, regarded themselves as 'disciples' of Cage.

Example 2: Cardew, C. (1968) *Schooltime Compositions* cover.

The *Great Learning*, originally titled *The Great Digest* until Cardew's self-critical revision of his work which took place around 1971, was strongly influenced by Christian Wolff's *Prose Collection*

(Wolff, 1968) written for English musicians during a stay in England in 1968. *Prose Collection* uses verbal instructions only, leaving a lot to the discretion of the player. It is designed for people 'who don't necessarily have a musical education'.

Cardew's *Great Learning* is a set of simple instructions using texts by Confucius which can be performed by a large group of people with no musical training. Typical is the scoring of Paragraph 7. The only equipment the performers need is their own voices. The text is broken up into short phrases. Performers intone pianissimo each phrase a given number of times, moving through the material at their own speed, an idea borrowed from Morton Feldman's 'people processes'. They start on any note they wish, but then change to a note they can hear another person singing. The resultant mass of slowly changing choral aggregates gradually coalesces onto one or two unison notes.

Cardew's involvement with the Communist Party, and later the Workers Revolutionary Party, is well known. But his influential Morley College evening classes in Experimental Music during the late 1960s and early 1970s pre-date his Maoist/Leninist conversion. Even then Socialist principles of equality, and a belief that musical creativity was a universal human ability and that access to it was a fundamental human right, were central to his philosophy. His acceptance of Confucianism at this time echoes strangely Cage's pre-occupation with Zen. Confucianism advocates 'correct behaviour' which grows out of 'ethical purity of inner thought'. The texts of *The Great Digest* are concerned with 'the development of an unassailable moral authority which Confucius locates *inside...* These texts express the (idealist) view that once you have set your own house in order all will automatically be well with society' (Nyman, 1999: 122).

The Scratch Orchestra

In 1969 Cardew with a nucleus of his Morley College students, and participants in the ICA *Schooltime Compositions* performance, formed the Scratch Orchestra based on the idea of collectivised creativity as summed up by Cardew:

40

Art, instead of being an object made by one person, is a process set in motion by a group of people. Art's socialised. It isn't someone saying something, but people doing things, giving everyone (including those involved) the opportunity to have experiences they wouldn't otherwise have had (Cardew; cited in Nyman, 1999: 131).

To some extent the Scratch Orchestra took its inspiration from Frederick Rzewski's Sound Pool. Rzewski's view that 'the act of music-making is self-exploration within and of a collective' was embodied in the European group Musica Eletronnica Viva. Sound Pool grew out of MEV's experimental work in the streets and piazzas of Rome and Venice in 1968. Such ideas are still alive today in the street parades of Vinko Globokar, Lorenç Barber's 'Urban Land-scapes', and the site-specific projects of Stephen Montague. Rzewski expressed his view of the universality of musical creativity as follows:

We are all 'musicians'. We are all 'creators'. Music is a creative process in which we can all share, and the closer we come to each other in the process, abandoning esoteric categories and professional elitism, the closer we can come to the ancient idea of music as a universal language (Rzewski; cited in Nyman, 1999: 130).

In 1968, Rzewski described a new function for the composer:

He is no longer the mythical star, elevated to a sham glory and authority, but rather an unseen worker, using his skill to help others less prepared than he to experience the miracle, to become great artists in a few minutes [...]. His role is that of organiser and redistributor of energies: he draws upon the raw human resources at hand and reshapes them, combining loose random threads of sound into a solid web on which the unskilled person is able to stand, and then take flight (Rzewski; cited in Nyman, 1999: 130).

The Scratch Orchestra, in its 'draft constitution' published in the June 1969 edition of *The Musical Times*, is described as: 'A large number of enthusiasts pooling their resources (not primarily material resources) and assembling for action (music-making, performance, edification)' (Cardew, 1969).

The Scratch Orchestra embodied the important idealistic notion that no one member had priority rights. There was no overall director. Each member of the orchestra in rotation had the opportunity to design a concert. Concerts took place in a wide variety of places, even on trains as in Harvey Matuso's ICES Festival (International Carnival of Experimental Sound). A Scratch Concert came close to Cage's concept of *Musicircus* except that the Scratch Orchestra consisted, ideally at least, of regular concerts given by a frequently meeting large experimental ensemble. The Scratch Orchestra therefore can be seen as one of the earliest examples of 'community music'. The constitution defined five basic repertory categories, some of them prophetic of later developments in Creative Music Making. Clause 1 anticipates Peter Wiegold's technique of group improvisation through a process of 'riff-building':

> Clause 1 – 'Scratch Music': Each member has available a number of accompaniments preferably sustainable continuously for indefinite periods, allowing a solo to be heard as such if one should arise.

Clause 2 resembles the approach of the Portsmouth Sinfonia during the early 1970s:

> Clause 2 – 'Popular Classics': Works familiar to several members only qualify for this category. One member plays a particle and the rest join in as best they can, playing along, contributing whatever they can recall of the piece in question, filling the gaps of memory with improvised variational material.

Clause 3 looks back to La Monte Young's text pieces:

> Clause 3 – 'Improvisation Rites': Initiated by 'short mainly verbal instructions'.

Clause 4 anticipates the mission of COMA with its emphasis on compositions playable by a range of amateur or unskilled musicians:

> Clause 4 – 'Compositions': '[...] either established experimental classics or specially written works by members, the basic requirements being brevity and a simple form of notation capable of being understood by both musicians and non-musicians'.

Clause 5 was concerned with 'Research projects – research into new methodologies' (Cardew, 1969; cited in Nyman, 1999: 132). For some Orchestra members 'research' meant exclusively study of music-workshop techniques used in Mao-ist China during the Cultural

42

Revolution. As a result, the influence of the Scratch Orchestra exceeded its ability to survive. After only three years, it was torn apart by disagreements between members of the Mao-Leninist Ideology Group led by John Tilbury, Keith Rowe and Cardew on one hand, and a less doctrinaire group of avant-gardists and experimentalists including Hugh Shrapnel, Michael Parsons and Howard Skempton on the other. Rod Eley charts the rise and fall of this remarkable and innovative project in *Stockhausen Serves Imperialism* (Cardew et al., 1974: 11–32).

Cardew's political philosophy

Cardew's adoption of extreme left-wing political principles caused him to react against the American experimental music of John Cage and his associates, and against the European avant-garde as typified by the music of Boulez and Stockhausen. Cardew, the most extreme of all the British composers of his generation during the 1960s, was steeped in the ideas of the two schools and, in compiling the book *Stockhausen Serves Imperialism*, rejected both.

His rejection of Cage and Stockhausen and, by implication, his own work written under their influence, was motivated by the realisation that if he were to move towards the goal of true socialisation of musical creation, then he must embrace musical styles and idioms which were intelligible to ordinary people. For Cardew, this meant the working class:

> In the age of large-scale industrial production, the largest, strongest and most revolutionary class is the industrial working class. [...] For the musician, the process of integrating with the working class brings unavoidable involvement with the ideological trends current in that class, both at the receiving end, among the 'consumers' of pop music etc., and at the production end, through leaving the avant-garde clique and integrating more with musicians working in the music 'industry' proper (Cardew et al., 1974: 8–9).

Looking forward to an imminent proletarian revolution, Cardew saw the avant-garde period as the last chapter in the history of bourgeois music. He explained the dwindling concert audiences in terms which anticipate Chris Small's gloomy predictions about the death of the western classical tradition (p. 63):

> The bourgeois class audience turns away from the contemporary musical expression of its birth agony, and contemporary bourgeois music becomes the concern of a tiny clique, taking a morbid interest in the process of decay (Cardew et al., 1974: 47).

Chris Small criticised Cage's adoption of Zen thought as too simplistic (Small, 1977: 149), but Cardew's rejection of Cage's use of Zen, and of Stockhausen's cultivation of mysticism, was more extreme. All such philosophies were morally bankrupt because they could lead to the acceptance of evil in the world as an inevitable part of life – starvation, political victimisation, exploitation, violation of human rights.

A self-effacing man by inclination, Cardew did not wish to draw attention to his own very considerable powers of musical creativity, but to use his talents to help and inspire other people to discover their own creative abilities. A car accident brought Cardew's life to an end in 1981. Various groups and individuals have continued to foster his work, or pay homage to his influence, among them the composer Barry Russell, whose own ensemble is named after Cardew.

Gavin Bryars

Many remember fondly the appalling renditions of popular classics such as Tchaikovsky's *Nutcracker Suite* and *1812 Overture*, and Strauss' *Also Sprach Zarathustra* (which the orchestra insisted on calling *2001*) by Gavin Bryars' students from Portsmouth Polytechnic who could barely play a note of music. The shelf-life of the Portsmouth Sinfonia was limited by a process of creeping proficiency as members got better at playing their instruments. Since its 'raison d'être' lay in harnessing musical ineptitude, the orchestra eventually started to lose its point, an intriguing reversal of the 'skill-gap'.

Gavin Bryars represents a group of composers who found an alternative route to a career in music and composition through British art colleges. During the 1970s, art departments in polytechnics and colleges of art and design provided courses in Complementary Studies to give students a more general education in social and cultural history. The challenge was to discover ways of working with students who were musically unskilled but eager to encounter new and experimental ideas.

Bryars' lasting legacy to community music is to be found in the 'Experimental Music Catalogue', a collection of compositions compiled between 1969 and 1975 using a variety of forms of notation including written text, simplified staff notation, and number charts, by experimental composers such as Hugh Shrapnel, Christopher Hobbs, John White, and Howard Skempton, grouped into various anthologies: String Anthology, Rhythm Anthology and so on. Pieces such as John Adams' *John Philip Souza*, Rzewski's *Les Moutons de Panurge*, or Hugh Shrapnel's *Bells* have found new currency today with COMA (Bryars, 1975).

The Portsmouth Sinfonia spawned offshoots such as the Promenade Theatre Orchestra and the Ross and Cromarty Orchestra whose director, Ivan Hume-Carter wrote a series of waltzes in which: '[…] anyone with little or even no knowledge could participate in the performance of any of the Waltzes […] simple tonal music of the orchestra accessible to all' (Nyman, 1999: 169).

Harrison Birtwistle

The 1960s mark the career beginnings of a number of other British composers who took up the torch of education and community work. School-teaching, or university or college lecturing has long been a bread-and-butter occupation for composers in the early years of their careers, but it is important to distinguish between those who saw education work as something second best – a stopgap before establishing a reputation for 'serious' work – and those who, like Kodály, were fully committed to education as a central part of their role.

Even Harrison Birtwistle, a composer of uncompromising musical style and single-minded dedication to his own compositional work, spent the early part of his life as a school master, and produced at least one work for secondary school children, a small music-theatre piece called *The Mark of the Goat*, commissioned in 1966 by BBC Schools Programmes for performance on radio by young people in the 13–15 age range.

The very practically written instrumental accompaniment includes parts for three clarinets, three players at one piano, and a large assortment of un-pitched percussion. The score contains elements of proportional notation, indeterminacy, and other features commonly found in contemporary music, but at a technical level within the capabilities of a key-stage 4 school music class (Example 3).

Example 3: Birtwistle, H. (1966) *The Mark of the Goat*, p. 20.

Peter Maxwell Davies

The pioneering work of Maxwell Davies in introducing techniques of contemporary composition into his classroom at Cirencester has been widely discussed, although it is worth pointing out that Maxwell Davies used traditional tonal patterns as his starting point in the classroom, as he describes in his own reports of his teaching at Cirencester:

> Because my own composition grew out of this stage many years ago, many visitors to the school have been surprised to see me insisting on chords I, IV and V to the extent of having children improvise on them cleanly and correctly in groups on simple chord patterns with voices and instruments resulting in an elementary but controlled polyphony (Davies, 1963: 109).

For Maxwell Davies, it was important not to deprive pupils of the 'common denominator of experience and communication' in order to create some hoped-for freedom from tradition. To do so was to remove the common ground from which all of us must start out in order to reach a 'natural and assured individuation'.

Beginning with *O Magnum Mysterium* (1960) and *Five Klée Pictures* (1960), Maxwell Davies has made an enormous contribution to the repertoire of music for school performance. As well as a host of music for solo instruments, small ensembles, and choirs, the list includes two operas *The Two Fiddlers* (1978), and *Cinderella* (1979) and the music-theatre piece, *The Rainbow* (1981). Longmans commissioned six new music-theatre pieces on subjects designed to appeal to young minds between 1989 and 1992: *The Great Bank Robbery, Jupiter Landing, Dangerous Errand, Dinosaur at Large, The Spider's Revenge* and *A Selkie Tale*.

During Maxwell Davies' time as Associate Composer with the Scottish Chamber Orchestra, the 'Strathclyde Concertos' project incorporated an important educational dimension for the whole community called *The Turn of the Tide*. It enabled children to integrate their own pieces into an orchestral score and formed the centrepiece of the 1993 conference of the Association of British Orchestras involving sixteen orchestras, forty thousand children, and a £300,000 budget.

David Bedford

David Bedford continues to have a far-reaching influence on music in education. Bedford's music has been used extensively as examples in influential text books on music education by theorists such as George Self and John Paynter, but his own personal contribution singles him out as one of the best early examples of a composer working in education. Bedford's influence can be summarised as follows:

1. As a school teacher and Composer-in-Residence at Queen's College, London from 1969–1981.
2. As a Composer of music for educational performance.
3. As animateur.
4. As member or chair of the PRS Composer-in-Education Scheme, and the Association of Professional Composers.

An early interest in John Cage expressed itself in the use of indeterminate scoring techniques in *Piece for Mo* (1963), and *Music for Albion Moonlight* (1965), and in live performances as pianist and melodica player of music by Cage, Cardew, La Monte Young and others. His involvement with popular forms of music, through collaborations with Mike Oldfield, brought him closer to musical styles 'intelligible to ordinary people' than Cardew was able to achieve.

Bedford realised the educational potential of techniques of contemporary composition during the earliest part of his career when Maxwell Davies was just beginning to attract attention for his work at Cirencester. The two pieces of *Whitefield Music* (1966 & 1967 respectively) are his earliest educational scores. Both are flexibly scored. An element of playfulness borrowed from Fluxus infects some of these early educational pieces including *An exciting new game for children of all ages* (1969) and *Balloon Music* (1973).

Always on the look-out for what detractors have described as gimmicks, Bedford conducted *Piece for Mo* from a specially constructed conducting console which gave signals by means of coloured lights. In *Some Bright Stars for Queen's College* (1970), he equipped the girls of the Queen's College Choir with plastic twirlers, and a year later invited the audience to join in on kazoos in *With 100 Kazoos* (BBC commission; 1971). Accusations of 'gimmickry' illustrate how

Bedford's attitude to music differed from other more 'serious-minded' composers. The 'gimmicks' and the poetic or descriptive titles were all intended to make his music more 'user-friendly', to make it appeal to the imaginations of ordinary young people who, he believed, could be alienated by direct exposure to avant-garde music.

In 1978 he wrote what has become perhaps his most celebrated work, *The Rime of the Ancient Mariner*. Taking its text from Coleridge's famous poem, it is cast as a music theatre piece with action, narration and choral singing. It sets out to provide material for several different levels of musical ability.

At its centre is a piano part which binds the music firmly together. Apart from the piano and double choir, the scoring is flexible. There are optional parts for wind, brass and strings of a standard easily within the capabilities of members of an intermediate level school orchestra. Players on kazoos, bottles, whistles, singing wine glasses, and other percussion make up the creative sound-effects group depicting ice floes, storms and other perils of the ocean.

Part of the educational purpose of the work was to introduce children to techniques of contemporary composition. Bedford combines elements of diatonic musical minimalism – for instance the melody of the well-known sea-song *For we're bound for the Rio Grande* repeated many times like a mantra (Bedford 1979: 97–107) – with improvisational and sound-effects material using proportional graphic notation like an avant-garde score (Example 4). There is, however, no scope for youngsters to compose their own material.

The Rime, commissioned by 'Music in Action', has become one of Bedford's most performed works. The most recent performance was at the Albert Hall, Nottingham, in February 2000 presented by City of Nottingham Education Authority, with choir and full orchestra plus sound effects from Nottingham Music School, and dancers from the city's Arts Plus provision. Alistair Conquer's comments on the performance appeared on Bedford's website:

> Bedford [...] was very pleased with the biggest performance of the piece that he had seen. Over 300 performers, including some with learning difficulties, sang, danced and played their way through the *Hebrides* Overture and David's *Rime*. We had a sell-out audience of over 600 and had to turn people away (Conquer, 2000).

Example 4: Bedford, D. (1978) Sound effects score *The Rime of the Ancient Mariner.*

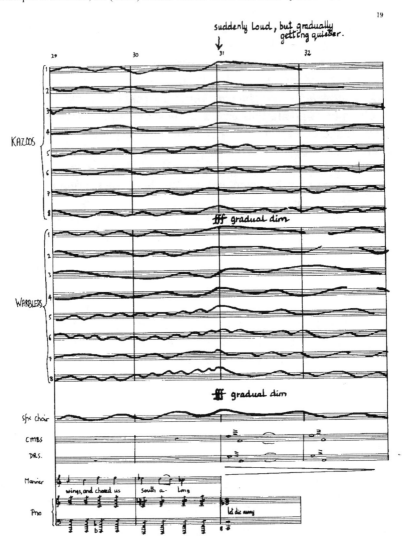

The success of *The Rime* established Bedford as a much sought-after composer of music for school performance leading to a string of commissions including works for youth orchestras, and in particular

50

for the British Association of Symphonic Wind Bands and Ensembles (BASWBE).

Bedford's commission for the Harlow Choral Society's 'Time-piece' project in 2001, co-ordinated by Sarah Tennant-Flowers, brought together junior-school choirs, the percussion quartet Ensemble Bash and the Hilliard Ensemble, and was also the focus for an extensive creative music project. The score invites the audience to take part by asking them to split into four groups to join in the singing of a four-part canon (rainbow: Track 01).

He was an obvious choice of composer for one of the annual COMA Summer Schools. The result was *Hetty Pegler's Tump* (1999) for amateur orchestra and voices. The choice of subject – A bronze-age barrow situated in the Cotswolds near Dursley in Gloucestershire which had been the inspiration for my own work for Dursley primary school with the same title in 1985 – reflects Bedford's recent move to a new house near Bristol.

Work as an animateur in creative workshops has formed an essential part of Bedford's career. He has always emphasised the difference between writing for children, and devising and directing projects in which children themselves compose. He was appointed Youth Music Director of the English Sinfonia in 1986, and a number of his works, such as *Seascapes* (1986), commissioned by the Scottish Chamber Orchestra, and *Frameworks* (1989) for the English Sinfonia, represent a kind of hybrid situation where students create their own music as part of a public concert with professional orchestra.

During my conversation with him in December 1998 he suggested five categories of project, arranged according to the degree of creative input of the participants.

Example 5: The Bedford Categories.

BC1. Interpretation of a fully written score.
BC2. Score containing opportunities for improvisation.
BC3. Written score which includes creative 'windows'.
BC4. Musical material generated in workshops assembled by the composer.
BC5. Fully creative project: all aspects devised within the group.

I include in Category BC4 projects in which the composer creates a conceptual or temporal framework at the start of the project into which creative ideas can be inserted.

Bedford's influence outside the UK has been minimal, but seeds were sown in 2000 when he was invited to spend a week with the Bakersfield Symphony Orchestra in California. Bedford conducted *The Sultan's Turret* and led a demonstration creative workshop with the Bakersfield High School encouraging students to compose.

David Bedford has also influenced the development of composing in education by directing financial support through the Performing Right Society Composer-in-Education scheme.

The Birmingham Arts Laboratory Experimental Sound Workshop

In *Experimental Music, Cage and Beyond* Michael Nyman acknowledges how far experimental music went towards 'channelling and releasing the creativity everybody has within them.' But there are many omissions. He makes no mention of Cardew's Morley College class, nor of the arts laboratories and arts centres which were another base for musical experimentation. Hugh Davies at the Drury Lane Arts Laboratory and musicians and composers such as Melvyn Poore, Jan Steele and myself at the Birmingham Arts Laboratory do not get a mention.

I was invited to join the Birmingham Arts Laboratory by Peter Stark in 1970. I founded the Experimental Sound Workshop there and ran it for five years, formulating my own creative workshop techniques based on my experiences at Cardew's Morley College class. The events presented during a series of annual festivals entitled 'Sound Symposium' are indicative of the methodologies which influenced our work. Cardew himself was a frequent visitor. He led a performance of paragraphs from *The Great Learning* and performed with the Scratch Orchestra in 1972. This was a formative time for the free improvisation movement. AMM with Cardew, Spontaneous Music Ensemble with John Stephens, and 'Amalgam' with Trevor Watts all appeared at the Lab.

A small but enthusiastic group took part in creative events with the Experimental Sound Workshop. Several members, who were students at Birmingham University such as Melvyn Poore, Keith Potter and Hilary Bracefield, went on to secure influential positions in contemporary musical life. Typical was the 1971 summertime project *The Super Spectacular Symmetry Show*. I provided a temporal structure based on the idea of a formant spectrum borrowed from Stockhausen's *Gruppen*. Stockhausen's fundamental durations vary from four seconds to a quarter of a second:

from: | at θ = 60   to: ε at θ = 120

Our piece was based on a single fundamental of one hour's duration with simultaneous formants of periods ranging between fifteen minutes and half a second, derived as squares of prime numbers. The structure – an example of BC4 – dictated when events should happen, but not what they should be. This was left to the ingenuity and inventiveness of the twenty or so participants who improvised on instruments, declaimed from novels, performed visible actions, or even let off army-surplus detonators, all co-ordinated by a large clock face which dominated the stage. The tendency of formant structures to accumulate towards nodal points, when all formants reach a simultaneous attack, gave the performance a built-in dramatic climax (Allen et al., 1998).

Participation was central to the work of the Experimental Sound Workshop. Like the Scratch Orchestra, we wanted to get sound and music out into the community, and into different everyday contexts. This led to presentations of sound sculpture and other environmental sound projects by artists such as Hugh Davies and Alvin Lucier. Interactive electro-acoustic sound installations such as *Locations*, *The Noise Factory* and *This Could Happen To You* were devised at the Lab and toured to galleries and arts centres all over England, Scotland and Wales, with one small tour to The Netherlands in 1975 attracting huge crowds. Even at this early date I was searching for new roles for the composer and new relationships between music and audiences.

The young Peter Wiegold was amongst the performers in a production of Tom Philips' opera *Irma* during the Media Fusions

The Arnolfini Music Workshop, Bristol

Wiegold was commissioned by Jane Wells, my predecessor at Arnolfini Music, to run a pioneering programme of school and community workshops in Bristol between 1976 and 1980. The project, supported financially by the Gulbenkian Foundation, consisted of a programme of creative music workshops in Bristol secondary schools, and Monday evening music workshops for adults. A series of six professional concerts by Wiegold's own ensemble, Gemini, coincided with end-of-term workshop concerts. Members of Gemini, including clarinettist Ian Mitchell, also participated in the workshops. The format developed by the Arnolfini project was thus one of the earliest examples of a model integrating professional concerts with creative music workshops.

The start of my work at Arnolfini, Bristol, in 1979 caught the tail-end of the Gemini project. Over ten years I promoted a series of educational projects built round concerts which formed part of the Arts Council Contemporary Music Network. These became the focal point for programmes of education workshops for schools, introductory concert talks, and discussion symposia focusing on featured composers. This was an approach geared not to the development of individual musical creativity in young people and adults, but towards providing opportunities for them to encounter different aspects of the work of particular composers. The format became one of the models for what came to be called the 'Holistic Principle' of music promotion.

Between 1982 and 1985, performances at Arnolfini Music by the Fires of London, the John Alldis Choir, and the Opera Factory of works such as Maxwell Davies' *Eight Songs for a Mad King,* David Bedford's choral work *The Golden Wine is Drunk,* and Birtwistle's *Punch and Judy* provided the focus of repertoire-based educational projects. None of the children were involved in creative composition work. They took part in performances of pieces written for children such as *5 Klée Pictures* (Davies, 1960), *The Rime of the Ancient Mariner* (Bedford, 1979) and *The Mark of the Goat* (Birtwistle, 1966). It was not until February 1986, with a project centred on the

Steve Reich Ensemble, that we began to encourage young people to write their own music.

Annette Moreau, Director of the Contemporary Music Network (CMN), described these projects as 'a model of how music promoters should behave' (Letter; Moreau to Laycock). However, educationalists and teachers frequently expressed misgivings about the educational value. Irene Macdonald complained that:

> The arts side is too often concerned with transmitting an appreciation of the product and with nothing else. The education side wishes to develop the individual even if, in some cases, the medium used is compromised by the process (Macdonald; cited in Winterson, 1998: 63).

Although the Network organisers felt genuine commitment to the idea of education, artists such as David Freeman or Steve Reich possessed none of the specialist communication skills essential in the classroom situation. We as music promoters did not have sufficient knowledge of current educational methodology to focus our planning on the specific educational needs of the teachers. This was our first encounter with the dichotomy between the 'child-centred' approach of the teacher and the 'style-centred' approach of the contemporary artist and musician.

At Arnolfini, I undertook three projects as composer and workshop leader. The first, in 1985, was *Bladud* (BC2), a music-theatre piece for Bathampton Primary School. Later, in 1988 in quick succession came *Hetty Pegler's Tump* (BC4), for Prema Arts Centre in Gloucestershire, and *Woden's Dyke*, (BC1) an 'operatic melodrama' with full orchestral accompaniment for secondary schools and intermediate orchestra.

These projects had important features in common. They took themes from the local history or legends of the places where they were performed, using my own libretti based on original research. *Bladud* took the ancient British myth of King Bladud who is said to have discovered the healing powers of the hot springs of Bath. *Hetty Pegler's Tump* was based on a fanciful story, created partly by the children who took part, set in the Bronze Age when this ancient round barrow was built. *Woden's Dyke* took reports from the Anglo-Saxon

Chronicle of the settlement of the Avon Valley by the Saxon chieftain Ceawlin of Wessex in the sixth century A.D.

All theses projects contained material suitable for different levels of musical skill, including creative sound effects groups, and music for trained instrumentalists. Musical material was derived from canons and rounds designed to give musical novices an experience of part-singing. Melodic material simple in character was incorporated into canonic structures of considerable complexity. *Bladud* was based on an eight-part double canon of two interlocking four-part canons of different musical character (rainbow: Track 02) (Example 6).

The projects also celebrated features of the local landscape, depicting a journey in music in various ways. Bladud, banished from his Iron-Age tribal home on Little Solsbury because of leprosy, takes a journey along the River Avon towards Bath. *Hetty Pegler* employed a conceptual process using contour elevations taken from an Ordnance Survey map of the ring of Cotswold hills surrounding the Uley valley as a musical score for improvising percussion group. *Woden's Dyke* contains a song describing the course of the ancient defensive wall called the Wansdyke, as well as orchestral interludes descriptive of the Wessex countryside, the peaceful backdrop to a violent story.

Woden's Dyke introduced secondary-school children to a wide variety of contemporary musical techniques including extended instrumental techniques, bi-tonality, atonality, and minimalist processes. It integrated modal and tonal melodic material, some of it in a quasi-folk idiom, into a stylistic continuum with avant-garde techniques at the other extreme.

The three projects differed in the degree of creative input required from participants. *Bladud* and *Hetty Pegler's Tump* grew out of a series of creative workshops in the schools. The OS map contour sections of *Hetty Pegler's Tump* provide windows in which children improvised during the final performance, whereas the final version of *Bladud* was composed by me throughout.

The orchestral material of *Woden's Dyke* grew out of improvisation workshops with the full intermediate orchestra using graphic score sections from Stockhausen's *Mixtur* as a starting point. An extract from the opening orchestral prelude shows examples of dissonant cloud textures using extended instrumental technique in proportional notation designed for intermediate orchestra (Example 7).

The appointment of Barry Russell as Arnolfini Musician in the Community in 1987 meant a return to the encouragement of musical composition in young people. The residency was 'community-centred'. Its aim was not to propagate the music of Barry Russell as a composer, nor was there a commitment to any particular musical style. It was overseen by a steering committee including teachers, directors of arts centres, and the Avon County Council Director of Community Leisure. The residency took in primary and secondary school children and several community centres. Russell's work with the mentally and physically handicapped was based on his own intimate knowledge of conditions such as Downes syndrome and cerebral palsy, and of their very particular characteristics and requirements.

Example 6: Laycock, J. (1985) extract from *Bladud – a wordscape with music.*

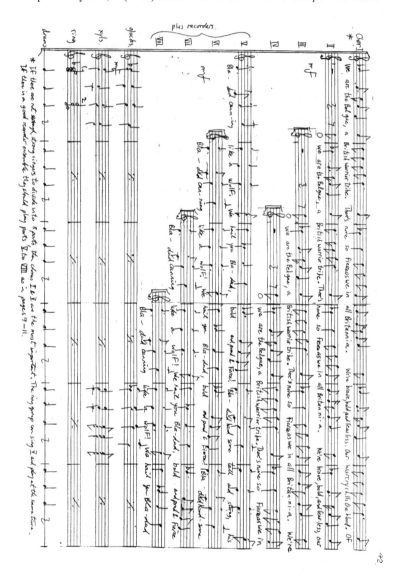

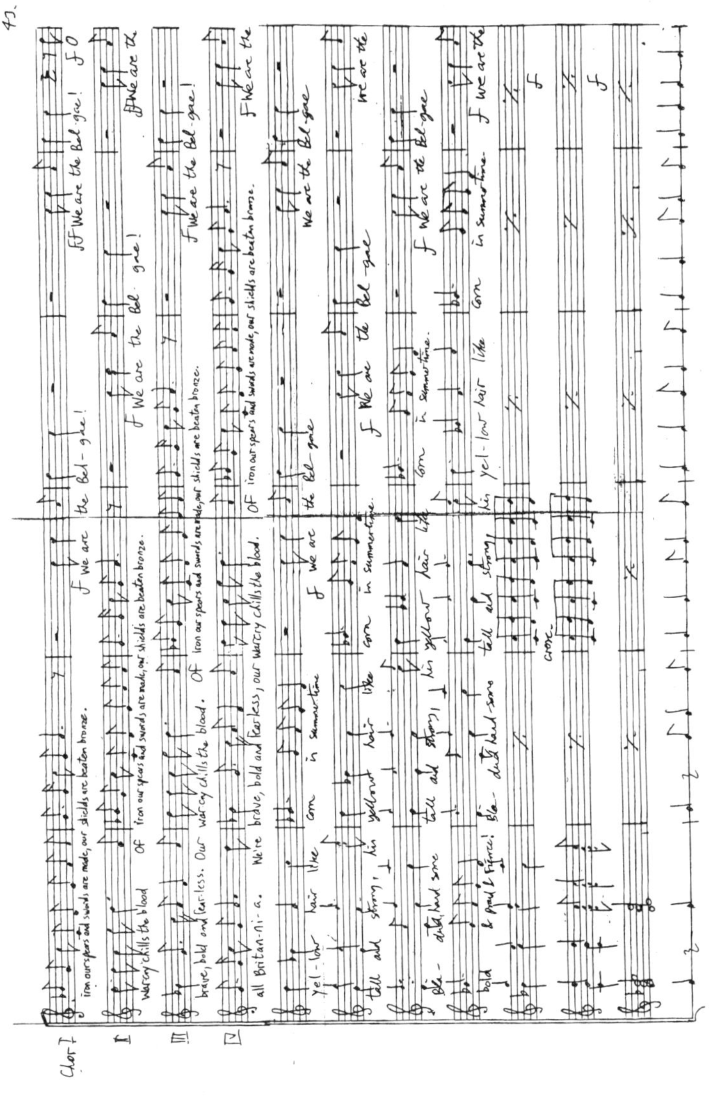
Chor I
II
III
IV
iron our spears and swords are made, our shields are beaten bronze.
We are the Bel-gae!
war-cry chills the blood
Of iron our spears and swords are made, our shields are beaten bronze.
brave, bold and fear-less. Our war-cry chills the blood.
all Britan-ni-a. We're brave, bold and fear-less, our war-cry chills the blood.
yel-low hair like corn in summer-time
tall and strong, his yellow hair like corn in summer-time
bold & proud & fierce!
yel-low hair like corn

Example 7: Laycock, J. (1988) *Woden's Dyke* Extract from orchestral prelude.

Chapter 2
Philosophical background

During the past century a rejection of the past tradition of music led to the abdication of personal responsibility for the creative process by composers such as Cage and Cardew, and eventually to a more positive realisation that their role could change to that of an inspirational catalyst for creativity in others. The value of the arts in society, the benefits of creativity, both personally and to society, the idea of artistic creativity for all, and the resultant problem of the 'skill-gap' (the need to cater for the musically gifted as well as the musically untutored) are recurrent themes in the writings of a number of composers, musicologists and educational theorists who have influenced the development of creative music-making.

The maxims of R. Murray Schafer

A particularly idiosyncratic and endearing approach to inspirational leadership is embodied in the ten maxims of the Canadian composer and music educationalist R. Murray Schafer, set out in his groundbreaking book *The Rhinoceros in the Classroom*. His approach is refreshingly iconoclastic, inviting us to take risks and to approach music-making with a spirit of adventure. From these ten maxims, I single out the following:

2. In education, failures are more important than successes.
3. Teach on the verge of peril.
4. There are no more teachers. There is just a community of learners.
8. [...] a class should be an hour of a thousand discoveries. For this to happen, the teacher and the student should first discover one another (Schafer, 1975: 132–133).

The philosophical writings of Michael Tippett

Michael Tippett, writing in part II of *Moving into Aquarius*, 'Poets in a barren age', has attempted to define the traditional role of the composer in society, a function he saw himself as carrying out well into the twentieth century:

> I am a composer. That is someone who imagines sounds, creating music from the inner world of the imagination. The ability to experience and communicate this inner world is a gift (Tippett, 1974: 148).

According to Tippett, the artist's fate is to be reviled, rejected, or merely ignored by a public which is 'deeply offended by any passion of the unusual, the rare, the rich, the exuberant, the heroic, and the aristocratic in art' (Tippett, 1974: 98). He blames this on what he sees as the essential conservatism of the public which 'seems to want no musical experience whatever beyond what it already knows' (Tippett, 1974: 97). Such a viewpoint brings Tippett to question the value of the artist in society:

> That the artist, whether composer, poet or painter, has a special gift, no one ever denies. But how valuable we think this gift is to society, and what is its real function there; these are matters not of fact but opinion (Tippett, 1974: 123).

His solution is not to define a new role, but to discover a justification which affirms the old one. Compelled by his own inner creative force, which will not be denied, his role is to write the music he wants to write, ignoring the mediocre tastes of the concert going public:

> I look, therefore, at public and patronage through the eyes of a dedicated person, who must do what he has to do, whether the issue is acceptable or not; [...] my passion is to project into our mean world, music which is rich and generous; [...] I hope to reject mediocrity as intensely as it rejects me (Tippett, 1974: 99).

Tippett regards it as his right and duty to compose whatever this inner creative force compels. Some distant posterity may eventually catch up with him, but it is almost a matter of indifference whether others are able to follow where he leads:

He (the artist) is accumulating our artistic capital, the results of which will last long after his own death. And to accumulate this kind of capital is his unwritten mandate [...] the mandate of the artist's own special nature, of his special gift, is to reach down into the depths of the human psyche and bring forth the tremendous images of things to come [...]. He creates, because without art, in this deep and serious sense, the nation dies. His mandate is inescapable (Tippett, 1974: 129).

Christopher Small: music in society

Chris Small, writing in *Music, Society and Education*, sees a serious dilemma confronting twentieth century composers from which any re-treat to an ivory tower of posterity is no solution:

We are forced once again to contemplate the melancholy fact that, notwithstand-ing the achievements of Debussy, Schoenberg, Stravinsky, Webern, Ives, Cage, Partch and many others, the experience of music in the western art tradition remains essentially unchanged. It remains as cut off, not only from that vaguely-defined group known as the people, but even from its immediate audience, as any music since the renaissance. It is still composed by highly trained and remote specialists, and played by professional musicians in concert halls and other spaces set aside for the purpose, and at times set aside from our everyday lives (Small, 1977: 168).

He seems to be hinting at that same ultimate death of a tradition which Cardew foresaw:

It is a sad but undeniable fact that a serious composer working in our society today is addressing a smaller proportion of the population than in any other period in the history of western music; not only is the audience for concert music a minority within the general population, but the contemporary composer is able to engage the attention of only a small minority of that minority (Small, 1977: 168).

Small argues persuasively for the development of musical forms in which all people can participate in a creative experience, giving, by way of example, a description of ordinary people making music in

Bali where, according to him, no gap exists between professional and amateur: '[...] the music is created and performed by farmers, merchants, even princes and children, who form themselves into clubs and play wherever and whenever they are called upon to do so' (Small, 1977: 41).

To illustrate the phenomenal powers of memory amongst musicians of non-literate societies, Chris Small quotes a passage from Hugh Tracey's study of African Chopi musicians:

> The ability of these musicians to imagine a work of symphonic scale without putting pen to paper challenges not only many western notions of the limits of musical memory but also assumptions concerning the necessity for notation (Tracey, 1940 cited in Small, 1977: 56).

Margaret Mead described Balinese musical life as:

> [...] a continuum within which the distinction between the most gifted and the least gifted is muted by the fact that everyone participates. The distinction between child and adult – as performer, as actor, as musicians – is lost (Mead cited in Small, 1977: 43).

What is to prevent such equal participation in artistic activities in a modern western industrialised society? The problem, according to Chris Small, lies in the limited expectations people have of themselves: '[...] it is in fact only a tiny minority of the population who think themselves capable of writing a poem, painting a picture, making a piece of music' (Small, 1977: 90). This basic lack of self-confidence is symptomatic of a central problem in contemporary society: 'the coming to power of the expert, of the person with knowledge in a particular field (since it is impossible for anyone to be an expert in everything) at his disposal' (Small, 1977: 90). Grave dangers lie ahead if this rift in society can not be healed and the drift towards philistinism and a new age of barbarism halted:

> The layman's ignorance of science is matched by the average scientist's lack of concern for the arts and what are known as humanities, producing a condition in our society mistakenly called the 'Two Cultures'. There are not two cultures, but one, though it is seriously, and increasingly, schizoid (Small, 1977: 70).

The educational theories of John Paynter

The development of creativity-for-all, as advocated by Chris Small, is central to the teachings of John Paynter whose far-reaching influence on music education is widely acknowledged. Through books such as *Sound and Silence* (1970) co-authored with Peter Aston, and *Music in the Secondary School Curriculum* (1982) which drew on the action-based research programme of the Schools Council Music Project, Paynter was one of the most significant voices to influence the introduction of composing into the 1988 GCSE syllabus and the National Curriculum.

The need to ensure the availability of music to all school pupils is a guiding principle of Paynter's work. In *Sound and Silence*, he and Peter Aston assert: 'Like all the arts, music springs from a profound response to life itself. It is a language, and as a vehicle for expression, it is available to some degree to everyone' (Paynter & Aston, 1970: 3). They hope that 'teachers will try to release the natural creativity in those they teach, whatever the age and ability of the pupils' (Paynter & Aston, 1970: 23).

This was the visionary philosophy behind the methods set out in Paynter's *Music in the Secondary School Curriculum*. Paynter quotes Tom Gamble, a teacher from Manland School, Harpenden, who took part in the Schools Council project: 'Whatever we do in class music we must aim to involve all children, and to involve them in a real experience of music'. Music in the classroom should be a core time-tabled classroom subject, available to all pupils (Paynter, 1982: 39).

Paynter asserts that the art most relevant to us is the art of our own time, but that a methodology based only on talking about and listening to new music is not enough. 'We need the professional artist but at the same time we must cultivate the artist within ourselves' (Paynter & Aston, 1970: 4). It is important to distinguish between 'Music for all' and 'Composing for all'. Holst encouraged his pupils to compose their own music, and to try it out on each other. Members of the Scratch Orchestra composed their own music, as well as playing it. But others have been less enthusiastic about the idea that all people have within them a creative as opposed to a re-creative musical impulse:

> Too often we are encouraged to regard music as a leisure activity, as though its only function is to entertain. This may have led us to emphasise re-creative rather than creative activities in school music; and although creative work in language, drama and the visual arts has quickly found general acceptance, creative work in music has often been challenged as being of doubtful value in itself, having little bearing on conventional musical education (Paynter & Aston, 1970: 6).

Just as Cardew grappled with the problem of finding a role for skilled musicians in forms of music which were meant to be accessible to all, Paynter was aware of a similar 'skill-gap' in education. According to him, choirs and youth orchestras catered for a minority, an apparent bias towards the musically gifted intended to ensure 'the continuing supply of suitable recruits for the orchestra' (Paynter, 1982: 16).

When resources are scarce it is all too easy for provision to be targeted at the most gifted. The more we exploit opportunities for extra-curricular ensembles and encourage talented pupils to increase their skills, the less spin-off there will be within the curriculum as a whole. 'Far from causing others to want to join in, musical activities assume an exclusive appearance, with a correspondingly weakening effect upon general class music' (Paynter, 1982: 16). For Paynter, the only logical approach is to advocate mixed ability groups allowing pupils to work at their own pace, ensuring that there is something everyone can do (Paynter, 1982: 52).

Paynter repeatedly emphasises the importance of 'education' as distinct from 'training': 'We educate through music. Our commitment is to education and not merely to music training' (Paynter, 1982: 91). He advocates an integrated approach. Breadth of understanding and experience is only possible when conscious efforts are made to remove the boundaries between subjects. Music is seen as a communal creative activity in which children of different levels of ability can work co-operatively alongside one another:

> [...] where music has been seen to flourish in the curriculum and to have something to offer to the majority of pupils it is almost always because the

teacher concerned has started from a firm conviction that he has an educational as well a musical duty (Paynter, 1982: 90).

Paynter has spoken out against the reliance on any one particular methodology. He prefers to lead by example rather than by pre-scription. Thus *Sound and Silence* contains the all-important warning, prompted perhaps by the experience of Carl Orff: 'The projects in this book do not constitute a method of teaching music. This must be avoided at all costs' (Paynter & Aston, 1970: 23). He took up the theme again in *Music in the Secondary School Curriculum*: '[…] no one method or syllabus will work in every given circumstance […] every teacher must develop strategies appropriate for his/her cir-cumstances and suitable for those pupils in that school' (Paynter, 1982: 32).

The integrated approach only 'works' if the teacher himself carries conviction, but this would be true of whatever method being used. Even a traditional 'rudiments of theory' and 'music appreciation' approach can bring results if the teacher has conviction:

> […] it is no use grasping at straws of new things to do simply because the old standbys have failed. For example, electronic sound sources and the range of possibilities in electro-acoustic music will certainly offer a new world of sound which may initially excite our pupils. But this will not work any better than singing or musical appreciation if we are not ourselves utterly convinced about it as music, and about its value in the educational process (Paynter, 1982: 67).

As a book, *Sound and Silence* set a pattern which was used again in *Sound and Structure*: that of a short chapter or series of chapters of introduction, followed by a long series of project-examples, each followed up by a commentary drawing out various general principles. In the introduction to *Sound and Silence*, Paynter and Aston set out the principle which underlies all the project-examples. The educational aim is to give children an appreciation of important classical and contemporary works in such a way that they gain the deepest possible understanding of the principles upon which the music is based. The principles are introduced first, followed by the musical examples which embody them. The same sequence of processes applies to each example in the book:

A. Introduction to the principle behind the project, intended for teachers rather than their pupils.
B. The project assignment itself, or in some cases, a series of graded assignments involving practical experiment with sound, or with musical instruments.
C. Some examples of responses to the same assignment by other pupils.
D. Examples of works written by professional composers which embody the principle introduced by the practical examples.

The authors maintain that pupils respond to these established works with more understanding and enjoyment if they have already experimented with similar ideas (Paynter & Aston, 1970: 11).

As Orff also found, placing the model after the experiment is important. If the model comes first:

> [...] we run the risk that it will simply be copied without understanding, whereas if it is placed after the experiment, then we can say: 'here is another composer making music like yours'. It is confirmation and enrichment (Paynter & Aston, 1970: 12).

Sound and Silence presents a sequence of thirty-six projects progressing from an exploration of the philosophical, associative and semiotic nature of sound towards an introduction of the technicalities of music, and finally to two projects inviting a more elaborate theatrical approach. The first few projects include 'What does music say?' and 'The music within us', which uses sounds of the body, the voice, or natural sounds such as twigs and leaves. Later projects explore movement and music, musical instruments, concepts of space and time, or short and long sounds, before moving on to more technically complex aspects of melody, harmony, modes, twelve-note rows, chance procedures and so on.

In *Sound and Structure* (1992), Paynter ingeniously avoids the 'linear logic' of conventional academic discourse. The examples are placed in a structure designed to indicate that there is no single correct order in which to use them. A chapter called 'Using this book' contains a flow chart reminiscent of some indeterminate contemporary scores encouraging teachers to work out their own route through the sixteen projects, grouped into four sections of four projects each:

Paynter's influence outside the UK can be traced in the introduction of composition into the International GCSE, the International American Schools' Music Programme, and the International Baccalaureate. His work in Oslo (Norway) and in Fiesoli and Bolzano (Italy) during the 1990s made him one of the earliest examples of the adoption of British methodologies in Europe.

A report in the magazine *beQuadro* of Paynter's work in Italy, co-ordinated by Centro di Ricercara e di Sperimentazione per la Didattica Musicale (Centre for Research and Experiment in Music Teaching) in Fiesole, consists of an introductory chapter followed by fifty-one examples of project reports. Eight different educational institutions took part. Project descriptions by each project co-ordinator are arranged in order of the participants' age groups from six-year-old children to students in higher education and adults. Each report is followed by Paynter's own commentaries (Paynter, 1997a). Here we see Paynter acting as inspirational leader, encouraging composition through his words of constructive critical comment, an approach described in his own article 'Making progress in composition':

> The word 'composing' means 'positioning (things) together', and when anyone has tried putting sounds together, and is pleased with the results, enough to remember them, then the teacher can start to teach – mainly by asking questions about what is presented (Paynter, 2000).

Keith Swanwick: musical development in the child

In his book *Music, Mind and Education*, Keith Swanwick proposes a systematic theoretical model to describe the development of musical awareness in children which also defines the role of the teacher. It is based on the writings of previous educational theorists and on practical research at the Institute of Educational Research of London University. His theories are embodied in the 'Spiral of Musical Development' (Swanwick, 1988: 76) (Example 9). This unites two previous models. Malcolm Ross distinguished four phases of musical development, categorised by age (Ross, 1984: 129–130):

ages:
0–2   Pure sensuous engagement
3–7   Musical doodling
8–13 Conventional musical production
14+   Music as personal expression

Basil Bernstein saw learning as taking place within a two-dimensional matrix (Bernstein, 1971). He labelled the two axies 'Classification' and 'Framing', each representing a continuum between 'weak' and 'strong'. 'Strong' framing was 'instructional', adhering to a strict method and timetable. 'Weak' framing allowed the pupil to develop at his or her own pace by a process of 'encounter'. Strong classification set a clearly defined goal, represented by stylistic conventions such as those of European classical music. Weak classification allowed the pupils to choose their own stylistic starting points (Swanwick, 1988: 122).

Example 8.

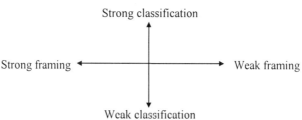

Ideally, the teacher achieved a balance between these 'weak' and 'strong' extremes. Swanwick realised that pupils progressing through Ross's four phases of development could be seen as oscillating between Bernstein's weak and strong framing at each stage in the process. Swanwick created his own four-phase progression which he saw as an improvement on Ross.

Example 9: The spiral of musical development (Swanwick & Tilman, 1986).

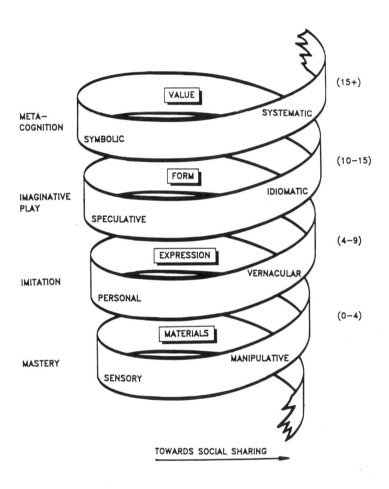

In drawing the spiral, Swanwick seems to have reversed the handedness of the Bernstein diagram. The small child first experiences a direct sensory encounter with the materials of sound. The teacher then offers elements of instruction described as manipulative, vernacular, idiomatic, and systematic (right hand side) which the pupil assimilates through processes of encounter described as personal, speculative, and symbolic (left hand side).

Swanwick modified Ross's age boundaries, sometimes by as much as two years, giving them more precise labels (Swanwick, 1988: 63). Swanwick's 'mastery of materials (0–4)' is first 'sensory' and then 'manipulative', merging Ross' 'Pure sensuous engagement (0–2)' with the early years of 'musical-doodling (3–7)'. Ross saw 'musical doodling' continue up to age seven, but Swanwick regarded the later years of this process as part of 'expression' through 'imitation' (4–9). This was at first 'personal', progressing towards imitation of a musical 'vernacular', equivalent to Ross' 'Conventional musical production (8–13)'. Swanwick's 'imaginative play' with 'form' (10–15) developed from 'speculative' to 'idiomatic'. The two came closest to unanimity when Ross credited the over-fourteens with an ability to use music as a form of personal expression. Swanwick saw this as a period when young people begin to give symbolic value to music, becoming more systematic as understanding increases (meta-cognition).

The second part of *Music, Mind and Education* is concerned with multi-cultural musical education. Swanwick emphasises the difference between dislikes based on knowledge, and prejudice based on ignorance (Swanwick, 1988: 95). Swanwick draws attention to the loss of common cultural traditions in modern industrialised society, blaming this on mass transportation and rapidly evolving communications systems. The common culture of our time is an electronic folk-culture based on Afro-American forms (Swanwick, 1988: 15).

Different social groups, particularly the young, use musical idioms as badges of identity to separate themselves from other people or other groups. This begins around the age of ten when young people are taking a 'speculative' attitude to music, listening to different styles and discovering which conform to their own self-image. The process reaches its full 'systematic' development at the age of fifteen when styles of music, fashions of dress, modes of behaviour, and idioms of speech, all identify them as belonging to a particular peer group. Musical likes and dislikes formed by the age of eighteen/nineteen are likely to remain with them throughout their lives.

However, because of its abstract nature, music can also transcend cultural boundaries: 'Music meaning is sufficiently abstract to travel across cultural boundaries, to step out of its time and place' (Swanwick, 1988: 101). This is the difference between words and music:

> Words produce in us some replica of the actual object or behaviour. But music communicates only through a combination of motoric and physical reflexes – pulse, tempo, pitch etc., and associated ideas remembered and learnt from childhood experience (Swanwick, 1988: 25).

He sees music as '[...] being free from literalness of represent-ation; being fluently expressive, but not naturally descriptive' (Swan-wick, 1988: 30). Although music is abstract, it is also 'metaphorical' and is able to raise images:

> [...] perhaps of hard edges, or of throbbing movement, of fleeting shadows, of massive substance, or of flowing tranquillity – and relate these in logically evolving structures that rise before us with the same ordered and sequential presence as poems and plays (Swanwick, 1988: 41).

The ability of musical structures such as melodic shapes, or chord progressions to adapt themselves to many different stylistic con-ventions is what he calls music's 'free-standing cultural autonomy'. He gives, as a striking example, the use of the chord sequence of Pachelbel's Canon in a pop song from Papua New Guinea (Swanwick, 1988: 107).

It is the job of teachers to open the eyes and ears of their pupils to this adaptability of musical forms: 'Teachers cannot be expected to be skilled in all the musics of the world, but they must be sensitive to many, and skilled in at least one' (Swanwick, 1988: 116). The teacher should help pupils to encounter and experience as many different styles and idioms of music as possible, drawing attention always to shared features: intervals, scales, modes, ragas, chords, note rows, ostinati, drones and so on, as much as to features which differentiate them.

Finally, Swanwick analyses the difference between music in school and in the wider community in terms of the Bernstein matrix (Swanwick, 1988: 118). Music in the community takes the form of encounter. Music in education is fundamentally instructional in intention, even if the process is based on a balance between encounter and instruction:

> The fundamental difference between musical encounter in the community and music education in schools and colleges is precisely the obligation of evaluation and criticism, of becoming *explicit*, which is characteristic of formal settings (Swanwick, 1988: 131).

The difference between school and everyday life is that school requires 'conscious knowledge'.

Swanwick challenges the professional music world. It is the task of music-educationalists to devise an effective curriculum which will open the ears and minds of young people to the full richness of musical idioms, but it is the job of music promoters in arts centres and concert halls to provide those opportunities for musical encounter which will feed and enrich the musical lives of young people (Swanwick, 1988: 138).

Paynter and Swanwick collaborated to produce the first issue of *The British Journal of Music Education* (BJME) in 1984. With Paynter as editor until 1998, the journal has become a forum for wide-ranging debate on music education. Composing in education has been a recurrent theme from Brian Loane's *Thinking about Children's Compositions* (Loane, 1984) and Peter Owens' *The Contemporary Composer in the Classroom* (Owens, 1986), to Paynter's own article *Making Progress with Composing* (Paynter, 2000).

The BJME also reflects Paynter's interest in music education outside the United Kingdom. Europe has been represented by articles on France (Terry, 1985) and Germany (Martin, 1985), a report on the 1985 Strasbourg Conference on Contemporary Music by Thomas Chatburn (Chatburn, 1986), and more recently Janet Hoskyns' *Music Education and a European Dimension* (Hoskyns, 1992).

In his introduction to the 1987 Nordic issue, Paynter warns against the presumption that the British have all the answers (Paynter, 1987). However, although BJME cannot claim to have produced an exhaustive survey of European practice, these reports do seem to indicate how small a part composition, or even contemporary music, has played in music-education there.

George Odam and child-centred music education

In 2000 BJME published George Odam's article 'Teaching composing in secondary schools – The Creative Dream' (Odam, 2000), discussing his research work in collaboration with Anice Paterson based at Bath Spa University College (BSUC). The influence of George Odam, together with members of his staff at the BSUC School of Music, has been crucial in the development of ideas about composing in education over a thirty-year period.

It was as a direct result of his influence that Bath Spa provided a context for projects involving composers in the community and the classroom which formed the basis of my own action-based research. The Composing in Education course, devised by Jo Glover as a BA half module, formed the academic component to composer-in-education projects that I ran at 'Rainbow over Bath'.

Odam's fascination with the educational potential of non-European music manifested itself early in *Angry Arrow* (Odam, 1968), consisting of traditional songs of native North American tribes arranged for performance by unison junior choir and flexible junior school ensemble. The score contains two 'creative windows'. Children create their own material using rhythmic ostinati, and compose words for an Indian battle-chant (BC3).

Tutankhamun (Odam, 1972), scored for similar forces and again held together by the piano, is more ambitious in its conception but contains no opportunities for creative composition by children. The choir often breaks into three-part rounds, an example of a widely used device to develop part-singing.

In these pieces, Odam exemplifies John Paynter's idea of an integrated approach to education – one in which there can be 'an exchange of ideas and enthusiasms between various curriculum areas' (Odam, 1976: 4). His production notes for *Inca* invite integration between music, drama, dance, art, geography, history, English and religious studies, and suggest the use of maps and tourist leaflets of Peru to support classroom projects. The creative windows, entitled 'The Sea', 'The Desert', or 'The Mountains', are supported by detailed work cards (Example 10).

Odam's book *The Sounding Symbol* (1995) focuses on three of his pre-occupations:

1. The importance of an integrated and child-centred approach.
2. The potential offered by non-western music and the development of memory in aural traditions.
3. The significance of brain function in cognitive perception.

He puts forward a wide-ranging definition of music education – one which advocates life-long learning but also contains an indication of that changed role for the composer which is central to my discussion:

> There is a commonly held opinion that music education is the province only of schools. My contention is that it takes place whenever a person endeavours to explain or reveal some aspect of music to someone else. Music education is not simply the business of schools and teachers. It is the business of parents who wish to introduce their children to music, of instrumentalists who teach others to play and who play to other people, of composers who write music for others – most particularly music for those of us who are modest in our skill. It is the business of composers who teach others to compose, of lecturers, tutors and professors of music and music education, of those who work as musicians in our communities, and of those who train others for a lifetime of working with music in some aspect (Odam: 1995, 6).

Example 10: Odam, G. (1972) *Inca* score windows p.7.

77

In examining the results of recent brain research, Odam was looking for a scientific basis for educational theories arrived at by empirical methods based on his own observations of what works and does not work in the classroom. He draws inspiration from John Sloboda's work in cognitive psychology (*The Musical Mind*, 1985), David Hargreaves' work in developmental psychology (*The Developmental Psychology of Music*, 1986), and the work of Prof. Paul Robertson and Dr. Peter Fenwick. Odam took an interest in developments in Positron Emission Tomography, which allows brain action to be studied through photographic images showing areas of increased activity. Early results appeared to support the theory, central to Odam's argument, that the right hemisphere deals with intuition, emotion and holistic thought, while the left is concerned with logical, cognitive and linguistic functions.

Odam draws attention to the importance of movement in the musical education of very small children. Movement learning, centred in the cerebellum, is fundamentally important to humans. Odam recalls the theories of Jacques Dalcroze when he declares that 'we begin to develop sophisticated thought processes in both the right and left brain only through the mediation of movement' (Odam, 1995: 13). This fundamental link between movement and music is expressed in the many African musical cultures, for example the Igbo concept of *nkwa* which combines singing, playing musical instruments and dancing in a single act. Carl Orff's idea of 'conducting as dance' exploited the same primal link.

The Sounding Symbol was published in 1995. Unfortunately for Odam, more recent research has tended to suggest different interpretations of the functions of the brain's left and right hemispheres. The findings of Stefan Evers at the University of Münster (Evers et al., 1999) and of Jean-Pierre Royet at Université Claude Bernard, Lyon (Royet et al., 2000), have thrown serious doubt on the presumption that emotions happen in the right hemisphere, and cognitive processes in the left. It now seems probable that in most humans, the brain exhibits a form of reversed 'handedness' in which the left hemisphere is the dominant area of brain function. The centre of consciousness, the part which processes immediate experiences, making sense of anything new, complicated or unfamiliar, is now thought to be located in the left frontal lobe.

However the evidence from brain-function research still confirms that the response to rhythm, physical movement, and melodic shape is a very primitive instinct in human beings, associated with the earliest development of the brain. Psychologists have noted the spontaneous development of 'song babbling' in children at around 18 months before they have begun to speak (Moog, 1976; Gardner et al., 1982 cited in Odam, 1995). Moreover, observations show that the ability to respond to music persists into old age, and is one of the last mental faculties left in advanced stages of Alzheimer's Syndrome and other degenerative conditions. Those who have given musical performances in old people's homes know very well the pleasure and stimulus which they bring. Music comes before speech and is still there after speech has disappeared. There is therefore no period of our lives which cannot be enhanced by the experience of music.

The longest of the eight chapters of *The Sounding Symbol* is entitled 'Teaching Composing'. Odam's primary aim is to propose teaching methods for children in school, but much of what he has to say is applicable at any age. He advocates teaching composition in what he calls a 'whole-brain' manner. His presumptions about the pre-cise locations in the brain of so-called right-brain functions of listening to sound, aural memory and spontaneous improvisation, and left-brain functions of writing music down, and analysing and describing it in words, must now be regarded as metaphorical. However his descrip-tion of the way these functions reinforce one-another is still valid.

He discusses Benjamin Britten's descriptions of his lessons with Frank Bridge. Britten was sent across the other side of the room while his teacher played the young composer's juvenile attempts on the piano, demanding to know if this was really what he had intended to write. According to Odam, such an approach strikes the right balance by forcing the young composer to remember the sounds he had first imagined, compare them with what he was now hearing, analyse the difference and express it in words.

Odam compares this with his own experience of composition lessons with Alexander Goehr, Jonathan Harvey and Hans Keller which were, in his view, entirely left-brain focused. Discussion centred on what was written on the page, without hearing what the music sounded like. As a student I remember similar, sometimes intimidating encounters with these same teachers, where, as Odam tellingly puts it: 'It was assumed [...] that the inner ear was completely and satisfactorily in operation in both teacher and pupil, leaving no need for sound actually to be used' (Odam, 1995: 55). Using the piano was seen as in some way inferior because it would impede development of our inner ear, and divert our attention away from the structural rigour of motivic unity, or of serial method, and tempt us to resort to 'mere effect'.

Odam's fifth chapter discusses aspects of teaching composition based on many years of his own experience, and on observation of other teachers in the classroom. His approach is always child-centred, and never based on a desire to evangelise for a particular musical style: 'The matter of musical styles is largely immaterial except in the sense that pupils need to have a wide experience of styles' (Odam, 1995: 56). In the later stages of music education pupils might be asked to produce stylistic pastiche, but teaching should always progress from the known to the unknown. Children's creative work must stem from the musical languages with which they feel comfortable: 'Style in musical composition should normally be the choice of the child' (Odam, 1995: 56). The use of musical vernaculars like rhythm-and-blues, reggae, soul and ballad was therefore of utmost importance as a point of departure:

> There should be a focus on the music of today's society, not defined exclusively as the music of today's youth culture, which is too particular, and largely ephemeral, but emphasising the foundations of music that is popular generally (Odam, 1995: 56).

Odam echoes Kodály in emphasising song as 'the earliest form of musical discourse'. Voices always come before instruments. In Odam's view, a combination of song and story is a very practical starting point because it combines right-brain function (mapping out the structure of the story and imagining relationships between characters) with left-brain function (telling the story in words). The use of short narrative texts written by children as a starting point for the composition of simple song melodies has become a well-tried method in classroom projects, as discussed by Coral Davies in *Say it till a song comes* (Davies, 1986).

Children also respond well to the use of sound to tell a story without words. Odam is well aware of contrary views on this subject. John Paynter has objected that the practice of always linking stories to music will foster the view that music represents something:

> Regrettably, in schools we still find a misleading emphasis upon the literal inter-
> pretation of music. Stories, pictorial ideas, notions of mood and 'atmospheric'
> meaning, programme notes and peripheral information have been pressed upon
> us in the name of musical understanding for so long that we have reached the
> stage where it is difficult even to question this practice (Paynter, 1992: 18).

Paynter has encouraged a more abstract approach, concentrating on the materials and 'constructional elements' of music. But Odam takes the view that children like to do both (Odam, 1995: 60). In pursuit of the 'abstract approach', one of the best ways to start children composing is simply to listen to what they do spontaneously, for instance unconsciously humming a simple melody or making random noises on a xylophone, and then follow up with an encouraging comment, inviting the children to repeat what they just did.

As children progress through the school system, those who have instrumental lessons begin to have an advantage in composition over those who do not, since they are much better equipped to try out and develop their musical ideas. Odam's practical answer to the 'skill gap' is to give children who have what he calls 'the privilege of instrument-al tuition' the responsibility of leading composing groups or producing songs for the whole class to sing. This gives them a chance to shine among their peers and helps to build confidence, an example of one of the social benefits which can come from music.

Odam's idea of music as part of an integrated approach to education comes across in his many ideas for cross-curricular links. He proposes a song about a historical event, exploration of the idea of division of a beat into mathematical fractions, or music describing the course of a river *à la* Smetana to back up geographical study. His suggestion of the use of geographical maps as a starting point for music was prompted by his own reading of Bruce Chatwin's *Songlines* (Chatwin, 1987).

Finally, Odam is well aware of the criticism that creative music-making has failed to educate children in the traditional technicalities of music. He is adamant about the need for an understanding of scales, keys and modes, and notational skills of reading and writing. He proposes that these should be understood by the end of key-stage 3 (age 11–14), so that teachers can approach their work in key-stage 4 (14–16) confident that the ground work had been done (Odam, 1995: 69). Unfortunately, no such assumption can be made, posing problems both for the advanced teaching of composition at 'A' level and in higher education, and for the encouragement of composition in adults.

Peter Wiegold, Ian Mitchell and the Gemini Ensemble

Odam emphasises that education must be 'child-centred'. Peter Wiegold's work has a much wider community base, and has focused on the release of creative energies within the individual composer or musician. For Wiegold the word 'centred' has a different significance, and refers to the achievement of an inner balance between mental and physical energies. It is from this state of alert but balanced readiness and composure that the workshop leader can be most effective in helping others to discover and realise their own creative musical potential.

But equally we cannot describe Wiegold's work as 'style-centred'. His aim is the discovery and release of creativity for its own sake, and for this purpose he has evolved a kind of general-purpose, accessible workshop style based on modal patterns, sometimes chromatically coloured, into which a wide variety of rhythmic, melodic and harmonic ostinati can be incorporated.

Wiegold, like John Paynter, seeks to avoid what he sees as the 'rigid imposition of skills and knowledge'. He does not advocate a 'creative free-for-all', but a 'third way' based on 'Continuous friction and stimulation between given material and student response, between the formal and the spontaneous' (Wiegold, 1997: 1).

Unlike the other figures discussed in this chapter, Wiegold has produced no books or publications. As a result his influence is often overlooked or, worse still, others have taken the credit for his innovations. His commitment to music education was encouraged by David Lumsdaine at Durham University (1972–1975). Wiegold also acknowledges the formative influence of a trip to India in 1979, and to Java to study Gamelan in 1981, and of his encounter with John Cage at the Gulbenkian Music and Dance Summer School in 1986. The influence of eastern forms of thought is seen in his use of Tai Chi, and his interest in Sufi poetry.

His exemplary work as director of the Gemini Ensemble from 1975 to 1985, and as Artistic Director of the Performance and Communications Skills (PCS) course at Guildhall School of Music and Drama from 1984 to 1996 has influenced a generation of composers and musicians. It is perhaps symptomatic of the lack of full recognition of the originality of his ideas that a report at the end of the first year of what was then called the MPCS course (Music Performance and Communication Skills) in the British Journal of Music Education, failed to mention his name (Renshaw, 1986). However Wiegold was later awarded an Honorary FGSM in recognition to his contribution to the School.

Clarinettist Ian Mitchell took over as director of Gemini in 1985 and continued the pattern of educational residencies established by Wiegold. Over twenty-six years, the number of projects undertaken by Gemini is too large to allow detailed description of all of them. In discussion with Wiegold and Mitchell, I have singled out those which were most significant. These include a residency in Manchester in 1983, initiated by Paul Robinson, Music Officer for the North West Arts Association. In the same year workshops at the Gardner Arts Centre in Brighton were memorable as the first to use Wiegold's 'backbone' principle discussed below.

The Merseyside Arts Residency in 1985, based at the Bluecoat Gallery, was formative. Initially Gemini made short intensive three-day visits to Merseyside in October and December 1984 as part of 'Music for Youth', a programme to encourage the development of participatory art-forms 'in areas where they are most needed' socially, geographically and artistically. They were invited back in 1985 to participate in an extended seven-month music residency as part of a long term plan 'to strengthen the relationship between professional educators and professional artists [...] [and] create more meaningful and longer-lasting resources than previously established through occasional schemes, visits or residencies' (Gemini, 1986: 4).

The outcome of the residency is well documented in a project report which gives a useful 'state-of-the-art' snapshot of the evolution of a model for an ensemble residency. It sits on the cusp of the change-over between Peter Wiegold and Ian Mitchell as Directors of Gemini. Mitchell saw it as the genesis of a blueprint for future school projects.

The project exhibited a degree of social inclusiveness in that its aim was to involve teachers, community leaders, school children of all ages, parents and community groups in music making in a contemporary idiom and 'to bring professional performance to as wide an audience as possible' (Gemini, 1986: 5). Secondary schools and their feeder primaries took part, and parents were involved, but only as members of concert audiences. Amongst its objectives we find breaking down the performance/audience barrier, giving people an opportunity to experience the fun of working with contemporary music, propagating a music workshop method, encouraging children to create their own music, and giving people the chance to widen their musical experience.

The residency took the form of three visits, one in each of the autumn, spring and summer terms. Each visit was of three weeks duration divided between three Merseyside Local Education Authorities (LEAs). According to one press report, the residency reached a total of around eight-hundred children (Bergen, 1986). Each LEA approached the project in different ways so that it represents a kind of control experiment.

Example 11: Gemini Merseyside residency 1985 timetable
(Reconstructed from information supplied in the project report).

Residency I: 10–29 November 1985

		morning	afternoon/evening	other schools:
week 1 Wirrall	day 1		Public concert, Bluecoat Gallery	
	day 2		Residency concert, Bluecoat Gallery	
	day 3	Marian High workshop	Woodchurch Community Centre	
	day 4	Marian High workshop	Woodchurch CC	
	day 5	Marian High workshop	Woodchurch CC	
	day 6		Residency concert, Glenda Jackson Theatre	
week 2 Sefton	day 1		opening concert	
	day 2	St. Wilfrid's High, Litherland: workshops	King George V College youth club	St. Elizabeth RCP school
	day 3	St. Wilfrid's High workshops	King George V College youth club	Our Lady Queen of Peace Juniors
	day 4	St. Wilfrid's High workshops	King George V College youth club	
	day 5	St. Wilfrid's High workshops	King George V College youth club	
week 3 Knowsley	day 1		opening concert	
	day 2	St. Paul's Comp., Halewood	workshop	West Vale Juniors
	day 3	St. Andrew's Comp., Prescot	workshop	Kirby C of E Juniors
	day 4	Ruffwood Comprehensive	workshop	Teachers Centre
	day 5	workshop	workshop	

85

Residency II: 26 January – 14 February 1986

		morning	Afternoon/evening	other schools:
week 1 Knows-ley	day 1		Concert at Christ's & Notre Dame College	
	day 2		Residency concert	
	day 3	St. Paul's Comp., Halewood	Workshop	West Vale Juniors
	day 4	St. Andrew's Comp., Prescot	Workshop	Kirby C of E Juniors
	day 5	Ruffwood Comprehensive	Concert, Knowsley Tertiary College	Plantation CP & Nursery schools
	day 6	workshop	Workshop	
week 2 Wirrall	day 1		opening concert	
	day 2	Marian High	Workshop	
	day 3	Marian High	Workshop	
	day 4	Marian High	Workshop	
	day 5	Marian High	Workshop	
week 3 Sefton	day 1		opening concert	
	day 2	Haghull High School	Bootle Youth Club	St. Elizabeth RCP school
	day 3	Haghull High School	Workshop	Our Lady Queen of Peace Juniors
	day 4	Haghull High School	Workshop	
	day 5	Haghull High School	Workshop	

86

Residency III: 5–23 May 1986

		morning	afternoon/evening	other schools:
week 1	day 1	Stanley High School	opening concert	
Sefton	day 2	Stanley High School	workshop	
	day 3	Stanley High School	workshop	
	day 4	Stanley High School	workshop	
	day 5		Concert at Southport Arts Centre	
week 2	day 1		workshop	
Knows-	day 2	St. Paul's Comp., Halewood	workshop	West Vale Juniors
ley	day 3	St.Andrew's Comp., Prescot	workshop	Kirby C of E Juniors
	day 4	Ruffwood Comprehensive	workshop	
	day 5		workshop	
week 3	day 1	Marian High	workshop	
Wirrall	day 2	Marian High	workshop	
	day 3	Marian High	workshop	
	day 4	Marian High	workshop	
	day 5	Marian High	Final concert	

Wirrall Borough carefully selected one school in a socially ad-
vantaged area, the Marian High School for Girls, for the entire
scheme. This was reflected in a strong commitment from the music
staff, and continuity of creative involvement of the key-stage 3
children who took part. The climax was a performance at the Glenda
Jackson Theatre in Birkenhead of a group composition depicting the
River Mersey in words and music. Stephen Pratt's evaluation indicates
a high level of interest from the rest of the school with full attendance at
the final concert by other pupils and teachers (Gemini, 1986: 8).

Sefton Borough chose a different school each week. Jolande van
Bergen, Music Officer for Merseyside Arts, praises Sefton's decision
to use the project as a training opportunity for peripatetic instrumental
teachers (Gemini, 1986: 15). However, Mitchell himself expresses
doubts about the success of this attempt to propagate their method and

leave a legacy of new skills amongst teachers who apparently failed to grasp any relevance it might have to their normal teaching programme (Gemini, 1986: 11).

Knowsley authority tried to spread the residency even more thinly, sharing it between three secondary schools and several primaries. One of the assessors praises Gemini's ideological commitment to breaking down barriers of social class, age and ability, reflected in the strategic choice of schools in this socially deprived area. Mitchell's candid reports of a general lack of commitment, including one incident of what he describes as insulting behaviour from a head-master, have an all-too-familiar ring.

The ensemble's work in the youth service seems to have been the least successful aspect. Mitchell's comments about the problems of working in youth clubs, where 'the informal structure militates against the success of one or two short visits' and the artists found themselves being used as 'a commodity for the evening if anyone wanted it', reveal how much harder it is to make an impact in this sector (Gemini, 1986: 12).

The report is less revealing about the actual workshop methodology. It reads like an ideological statement with phrases like 'Gemini workshops involve all levels of music making from simple skills exercises to creative work' and 'Each member of a workshop had an integral part to play regardless of previous music experience (or lack of it!)'. There is no detailed description of the progression of ideas, but the list of activities is a characteristic mixture of ingredients containing the seeds of Wiegold's later, more fully-developed four-phase model:

- Games to bring everyone together and practice actual rhythmic concentration and performance skills.
- Exercises exploring new sounds, trying patterns, inventing notations, following the Gemini players and improvising on given ideas.
- Discussion: What is music for? What are the basics of musical language?
- Creative work: Creating something from scratch together with the Gemini instrumentalists on a given theme or idea.
- Involvement of elements of theatre, movement, mime and poetry, drawing together the various earlier workshop activities to show them in operation.

Mitchell has emphasised the importance of the strategic planning which lay behind the ten-year residency in London Boroughs, initiated by Derek Warby for Greater London Arts in 1987. Gemini undertook projects all over the Greater London area in places of widely differing socio-economic character, particularly in Barnet and Enfield. These followed a timetable of teacher training days, followed by workshop visits and final concerts, sometimes staged at the South Bank. Projects adopted a variety of themes such as the 1988 'Radio project' in Barnet with Bruce Cole and the 'Music and Movement' project with Sue Maclennan in Streatham in the same year. The ensemble was able to visit the same schools repeatedly and to forge long-lasting beneficial relationships with them.

Spitalfields Festival endorsed this principle of lasting relationships when, in 1992, Simon Foxley invited Gemini to lead a regular programme of primary workshops for the Festival. The partnership ended when Philip Flood took over in 1998.

Gemini's touring schedule reflects the patchiness of interest in creative music in this country. Projects were scattered widely over the country. The ensemble simply went where it was invited. An involvement with the English National Opera Baylis programme led to performances in 1990 of Nicola LeFanu's *The Green Children* as part of the King's Lynn Festival, reflecting the ensemble's long-term commitment to women composers.

Gemini's creative project work outside the UK has been minimal, which is surprising in view of its exemplary programme policy. Apart from Mitchell's own occasional conference visits to Europe, only a three-day visit to the International Society for Music Education conference in Canberra, Australia, in July 1988, a ten-concert tour of the Sultanate of Oman in 1993 which included three creative music workshops, and a lecture-demonstration in Riga, Latvia, have given the ensemble any opportunity to propagate its techniques outside this country.

The workshop methodology of Peter Wiegold

After leaving Gemini in 1985, Wiegold continued to conduct and lead workshops with other ensembles and orchestras. He has maintained a relationship with the Composers Ensemble, including several educational projects initiated by 'Rainbow over Bath' which I will discuss in later chapters. He has described his time at the Guildhall School as 'ten years of laboratory'. It was during this time that a more systematic analysis emerged of the way that the creative process progresses during a music workshop.

Working each year with a carefully selected group of fifteen one-year postgraduate students, the aim of the course was to create a new kind of musician capable of 'understanding people as well as an instrument' – one who was not just an expert on his or her instrument, not even simply a good all-round musician, but a good communicator, educator, and inspirational leader as well, able to enter any situation, professional or community, and stimulate other people to develop their own musical creativity – just as Kodály advocated in his famous address of 1956.

Wiegold stresses the importance of a clear timetable for creative work. His Monday evening adult sessions at Arnolfini always began with a period of warm-up exercises, followed by discussion of ideas and concepts, moving on to creative improvisation or group work, and finally to performance of the results. At the Guildhall PCS course he established a two-day working pattern, repeated during each week.

Day one began with an hour of Tai Chi, when the whole group worked together in what Wiegold has described as a 'grounding activity', followed by two hours of theatre improvisation including mime, movement and use of words. The afternoon consisted of an hour and a half of free improvisation on instruments or voices, ending with a seminar on some aspect of musical or cultural history, 'tracing the progression of music from Bach to Stockhausen'.

Day two concentrated on group practical work, exploring the technicalities of composition in a workshop context. Sessions ranged widely over the use of classical and jazz chord sequences, rhythm including Afro-Caribbean drumming, and formal structures including use of Indonesian number sequences. The day was broken up with an hour of silent meditation. The course also included placements in classroom or community contexts in Tower Hamlets seen as a form of apprenticeship.

Wiegold learnt early that no system or structure is perfect. He was aware that in an organic situation such as the PCS course, relationships between fellow students and between teachers and students, can break down, or that the group can lose focus, with seriously detrimental effects on the students' learning process. He therefore built regular crisis meetings into the timetable.

More recently Peter Wiegold has set out the four phases of a creative music workshop in a project proposal for 'Rainbow over Bath':

1. Preparation: Focus attention – set tone – encourage spontaneity – build ensemble.
2. Presentation: Learn practical skills – learn and explore materials – learn forms and processes – find an individual response to these – deepen tone of workshop.
3. Realisation and composition: Set themes – set materials – demonstrate processes, especially the 'backbone' process – set tasks (individuals and groups) – realise – discuss – coach – refine.
4. Rehearsal and Performance: Rehearse – focus on communication – perform (Wiegold, 1997: 1–2).

'Preparation' includes warm-up games and 'centring' exercises designed to establish a mood of concentration and listening. The use of musical games is central to Wiegold's approach, but it would be wrong to regard him as the sole originator. Although classical musicians and singers regularly put themselves through an individual daily routine of technical exercises to loosen up fingers, lungs and voices, they do not traditionally take part in group warm-up games designed to focus mind, body and intellect in the way that Wiegold advocates. The practice found its way into music via experimental theatre and dance companies.

I first encountered the idea of the group physical warm-up in 1971 with companies such as 'Moving Being' or 'The Brighton

Combination' at the London and Birmingham Arts Laboratories. At this time the Spontaneous Music Ensemble and AMM were regularly touring small venues offering a package of improvisation workshops linked to evening concerts. A music workshop in Birmingham in 1971, led by John Stephens, was my first experience of interactive music games in which participants sat or stood in a circle, passing sounds from one person to the next. Many of Trevor Wishart's musical games, published in *Sounds Fun* (1975) and *Sounds Fun 2* (1977), are based on the 'sitting in a circle' model.

'Tuning' (Example 12) in which the object is: 'To generate an endless thread of interesting melody [...]' (Wishart, 1977: 16), is typical of what has become a standard format. It has been subjected to endless variations shared amongst an ever increasing community of practitioners. The origins can no longer be traced with any certainty.

Wiegold's second workshop phase, 'Presentation', includes the introduction of rhythmic structures, modes, harmonies and so on, moving on to ideas of copying, extending, adding and responding to changes. This can be a time to introduce improvisation. Wiegold suggests two ways of starting the process:

1. Riff building in which participants create simple ostinato patterns which fit and complement one another. Wiegold defines a riff as 'a musical idea that remains stable and in some sense repeats'. Patterns are often held together by a rhythmic *clavé* pattern which provides a central anchor to the sound, an idea borrowed from Latin music.
2. Free improvisation to encourage a wide and dramatic use of colour and gesture. The workshop leader may set limits such as 'play only three notes', 'play extremely quietly', 'use only trills', or 'start and stop on cue' (Wiegold, 1997: 4).

Wiegold is careful to explain the importance of a particular process or activity. He explains the value of improvisation in the following terms:

Starting improvisation in these two completely contrasted ways gives a broad sense of permission to what follows – a musical world that can go from the tightest group rhythm to a unique individual instrumental colour (Wiegold, 1997: 4).

Once an improvised ostinato pattern has been established, and has become 'cohesive and atmospheric', Wiegold draws out solos from the larger ensemble. The process helps even the most timid and inexperienced of participants to gain confidence in their ability to hold their own, or simply to take a risk, let go, and see what happens. In practice, the process is directed by Wiegold from the keyboard, sometimes supported by one or more instrumental assistants, professional musicians such as clarinettist Duncan Prescott who is capable of improvising an intricate melodic cantilena over the pulsing accompaniment of ostinato patterns.

Recorded examples on the Rainbow website show four progressive stages in the process during a workshop at the Hogeschool Alkmaar Conservatorium in December 1999. Wiegold can be heard encouraging players to introduce new elements and make changes:

rainbow: Track 03: Riffs enter in sequence leading to clarinet improvisation.
rainbow: Track 04: Players add parallel harmonies to one of the riffs.
rainbow: Track 05: The texture is refined to singing voices alone.
rainbow: Track 06: The final moments of the improvisation.

'Realisation and Composition' is the phase during which tasks are set and compositional models are given. A large group may decide to divide into smaller creative sub-groups, each deciding what form of leadership to adopt. The workshop leader will provide starting points such as a theme or a description of musical atmosphere, and will also set time limits: 'come back in twenty minutes', for instance or, more precisely, 'come back in twenty minutes with only the very first sound of the piece'.

A compositional model might take the form of a composition drawn from repertoire, or a live demonstration of a compositional process. It could take the form of what Wiegold calls a 'backbone', consisting of an ostinato, harmony, rhythm or a combination of these elements prepared in advance by the workshop leader: 'A backbone is like a clavé. It carries the key to the piece. It also expresses the whole structure of the piece, the railway line and the stations of the journey, as it were' (Wiegold, 1997: 7).

Feedback and refinement are a vital part of the process of 'realisation and composition'. Groups who have created material in response to the workshop leader's starting points perform the results of their work, subjecting it to critical examination by other participants. The process can be difficult because it often means modifying or rejecting some people's ideas. Wiegold sees this as a moment to adopt a more traditional instructional approach. 'A balance is needed between teaching compositional craft and encouraging individual creative autonomy' (Wiegold, 1997: 8).

Finally, when the material created in the workshop is set, a period of rehearsal allows the group to concentrate on performance skills. Wiegold is certain of the value of the live public performance:

> [...] the thrill of going before an audience and 'risking all' is something very special in the performing arts, and whatever background and experience the participants have, performance can be very exciting and leave a lasting memory (Wiegold, 1997: 8).

Wiegold's former students have carried his influence into many areas of musical life. When he resigned as Director of the PCS course in 1996, his former student Sean Gregory took over. Wiegold is widely recognised as conductor, workshop leader and animateur, skilled in working at many different levels of age and ability. He works as 'player trainer' with professional ensembles and orchestras in this country such as the London Sinfonietta, the Composers Ensemble, Lontano and the Park Lane Music Players.

His work in Canada with Symphony Nova Scotia and 'Upstream' Canada, and in Finland with the Joensuu City Orchestra, has begun to propagate his ideas abroad. Recently he led a project in The Netherlands co-ordinated by the London Sinfonietta and the Dutch trust Netherlands.dot.comp providing professional player training workshops in Den Haag. His methods have even begun to reach into the field of commercial management leadership training schemes with courses organised by the Swedish firm Erikson, a novel example of the changing role of the composer in society.

Example 12: Wishart, T. (1977) Game from *Sounds Fun 2*.

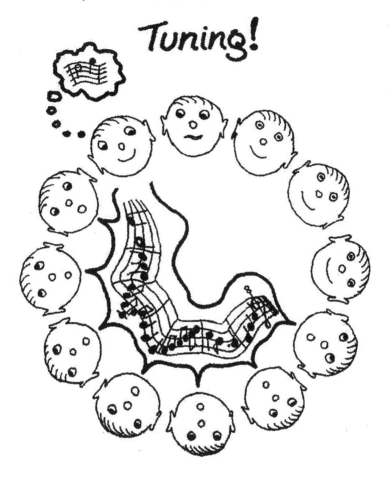

1. Students at a workshop with Peter Wiegold at the Hogeschool, Alkmaar.

2. Group improvisation led by Peter Wiegold at the Hogeschool, Alkmaar.

Chapter 3
Private trusts and government policy

Various reports, either independent or government sponsored, have influenced the policies of arts funding agencies over the past forty years, both in the UK, and in Europe. These in turn have influenced the development of creative music-making by setting priorities for financial support. Government bodies such as the Arts Council, Regional Arts Boards and organisations in the education sector, together with various private organisations such as the Calouste Gulbenkian Foundation, have contributed to a lively interchange of ideas, but the progression has not been smooth. The enactment of clear-sighted and sometimes even visionary policy has been held back by political expediency, foot-dragging and lack of continuity.

A conference at the South Bank Centre in London on 22 May 1996, which revealed a depressing picture of lack of continuity in the Arts Council's music education policy at that time, was the inspiration for my study. Several case-studies were held up as examples of 'best-practice' but they were presented uncritically. There was no serious examination of the practical needs, such as liaison with schools and teachers, or the importance of preparation and follow-up work. No reference was made to the valuable work in the field of 'Composers in Education' done by the Performing Right Society, nor of the resource material available from Colleges like Guildhall and Bath College of Higher Education. The conference even ignored the Contemporary Music Network's own archives from the 1980s, when its education policy was being formulated (Laycock, 1996: 6). It was this apparent lack of a well-informed overview which made me aware of the need for a comparative study.

The Calouste Gulbenkian Foundation

The Gulbenkian Foundation (CGF) has had a fundamental impact on arts education in this country through its reports and funding schemes. The 1973 Artists in Schools Scheme in which seven local education authorities collaborated, included a composer in residence at Ebenside School, Cleator Moor, Cumbria, a post held by David Cain in 1974 (Braden, 1978: 65).

The 1978 CGF report *Training Professional Musicians* emphasised re-creative rather than creative music. It had many sensible things to say about the training of performers, but little about composers. The provision of music centres for young people was discussed, but the emphasis is always on performance. Its recommendations concerning the role of music colleges made no mention of composition: 'We propose, therefore, that the music colleges should concentrate mainly on the training of intending performers and instrumental teachers' (Gulbenkian, 1978: 75). Not until the end of Chapter 3 is there any mention of the young composer:

> The young composer should be helped by the simple means of being performed as he develops. We recommend that the Arts Council of Great Britain should consider making more funds available for the preparation and playing of new music by promising young composers as soon as they emerge from full-time study (Gulbenkian, 1978: 84).

The 1982 CGF Report *Artists in Schools* set the tone for the development of creative arts in education for several decades. It put forward compelling philosophical arguments for the importance of artistic creativity in young people and expressed eloquently the need for cultural and artistic awareness amongst all members of an industrialised and technological society:

> Without the balance that an education in both the sciences and the arts can give, we should have a society undignified by a predilection for beauty in art and dignity in relationships. We should have rather a nation of beings with heads like computers, hands like robots and hearts like Caliban's (Gulbenkian, 1982: 25).

In as much as the 1982 Gulbenkian Report concerns all the arts, its general conclusions apply to music. The report asserted that: 'Creative thought and action should be fostered in all areas of education. In the arts they are central' (Gulbenkian, 1982: 26). It identified a number of compelling functions for the arts in a healthy society:

> [...] they can help to develop qualities and abilities that have very practical applications: grace, poise and balance in gesture and movement; sharpness of vision, hearing and touch; a high degree of co-ordination between hand and eye; and ability to express oneself in precise terms [...]. The visual arts, drama, dance and music [...] can have valuable therapeutic functions in the treatment of some physical or emotional disorders [...] they provide [opportunities] for recreation of the individual, in giving him or her different perspectives and challenges away from the pre-occupations of the everyday business, industrial or domestic worlds (Gulbenkian, 1982: 26).

The report saw the arts as a means of developing individual qualities of confidence and self-esteem. The skilful exercise of the arts called for discipline, dedication and attention to detail. They were of central importance to human beings whatever their social and economic circumstances. The arts were not to be seen simply as pastimes, whose importance increases as the opportunities for 'real' work decline.

Like George Odam (Odam, 1995: 9), the report found justification for its view in psychological studies of brain function. Education had concentrated too much on 'the rationality of the left-hand hemisphere at the expense of the more sensuous, intuitive and holistic aspects of consciousness and perception' (Gulbenkian, 1982: 25). It drew attention to the difference between 'convergent' thinking and 'divergent' thinking typical of the arts which showed 'ingenuity, inventiveness, unconventionality and the ability to innovate and solve problems' (Gulbenkian, 1982: 34).

Getting children to think and work creatively was a matter of the highest educational importance: 'To encourage creative work we must put a premium on the pupil's own original ideas whenever possible' (Gulbenkian, 1982: 34).

Creative work must meet seven 'conditions of creativity':

1. It must involve making or producing something.
2. It must be someone's personal achievement.
3. It must be in some way novel, original, different or distinctive.
4. It must be the product of conscious and deliberate activity, rather than chance, luck or serendipity.
5. It must be of high quality.
6. It must take account of context, in relation to the person's particular sphere of expertise.
7. It must show consistency of output – an ability to produce quality on more than one occasion (Gulbenkian, 1982: 30).

Many of the 1978 and 1982 recommendations have been acted upon. The introduction of composition into the GCSE and 'A' level syllabuses, the focus on child-centred music education, the formulation of the National Curriculum, the establishment of Saturday-morning music centres, the development of the Artists in Schools movement, and the creation of specialist music schools such as Chethams, Purcell, Menuhin and Wells Cathedral all seem to owe something to the climate of opinion created by the 1982 Gulbenkian Report.

The Arts Council of Great Britain and its successors

The Gulbenkian report had a fundamental influence on Arts Council policy. Julia Winterson has provided an excellent summary of the significant landmarks in the development of UK government policy towards the arts in education since the early 1960s (Winterson, 1998). Acknowledging the importance of Jennie Lee's appointment as Arts Minister by the Wilson government, and the influence of her white paper *A Policy for the Arts* (Lee, 1965; cited in Winterson, 1998: 20), Winterson emphasises the initial resistance of the Arts Council to supporting education. It was not until the appointment of Roy Shaw as Secretary General (1978–1983) that the Council began to develop a serious commitment to arts education. It was Shaw's aim 'to make excellence accessible'. Irene Macdonald, the first Education Liaison Officer, framed the Council's fledgling education policy in her paper *Professional Arts in Schools* (Macdonald, 1980).

It was through the Contemporary Music Network that the Council took its most important early steps in establishing a music education programme. As Andrew Peggie rightly pointed out, when the Network was annually touring twelve expensive and highly trained ensembles around the country, attempts must constantly be made 'to bring them and their music into meaningful contact with the local community' (Peggie 1986: 39). The network committee, convened by Annette Moreau, included education specialists such as John Paynter, and also myself as an active promoter of educational projects at Arnolfini, Bristol.

Roy Shaw's principle of 'the pursuit of excellence' was framed in *The Glory of the Garden* (1984), but unfortunately the enactment of its proposals did as much harm as good by re-distributing a diminishing cake, with inevitable unfairness. At this time the Arts Council and the Regional Arts Associations adopted a policy of forcing orchestras and arts centres to embrace educational and community work as a condition of funding. Some accepted the challenge with enthusiasm. Others engaged in reluctant tokenism to qualify for the funding, a situation which Julia Winterson still found to be the case in 1996 (Winterson, 1998: 200).

If the funding bodies were to be fully accountable, it was essential to monitor the effectiveness of educational projects. Andrew Peggie's *Music Education Projects, Monitoring Reports* was published in 1986. The need for evaluation has been taken up many times since, for instance by Anthony Jackson of Manchester University in: *Anecdotes are no longer enough* (Jackson, 1995). Calling for greater rigour in evaluation work he finds that: 'Academic research has a vital role to play in identifying, testing and helping to implement models of evaluative methodology that will be of benefit to companies, funders, and, most of all, to potential audiences of the work' (Jackson, 1995: 1).

The Arts Council's 1986 Music Education Policy resulted in the creation of a scheme of musicians in residence. Fourteen animateurs were appointed by Stephen Firth. They included Hugh Nankivell at

Tyne and Wear Museum, David Price at the Abraham Morris Centre, Manchester, and Barry Russell at Arnolfini, Bristol (p. 57).

The artists-in-schools movement

Throughout the 1980s composing in education was part of the wider movement of artists in schools inspired by the 1982 Gulbenkian report. By the early 1990s there were many schemes all over the country. Some were well managed. Others failed to realise their full potential. It was this situation which inspired *Artists in Schools* (1992) by Caroline Sharp & Karen Dust, a handbook designed to help teachers and artists with their project planning. The seven chapters of this well-organised book are packed with useful practical guidance, taking us step by step through a successful project:

1. Benefits and frustrations.
2. Artist's guide to getting started.
3. Teacher's guide to getting started.
4. Project planning guide.
5. Project in action.
6. Evaluation.
7. Resources, contacts, further reading.

The book is based on a wealth of practical experience. Sharp was Senior Research Officer for the National Foundation for Educational Research, and Dust was part-time Education Officer at Eastern Arts. The first chapter lists many of the benefits of arts-education projects well rehearsed in the 1982 Gulbenkian report. Benefits for pupils include insight into the professional arts world, understanding and developing artistic skills and processes, and the enthusiastic enjoyment of participation in positive working relationships. Benefits for teachers and schools include enrichment of the whole curriculum, focus on personal and social issues, opportunities to form closer relationships with pupils, links with other schools, involvement of parents and the wider community, and projection of a positive image of the school (Sharp & Dust, 1992: 7).

The fact that only three benefits are identified for artists, including reaching a wider audience, opportunities to work with others, and helping them to develop their abilities, is symptomatic of the child-centred approach of this book. The advice on project planning and implementation is based on sound principles of child-centred education, while at the same time persuading artists to ask themselves searching questions about their own motivation in undertaking education work.

The book proposes three levels of involvement for the artist in school:

1. Making – commissioned work in progress by artist or composer in residence.
2. Presenting – artist presents work in live concerts, exhibitions, readings, etc.
3. Instructing/facilitating – workshops, composer-in-education schemes, etc.

An ideal project might include elements of all three, resulting in the kind of 'holistic project' about which more anon.

However, the book does not advocate risk-taking. This is not an approach based on Schafer's maxim: 'teach on the verge of peril'. The sections entitled 'what could go wrong?' (Sharp & Dust, 1992: 11) are particularly revealing. Realistically one should expect things to go wrong. There are risks in the arts, and a project which sets out to anaesthetise itself against them is cutting itself off from one of the real benefits of an artistic project: the excitement of discovery in uncharted seas.

In *Artists in Schools – a review* (1998) David Odie & Garth Allen provide a comprehensive survey of the development of the artists-in-schools movement. They trace its development from the Cockpit Arts Workshop, which opened in London in 1970 funded by ILEA (Tambling 1997: 44; cited in Odie and Allen, 1998: 10), and the introduction of 'Theatre in Education' companies. They single out the visionary Drumcroon Education Art Centre, Wigan in 1980. The aim of the 'Artist in Wigan Schools Scheme' was to place an artist in every school in the LEA, and:

To give all Wigan's young people irrespective of age – their teachers and the local community access to the range, breadth and variety of the visual arts through the main focus of contemporary makers, taking into account such issues as race, gender and special needs (Taylor, 1991: 9; cited in Odie & Allen, 1998).

Odie and Allen go on to assess the impact on arts provision of the 1988 Education Reform Act (ERA) and the introduction of Local Management of Schools (LMS) (Odie & Allen, 1998: 13). Previously many arts organisations received direct support from LEAs, but after LMS, they could only be supported on a piecemeal basis by individual schools. Far too many schools, faced with setting their own priorities, regarded the arts as dispensable. There was a resultant 'triumph of quantity over quality', a shift away from participatory projects and an increase in performance-only large-audience events (Jackson, 1995: 26; cited in Odie & Allen, 1998: 13). The ERA (1988) outlined the need for a broad curriculum emphasising 'spiritual, moral, cultural, mental and physical development', but defeated its own objectives by making some arts subjects optional, especially at key-stage 4, while the pressures of the National Curriculum timetable gave teachers less freedom for creative projects (Odie & Allen, 1998: 13).

Odie & Allen compare research into the growth of arts education agencies (AEAs) including two studies commissioned by the Paul Hamlyn Foundation (Harries & Shaw, 1994 and 1995), and the Arts Council's document *Leading Through Learning* (1997) which revealed two contradictory trends:

1. A significant increase in educational activities funded by the Arts Council and the Regional Arts Boards.
2. A significant disappearance of committed arts-education organisations such as Theatre-in-Education.

Leading Through Learning claimed a huge growth in educational activity among artists and arts organisations, successfully countering the downward trend in LEA-supported projects. A second report *Arts Organisations and the Educational Programmes* revealed that 78% of arts organisations funded by the Arts Council or the RABs had educational programmes and that 63% had dedicated officers running them (Hogarth, Kinder & Harland, 1997: 6). But Odie & Allen question the significance of these claims, suggesting that the true picture was rather patchy, with good provision in some areas, and almost none in others (Odie & Allen, 1998: 19), a view supported by *The Heart of the Matter – Education Research and Development Initiative* (ERDI) (Rogers 1997). ERDI supported twenty organisations in its first year, including Arnolfini and the Cheltenham Festival. Rogers contended that arts organisations should be building education into the core of their programmes, but found that too many saw education as primarily a marketing device to attract new audiences.

The report *Developing Arts Education Agencies* (Rogers, 1998) published by the Arts Council (by now reconstituted as the Arts Council of England), estimated that there were over sixty AEAs, amongst them the south-west-based Wren Trust for folk music, the Devon Arts in Schools Initiative (DAISI), Bolton, Bury and Rochdale AISA which raised half a million pounds over three years, and the London Education Arts Partnership (LEAP). This might imply a coherent network, but in fact shows a very patchy picture (Odie & Allen, 1998: 31).

National Lottery schemes of the Arts Council of England

During September 1995, Lord Gowrie, then Chairman of the Arts Council of England, announced the initiation of the National Lottery Arts Capital Fund. A nation wide consultation process took place to enable the Council to formulate its strategy for spending the lottery bonanza. Consultation with the musical community led to the green paper *Striking a New Note* (February 1996) which drew on the views of 'many composers, creative musicians, promoters, publishers, broadcasters, journalists and administrators concerned with new music.' Gowrie expressed determination that 'the process will lead to a celebration of new work, and great variety, in the next millennium' (Gowrie, 1996: 1).

Striking a New Note formulated a 'holistic approach' to new-music promotion, the origins of which can be traced back to the 1978 Gulbenkian Report which acknowledges that: 'Over the past decade opportunities for composers have been improving [...] [that there were] more grants available [...] [and an] increasing fashion for first performances, with the BBC and commissioning bodies anxious to discover gifted young composers' (Gulbenkian, 1978: 23). However, the report found that the 'exclusively serious composer', defined as one 'who does not want to specialise in films or TV or other forms of popular music', was unable to earn a living solely by composition. The size of fees did not bear any relation to the amount of time spent on the composition, and composers did not often get sufficient opportunity to hear their work performed. Although more festivals, orchestras, chamber groups and individuals commissioned new works, they did not give sufficient opportunity for second and third performances. The report concluded that: 'the opportunities and rewards for composers do not match the quality and variety of the work that is being produced in Britain at the present time' (Gulbenkian, 1978: 23).

The model was beginning to emerge in *A Fairer Hearing* by Keith Allen and Phyllida Shaw in which they stated:

> [...] funding bodies should be looking to support a package that includes a commission fee, the production of performing materials, the participation of the composer in rehearsals, the premiere and its associated costs and the recording of the premiere (Allen & Shaw, 1993; cited in Gowrie, 1996: 29).

'Striking a New Note' summarises the approach as follows:

> The holistic approach would acknowledge that the creation of new music is a flow which starts with the original creative idea, moves through preparation, rehearsal and performance and ends up with the listener. Funding should reflect that process, linking money for creation with money for production – and these production funds should recognise that a piece is rarely perfect on its first hearing. The funding should allow for post-premiere revisions or reworking (Gowrie, 1996: 2).

Educational and community work did not form part of these early holistic models. *Striking a New Note* advocated a number of practical measures, adding to its list activities of an educational nature and implying that these would all be eligible for support from the National Lottery. Strategies were needed to attract and hold on to a wide range of new audiences, especially the young. Promoters, producers, composers and creative musicians all needed to offer 'ways in' to new work – whether through education and outreach programmes, pre-performance talks or any other mechanism (Gowrie, 1996: 9).

Existing composer-in-residence schemes provided a model for the integration of education and community work into the holistic model. Job descriptions varied. At one extreme was the 'composer-in-association' model in which the composer was expected to do no more than produce a given number of commissions. At the other extreme was the composer as educational or community animateur (Gowrie, 1996: 54–55).

My own view was uncompromising and is summed up in an un-attributed remark: 'One composer went so far as to propose that additional work – talks, workshops, education programmes – should be a compulsory condition of receiving public commissioning funds' (Gowrie, 1996: 73). The Green Paper stopped short of wholehearted endorsement of my view, but its reasons are interesting, and underline the need for training in the skills of animateurship: 'This is probably over-prescriptive, especially as it might involve individuals doing work which they hated and for which they were totally unsuited' (Gowrie, 1996: 73).

Considerable discussion followed *Striking a New Note*, including my own lengthy response document (Laycock, 1996). Educational schemes developed by orchestras and arts centres could support the aims of the National Curriculum, resulting in 'future generations developing a more sophisticated awareness of music'. However, such a policy would not work out in practice unless there were more teachers who understood its significance. If they were not fully committed to the policy, and were relatively poorly informed about new trends in composition, we would end up with several generations of people 'who were neither skilled in traditional methods, nor understood anything about new music' (Laycock, 1996: 3), a view supported by several commentators (Odie & Allen 1998: 14; Rogers 1998: 18).

The consultations led to the publication, in November 1996, of *Creating New Notes*, the Arts Council's policy for the support of new music in England. This in turn influenced the formulation of the music policy of the new 'Arts for Everyone' lottery programme. The Capital Lottery Programme had provided much-needed funds for the provision of new buildings to house the arts or for the improvement of existing facilities, but it was heavily criticised for failing to support the activities which took place inside them. 'Arts for Everyone' (A4E) was intended to answer these criticisms.

The scheme was organised in three tiers. Applicants were asked to measure up to one or more of a set of five priorities, according to the scale of their projects and the size of their funding requirements:

1. Encouraging new audiences to experience high quality arts activities.
2. Encouraging and developing participation in arts activities.
3. Getting more young people involved in arts and cultural activities.
4. Supporting new work and helping to develop its audience.
5. Building people's creative potential through training and professional development.

'Rainbow over Bath' was one of a number of organisations which received generous three-year awards from A4E. All the projects funded by the scheme had come to an end by 2001. It is unfortunate that the relative generosity of the scheme was not continued by its successor, the Regional Arts Lottery Programme, where smaller awards and terms limited to one year were again the norm. There was widespread frustration at the dismantling of many important and forward-looking initiatives, with resultant loss of continuity.

There has been an incomprehensible refusal to recognise the value of the wealth of knowledge and experience gained through A4E programmes or to take account of the many important conclusions and recommendations about future action emerging from evaluation reports. Major staff changes at the Arts Council and an unexpected shake-up of the system of Regional Arts Boards may ensure that the future is once again about to ignore the lessons of the past.

Several other recent reports have suggested that the march of progress may not be all in one direction. Eighteen years after the 1982 Gulbenkian report it was apparently still necessary to argue the case for artistic creativity in education in the report *All Our Futures* (1999) by the National Advisory Committee on Creative and Cultural Education (NACCCE) chaired by Kenneth Robinson, and commissioned by David Blunkett and Chris Smith: 'The economy needs scientists and technologists with a broad understanding of cultural and social processes' (Robinson, 1999: 75). The fact that the writers of *All Our Futures* needed to reiterate so many intellectual justifications borrowed from the Gulbenkian report in support of its claims invites gloomy conclusions about the importance given to the arts in our materialistic contemporary society.

All Our Futures parodies the title of the report *Half Our Future* which, in making new proposals on 'the education of pupils aged thirteen to sixteen of average and less than average ability' (Newsom, 1963: xv), was responsible for a radical democratisation of the English education system, including the raising of the school leaving age to sixteen and the introduction of the Certificate of Secondary Education (CSE) as an alternative to 'O' level. There is a clear implication that the aim of *All Our Futures* is to democratise artistic creativity.

All Our Futures proposes a systematic set of definitions of creativity. It sees a fundamental need to foster creativity in all areas of human life: 'Many people associate creativity primarily with the arts [...] but creativity is not unique to the arts. It is equally fundamental to advances in the sciences, in mathematics, technology, in politics, business and in all areas of everyday life' (Robinson, 1999: 27). Creative thinkers are essential to the progress of mankind because they can 'lead us to new horizons' (Robinson, 1999: 34). The report's assertion that the arts encourage and develop creative thought and action echoed the 1982 Gulbenkian report almost word for word.

All Our Futures analyses three different categories of originality, complementing the Gulbenkian's 'seven conditions of creativity' (p. 100):

1. Individual: in relation to one's own previous work; something the individual has not previously achieved.
2. Relative: in relation to one's peers; something not previously achieved by others in a school or group.
3. Historic: in relation to everyone's output in a particular field; something of true historical originality (Robinson, 1999: 30).

We should expect everybody to achieve some level of originality as defined by the first two categories. To create work which is original in relation to one's previous work is another way of defining individual progress. To create work which is original in relation to other members of a group is to express one's own individuality of character or feeling. By contrast, the third category is extremely rare, and the possession of such originality, in Tippett's words 'the ability to experience and communicate this inner world' (Tippett, 1974: 148) is a gift. But let none be discouraged by Tippett's view of himself! Not everyone possesses this rarest of gifts, but all can and should strive to achieve whatever kind of creative originality they are capable of, and take from it pride and self-fulfilment.

The National Federation for Educational Research

A year after *All Our Futures*, Robinson was accusing the government of 'neglecting to promote, refusing to accept and failing to act upon its findings' (Elkin, 2000). In November the National Campaign for the Arts took up the cudgels by publishing a free summary of *All Our Futures* sponsored by the Gulbenkian and Paul Hamlyn Foundations. How can the government's reticence be explained? Was this an example of an emerging 'not-wanting-to-hear' mentality, or were they waiting for the publication of the report of the National Federation for Educational Research (NFER)?

The NFER, under the guidance of its 'Arts Matter' steering group, chaired by Prof. Eric Bolton, published *Arts Education in Secondary Schools: Effects and Effectiveness* in October 2000. This weighty six-hundred-page report is the result of three years research, funded jointly by the Arts Council of England, the Association of Business Sponsors of the Arts, British Telecom, the Gulbenkian Foundation, the Local Government Association, two local education authorities and two industrial sponsors. It specifically examined the responses of pupils to artistic activities in their schools. There were four categories of research:

1. In-depth case studies of arts education in five secondary schools. The schools were chosen strategically to represent different social, urban and rural environments.
2. Data analysis of information compiled through NFER's 'Quantitative Analysis for Self-Evaluation' project (QUASE). Data from one hundred and fifty two schools with up to three cohorts of year-11 GCSE pupils between 1994 & 1996 was analysed, a total of 27,607 pupils.
3. A year-11 survey of pupils and schools by means of a questionnaire distributed among a total sample of sixty schools. A total of 2,269 pupils responded from twenty two schools.
4. Interviews with employers and employees in twenty companies throughout the UK on the relationship between arts education and the world of work.

In the case of schools with strong reputations in the arts the report seems to support the intellectual model offered by 1982 Gulbenkian report: 'Numerous and wide-ranging effects were reported by pupils who were performing well in at least one art-form'. Pupils mentioned 'advancements in the technical skills and knowledge associated with specific art-forms [...] a sense of fulfilment in their own achievements, social skills, self confidence, expressive skills and creativity.' Many of these effects are 'highly pertinent to the task of tackling disaffection and social exclusion amongst young people' (NFER, 2000: 565).

It has often been claimed that the arts boost academic performance. *Arts-based projects in schools,* a study undertaken in selected London primary schools, found that arts projects developed children's confidence, concentration and creativity (Hedges, 2001: 5). However, the NFER report found no evidence for any improvement in general academic performance at GCSE. There was some evidence that arts skills were transferable (NFER, 2000: 566), though art and drama scored higher in this respect than music. However the report admits that differences in the patterns of response between schools was attributable to variations in teaching methods. It also found that there were 'considerable inequalities in the provision of arts education available to pupils.' Few schools taking part in the survey made effective provision for all the major art-forms, and many were 'falling well short of the standards set by the best' (NFER, 2000: 567).

In its analysis of its own QUASE data, NFER admitted: 'That music in particular can have a positive transferable impact on GCSE performance in the core subjects, is undoubtedly one of the possible and plausible interpretations of the results' (NFER, 2000: 190). But there is an ironic tone in the report:

> Proponents [...] could argue that the findings are consistent with the view that, for some pupils, studying music is a highly positive and rewarding experience which nurtures generalised and improved self-esteem and motivation and which in turn affects learning and performance in English, maths, science and other subjects (NFER, 2000: 190).

However the report questions the direction of causality, proposing what it calls the 'backwash effect' defined as 'the effect of predicted GCSE performance on the take-up of arts subjects in the light of pupils' academic attainment and experiences during key-stage 3.' It was the high attainers who tended to take up music, rather than their high academic attainment being influenced by studying music.

More depressingly, arts education was having a limited impact on the generality of pupils. Most pupils in year-11 indicated that the arts had made no impact on them at all. Some pupils in the 'case-study' schools saw music as 'special' and 'for the élite', and the report was forced to conclude that 'the rhetoric of the "arts accessible to all" was not always born out in reality' (NFER, 2000: 567). Perhaps most depressing of all were the conclusions that music 'registered a more limited range of outcomes compared with art and drama, had very low numbers enrolling for it at key-stage 4, and relative to other arts subjects, received lower levels of enjoyment in GCSE courses' (NFER, 2000: 568). Even so, the arts were seen by many members of senior management in schools 'to impact on the whole school ethos mainly by encouraging a positive cohesive atmosphere through enhancing pupils' enjoyment, self esteem and achievement' (NFER, 2000: 568).

The report concludes that there is an urgent need to tackle the quality of music teaching by mounting a programme of continuing professional development, and by recruiting teachers with specialist expertise in the arts and encouraging them to remain in the profession. The report acknowledges the beneficial outcomes of the arts but advocates a new sharing strategy to reverse 'the trend towards selective policies that extend inequalities between schools and which result largely in the best schools for the arts becoming even better' (NFER, 2000: 572).

Do the NFER's gloomy findings invalidate the theoretical rationale of the 1982 Gulbenkian report? I believe not. Many have criticised the NFER report for the small size of its sample, and have questioned if it can be seen as representative of the national picture. Many practitioners find that the report does not reflect their own more positive experience. What NFER really found was that, in the small sample of schools which it investigated, arts education and, in particular, music education was falling short of the idealistic goals which had been set for it in the 1980s. This is no reason to give up.

However the report does indicate the dangers of complacency, and adds more substance to the findings of Julia Winterson. She also found that claims of originality for high-profile music education projects were not borne out by the evidence (Winterson, 1998). The objectives stated in project summaries which formed part of the grant applications for project-funding were not being met. Visits by professional musicians were too often seen as an enjoyable diversion.

Eventually, in September 2000, the government took action by announcing an increase of £100 million in subsidy to the Arts Council. This was quickly reflected, in January 2001, by an announcement from the National Foundation for Youth Music (NFYM) of a £10 million grant towards the establishment of twenty 'Youth Music Action Zones' across the United Kingdom. At the same time the recognition that the role played by creative arts in the schools curriculum needed clarification resulted in the introduction of the Artsmark Award in

January 2001 as a benchmark of excellence and a symbol of recognition.

Unfortunately, although the NFYM can dispense project grants in the region of £20,000, its ability to support artists-in-schools projects of the kind advocated in *All Our Futures* is severely hampered by a condition which dictates that only 30% of any grant can be used to support school-based activities. The emphasis must be on projects for young people out of school hours, a short-sighted and politically motivated condition which has the effect of limiting the involvement of class teachers and thus reducing the effectiveness of creative projects.

Other trusts and foundations

A number of private foundations other than Gulbenkian have supported arts education and community work. I shall examine the Performing Right Society's 'Composer in Education' scheme, initiated in 1990, in detail in Chapter 13. The Paul Hamlyn Foundation, Esmée Fairbairn Charitable Foundation, the Foundation for Sport and the Arts, and the Baring Foundation, which set up its 'Arts in Education and in the Community – Small projects Fund' in 1998, have become increasingly influential. Esmée Fairbairn chooses to fund projects according to an exemplary set of eight 'guiding principles':

- Projects giving priority to culturally deprived rural and urban areas.
- Projects which help to foster a free and stable society.
- Projects which are innovative and developmental.
- Projects which aim to make a practical impact by active participation of the community.
- Projects with black and minority ethnic groups.
- Projects which include disadvantaged groups such as disabled people.
- Projects organised in partnership with other agencies.
- Projects which include effective assessment and dissemination of results and conclusions (Fairbairn, 2001).

Arts funding policy in Europe

At a European level too, there has been a growing awareness of the social impact of the arts, as reflected strongly in the funding priorities of the EU Culture 2000 programme, though less so among other national or regional government funding agencies outside the UK.

Most large European nations and some smaller ones possess comparable structures of local, regional and national funding. In France, for instance, the role of the Arts Council of England is represented by the Ministère de la Culture et de la Francophonie with its regionally-based DRAC offices (Direction Régionale des Affaires Culturelles), and third tier of Délègues Départmentals. The role of Regional Arts Boards is represented by the Offices Régionals de la Culture. The ARCAM office (Association Régionale de Culture, Arts et Musées) for the region of Provence Alpes Côtes d'Azur takes a more proactive role than British RABs by organising educational events at the level of adult and community courses. The role of local districts and counties is represented by cultural offices within the Departements themselves which also relate to the Délègues Départmentals.

Unlike the British Music Information Centre (BMIC), music information centres (MICs) in Holland (Gaudeamus Foundation), Austria (Music Information Centre Austria – MICA) and France (Centre de Documentation de la Musique Contemporaine) are also constituted as charitable foundations with funds at their disposal, and can take a proactive role in the formulation of policy, and the funding of contemporary music events. MICA, for instance, influenced the appointment Christoph Cech as composer in residence and animateur at the Festspielhaus, St. Pölten near Vienna, in 1997/1998.

Many European countries also possess a framework for funding international work along the lines of the British Council and Visiting Arts in this country. The Association Français d'Actions Artistiques (AFAA) helps to fund foreign tours by French artists, usually by contributing to travel costs. Directie Culturele Samenwerking en

Voorlichting Buitenland (DCSVB) plays a similar role in The Netherlands.

Cultural collaboration has been the key phrase for the funding programmes of the Culture Unit of the European Union. The Kaleidoscope programme, established in 1996, was the first European Community programme in support of culture, enacting Article 128 of the Treaty of European Union. Kaleidoscope supported projects with a European dimension involving partnerships between organisations from different member states. Its aim was the promotion of knowledge and transmission of culture and cultural experience of the European people. It also aimed to improve the skills of artists and of others in the cultural sector, and to improve access to culture for all citizens (European Commission, 1996a).

The Kaleidoscope programme comprised two actions. Action 1 required partners from a minimum of three member states. Action 2 was for 'large-scale European co-operation actions' between four or more partners. There was an emphasis on 'networks which promote access to culture for people from a diversity of social and regional backgrounds', and on projects for young people. Specifying a minimum number of partners ensured that the programme extended beyond simple two-way cultural exchanges typical of the town-twinning movement. The concept of 'added value' was crucial. Kaleidoscope gave only 25% of project costs. Partnership funding was essential (European Commission, 1996b: 18). An important sub-clause to the conditions provided for the involvement of 'third countries' which were parties to the European Area Agreement, such as former Warsaw Pact countries and former members of the Soviet Union. Projects were selected according to nine criteria:

1. High cultural and artistic quality.
2. Encourages artistic creation.
3. Encourages cultural exchanges.
4. Provides real added value at Community level.
5. Establishes lasting co-operation.
6. Innovatory or exemplary.
7. Increases access to culture.
8. Potential socio-economic impact.
9. Can be evaluated after the event (European Commission, 1996b: 19).

In 1996, thirty-six music projects were supported under Action 1, and one under Action 2. Grants varied between ECU 6,000 up to the maximum of ECU 70,000, a total of ECU 7.5 million. 'Rainbow over Bath' received ECU 36,000 for its project 'Rainbow across Europe II'. Kaleidoscope required projects to be co-ordinated by one lead organisation. Only two other successful music projects were co-ordinated by lead-organisations based in the UK, while six involved UK institutions as 'co-organisers'.

Seven music projects can be identified which, like 'Rainbow across Europe' contained some element of workshop or music education for young people. Among these were the Philharmonia Orchestra's 'Ligeti Project' with Société Philharmonique de Bruxelles, and Théâtre du Chatelet of Paris. A 'European network for the training services of opera houses' led by La Monnaie de Munt of Belgium, with co-organisers Opera National de Paris, Het Muziektheater of Amsterdam and Hamburgische Staatsoper, was the forerunner of the now very successful 'RESEO' (Réseau Européen des Services Educatifs des Maisons d'Opéra – European Network of Education Departments in Opera Houses). Community Music Wales collaborated with organisations in Ireland and Germany to organise the 'European Youth Community Music Collaboration'. Several projects were based on a competitive model including the 'European Female Composers Competition' organised by the Dutch Chamber Choir Mnemosyne, with Germany's Frau und Musik Internationaler Arbeitskreis, and the Dorset-based 'Chard Festival of Women in Music' (European Commission, 1996a).

It was envisaged that Kaleidoscope would run for only three years until 1998. In fact it was extended by a further year. 'Rainbow over Bath' won a further award in 1999.

Kaleidoscope was replaced by the Culture 2000 programme. The Culture Unit ran a pilot scheme in early 2000, with the first full programme in 2000/2001. The objectives were more ambitious and wide-ranging than Kaleidoscope, and were set out in a detailed 'Communication' published by the European Commission in May 1998 described as 'The First European Community Framework Programme in Support of Culture (2000–2004)' (European Commission, 1998b). With a much larger budget to spend (EURO 167 million over five years), the Culture Unit could afford to offer more than added value, with grants up to 60% of total project costs. It also imposed a more detailed set of aims and objectives.

Culture 2000 was the Culture Unit's response to Agenda 2000, adopted by the commission in July 1997 and intended to meet what the Commission saw as the 'great challenges now facing the European Union'. A consensus emerged that 'culture' is no longer restricted to 'highbrow' culture, but covers also 'popular culture, mass-produced culture, everyday culture' (European Union, 1998b: 3). The 'great challenges' included:

- Acceleration of European integration towards a twenty-six-country union.
- Globalisation: Will integration rob individual cultures of their individuality, or expand the range of possibilities for cultural expression? The Communication re-assures us that 'the public need not consider the Union as something which dilutes their cultural identities, but rather as something which guarantees the existence and flowering of their cultures' (European Union, 1998b: 3).
- The information society: New information and communication technologies can contribute to the realisation of cultural aims, 'including the dissemination of culture, and the promotion of cultural and linguistic diversity' (European Union, 1998b: 4).
- Employment: Cultural activities represent an important reserve of jobs.
- Social cohesion: As a result of unemployment and insecurity, social exclusion is becoming a serious issue. Cultural activities can help the marginalised, particularly young people, to reintegrate into society. All European cities now deal with issues of multiculturalism: 'The European Union now needs to promote integration on the basis of fundamental issues of human rights, freedom, solidarity and tolerance' (European Union, 1998b: 4).

Agenda 2000 highlighted the role of culture in the process of enlargement. Closer links with the accession countries of central and eastern Europe would provide an enriched experience for all. Agenda 2000 also encouraged inward focus on marginalised communities within each country, including issues of rural deprivation and poverty. It advocated a policy of diversification of cultural activities in rural areas. It emphasised the need to preserve vernacular cultural heritage and folklore and to develop opportunities for training and dissemination of knowledge.

Culture 2000 was not intended to replace the cultural actions of member states, but to encourage co-operation between them and 'bring the common cultural heritage to the fore' (EC Treaty, Art. 128; cited in European Union, 1998b: 6). It also aimed to correct the shortcomings of the previous Kaleidoscope (arts), Ariane (literature) and Raphäel (heritage) programmes which it replaced. Such failings included excessively bureaucratic procedures, creation of too many small-scale projects without long-term impact, and failure to create lasting structures of partnership. These echo the problems of arts funding in the UK, including long-term insecurity engendered by reliance on one-year project funding.

There were three 'Actions' covering innovative projects with a minimum of four partners, large-scale integrated projects covered by 'structured, multi-annual cultural co-operation agreements' between seven partners; and special cultural events, in particular European Cultural Capitals. The fund would be open to the fifteen EU member states. The accession states could participate, but could not gain financial advantage from EU money. This was a backward step. Kaleidoscope had allowed accession countries to enjoy equal partnership arrangements.

Unfortunately, Culture 2000 was not immune to some of the bureaucratic problems which had dogged Kaleidoscope. If anything, the application form was even more complicated. It ran to over a hundred pages in the case of the 'Rainbow over Bath' submission for 2000. The results were not finally announced until January 2001, by which time, many of the events, such as the International Society for Contemporary Music (ISCM) World Music Days in Luxembourg had already taken place without knowing if they would be successful in attracting funds or not.

The great majority of successful projects were in Action 1, and were therefore of only one year's duration. Of fourteen music projects, two involved British co-organisers. The most interesting is the '1st International Forum of Young Composers' organised by the French group *Ensemble Aleph* which collaborated with COMA at the 1999 Bath Festival, and is now co-operating with seven European co-organisers including the British Section of the ISCM, the French Music

Information Centre (CDMC) and the Faculty of Music at Corfu University.

Oxford City Council was the lead organisation in a 'Young Europeans' International Music Event'. This collaboration with City Councils in Bonn, Grenoble and Leiden, and with the Orchestra of St. John's Smiths Square, brought together young professionals and amateurs from five nations in performances of Britten's *Noyes Fludde*, a puzzling choice of work considering the enormous range of music-theatre works now available for young people to perform as discussed in Chapters 1 and 2 of this book. The project claimed to focus on 'social integration and citizenship in a pan-European context, intercultural dialogue and development of new forms of expression' (European Commission, 2001: 44).

Two projects, the European Internet Chamber Opera based in Austria, and the 'Operas à Capella pour Enfants 4th Opera Virtuel' organised by Voix Polyphoniques of France, exploit information technology, the latter using folk song material of Kodály and Bartok. 'New Music Live', an Electro-acoustic project with workshops for students led by the Gaudeamus Foundation in partnership with CDMC Spain (Centro para la Difusion de la Musica Contemporanéa), Eesti Kontsert of Estonia, and the 'Information Centre for New Music Germany', had a proportion of its grant deducted because of the inclusion of Estonia, an accession country.

There were only two projects, each of three years duration in the large-scale Action 2. One of these, a folk music and dance project organised by 'Fédération des Associations de Musiques et Danses Traditionelles de France', with the British 'Folk Arts Network', and the Sibelius Academy of Finland, alongside twenty-one other co-organisers from Italy, Greece, Norway, Spain, Austria, Belgium and Ireland, reflects the EU's aim of preserving and celebrating indigenous folk cultures. The other project in Action 2 was the Belgian opera project 'RESEO' in an enlarged form with collaborators including English National Opera and companies in Italy, Norway, Spain, Amsterdam, Stuttgart, Paris, Salzburg, Finland and Sweden. Of all the projects in the current round, this one conforms most closely to the British model of creative workshops for young people.

Part 2
The theoretical model

Chapter 4
Towards a theoretical model

Faced with so many disparate manifestations of Creative Music-making throughout the twentieth century, the time has come to devise a theoretical model capable of making sense of the overall picture. Educational theorists like Swanwick, Paynter and Odam have been able to develop coherent analyses of methodologies concerned primarily with creativity and composition in the classroom. What is required now is a model which will provide tools for critical evaluation and a predictive framework indicative of directions for future development within a wider social context.

The model I propose is taxonomic in nature in that it provides a systematic set of descriptive classifications. It is also a 'model' in the sense of a pattern of excellence to be copied, or towards which project organisers may aspire. The model is 'theoretical' in the sense that it is an exposition of abstract principles to be followed in the formulation of creative music projects – theory as opposed to practice. Although I give many practical examples which exemplify different aspects of the model in action, it is 'predictive' in that it suggests other possible applications. It is therefore 'speculative' in that these applications require further field-testing, and also because of the possibility that creative projects may arise which do not fit into it, indicating a need for further refinements of the model itself.

Society and community

The title of my book speaks of the composer's role in 'society', a word which derives from Latin *socius*, meaning 'a companion'. 'Society' has a variety of related definitions, but for the sake of discussion, I define it simply as the mass of people in the civilised world. They can be seen as relating together in sub-groups or 'communities'. Wherever a project is located, it must always encounter and engage with the people who belong to a particular 'community'. The composer Hywel Davies has described 'community' as the resources at his disposal for a given musical project. He takes the view that it is pointless to compose in a generalised way for amateur brass band or choral society. He prefers to meet people already working at an amateur level in a given community, get to know them, and take their strengths as his starting point (Conversation 18 April 2001).

Human communities can be defined by a number of different factors. Geographical proximity is only one of them. Other factors include shared interests, age, ability, nationality, ethnicity, height, weight, gender, sexual orientation, socio-economic classification, state of health and so on. But not all these categories are useful in the context of a model applicable in the field of music. I propose to define 'community' according to a simplified list of five parameters chosen for their relevance in discussion of music:

1. Shared interests.
2. Similar age group.
3. Similar level of ability.
4. Geographical proximity.
5. Similar types of people.

The fifth is a generalised parameter embracing all other categorisations according to ethnicity, nationality, socio-economic classification and so on. We all belong simultaneously to communities which can be defined with reference to each of these five factors. We all live somewhere, we all share interests with other people, and we all belong to a peer-group of the same age.

Bernstein's diagram set curriculum classification and framing as the two axes of a two-dimensional matrix. I propose to look at the factors which define community in the same way. When Swanwick applied the Bernstein diagram to music education, he interpreted 'classification' as 'musical style'. In my list of parameters which define community, 'shared interests' could mean 'an interest in music'. But it could also mean 'an interest in a particular style of music'. This suggests a similarity between Bernstein's 'classification', Swanwick's 'musical style' and my 'shared interests'. I shall therefore re-label the five axes which define a community as follows:

1. Classification.
2. Age.
3. Ability.
4. Places.
5. People.

Bernstein's 'classification' axis represents a distinction between two different approaches to learning: a child-centred approach (weak) and a subject-based approach (strong). In musical terms, Swanwick saw this as a distinction between child-centred (weak), and musical-style-based (strong). When we apply this to a community context, we can substitute 'community-centred' at the 'weak' end of the axis.

However there is a difference between Swanwick's 'musical style' axis and my own. Swanwick is using the terms 'weak' and 'strong' to analyse differences of approach to musical style in a teaching situation. I am using 'musical style' as a refinement of the 'shared interest' parameter to define categories of community – for example, the community of jazz lovers, or a community of devotees of the music of Terry Riley. Swanwick's diagram is not concerned with what the musical style actually is, but only with the attitude of teacher and pupil towards it. In theory, a teacher with a class of thirty children who wishes to adopt a weak approach to classification by following Odam's advice that 'Style in musical composition should normally be the choice of the child' (Odam, 1995: 56) might be faced with thirty different individual preferences of musical style. If he adopts a 'strong' approach, he will dictate what the class is going to study, for example, only the music of the western classical tradition. Alternatively he might adopt a balanced approach, striking a compromise by choosing to focus on a narrower range of those styles which he regards as educationally most significant, but at the same time responding to some of the style preferences expressed by his pupils.

Qualitative, quantitative and categorical aspects

I therefore make a distinction between 'qualitative' and 'quantitative' aspects of 'classification'. The qualitative aspect concerns the one-to-one relationship between pupil and teacher: musical style dictated by the teacher (strong), or left to the choice of the pupil (weak). The quantitative aspect concerns the teacher's relationship with the whole class: the range of musical styles to be encountered. We can apply the same analysis to a creative music project. A 'strong' approach would focus on one particular style, or even a particular work by a featured composer. A 'weak' approach would embrace a wide range of different musical styles.

The use of the word 'quantity' seems to imply numerical value. This is not intended, nor is it desirable. I am using 'quantitative' in a comparative sense. In comparing one project with another, I see the range of styles as wider or narrower, without necessarily counting how many styles there are. Why is this not desirable? Because to do so I would have to define 'boundaries', something that I shall be arguing against. However a simple list of stylistic forms used in a project can be useful. It represents the 'categorical' aspect of the 'classification' axis. But just as 'quantitative' does not imply numerical value, so 'categorical' does not imply 'stylistic boundaries'. I prefer to see musical style as a continuum in which particular stylistic categories stand out as nodal points. Musical style depends on the interaction of many different factors including subtle nuances of melody, harmony, and rhythm. Henri Pousseur created a continuum of musical style when he devised a series of transformations through historic styles of European classical music in the piano piece *Miroir de Votre Faust* which formed part of his opera *Votre Faust* (Pousseur, 1960–1968). I see Pousseur's transformations as another example of what Swanwick called 'music's free-standing cultural autonomy' (Swanwick, 1988: 107).

How do these 'qualitative', 'quantitative' and 'categorical' aspects apply to the other axes? In their 'quantitative' aspects, the 'age', 'ability', 'places' and 'people' axes are measures of how all-embracing

126

a project is: how wide is its age-range, or its geographical spread, for example.

At first sight, 'age' may appear to be a quantity and not a quality. However we are not concerned with counting the number of years a person has been alive, but with the qualities of mind, imagination and inventiveness associated with each phase of life. A iist of life's phases, marked by 'rites of passage' such as leaving school, first job, marriage, the birth of children, retirement and so on, represents the 'categorical' aspect of 'age'. Ross's four phases of a child's musical development (Ross 1984: 129–130) discussed in Chapter 2 (p. 70), or the key-stages (KS) of thc currcnt national curriculum in use in English and Welsh schools are other examples of age categories:

KS 1: ages 5–7; Years 1 & 2.
KS 2: ages 7–11; Years 3 to 6.
KS 3: ages 11–14; Years 7 to 9.
KS 4: ages 14–16; Years 10 & 11.

In its 'qualitative' form the 'ability' axis could be labelled 'less able/more able'. The categories can be represented by graded standards such as beginner, intermediate and advanced. But in its 'quantitative' form we should guard against misinterpreting 'strong/weak' as 'less able/more able'. What we are looking at here is the spread of ability, so that 'strong' means 'narrow range', and 'weak' is equivalent to 'wide range'.

The categorical aspect of 'people' defines them according to membership of different social, ethnic, national and other groups. The categorical aspect of 'places' could be represented by a list of administrative units of government, or as a list of actual geographical locations. The Qualitative aspects of 'places' and 'people' are more difficult to define, and I will discuss them later.

A framework for evaluation

So far I have been using 'weak' and 'strong' in the same way as Bernstein and Swanwick. No value judgements are implied. The analysis is purely descriptive. In the Bernstein diagram, a traditional teaching approach of instrumental instruction in the classical/romantic repertoire lies at the 'strong' end of both the 'classification' and 'framing' axes. Such an approach is not necessarily right or wrong. It is a question of choosing the most appropriate approach in a given situation. If the aims are to encourage musical creativity, to break down artistic and cultural boundaries, and encourage openness to new musical ideas, it can be argued that a 'strong classification; strong framing' approach will not achieve them. In this case 'strength' would not be a positive quality.

The problem with the terms 'weak' and 'strong' used without reference to the Swanwick spiral is precisely this avoidance of value judgement. The Bernstein analysis is unable to indicate whether a given approach will be positive or negative in its effect. It implies that a balanced approach is desirable. One which veers too far either to the 'weak' or the 'strong' is likely to be less effective.

We might alternatively substitute the word 'open' for 'weak', and 'closed' for 'strong', in which case the implied value judgement is reversed. It is difficult to find pairs of opposites which do not carry some implication of value. The words 'weak' and 'closed' seem to carry negative connotations, while 'strong' and 'open' carry positive ones. The four terms can therefore be set in the following cross-over pattern:

strong (positive)   weak (negative)

↖   ↗

↙   ↘

closed (negative)   open (positive)

I can now choose either the positive or negative version of each term thus implying a definite value judgement. For instance we could say that a project which is located towards the 'weak' end of the 'framing' and the 'classification' axes is 'open' because it provides the widest opportunity for creativity. The 'openness' of Bernstein's weak framing and classification is equivalent to the approach of the Zen master in guiding his pupil towards enlightenment. Master does not instruct pupil, but requires him to discover his own path towards enlightenment. Neither does he define what enlightenment actually is, so that both framing and classification are 'open'.

The aim of my study is to discover and analyse new approaches to musical creativity, so I will be looking for projects which Bernstein would describe as 'weak' in the 'classification/framing' matrix, but which I would judge to be 'open'. The terms 'strong', 'weak', 'closed' and 'open' are evaluative terms. Their use is based on my professional judgement of a particular project. My criteria are similar to those applied by Julia Winterson. For example, she criticises the lack of coherent rationale of music companies in their struggle for survival '[…] using extraneous styles in order to entice young people into their organisation's sphere of interest and therefore make the product more marketable' (Winterson, 1998: 200). This is typical of what I would describe as a 'weak' approach to classification.

The choices between 'strong' or 'closed', and between 'weak' or 'open' are based on my judgement of the coherence of the rationale behind the project-leader's policies. 'Strong' and 'closed' are positive and negative equivalents of the same thing; likewise 'open' and 'weak'. No material difference in the project itself is indicated but rather in the attitude of the project leader or participants. Such differences of attitude are, however, likely to have far-reaching effects in terms of the project's long-term legacy. The choice between 'strong' or 'open', and between 'closed' or 'weak', on the other hand, does reflect a material difference in the project: narrow or wide range of musical styles, use of instruction or encounter, and so on. Thus the crossover diagram shown above is not another two-dimensional matrix like 'classification/framing'. It could be seen as more like a 'thickening' of each axis, represented diagrammatically as a 'twisted skein' (Example 13).

Example 13.

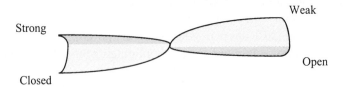

Strong

Weak

Closed

Open

These four evaluative terms do not apply equally to the qualitative, quantitative and categorical aspects of all the axes. A 'qualitative' evaluation of a project in the 'age' or 'ability' axes will focus on the effectiveness of the actual workshop methodologies for people within a specific age or ability range. A 'categorical' evaluation of a project in the 'places' and 'people' axes will examine the approach to different social, ethnic, national and other groups.

Scale and duration

In practice, moments when the entire age and ability ranges of a large-scale project are represented in a single workshop session are rare. The project is more likely to consist of a series of small group workshops, typically class-groups of thirty children. The participants would not all meet together until the final rehearsal period, typically an intensive day in which the whole project is put together before an evening public performance.

The scope of a project can be measured in terms of its duration and number of participants – a two-dimensional matrix consisting of axes which can only exist in a quantitative form (Example 14).

Projects of larger scale or duration can be assembled from a number of small-scale components which come together in a final workshop-day and performance. Although the overall project might aim to include many age-groups and abilities, the small-scale components, for practical reasons, would be precisely targeted. I would describe the individual components as 'strong' as to age and ability, implying that limitations of this kind are a positive benefit, while the project as a whole would be 'open' implying that, at this level, social inclusion is a wholly positive objective.

Example 14.

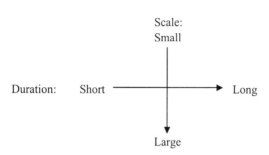

Similar considerations apply with 'places' and 'people'. In small-scale workshops, working in specific geographical locations, and with specifically defined social groups, a well-thought-out strategy, accurately targeted, would make this approach 'strong' rather than 'closed'. But the objectives of the project as a whole would be 'open' rather than 'weak'. Something different happens when the project moves towards the climax of a final workshop and concert on the same day and in the same place. Geographically, the project becomes very 'strong', but achieves maximum 'openness' in the social axis. Arguably this is an ideal combination since many people from different social and cultural backgrounds come together to take part in a common celebratory climax.

The difference between an approach leading to large-scale group performance and one leading to detailed individual creative work, represents two contrasting schools of thought. I list some of the pros and cons, analysing different aspects of large-scale group projects as 'open' or 'weak', and those of small-scale projects as 'closed' or 'strong'.

A well conceived holistic project should achieve a balance between the two in order to combine the positive effects of both approaches (see Example 15).

Example 15.

Individual project work:

1. Workshops can be precisely targeted at specific age and ability groups.
2. Encourages individual creative work.
3. All work is given equal prominence.
4. Priority is given to detailed work and there are many opportunities to explore ideas in depth.
5. Participants are likely to progress on an individual basis.
6. The emphasis is on quality of ideas and their realisation.
7. Final concerts can be relatively simple to plan and co-ordinate.

Large group performance:

1. There is too little focus on the needs of specific age and ability groups.
2. Discourages individual creative work.
3. Individual contributions are devalued.
4. Too little attention is given to small details, and there is little opportunity for in-depth work.
5. It is difficult to monitor progress of individual participants.
6. The emphasis is on quantity rather than quality.
7. Lack of planning can lead to chaotic and badly managed final concert.

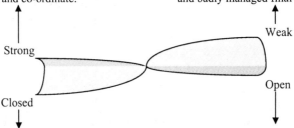

Strong

Weak

Closed

Open

1. Participants only meet others in the same age, ability or community group.
2. Smaller-scale concerts engender less excitement and enthusiasm.
3. There is little opportunity for collaborative work.
4. Individual work more exposed leading to nervousness and lack of confidence.
5. Concerts with too many individual items may lack overall coherence.
6. The audience is small and there is no sense of occasion.
7. The concert fails to achieve a memorable climax.

1. There are many social benefits, such as new friendships and social mixing.
2. Working together with a large group brings creative stimulus.
3. There are many opportunities for collaborative group work.
4. Working in a large group is good for individual self confidence.
5. The workshop leader gives coherent shape to the final concert.
6. A large audience rewards the performers with enthusiastic applause.
7. Catharsis of final concert generates an experience remembered for years.

The framing axis – instruction and encounter

How do the four evaluative terms apply to 'framing'? Swanwick replaced of the terms 'strong' and 'weak', with 'instruction' and 'encounter'. According to him, a properly balanced musical education involves instruction and encounter in equal measure. Musical education consisting only of regimented technical exercises, and formulaic 'correct' interpretations of a restricted repertoire of music would be as unbalanced as one in which the pupil did nothing but indulge himself in completely free and uncontrolled improvisation (Swanwick, 1988: 122).

The notion of balance between instruction and encounter in the 'framing' axis is reminiscent of Peter Wiegold's principle of the 'third way' which likewise seeks a balance between freely developing creativity and the discipline provided by technical mastery and intellectual control. George Odam expresses such a balance in terms of teaching in a 'whole-brain' manner, using both hemispheres (Odam, 1995: 55).

Paynter too advocates a middle way. Too rigid an adherence to any one particular 'rule system' would be creatively sterile, but total freedom would encourage cultural anarchy: 'To acknowledge the importance of the individual is not to advocate an anarchic society in which everyone "does his own thing". It is simply to recognise our responsibility in helping people to maintain self-respect through self-realisation' (Paynter, 1982: 30). Paynter, therefore, does not deny the importance of a disciplined approach, although he does recognise a difficulty. Surrounded by so many 'rule-breakers' in 1970, it was difficult to choose which particular set of rules had the most relevance as a starting point:

> [...] how could school pupils possibly start to compose before they had first mastered the rules? But which rules? It is certainly useful to examine the variety of ways in which composers have solved problems of balance and structure in harmonic and contrapuntal music, but so much depends upon how these things are studied (Paynter, 1982: 99).

How we evaluate the positive and negative aspects of 'framing' depends on whether we are looking at the role of 'teacher' or 'learner'. The learner will be either well-motivated, that is to say eager to learn, committed and engaged, or poorly motivated, that is to say resistant, disengaged and sceptical (Example 16a).

Example 16a.

Learner:

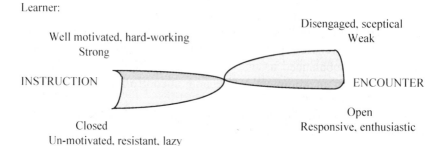

Well motivated, hard-working
Strong

Disengaged, sceptical
Weak

INSTRUCTION

ENCOUNTER

Closed
Un-motivated, resistant, lazy

Open
Responsive, enthusiastic

The teacher will be either enthusiastic about the music, and committed, inspirational and authoritative in approach, or concerned only with the mechanics, and dogmatic and inflexible in approach (Example 16b).

Example 16b.

Teacher:

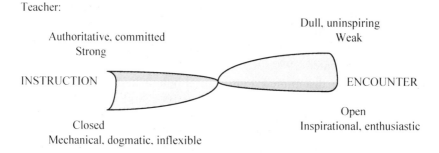

Authoritative, committed
Strong

Dull, uninspiring
Weak

INSTRUCTION

ENCOUNTER

Closed
Mechanical, dogmatic, inflexible

Open
Inspirational, enthusiastic

Another way to look at the relationship between teacher and learner is in terms of the framework shown in Example 16c.

134

Example 16c.

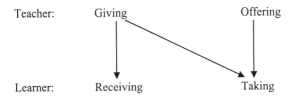

Teacher: Giving   Offering

Learner: Receiving   Taking

The 'giving/receiving' interchange is 'instructional'. It is the teacher who takes the initiative. The attitude of the teacher is either 'strong' or 'closed' as defined above. In order for the instruction to take place effectively, the pupil must be receptive. The pupil's attitude is either 'weak' or 'open', again as defined above.

The 'offering/taking' interchange is one of 'encounter'. It is the pupil who takes the initiative. The attitude of the teacher is either 'open' or 'weak'. In order for the encounter to take place effectively, the teacher must offer freely and generously, but the pupil must be able to exercise good judgement. The pupil's attitude is either 'strong' or 'closed'.

In a 'giving/taking' interchange, 'strong' or 'closed' attitudes on both sides may reinforce one another, leading either to disagreement and conflict or, perhaps, to a fiery relationship with spectacularly fruitful outcome. An 'offering/receiving' interchange, on the other hand, will never get off the ground since neither side takes any initiative.

Can 'framing' also have a quantitative aspect? So far I have analysed only the qualitative aspect at the level of one-to-one inter-action between student and teacher, or between workshop leader and participants. But 'framing' takes on a quantitative aspect when applied to a whole project. 'Strong' and 'weak' refer to the range of different 'formats' used during the course of a creative-music project. What actually are these 'formats'? They represent the categorical aspect of 'framing'.

What about evaluation of the quantitative aspect of framing? A project which used a wide range of different formats varying between instruction and encounter could be described as either 'open' or 'weak', while one which employed only 'encounter' would be either 'strong' or 'closed', even though, in Swanwick's version of the Bernstein diagram, 'encounter' is synonymous with 'weak'. Qualitative and quantitative aspects appear to be in conflict. The conflict is resolved when we realise that an evaluation of quantitative aspects focuses on the attitude of the project organiser, rather than on the use of specific methodologies. Uncritical adherence to an orthodoxy which stated dogmatically that only freely creative encounter methods were valid would be judged as 'closed', even though the methods themselves were superficially 'open'. A well constructed project, employing a balanced variety of 'strong' and 'open' formats, including a public concert, world premieres of commissioned works, introductory talk, creative music workshops, composition seminars and so on, would be judged as 'open'. On the other hand, a poorly articulated policy, following the latest fashion by trying to incorporate as many different approaches as possible, would be judged as 'weak'.

The action axis – active and passive

I have been discussing eight different parameters to be considered in describing and evaluating a creative music project. Two of them, 'framing' and 'classification', describes people's relationship to the creative project. I now want to put forward two other factors which are concerned with this relationship.

So far I have only considered the experience of those taking part in a project. But audiences, too, play an essential role, particularly at the final stage. The Bernstein diagram was designed to describe how children learn, a process involving at least some active participation. Consideration of the role of the audience suggests a new parameter: active/passive. By 'active' I mean participation in the act of performing or composing music, or in directing others to make music, for instance, as a conductor. By 'passive' I mean an experience of music which happens only in the mind, whether it is heard through the ears, or imagined by the 'inner ear'. The word 'passive' seems to carry a pejorative tone. I prefer to use 'participating' and 'listening' as the opposite terms in this new axis which I shall call 'action'.

What happens when positive and negative evaluations are applied to 'action'? We can distinguish between active 'listening' to music, and passive 'hearing' of music. 'Listening' could be seen as 'knowledgeable and well-informed', or at least 'attentive and alert', while 'hearing' treats music as background 'muzak', although as Vernon Lee has pointed out (Lee, 1932), passive 'hearing' should not necessarily be seen as an entirely negative way of experiencing music. George Odam has emphasised the importance of the 'active' form of listening, identifying it as a 'whole-brain' task which engages us in involuntary physical activity as well (Chapter 2, p. 78; and Odam, 1995: 83). Recent research has indicated variations in brain function associated with different attitudes of listening (Evers et al., 1999).

Positive and negative evaluation of 'participation' suggests a distinction between committed engagement and mechanical, formulaic playing. We either take part with all the emotional and intellectual powers of our being, or, like the apocryphal brass section in Wagner's 'Ring', we are so disengaged that we feel entitled to retreat to the bar during the quiet bits.

Is it possible to talk of a categorical aspect of 'action'? The extreme ends of the 'action' axis represent a traditional situation in which the participants take part in rehearsals and perform during the final concert while the audience sits and listens. But we cannot separate the act of listening from the act of performing. Music is a form of communication between human beings. Performers must listen to one another in order to keep in time, or in tune, or to preserve a good sound balance, unless specifically required not to do so for some special aesthetic reason. The presence of an audience creates that 'sense of occasion' which contributes to the final cathartic experience. But there are many examples of situations such as the congregational singing of Lutheran Chorales during a Bach Cantata, a sing-song in an old people's home, a 'Scratch' performance of Handel's *Messiah*, the singing of *Land of Hope and Glory* or *Jerusalem* at the last night of the BBC Promenade Concerts, or the round in David Bedford's *Time Piece* (p. 51), in which audience participation is invited, blurring the lines of demarcation.

The creativity axis – creative and re-creative

The creativity axis concerns the differences between composer and performer. The relationship between composer, performer and listener can be described in terms of a triangular partnership where the composer is creative, the performer re-creative, and the listener a passive receiver. Jean-Jacques Nattiez sees the musical work as existing on three levels:

> Immanent – the physiological impact of the sound on the neurological network.
> Poietic – the meaning of the work as seen from the composer's point of view.
> Esthesic – the meaning of the work as interpreted by performer or listener.

For Nattiez the composer's role is creative – in the Poietic realm (from Greek – Ποιος – 'something created as a work of art'), while that of both performer and listener is re-creative – in the Esthesic realm (from Greek Εσθης – a garment, therefore 'something clothed') (Nattiez, 1985: 3). These two terms define what I shall call the 'creativity' axis.

Can there be a 'categorical' aspect to the 'creativity' axis? The Bedford Categories (p. 51) represent a continuum which can be seen as one way of defining different positions along the creative/re-creative axis as shown in Example 17.

Example 17.

BC1. Interpretation of a fully written score.   re-creative
BC2. Score containing opportunities for improvisation.
BC3. Written score which includes creative 'windows'.
BC4. Material generated in workshops
     (composer provides framework).
BC5. Fully creative project
     (all aspects devised within the group).   creative

By working directly with the composer as workshop leader, in a project which includes creative windows, participants are drawn into the poietic realm of the composer. In creating material for the windows, they all share the excitement of the act of creation. In working with him on the re-creative process of performing the composer's own

138

non-window material, they come closer to an understanding of his uniquely poietic viewpoint.

How can positive and negative evaluations be applied to the 'creativity' axis? This is perhaps one of the most difficult aspects to deal with in discussion of creative music projects. How can there be any basis of comparison in the poietic realm between the uncertain, stumbling musical output of a small child, and the work of a mature and experienced composer or improviser, or, in the esthesic realm, between the unskilled scrapings of the beginner and the assured accomplishment of an advanced performer?

In the 1970s free improvisation and the use of graphic scores in the classroom as advocated by John Paynter was a revolutionary and liberating idea, but it has encouraged the lazy presumption that the disciplines of music are no longer necessary or relevant, a point picked up by the Gulbenkian report. In advocating the need to encourage creative artistic activity in young people, it warns against the uncritical acceptance of anything and everything which a pupil may produce:

> We do not however share the view of some past advocates of the arts, that this amounts to a need to encourage 'free expression'; that any response is acceptable from pupils because it is their response; that anything produced is worthwhile simply because it has been produced (Gulbenkian, 1982: 29).

According to the Gulbenkian, it was the role of the teacher to provide a framework within which creative activity could take place, not simply letting things happen in the name of self expression, nor imposing rigid structures, but striking a balance of freedom and authority. The Gulbenkian's 'Seven conditions of creativity' (Gulbenkian, 1982: 30) and the three categories of originality set out in *All Our Futures* (Robinson, 1999: 30) go some way towards providing evaluative frameworks for musical creativity.

Building a multi-dimensional matrix

The ten axes which I have defined so far in this multi-dimensional matrix fall into several groups. 'Framing', 'action', and 'creativity' are concerned with the relationship of participants to the creative process. 'Age', 'ability', 'places' and 'people' are 'community parameters'. Of these, 'Age' and 'ability' are measurable characteristics of the participants which affect their level of response to a creative project. 'Places' and 'people' group people according to geographical, national, ethnic, socio-economic, and other factors. 'Classification' occupies a pivotal relationship with all these groups. The two axes of the 'scope' matrix, 'duration' and 'scale', are concerned entirely with statistical aspects of a project.

It is impossible to represent such a complex matrix on a flat sheet of paper. I intend therefore to explore some of the relationships between different groups of two and three axes. The following is a list of the ten possible pairs of the five 'community' parameters:

Classification/places	Places/people	Age/places
Classification/people	Age/ability	Age/people
Classification/age		Ability/places
Classification/ability		Ability/people

I will discuss the wider implications of some of these groupings later. 'Classification/places' will lead to a discussion of the link between musical style and geographical location as expressed, for instance, through national and regional folk-music styles. 'Classification/people' raises issues of musical style as an indicator of social divisions within society. 'Classification/age' focuses our attention on music as a badge of age and peer group. Discussion of 'Classification/ability' focuses on issues of stylistic integrity and compromise in the interests of accessibility. Consideration of 'places/people' will lead to a discussion of the geographical location of projects.

'Age/ability' is a closely linked pair which shows clearly the distinction between quantitative and qualitative aspects. Example 18 shows, in a highly simplified manner, a hypothetical individual's development of ability with age as applied to some particular area of musical skill such as piano playing.

Notwithstanding the search for eternal youth, we have no choice about moving through life from youth to old age. Ability is a different matter. The smooth dotted curve indicates a notional maximum potential, limited by hereditary physical characteristics such as size of hands or by mental capacity, innate intelligence and so on. Above it lies an unattainable zone. The irregular black line represents the level of skill actually achieved in life, a level which may even deteriorate through lack of practice. The 'grey area' between is a 'could-do-better' zone. Part of a class teacher's role is to help pupils to narrow the gap by realising more of their potential.

Example 18: The qualitative aspect of age/ability.

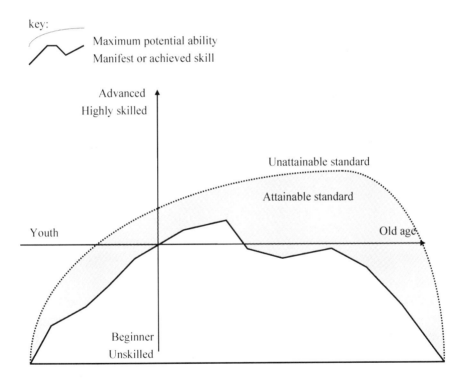

In creative music projects we find ourselves working with individuals for only a few days or weeks in their lives. We must 'take them as we find them', represented in the above diagram by the point of intersection between the two axes. We concern ourselves primarily with where they are now on the 'manifest skill' line. We help them to make small improvements in aspects of musical ability which they are less likely to get from individual music lessons. These include ensemble skills, collaborative group work, creativity through co-operation, and aesthetic awareness. Hopefully we can influence the future direction of the 'manifest skill' line.

The quantitative aspect of age and ability, on the other hand, is concerned with aspects of the conception of a creative project as a whole. In this case there are no 'unattainable zones' (Example 19a).

Example 19a.

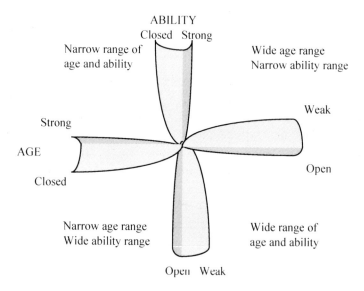

In this quantitative 'age/ability' matrix the point of intersection between the two axes indicates where a particular project is located. Example 19b shows both the 'age' and 'ability' axis shifted towards 'open' or 'weak', indicating a relatively wide range of age and ability.

(Arrows point from narrow to wide range, but imply no direction of progression.)

Example 19b.

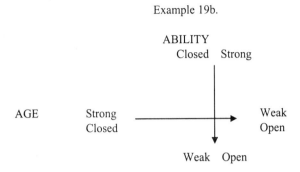

Adding to this 'plane', a third 'quantitative' axis such as 'classification', creates a three-dimensional quantitative 'space' (Example 20). A centralised point of intersection could indicate a typical or average project with, for example, a balanced approach to classification, a range of ages from upper juniors up to GCSE, and an average spread of abilities within this age-range.

The limitations of two-dimensional geometry force me to leave to the imagination of my readers the effect of completing the full five-dimensional 'Community matrix' by adding axes for 'people' and 'places'. The point where the axes intersect indicates the specific position of any creative project in this five-dimensional quantitative matrix. Shifting any of the axes shifts the point of intersection.

Example 20.

Narrow range
of age, ability
& style

Wide age range;
Narrow range of
ability & style

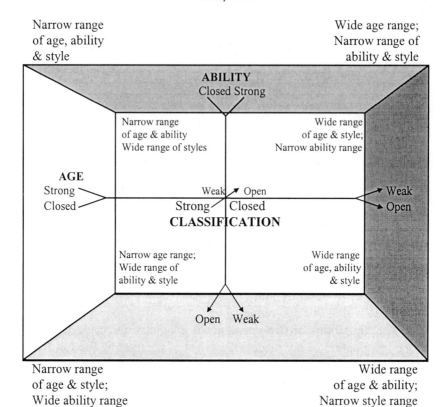

ABILITY
Closed Strong

Narrow range
of age & ability
Wide range of styles

Wide range
of age & style;
Narrow ability range

AGE
Strong
Closed

Weak   Open

Weak
Open

Strong   Closed
CLASSIFICATION

Narrow age range;
Wide range of
ability & style

Wide range
of age, ability
& style

Open   Weak

Narrow range
of age & style;
Wide ability range

Wide range
of age & ability;
Narrow style range

Action and creativity – the holistic model

What happens if we construct a two-dimensional matrix in which the two axes are 'creativity' and 'action'?

Example 21a.

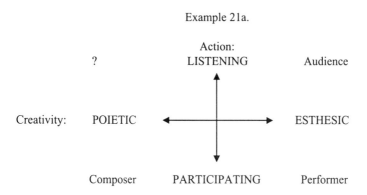

Such a diagram describes the familiar composer-performer-audience relationship, but who occupies the empty corner? Can we identify an individual who is not involved actively in the performance of the music itself, but nevertheless takes on a creative role in relation to its presentation to the listening public? The role described seems to be that of producer, concert promoter, project administrator or entrepreneur. Without a person or team of people fulfilling these enabling functions, no musical project of any kind can happen.

Example 21b.

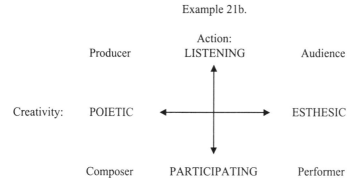

145

The conventional communication between composer and performer is represented by a diagonal line. In performances of music from the distant past the communication is through time, and in only one direction. When the composer is alive, the possibility of two-way interaction across this simple matrix exists. The matrix suggests the possibility that audience or performer may communicate with composer, or that composition itself may be a collaborative act, for instance, between composer and performing artist working together in creative partnership.

The two-dimensional action/creativity matrix in its qualitative form seems to describe only the formal concert situation. When it intersects with 'framing' to form another three-dimensional 'space', we see how concerts, workshops, introductory talks, recordings, documentation and forms of audience participation can interact in a holistic experience of music (Example 22).

This action/creativity/framing matrix is a way of categorising the formats available within the context of a holistic project. It is also a systematic description of the formats which make up the categorical aspects of 'framing', 'action' and 'creativity'. The matrix implies that a truly holistic music project – one from which we want to wring out every drop of educational benefit – should consist of activities corresponding to all eight categories. It does not dictate what those activities should be, but indicates the function they fulfil. Thus several different activities may occupy the same position, and can be seen as equivalent. For example, an individual music lesson and a full rehearsal of the local choral society are both participatory instructional activities in the esthesic realm. In this case the differences are to do with the number of people taking part ('scale' axis). In the case of a folk band, the style of music ('classification' axis) may indicate the difference. A ceilidh rather than a formal concert might be seen as the most appropriate format for a participatory encounter in the esthesic realm. I will refer to this diagram in future as 'The Holistic Model' to distinguish it from the larger 'Theoretical Model' of which it forms part (Example 22).

Example 22: The Holistic Model.

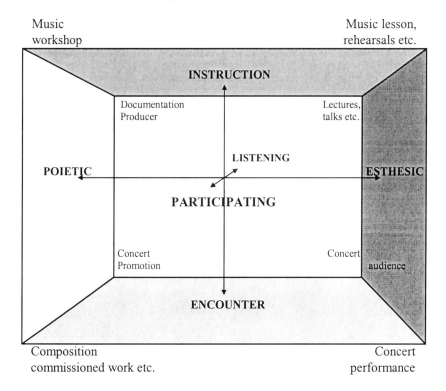

Music
workshop

Music lesson,
rehearsals etc.

INSTRUCTION

Documentation
Producer

Lectures,
talks etc.

LISTENING

POIETIC

ESTHESIC

PARTICIPATING

Concert
Promotion

Concert
audience

ENCOUNTER

Composition
commissioned work etc.

Concert
performance

Action and creativity – the community of learners

In a traditional teaching/learning situation there are those who learn and those who teach, but in the more flexible context of creative music-making projects, all participants, including the workshop leaders, may have something to learn and something to teach. As Schafer says in his 4th maxim: 'There are no more teachers. There is just a community of learners' (Schafer, 1975: 132–133). Adding a vertical axis of 'ability' to the 'action/creativity' matrix creates another 3-dimensional 'space'. Composer, performer, audience and producer become the four cornerstones of this 'community of learners' (Example 23).

Example 23: The community of learners.

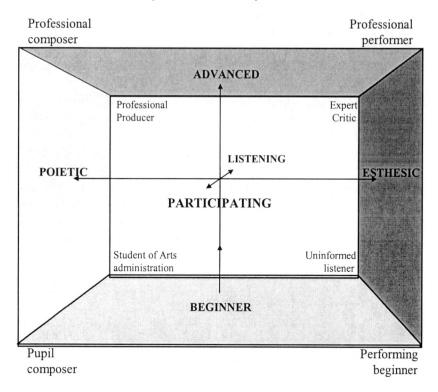

Professional composer

Professional performer

ADVANCED

Professional Producer

Expert Critic

LISTENING

POIETIC

ESTHESIC

PARTICIPATING

Student of Arts administration

Uninformed listener

BEGINNER

Pupil composer

Performing beginner

In what Chris Small has called our 'schizoid culture', with its tendency towards specialisation, learning could simply mean staying in one place on this matrix, and becoming a better composer or performer, or a better (i.e. more knowledgeable) listener. There are therefore two different kinds of progression in the 'Community of learners': horizontally across the action/creativity plane where 'progress' is measured by increasing versatility through the accumulation of a wider range of skills; and from bottom to top, leading to greater and greater skill in one specialisation.

What distinguishes learners from teachers is the direction in which they face along any axis. To borrow a metaphor from the Gulbenkian: 'It is the teacher's job to show the pupils the ropes. It is up to the pupil to climb them' (Gulbenkian, 1982: 33). In my definition 'teacher' includes all those, who, by their inspirational leadership, show others how to progress along one or more of the axes of the matrix. They may be conductors, instrumental teachers, class teachers, or workshop leaders. They look back along a particular axis towards those who follow. Ideally they will possess a breadth of knowledge and experience spreading across the whole action/creativity plane, but most will inhabit an uneven landscape of hills and valleys in which some skills are more developed than others. Learners face forward, trying to see further along the axis, but only able to make out dimly what lies ahead. But teachers are learners as well and, to some extent, learners are teachers, and so all must be 'Janus-faced' (Example 24).

When progression takes place horizontally across the action/creativity plane, composer can become performer, and listener can become performer or composer. When jazz musicians improvise using a 'standard', they locate themselves somewhere midway along the 'creativity' axis. In Nattiez's terms, their response to the 'standard' is Esthesic, but their attitude to what they actually play is Poietic. This is just one example of the kind of fluidity and adaptability which is required of the skilled and experienced workshop leader, and which creative music projects should aim to encourage in their participants. Particularly when we want them to progress from 're-creation' towards 'creation', and from 'listening' towards 'participation'.

How does the 'community of learners' interact with the 'holistic model'? There are two ways of integrating them to provide a fuller picture. Adding an 'ability' axis to the 'holistic model' invites us to consider the role of skilled and unskilled individuals in every type of activity represented by the eight corners of the matrix. This is one of the ways in which the theoretical model is predictive. It is useful as a management tool to show possible deficiencies in a project's holistic policy. Adding a 'framing axis' to the 'community of learners' is equivalent to erecting versions of the Swanwick Spiral like pillars on each of the four cornerstones of 'composer', 'performer', 'listener' and 'producer' (Example 25).

Example 24 is a chart summarising the characteristics of the ten axes of the theoretical model, grouped according to type. The qualitative, quantitative and categorical aspects of each one are tabulated, indicating the evaluative criteria.

Example 24: Chart of the ten axes of the theoretical model.

Group 1:	Qualitative	Quantitative	Categorical
Classification	Style/person-centred	Range of styles	Continuum of styles
Evaluation:	Strong ↖ ↗ Weak Closed ↙ ↘ Open	Strong ↖ ↗ Weak Closed ↙ ↘ Open	

Framing	Instruction→Encounter	Range of formats	Holistic model
Evaluation	Strong ↖ ↗ Weak Closed ↙ ↘ Open	Strong ↖ ↗ Weak Closed ↙ ↘ Open	

Group 2:	Qualitative	Quantitative	Categorical
Action	Listening → Participating	Range of formats	Forms of
Evaluation:	Committed ↖ ↗ Hearing Formulaic ↙ ↘ Listening	Strong ↖ ↗ Weak Closed ↙ ↘ Open	participation

Creativity	Esthesic→Poietic	Range of formats	Bedford categories
Evaluation:	Gulbenkian 'Condi- tions of Creativity'	Strong ↖ ↗ Weak Closed ↙ ↘ Open	

Group 3:	Qualitative	Quantitative	Categorical
Places	Near → far	Geographical range	Geographical locations
Evaluation:		Strong ↖ ↗ Weak Closed ↙ ↘ Open	Effectiveness of strategic planning

People	Culturally near → far	Inclusiveness	Communities
Evaluation:		Strong ↖ ↗ Weak Closed ↙ ↘ Open	Response to needs and desires

Group 4:	Qualitative	Quantitative	Categorical
Age	Youth → old age	Range of ages	Phases of life
Evaluation:		Strong ↖ ↗ Weak Closed ↙ ↘ Open	How appropriate is the methodology?

Ability	Less able → more able	Range of abilities	Graded standards
Evaluation:	Manifest ability	Strong ↖ ↗ Weak Closed ↙ ↘ Open	Appropriateness of methodology.

Group 5:	Qualitative	Quantitative	Categorical
Duration	Short → long	Length in time	
Scale	Small → large	Number of participants	

150

Example 25: The Community of Learners with landscape.

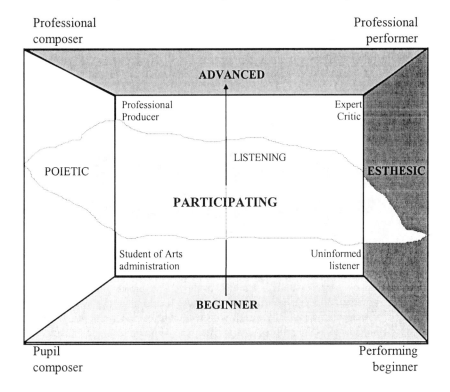

Applying the theoretical model: a case study

As an example of how the ten axes apply in practice, I put forward an analysis of the London Sinfonietta's Pentonville Prison project. The Sinfonietta has, for a number of years, undertaken a music project at Pentonville Prison. In October 2000 the project was based on the music of John Tavener. The outcome was a performance of *In One Single Moment* with soprano Mary King, a chorus of prisoners, and members of the Sinfonietta, conducted by Terry Edwards.

The work focuses on the theme of sin and redemption. It is a cantata based on the story of the two thieves, one repentant and the other unrepentant, who were crucified next to Christ. Prisoners also composed their own music in response to the theme of *In One Single Moment*. The following analysis of the project is from the point of view of the participants in the project:

- Classification: 'strong'; The decision to focus entirely on the music and style of John Tavener was based on well-thought-out principles.
- Framing: 'strong'; The objective of rehearsing and performing Tavener's composition was 'instructional'.
- Action: 'participation'; The project aimed to encourage committed participation.
- Creativity: balanced between 'esthesic' and 'poietic'; One of the aims was to encourage prisoners to create their own music, as well as performing in Tavener's work. Therefore creativity was open in its quantitative aspect.
- Places: 'closed'; Location was entirely limited to the prison, although the decision to work in a prison reflects the 'openness' of the Sinfonietta's geographical policy.
- People: 'open' within a 'strong' context; The project took all comers regardless of ethnic or religious differences. The group of eighteen volunteer participants was racially mixed with twelve black and six white, but was limited entirely to inmates of the prison who could be seen as members of a strongly defined social group.
- Age: 'weak'; Age was not a significant parameter. The only limitation was set by the age range of the prison population.
- Ability: 'open'; The project tended to favour prisoners with some playing or singing ability, but the aim was to take all comers.
- Duration: five weeks.
- Scale: A small group of eighteen prisoners with soloists from the London Sinfonietta. The small scale of the project spread over a five week duration allowed an emphasis on detailed individual work.

Some factors can be analysed differently from the audience's point of view. For them 'framing' took the form of 'encounter' rather than 'instruction'. Therefore the project as a whole offered at least two forms of framing, an example of quantitative openness. The musical likes and dislikes of individual members of the audience are likely to be summed up by the phrase 'I know what I like, and I like what I know', a typically 'closed' response. It must therefore be one of the aims of the project to educate through 'encounter', helping listeners to progress towards greater 'openness' in their response to the music. A formal introductory talk might 'strengthen' the experience, although endemic cynicism among the prison population might limit any widely beneficial effect. Alternatively an approach focusing on less tangible factors which come under the heading of emotional response might be more effective. A period of meditation or reflection on the theme of spirituality, so important in the music of John Tavener, could have had the effect of opening the mind and making listeners better equipped to 'encounter' the performance in a way which would transform a 'weak' response into a more positively 'open' one, allowing prisoners to discover their own inner sources of 'strength'.

The organisers of the London Sinfonietta prison project would have seen it as one part of a much larger education and community programme. Although the Pentonville project scored as relatively 'strong' on the 'framing' axis, this would not be typical of the Sinfonietta programme as a whole which tends to encourage projects clustering at the 'open' end of the axis. Example 26a shows pairs of quantitative axes intersecting to give a descriptive project profile of the London Sinfonietta prison project.

Example 26a.

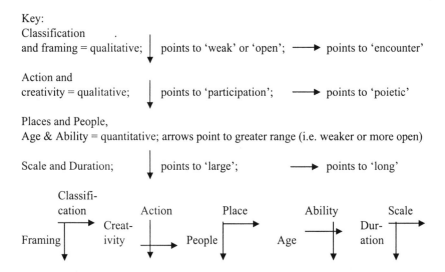

Key:
Classification
and framing = qualitative; points to 'weak' or 'open'; ⟶ points to 'encounter'

Action and
creativity = qualitative; points to 'participation'; ⟶ points to 'poietic'

Places and People,
Age & Ability = quantitative; arrows point to greater range (i.e. weaker or more open)

Scale and Duration; points to 'large'; ⟶ points to 'long'

The orchestra's aim is to propagate contemporary music, and its workshop programme is almost always repertoire-based. However, it will usually seek to achieve this aim by beginning from the 'open' end of the classification axis, and moving towards the 'strong'. At the start musical style would not be defined, allowing participants to choose their own most familiar musical vernacular as a starting point. The project would move towards the 'strong' classification of a Sinfonietta repertoire work as shown in Example 26b which assumes a balanced framing approach.

Example 26b.

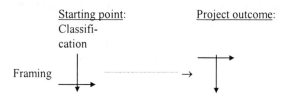

Less often it might progress not towards producing work in a given style, but towards helping young composers to discover their own voices. In this case they might be given an opportunity to encounter a great many different musical models. The project would not move towards 'strong' classification, but rather from 'weak' to 'open' in the quantitative aspect. However progression towards 'strong' classification in the qualitative aspect in the sense of 'discovering one's own voice' would be a desirable outcome for individual students whose own compositional style might, as a result, become more clearly developed.

Structure in time – the four-phase model

How is progression to be achieved? The framing axis intersects with 'action', 'creativity', 'age' and 'ability' in their qualitative aspects, defining the processes by which progression takes place. The level of an individual's 'action/creativity plane' in the 'community of learners' matrix rises as a result of processes which lie somewhere on the instruction/encounter axis through the acquisition of knowledge, understanding, musicianship and technical skill.

The Swanwick spiral can be seen as an intersection between classification, framing, age and ability or, rather, an ability axis skewed by age. In the horizontal axis, the spiral oscillates between instruction and encounter. The single vertical axis represents a simultaneous progression of ability with age, and from weak to strong classification, using the terms 'weak' and 'strong' here in Bernstein's original sense. The spiral describes a progression in time. It shows an alternation between four modes of personal encounter, and four modes of instructional interaction with a teacher.

It is possible to see a resemblance between Swanwick's four-phase structure of Mastery, Imitation, Imaginative play, and Meta-cognition, the four workshop stages A, B, C, and D of Paynter and Aston, and Wiegold's sequence of Preparation, Presentation, Realisation and Performance. Paynter puts forward an alternative four-phase model in *Sound and Structure* (Paynter, 1992: 23). At 'Rainbow over Bath', without at that time being familiar with the Swanwick spiral, I developed a model timetable for creative projects consisting of four visits by a team of workshop leaders, alternating with creative work supervised by class-teachers.

All these models describe a progression in time, and a process of encounter between learner and teacher. But how closely do they resemble one another in other respects? There are differences of time-scale. Ross and Swanwick describe an educational process taking place over some fifteen years. Paynter, Aston and Wiegold are concerned with processes lasting days or perhaps hours. Ross and Swanwick are describing the development of individual children, whereas the others are concerned with class or group work. However Swanwick suggested that his spiral could also be seen as a metaphor of how we all encounter a piece of music for the first time (Swanwick, 1988: 77). Example 27 shows a simple step by step comparison of the models.

Can we draw out any other principles from which to construct a general model for a structure in time? I have already shown how Swanwick based his progression on Ross (p. 70). When we place

Swanwick, Paynter and Wiegold side by side, a more complex picture emerges. Wiegold's 'Preparation' includes warm-up games and 'centring' exercises. The element of play is all-important. Purposes include getting to know one another if participants are strangers (see Schafer's eighth maxim: '[…] the teacher and the student should first discover one another'), and establishing an attitude of listening and working sensitively together. Musical instruments may be used at this stage in a playful and exploratory manner. Such an attitude of playing about with sound is implicit in Swanwick's 'Mastery' phase where the young child is interested in the noises that things make and in sound as a raw material, rather than in its musical qualities.

Example 27.

Ross	Swanwick	Paynter & Aston (*Sound & Silence*)	Paynter (*Sound & Structure*)	Wiegold
Sensuous engagement	Mastery	A: Introduction of idea or concept	I. Sounds into music	Preparation
Musical doodling	Imitation	B: Project assignment	II. Musical ideas	Presentation
Conventional & musical production	Imaginative play	C: Show examples	III. Thinking and making	Realisation composition
Music as personal expression	Meta-Cognition	D: Encounter with the model	IV. Models of time	Rehearsal & performance

This exploratory stage appears to be missing from the Paynter/Aston model which cuts straight to an introduction of the idea or concept upon which a given task is to be based, although this element of playfulness with sound may form part of 'Project assignment'. The 'Sounds into music' phase of Paynter's 'Sound and Structure' model however does represent a transition from exploration of raw materials towards Wiegold's second phase.

156

Wiegold's 'Presentation' is concerned with the materials of music itself: rhythmic structures and modes. During this phase, participants encounter forms and processes and begin to use sound to create musical structures through improvisation. Such a process is equivalent to Swanwick's 'Imitation' phase (Ross's 'Musical doodling') in which the young child assimilates the forms of a musical vernacular. Wiegold does not begin to move towards the setting of specific musical tasks until the second phase is drawing to a successful conclusion. Only at the end of the 'Presentation' phase will he begin to introduce an idea or concept equivalent to the Paynter/Aston phase A.

Wiegold's process of 'Realisation and Composition' forms the substantial part of the project. Swanwick's idea of 'Imaginative Play', and Paynter's 'Thinking and Making' sum up the process perfectly. Workshop participants are given a project assignment equivalent to one of Paynter's examples from 'Sound and Silence'. They then work individually or in small groups, bringing the results back to the whole group to show what they have created. In the Paynter/Aston model the process is divided into two separate phases of B: Project assignment; and C: Showing and sharing examples of each other's work in response to the same musical concept.

Wiegold's fourth phase is one of consolidation and refinement leading to public performance. Likewise, it is only at Swanwick's 'Meta-cognition' stage that the young person is seen as confident enough to use music as a form of 'personal expression' where it achieves full symbolic value, and a systematic and coherent form. Paynter's 'Models of Time' also suggests musical ideas brought together into a formalised temporal structure.

It is at this final stage that Paynter and Aston advocate revealing the historical model on which a creative project was based. Their approach is 'open' in that students encounter ideas and concepts in a creative and imaginative way, and are shown the musical model only at stage D: the end of this process (Paynter/Aston, 1970). Bringing the model forward in time 'strengthens' the process by making it more instructional.

My observations of a project in the 'Discovery' programme at the London Symphony Orchestra, led by Richard McNicol, suggested that 'encounter' may be more effective with younger children. Under-

157

graduate students from Royal Holloway College taking part in a project based on the music of Janácek felt patronised when the musical model was not revealed to them until halfway through. They were thirsty for knowledge of Janacek from the start in a way that primary school children would not have been.

However, the Swanwick spiral implies a child's encounter with a musical vernacular at the very earliest phase, and certainly at the 'Imitation' phase, otherwise there is nothing to imitate. A specific musical model (or perhaps several parallel alternative but similar models) is implicit at the start of Wiegold's 'Realisation and Composition' phase.

Encounter with the musical model is not a one-off event, but a gradual process of assimilation. Perhaps some aspect of the model is revealed at the beginning of 'Realisation', but, for practical reasons, participants must wait for a complete revelation until the final public concert. Such a relationship is built into Bedford Category 1, 2 or 3 when amateur or school performers take part in early rehearsals of fully composed sections of a work, and then participate in the celebratory excitement of the world-première. In practice, nearly all the 'Rainbow' projects which I shall be discussing in later chapters included a final professional concert equivalent to Paynter's stage D.

So there is close resemblance between four of the models. Not forgetting that the flow-chart in Paynter's 'Sound and Structure' invites teachers to devise their own route through the sixteen project examples, my diagram is based on Paynter's published order which seems to be the most natural one. Only Paynter and Aston in 'Sound and Silence' came up with a substantially different pattern. I have already discussed the position of Paynter's stage D. How significant are the other differences? There seems to be a deficiency in the Paynter/Aston model in the absence of exploratory play. But conversely the other models appear to lack an introductory phase, particularly Wiegold's, where firm aims and directions are not defined until well into the creative process. This can be a problem with the Wiegold model when participants are baffled about the purpose of the games they are being asked to play.

Thus we encounter again the difference between the clear objectives of a formal education process, and the open-ended approach of the creative music project (Schafer's 'Hour of a thousand discoveries': Schafer, 1975: 132–133). Actually, Wiegold himself has a clear idea about the nature of the process if not about its precise outcome. Even 'openness' of this kind is a conceptual aim which can be expressed in advance. In a typical Wiegold project, the Paynter/Aston phase A (introduction of idea or concept) actually happens during an introductory session such as a teacher's Inset day.

The resemblances I have shown between the five models are perhaps not so surprising. They all describe a progression from a first encounter with the raw materials of music, passing through greater and greater elaboration towards a more fully developed experience. One way to interpret the phases is to see them as encounters with music at progressively 'higher orders' of musical organisation. Phase 1 might be concerned with single sounds or notes, phase 2 with sounds grouped together in phrases, phase 3 with complete melodies, and phase 4 with the organisation of those melodies into complete musical forms.

In 1968, I experienced an early example of the four-phase model which led students through successively higher orders of musical organisation. On a four-week composition course at Dartington Summer School, the French composer Pierre Mariétan based his teaching approach on musical forms developed by Stockhausen. Week one concentrated on single notes and sounds – a 'pointillist' approach. Week two explored 'groups', concentrating on statistical parameters such as pitch range, dynamic envelope and so on. In week three we studied 'collective' forms in which contrast, and the organisation of ideas into a coherent sequence became important. Finally, in week four, we studied 'moment' form, focusing on the use of a single musical element to unify a whole composition, or large section of a composition. The course was based on Mariétan's own interpretation of the forms. Stockhausen himself saw moment form as part of a separate set of categories: 'Entwicklungsformen', 'Reihungs-Formen' and 'Moment-Formen' (dramatic, suite and moment form) (Stockhausen, 1963: 250–251).

The five Bedford Categories can be analysed in terms of when the lead composer takes control of the creative process from the participants, or, to put it another way, at which phase in the model the participants cease to make a creative input. In BC1, the composer takes full control of the entire creative process. In BC2, the composer takes control from phase 2 onwards, having provided, at a phase-1 level, opportunities for improvisation which encourage an attitude of playfulness with sound typical of Wiegold's 'Preparation', or Paynter's 'Sounds into music'. In BC3, 'windows' in the score allow participants to take their creative responsibility as far as the invention of musical ideas, while the composer takes control from phase 3. In BC4, participants create all the musical material of the composition up to the phase which Paynter describes as 'thinking and making'. The composer then takes charge of the overall structure of the piece, a pre-occupation appropriate to phase 4. In BC5, participants take responsibility for the entire process right up to the creation of what Paynter calls 'models of time' (Example 28).

Example 28: Analysis of the Bedford Categories in terms of the four-phase model.

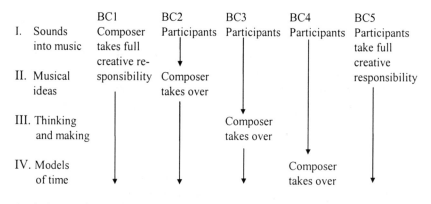

Analysis according to the Action/Creativity matrix:

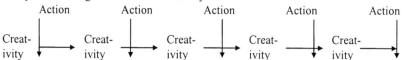

Other structural models have been proposed for arts education projects, among them the pamphlet *Artists in Residence – A framework for schools* prepared in 1983 in collaboration with Gemini by

160

Rosalyn Asher, Music and Performing Arts Adviser for the London Borough of Enfield. Asher's model has six stages (Example 29).

Example 29: Rosalyn Asher structural model.

Stage 1. Preparation, including identification of need, aims and objectives.
Stage 2. Preparing the specification – target groups, resources, budgets etc.
Stage 3. Initial contact with artist.
Stage 4. Initial meeting and planning with artist/s.
Stage 5. The project – process to include monitoring, review, renegotiating, recording and evaluating.
Stage 6. Summative evaluation meeting (Asher, 1983: 3).

Asher's perspective is that of an arts-in-education administrator. Her model stresses the planning stages of the process. The single preparatory phase in the Paynter/Wiegold model is represented by no less than four separate stages in Asher's model, whereas she avoids all theoretical analysis of the creative process, lumping it together into one single stage called 'the project'.

Example 30 shows a modified structure indicating more precisely how the phases of the respective models dovetail with one another. In all further discussion, I shall refer to this as 'the four-phase model' and to the larger sequence in which it is embedded as 'the three-stage structure'. The headings of the three stages of the larger structure provide titles for Part 3 of this book.

Example 30.

Ross	Swanwick	Paynter/Aston *Sound &* *Silence*	Paynter *Sound &* *Structure*	Wiegold	Asher

1st stage: Before the project starts

		A: Introduction of idea or concept		(INSET or introduction)	Preparation
					Specification
					Contact
					Planning

2nd stage: The project in action

Sensuous engage- ment	Mastery		I. Sounds into music	Preparation	The project
Musical doodling	Imitation		II. Musical ideas	Presentation	
Conventional musical produc- tion	Imaginative play	B: Project assignment	III. Thinking and making	Realisation & composition	
Music as personal expression	Meta- Cognition	C: Show and share examples	IV. Models of time	Rehearsal & performance	
		D: Encounter with the model			

3rd stage: Project outcomes

| | | | | | Evaluation |

162

Chapter 5
Classification

In the remaining three chapters of Part 2, I will discuss wider issues raised by some of the pairs of 'community' axes beginning with combinations of 'classification' with 'places', 'people' and 'age'.

The categorical aspect of the classification axis

The categorical aspect of classification can be represented by a list of musical styles, but faced with such a huge variety, it is useful for the purposes of discussion to break them down into four categories as seen from a European perspective:

- European classical styles and their derivatives.
- Indigenous folk music from native European people.
- Popular and commercial musical styles.
- Folk and classical music of non-European minority communities.

Because any point in a multi-dimensional matrix must occupy a position on all axes at once, it will sometimes be difficult to confine discussion purely to style, without referring sometimes to other axes. Each of the above categories relates to 'people', 'places' and 'age' in different ways.

Geographically, European classical styles are, with certain exceptions, relatively 'weak' in that they tend to obey a generalised set of musical conventions which do not typify particular regions of Europe. However, such music tends to define people by social groupings and age, again with some exceptions. Popular and commercial musical styles are also geographically 'weak', but can be 'strong' or even 'closed' indicators of social and age divisions. By contrast, folk musical styles, and the cultures to which they belong, have a 'strong' relationship with geographical location, but cut across age and social groups. There are two kinds of geographical focus. A folk culture may reinforce indigenous national or regional groupings; or, in immigrant communities, it may serve as a link with the culture left behind in a country of origin.

Classification equates with the definition of community according to 'shared interests'. When the 'classification' axis intersects with the 'weak' end of the 'places' axis, geographical location is not defined:

Members of such a 'shared interest' community may be dispersed widely over the country or the world. Thus the International Society for Contemporary Music serves the international community of people interested in contemporary classical music. Festivals such as the annual World Music Days bring members of that community together in one place at the same time to celebrate their common interest. To demonstrate that there is no hierarchy among nations, the festival takes place in a different country every year.

Such gatherings often invite accusations of 'élitism' from the local community who see themselves as excluded. To test whether such accusations are well founded, we might ask whether they could equally well be levelled at, say, a motorbike convention. Not all of us want to ride motorbikes, nor do we see this activity as part of our self-view. The community of motorbike enthusiasts is a self-selecting 'élite', but provided they don't block the road, or churn up the countryside, or disrupt the peace with noisy engines, nobody in a free society would wish to curtail their right to come together in a celebration of their shared interest. Likewise, there can be no objections to festivals and events which celebrate contemporary music, folk music, jazz, rock and roll, early music, or any of the other very many musical styles and idioms, although in some cases there may be

164

styles and idioms, although in some cases there may be similar objections about traffic dislocation, environmental damage or noise pollution.

However, I am making more far-reaching claims for music than I am for bikers who are in any case not in receipt of public money. The danger comes when we take a wholly exclusive and intolerant view of other people's music, and by implication, of them as people. Music has the ability to reinforce boundaries, but also to bridge them. In the case of publicly funded bodies such as festivals, it has to do both at the same time. There are few style-based festivals which do not now take seriously their duty to make their programmes accessible to some extent to a wider community, that is to say, to the community around them as defined by geographical proximity rather than by 'shared interest' in a particular musical style. The programme of 'mass participation events' during the 2002 ISCM World Music Days in Hong Kong in October 2002 is just one example. One of the aims of this study is to determine the success of such community programmes.

Swanwick showed how potent badges of identification can be in separating different social, ethnic and peer groups within society (Swanwick, 1988: 91). People habitually use music in this way, rejecting those styles which do not conform to their 'badge'. Ethnicity, territory, nationality, class, socio-economic status, support for a particular football team, or membership of a particular social sub-group can all be defined and reinforced by the kind of music which 'belongs' or does not 'belong' to 'us'.

Such an approach to music emphasises the divisions in society. Its opposite is an approach which minimises differences and seeks common ground, using music to cross over community or geographical boundaries, bringing together different age groups, ethnic groups, or musical interests. Both approaches can have positive and negative effects. During the course of my research, those projects I rated most highly combined successfully the positive aspects of both approaches. This is not the same as looking for a 'lowest common denominator'. I agree with the sentiments expressed by the European Community Framework Programme. We must discover 'highest common factors' moving towards a form of cultural unity which celebrates and preserves the diversity and richness of cultural forms, at the

165

same time as emphasising a common humanity. Example 31 characterises the positive and negative effects by setting certain key words in an orthogonal pattern using the four evaluative terms.

Example 31: Unity and diversity.

Unity, Authenticity, Distinctiveness	Uniformity, Eclecticism, Mediocrity
Affirmation of tradition	Indifference to tradition
Loyalty, Self-reliance, Independence	Disloyalty, Subservience, Dependency
Autonomy, Identity	Conformity, Anonymity

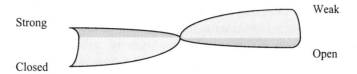

Strong   Weak

Closed   Open

Division, Orthodoxy, Conservatism	Diversity, Experimentation, Innovation
Prejudice against other tradition	Respect for other traditions
Hostility, Competition, Alienation	Trust, Collaboration, Integration
Exploitation, Social exclusion	Equality, Social inclusion

At an international level, division leading to conflict gives rise to warfare. One of the primary motivations for the creation of the European Union was to foster a climate of cultural and economic cooperation in which war could never again break out between the nations of Europe. In Britain, many people feel a sense of British-ness which is stronger than their sense of European-ness. Other Europeans are seen as 'them' in contrast to the 'us' of the British, reflected in a degree of defensiveness which is at the root of Euro-scepticism. Cultural and artistic exchange is one way to break down attitudes of defensiveness, prejudice and hostility, and this is why the new Cultural Framework Programme of the European Union was formulated: 'Culture, through cultural exchange and dialogue, consolidates peace, which is one of the primary goals of European integration' (European Commission, 1998b: 10).

European classical styles and their derivatives

Techniques of creative music making discussed in this study have arisen almost exclusively from composers and educationalists with a background in Western European classical music and a particular commitment to the most contemporary developments of that tradition. John Paynter and George Self explored the potential of using ideas in the classroom derived from the work of contemporary composers. There was an element of evangelism in their work. They wanted to share their own excitement at the creative opportunities of new compositional techniques with young people.

John Paynter saw these techniques as especially useful in the classroom because of the way they dealt with the components of sound. Teacher Tom Gamble advocated techniques used by contemporary composers because: 'They are working with sounds; ordering, developing, shaping them to form a coherent sound object which is musically expressive and interesting' (Gamble; cited in Paynter, 1982: 39). But the unfamiliarity of this material to almost all the children in his classroom posed an immediate problem. Even though the aim was to open pupils' ears and minds to the creative possibilities of the new music, in *Music in the Secondary School Curriculum* Paynter advocates that: 'Pupils' existing interest in music should be used as a starting point' (Paynter, 1982: xiii).

Indigenous folk music from native European people

Early in the twentieth century, Kodály advocated the use of musical material from the indigenous folk tradition as the single most important starting point for the training of Hungarian children. Pál Járdányi summed up the teaching aims of Bartok and Kodály as follows: '[...] to teach the *educated* people to be *Hungarian*, and to *educate* the millions of *Hungarians*' (Járdányi, 1961: 21). Kodály set folk music at the centre of musical education in school and kinder-garten, and sacrificed to it his best time and energy. As he wrote in *Corpus Musicae Popularis Hungaricae*:

> Anyone for whom the treasury of folk songs is not a dead museum but a living culture, which has only been checked in its development, will peruse even such unassuming tunes as these with the excitement of constant discovery. They are full of bustling life; a child's imagination and ingenuity clothing some simple basic forms into a thousand guises (Kodály, 1951; cited in Kodály, 1974: 53).

According to Kodály 'the first musical language a child must learn is his own' (Kodály; cited in Járdányi, 1961: 21). But what was 'his own language'? Even in those early days, the task was not a straightforward one, for most town children brought 'another kind of music from home'. Already forms of popular and commercial music were driving out indigenous Hungarian folk music from its previously held central position in national cultural life. Children had to relearn their musical mother language, forgotten by their parents, 'because it is as important to the people and the nation as the spoken language' (Járdányi, 1961: 22).

For Kodály, folk music was living music, not fabricated like so much former teaching material. It was music of the best kind: an endless series of works of art. He advocated the use of folk music because:

> The naïve, simple and self-explanatory mode of expression, the clearly arranged, short forms entirely suit the heart and mind of the child. […] Its chief scale, five notes without semitones, can be sung easily and well in tune: it is much easier for the child than the diatonic scale with seven notes and semitone intervals as well (Kodály; cited in Járdányi, 1961: 22).

The champions of the Kodály method have made great claims on its behalf. Cecilia Vajda's book *The Kodály way to music* was launched in 1974 with a foreword by Yehudi Menuhin in which he refers to what he sees as the special affinities between Hungarian and British musical traditions: 'Choral singing has always been the backbone of British musical expression and nowhere in the world are there as good Choral Societies, nor is their greater dedication to the noble choral works of music' (Menuhin, 1974: iii).

In 1974 it was still possible in Britain to see the choral tradition as one of the most important starting points for musical training: '[…] there is certainly no finer form of expression than the communal one of choral singing and when begun at a very early age it enhances the sense of belonging both to a community and to a tradition' (Menuhin, 1974: iii). Menuhin therefore advocates the adoption of the Kodály method in this country, describing it as 'this exemplary path'.

It is difficult now to take this book seriously. On looking through two hundred and nineteen pages I saw hardly a single tune which I recognised. It is unlikely therefore that British school children would find any starting point of familiarity. Kodály's method was based on taking, as a starting point, tunes and musical games the children already knew, or which were at least part of a musical tradition they or their parents had only recently lost touch with. Throughout most of England, we have lost touch with almost all of our indigenous folk tradition, and, regrettably, the only sources of melodic material now familiar to most people are popular culture and the mass media. It seems we can only make something like the Kodály method work if we substitute tunes like 'I wanna be your lover baby' or the latest Blur hit for 'The Lark in the Clear Air' or 'Brigg Fayre' which few know anymore.

Kodály himself was well aware of the threat to the folk tradition: 'Little by little, all over the world, folk music will be destroyed by technical and social development and the expansion of civilisation. Mechanical music penetrates the life of even the most hidden villages' (Kodály; cited in Járdányi, 1961: 23).

This situation is no more starkly exemplified than in the Balkan countries. Visits to Bulgaria during 'Rainbow across Europe' projects showed just how strongly the legacy of Kodály survives today and how these countries have managed to ward off the threat to their folk cultures. Recently set free from the puritanical constraints of former Communist governments, the signs of a people enjoying social liberation are all about you. In most large towns, clubs and discotheques pound out English and American rap music, and the shopping streets are becoming depressingly full of branches of McDonalds and The Bodyshop. But the hedonistic pursuit of these manifestations of 'global mass media' coexists with traditional culture.

In Bulgaria, folk music is very much alive, rubbing shoulders with mass, commercialised popular music. The same youngsters who are bopping to four-in-a-bar rap music till the small hours are enthusiastically giving up several nights a week or large parts of their weekends to play or sing traditional music to the highest standards. It is taught in the schools to enthusiastic children who would just as soon spend a couple of hours singing and playing together on traditional folk instruments as kicking a ball round the playground. They encounter traditional modes, melodic forms, and the mind-bending rhythmic complexity of additive time signatures.

How long can this last? It is an aspect of Balkan life from which we, as apparently 'culturally dominant' Western Europeans, can learn an important lesson. In Bulgaria 'Rainbow over Bath' could and did use the folk tradition as the starting point for a creative project since it was, in a real sense, the pupils' own music.

What lies behind the enviable success of nations like Bulgaria in preserving their folk traditions? Today, the former Communist regimes of all the countries of the Soviet block are reviled by most of those who were forced to live under them. One of the few positive legacies was the state's support of all forms of folk culture, especially music. There is an ever-present danger that, with the rejection of Communism and the rush to embrace the Western consumerist way of life, all values which were associated with the old régime, including the state patronage of folk culture, will be thrown out. In Bulgaria, at least, folk music and dance are still supported by state patronage at various schools and conservatoires such as the National Academy of Folk Music and Dance Art in Plovdiv.

Professor Nikolay Stoykov, Head of the Department of Folk Music, is a composer who has forged a personal style steeped in the melodies and rhythms of Bulgarian folk music, successfully integrating them into the context of a dissonant contemporary idiom using proportional notation and indeterminate scoring, applying it equally to works for professional ensembles and orchestras, and to a vast repertoire of music for young people. Typical is his *Ala bala nica* (1989), a divertimento for children's choir, piano and percussion band based on Bulgarian folk-tales. This sparse score makes effective use of silence between fractured gestures, and dramatic climaxes built out of accumulations of simple diatonic ostinati (Example 32). The recorded extract is taken from a performance in Bath not by Bulgarian children, but by members of the South West COMA group in March 1999 (rainbow: Track 07). It features a traditional bagpipe melody referred to later in this chapter (p. 174).

Example 32: Stoykov, N. (1989) *Ala Bala Nica*
from 'Shtoorche Svirche', pieces for children's choir, Moozika, Sofia.

The secret of the preservation of Balkan folk music must also lie in its intrinsic qualities. It is noted for its dynamism and excitement, its rhythmic drive and vitality, and its use of irregular metrical structures, often delivered at unbelievable velocity, by young men to whom it is a matter of masculine pride to achieve feats of musical dexterity and outdo their friends in virtuosity, like the musical equivalent of break-dancing. Vocal music on the other hand is the province of women and girls, typified by the world-famous *Mystère des Voix Bulgares*. It is a matter of female pride to learn to sing at an early age in the characteristically harsh, guttural Bulgarian style, and to perform the traditional girls' two and three-part singing games. Music which has such a hold over the social life of the country would be difficult to dislodge.

The greater problem for Bulgarian culture is not survival within its own boundaries, but to gain acceptance and understanding in Europe as a whole. I have already discussed the importance which the European Union 'Agenda 2000' attaches to cultural diversity, and to the preservation of regional and folk-lore cultures. One of the central aims and objectives of the Culture 2000 programme has been to encourage cultural exchange programmes which preserve cultural diversity, celebrate the diverse cultures of Europe, and make them widely accessible.

The enthusiastic support of folk cultures is not confined to Eastern Europe. It typifies the fringes of Europe, whereas the central countries are impoverished by comparison. In 2000, 'Rainbow across Europe' explored new collaborations in the Republic of Ireland and Finland. In Ireland, both north and south, there is a living and thriving culture of traditional music. Here, state patronage by Communists cannot explain its survival against the ravages of commercial and popular music. Neither was there a Kodály or a Bartok to keep alive the tradition.

Can the survival of Irish folk music simply be explained by the qualities of exuberance and virtuosity it seems to share with Bulgarian music? Folk music is one of the badges of nationality. The strong survival of folk culture in these smaller countries grows instinctively out of a need to affirm national identity in contrast to the larger, more self-confident central nations.

The importance attached to folk music in Finland is exemplified by the establishment of a Department of Folk Music under Professor Heikki Laitinen at the Sibelius Academy in Helsinki. The Academy was one of the co-organisers in a three-year project funded by Culture 2000. There has been a revival in popularity of traditional instruments such as the Finnish kantele, or zither, and the ancient shaman's drum, the quodbas. There are interesting similarities between the playing styles of the quodbas, the Irish traditional bodhran, and the Bulgarian timpura. Strong affinities exist too between the singing style of the Finnish women's folk choir, such as *Mnaiset* (Folk Voices, 1999: Track 1), and Bulgarian women's choirs like *Vai Doudoulay* (*Vai Doudoulei & White, Green and Red*, 1998: Track 3).

Among the most striking examples of music as a badge of nationality are the Estonian Song Festivals. According to Toomas Haug, Estonian history 'is essentially bound to song, singing together and choir singing', based on the concept of 'the singing nation' (Haug, 1994). Estonia was a province of the Russian Empire during the nineteenth century, and the first Estonian Song Festival, which took place in 1869, became a focus for Estonian nationalism. Song Festivals continued during the Russian imperialist occupation and throughout the Soviet period under strict cultural censorship, but during the 1988 Festival, now called the 'Singing Revolution', songs from the traditional repertoire were performed again for the first time in sixty years.

What is so special about the Estonian Song Festivals? Other countries have festivals of folk music and song, but in the Estonian Festivals the songs are performed 'en masse' by a vast choir of ordinary Estonian people in the arena of the Talinn Song Festival Grounds. It is alleged that over three hundred thousand people took part in the 1988 'Singing Revolution', more than a quarter of the population of this tiny nation:

> Maybe the force of singing is mysteriously conditioned by the size of a nation, since only a small nation can fit in the huge grounds as one family, so that the voices of singers from one side can reach the ears of the entire nation (Haug, 1994).

These songs are not 'folk music', if we define that term as traditional music of anonymous authorship, handed down through the generations by aural transfer. Songs such as *Mu Isamma On Minu Arm* (*My Homeland is All My Joy*) by Aleksander Kunileid which sets lyrics by Lydia Koidula, the leading poetess of the so called national awakening period around 1918, typify this tradition. There are no stylistic elements to identify the songs as 'typically Estonian'. They are written in a straightforward diatonic idiom with memorable tunes, and conventional four-part harmony which could locate them anywhere in Europe – geographically 'weak'. The style is deliberately simple so that anyone can sing them. The 'strong' geographical focus is to be found entirely in the words (Estonia, 1994: Track 2).

As the matrix analysis at Example 33 shows, this massive demonstration of nationhood expressed through music is 'closed'. Although foreigners are welcome to attend the festivals, only people who know the songs can participate in any meaningful way. The Festivals are 'closed' as to people, place, classification and framing. Only in age and ability are they 'open' because any Estonian, regardless of age and singing ability, can and does join in. Thus part of the uniqueness of these events is expressed through extreme positions on the action, places and scale axes. A significant proportion of an entire nation participates in the 're-creation' of traditional songs.

Example 33: Matrix analysis of the Estonian Song Festivals.

Musical style can also be a badge of identity within smaller geographical regions. The folk music of Bulgaria really consists of a number of closely related but essentially different musical cultures. The collaboration between Plovdiv and 'Rainbow over Bath' brought us into contact with two regional traditions. Differences of musical style typify specific regions of the country. The highly individual women's vocal style of Thrace was represented by the female quartet Vai Doudoulay. On a visit to Bachkovo Monastery we encountered the instrumental music of the Rhodope Mountains. The area is famous for its annual folk festival of which the high point is the performance of the hundred Kaba-Bagpipes, again, like the Estonian Song Festivals, a collective expression in music of ethnic identity though on a much smaller scale. The medley of bagpipe melodies includes the one quoted in Stoykov's *Ala Bala Nica* (Kaba bagpipes, 1996: Track 1).

174

Example 34: Matrix analysis of the hundred Kaba-Bagpipes.

Vai Doudoulay were at the time collaborating with our hosts, the *White, Green and Red Jazz Formation*, in a very unusual fusion of jazz-rock idiom with Bulgarian folk-singing. The different perceptions which Bulgarian and British audiences had of these cultural fusions was instructive. When 'White, Green and Red' play in their own country, audiences want to hear an imitation of funky jazz-rock in 4/4 time in a British/American style familiar to Western audiences. But when the band visited Britain, audiences here wanted to hear those Bulgarian modes and additive time-values, something at which the Bulgarians were experts, but which stretched the capabilities of British musicians (*Vai Doudoulei & White, Green and Red*, 1998: Track 3).

It is this very richness of cultural forms which the European Union, through the Culture 2000 programme, now wishes to protect. It is an aim which we should wholeheartedly support, whatever limitations we put on the term 'Europe'. Given that the current administrative borders are as they are, it is only logical that if financial resources are to be made available within the Union, then they should be used to put our own European back yard in order.

Unfortunately, in many Western European nations, the process of dumbing down has already gone too far. Can folk music any longer provide a useful starting point for musical education when the tradition has all but died apart from small groups of enthusiasts and devotees? English folk music is undergoing a revival, and it is to be hoped that the programme supported by Culture 2000 will help to regenerate other dying traditions across the continent. To win over most young people requires as much evangelical fervour as any other minority musical form, including contemporary music.

The following incident serves to exemplify this point. Part of our collaboration with 'White, Green and Red' included a creative project in Plovdiv in September 1999, led by British composer Barry Russell with the Cornelius Cardew Ensemble. A hundred and eighty young people from Plovdiv schools, including two folk bands and two folk choirs, took part. What resulted was a fifty-minute work created by the children in collaboration with the composer. The score incorporated the beautiful British folk-song melody *The Lark in the Clear Air*. The Bulgarians were beguiled by this sinuous tune from another country, and thought it just as exotic as we might regard a Bulgarian melody. Yet a straw poll among British students at a seminar in Bath revealed that none of them knew the melody or had even heard of it.

Popular and commercial musical styles

The music which is most familiar to the vast majority of young people is the music they hear every day on Radio 1 or 'Top of the Pops'. If we want to obey Paynter's admonition to use pupils' existing interest in music as a starting point (open classification), then we have to start from the commercial and popular music which has become the 'folk music' of this modern industrialised society.

Classification

Age

Attitudes about the role of popular music in education have progressed significantly in the last forty years. The dismissive attitude of Wyndham Williams from Huddersfield College of Technology, expressed in the proceedings of the Fourteenth Symposium of the Colston Research Society, held at the University of Bristol in 1962, typifies the earlier period. He invites the delegates to agree on a definition of 'what we are meaning by "music" [...]', because '[...] 99% of our young people are adherents of and followers of the Juke Box Jury Top Ten. If we consider that as music, then we need not

176

bother about converting our young people to music' (Lowery, 1963). Since then, many educationalists, notably Piers Spencer (Spencer, 1981), have explored the potential of popular music in the school curriculum, both as a starting point for creative work, and an educational activity in its own right.

Treatment of a model drawn from popular music was a widely-used device in the last century and there are some ingenious examples, particularly amongst 'Experimental' composers (as defined by Nyman). In Hugh Shrapnel's *Sing*, well-known songs of different periods were sung, whistled or hummed very quietly, and changed in some way so that the tunes were still recognisable, but not immediately identifiable. Michael Chant produced 'snapshot versions' of pop tunes such as *Boom Bang a Bang*. In *Of Over Fond* he used songs from the Beatles' *Revolver* album. Nyman based all the music from the Greenaway film *The Draughtsmans' Contract* not on popular music but on re-workings of ground-bass compositions by Purcell, using them as the basis for canonic processes.

The idea of popular music as a starting point lay behind the 'Rainbow over Bath' project 'Igor's Boogie', devised with the Composers Ensemble, and led by composers Deirdre Gribbin and Philip Cashian in March 1999. It was designed as a holistic project with educational workshops, concerts of children's compositions, and a final professional concert with first performances of commissioned works. The project was related to a concert by the Composers Ensemble in which the programme consisted of musical treatments of popular music by established contemporary composers. During the education project, school pupils took a favourite pop song as the starting point for their own compositions.

The inspiration for 'Igor's Boogie' came from the music of Frank Zappa. The educational workshops were 'open' as to 'classification' in that they used vernacular musical idioms as a starting point. The aim was to progress towards a 'strong' outcome in the sense of encouraging children to compose music in a contemporary style. The opportunity to encounter several excellent models of such a process being used by professional composers was given in the final concert (Stage D in the Paynter model). The project as a whole was relatively 'open' in the age-and-ability matrix in that it involved young people at several different key-stages, and provided educational opportunities at a more adult level in the form of the screening of a video about Zappa.

Example 35: Matrix analysis of the 'Igor's Boogie' project.

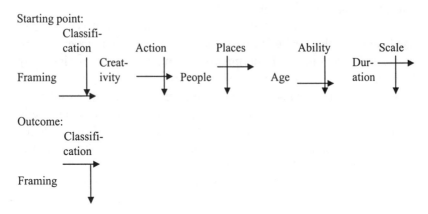

Starting point:

Outcome:

Groups of junior school children and 'A' level students worked on a creative composition project with the Composers Ensemble. A team of composers and musicians consisting of Deirdre Gribbin, Philip Cashian and Philip Sheppard, with additional support from Peter Wiegold, visited the schools every three weeks. The results were presented in two separate concerts. In the first, twelve compositions written by GCSE and 'A' level students were performed by members of the Composers Ensemble, conducted by Peter Wiegold. In the second, a hundred and sixty primary school children performed their own group compositions created in class sessions (Paynter's stage C). A few succeeded in progressing stylistically beyond the musical model as in an example from Moorlands Junior School created with the strong support of the class teacher Robin Benton. Called *Golden Strings,* it is based on Cher's *I Believe,* and the theme from *Titanic* (rainbow: Track 08).

The final evening concert by the Composers Ensemble was preceded by a screening of a video about Frank Zappa. The programme contained works by Deirdre Gribbin, John Woolrich, Simon Bainbridge, Franco Donatoni, and Thomas Adès, as well as songs and instrumental numbers by Frank Zappa including the song *Igor's*

178

Boogie arranged by Philip Cashian. All the works in the programme shared the theme of composers' treatments of a favourite piece of popular music. Singer Mary Wiegold and cellist Phil Sheppard both performed. Thus all members of the workshop team participated in this final concert in some way.

At many levels the project was a success. However, it stumbled into several of the pitfalls which commonly beset such holistic schemes. Very few of the school pupils attended the final evening professional concert, and thus did not encounter the model at all (Paynter's stage D). Nor did they see members of the workshop team working in their other roles as performers and composers. At a public and adult level the project only educated by 'encounter'. The opportunity to provide an element of 'instruction', in the form of a verbal introduction to the Zappa video or to the works in the concert, was missed, and very few people in the audience were even aware that the public concert had formed part of a larger project. As a result only a very few people other than the organisers of the event and the workshop leaders actually experienced the full holistic impact, which is rather beside the point.

Such failings were not the fault of the artists or ensemble, but of the hard-pressed and under-funded organisers (myself and the rest of the 'Rainbow over Bath' team) who were unable to persuade school teachers of the importance of the final concert. But equally those hard-pressed and under-resourced teachers failed to grasp the educational value of this opportunity for musical encounter or, if they did, were too pre-occupied with their classroom duties to do anything about it.

Was the project based on a valid conception? In the hands of professional composers such as John Woolrich or Deirdre Gribbin, the outcome of a musical process based on treatment of a favourite piece of popular music was unmistakably their work, recognisable by hallmarks of style. However, to the children taking part in the project, the work of these composers is unknown, and their style unfamiliar. Would the fact that these pieces grew out of treatments of popular material in itself make the end result any more accessible to the young people, even if they had attended the final concert? Or were the Composers Ensemble guilty of the same lack of coherent rationale discussed by Julia Winterson (Winterson, 1998: 200)?

However, if the end-product of a creative process based on treatments of familiar popular material sounds like another piece of pop music, then there has been no progression and the process has been of little value, unless the aim actually was to reinforce the desire of the boys to become mini Liam Gallagers and the girls to be just like Posh Spice in a kind of glorified Karaoke machine masquerading as education and legitimised by a travesty of modern educational theory.

This presents a serious dilemma to the contemporary composer and workshop leader who has strongly defined the aim of his project in terms of a specific style of contemporary classical music, seeking an outcome with strong classification. The dilemma is intensified if, on ideological grounds, he wants to adopt an open-framing approach.

Such a dilemma is avoided by the Valley Song-writing Project undertaken at the Blackwood Miners Institute, Caerphilly, led by singer/composers Hugh and Tony Williams, and supported and evaluated by the Performing Right Society. Here, annually for the past four years, up to two hundred junior school children (key-stage 2) have worked with these two charismatic and skilled workshop leaders to write songs which are then professionally produced, arranged and performed before an audience of delighted parents and friends.

In the people/places matrix, the project is well-conceived in that participating schools are chosen strategically within a clearly defined geographical area. Over a three-year period, most of the junior schools in the Caerphilly and Blaenau Gwent districts can take part, so that an entire year-group across the two districts will encounter the project at some time during key-stage 2.

There is no doubting the enthusiasm with which the youngsters throw themselves into this activity. Working in small groups they produce tunes through well-tried techniques with lyrics based on subject-matter close to the children's normal life experience such as shopping, pets or holidays. The tunes they produce are typical of a rather generalised popular musical vernacular. The Williams brothers insist that the limited aim of the process – simply to produce lyrics and melodies – is the secret of their success when working with this age-group.

The children's melodies are typically repetitive, employing only three or four notes within a narrow compass. The children are not encouraged to produce their own accompaniments or arrangements, nor to move beyond the limitations of the given style. Instead, when the children's creative process is complete, Hugh and Tony take the melodies to their own professional studio and arrange them for guitar, synthesiser and drum machine to a highly polished professional standard. The children then come into the studio for a few hours – an exciting and potentially educative experience in itself – to dub their voices on top of the backing tracks (rainbow: Track 09).

At the concert performance I heard at the Institute on 20 March 2001, in front of a large and supportive audience of parents and friends, the children from each of the four schools performed five of their own songs, often with rehearsed hand-gestures and physical movements as part of a well-produced presentation. However, it quickly became clear that they were 'singing along' to the professionally produced arrangements, and that this was not a truly live performance at all.

This approach to musical style is typical of the 'imitation of vernacular' which the Swanwick spiral sets between the ages 4–9, and is appropriate to key-stage 2. But I feel uncomfortable about the professional polish and the aping of practices derived from the commercial music world. This project comes dangerously close to reinforcing those stereotypes which lead to growing conformity as a result of the influence of global mass media as described in the Culture 2000 paper (European Commission, 1998b: 3).

The Swanwick spiral invites a more exploratory approach at, and above key-stage 3. Above the age of nine, the process can become more speculative, and it is essential that projects should develop beyond their vernacular starting point. The starting point must indeed be something which is familiar, but there must be development towards some unknown new destination. Otherwise the process is not educative but merely reinforces existing musical habits.

Projects like the Valley Song-writing Project are of enormous value in awakening children at key-stage 2 to the potential musical creativity within them, and building confidence in that creativity. But if their full potential is to be realised, such projects must be integrated into a planned developing programme which takes the children into more speculative areas of musical discovery through key-stages 3 and 4. In their report *Musicians go to School* (1993) Pratley, Rhydderch and Stephens refer to these different requirements at primary and secondary level, finding that primary school teachers will seek general support for music, whereas secondary teachers are more likely to need help with specific deficiencies.

Must every project be in some sense a voyage of discovery? Should we let young people set out only on a journey of which both the route and the destination have been firmly defined in advance, like a train journey from Bristol to York? Or can we expect children to embark with their workshop leader on Schafer's 'hour of a thousand discoveries' (Schafer, 1975: 132–133), like the popular conception of Columbus setting off to find out what lies on the other side of the Atlantic without even knowing if there *is* anything there at all? In terms of 'classification', we can discern three stages of development:

1. Exploration of a specific musical vernacular; Children internalise the characteristics of a musical language through creative activity. For them this is a voyage of discovery, although the teacher is familiar with the destination.
2. Growing acquaintance with a wider and wider range of musical styles and idioms; Children encounter a rich variety of musical experiences, and begin to form preferences, informed by knowledge. For them this is still a voyage of discovery, and so it will be to some extent for the teacher or workshop leader.
3. Exploration and development of new experimental forms, including stylistic fusion, and discovery of a personal 'voice'; By this stage, creative outcomes should not be defined in advance. The skill of the teacher or project leader consists not in knowing all the answers, but in how to deal with the unexpected, focusing on those creative accidents which should constantly arise during an inspiring music workshop, and integrating them into the final outcome.

Folk and classical music of non-European minority communities

The exploitative nature of the world of popular music may rule it out as a legitimate starting point for creative music-making on moral grounds. Some project leaders may decide to adopt a pragmatic

182

attitude, allowing teenagers to play and sing in a style which they know and understand to begin with: 'They will tend to have pronounced likes and dislikes and their first need will be to be able to play and sing what they like, in a style as near as possible to the model they admire' (Paynter, 1982: 116). Only later will they draw the pupils away from familiar ground, opening their ears to a wider experience of music in all its multiplicity of forms.

For others, the commercialism of popular music may present an insurmountable ideological barrier. They must look for other living traditions of music present in our society which are still close to their 'grass roots', or spring 'from the soil' in some way, and possess something which can be defined as genuine 'soul'. Such thinking has led to the widespread adoption of African drumming rhythms and chants, rhythms borrowed from Bhangra disco, Salsa, Samba, Reggae and many other popular forms, as well as Indonesian Gamelan, not only as the starting point but sometimes as the central raison-d'être for creative music projects. *Striking a New Note* advocated an approach to classification which was as open as possible:

> This review is taking as its starting point the belief that the term 'New Music' should include the widest possible range of original music being created in this country today. In stating that, it also acknowledges that music should be a spectrum, not a hierarchy (Gowrie, 1996: 14).

The writer goes on to emphasise the richness and variety of contemporary musical forms, and to give specific examples:

> British contemporary music includes not just work which derives from the Western classical tradition, but also jazz, ambient, house and jungle among a host of other styles, the roots of which lie in many other cultures. As a result of this diversity, the country's musical life is extraordinarily rich and this is a great source of strength which should be celebrated (Gowrie, 1996: 14).

Such openness to other musical styles has not always been easy for Western contemporary classical composers to accept. Thus Cage's *Water Music* engendered a degree of scandal amongst his purist contemporaries in 1952 by reintroducing 'sounds that were from a musical point of view, forbidden at that time...banal musical sounds such as octaves, 5ths and dominant 7ths' (Nyman, 1999: 51). John Tilbury describes a version of Stockhausen's *Plus Minus* made by Gavin Bryars of which the composer himself disapproved:

> The result was quite ravishing – the sheer sensuality of the sound of each was enhanced by the other. In this respect things have changed radically over the last five years. Previously our attitude had been quite ascetic, in fact we had a horror of any kind of indulgence and it was felt necessary to destroy 'beauty' wherever it occurred (Tilbury; cited in Nyman, 1999: 157).

The idea of using 'exotic' musical elements is nothing new. Henry Cowell's *United Quartet* (1936) introduced 'music from every time and place'. Carl Orff's fascination with the timbral qualities of exotic musical instruments was the inspiration for the 'Instrumentarium' (Orff, 1978: 68–136).

From the beginning of their collaboration Orff and Gunther were experimenting with tone colour through the introduction of many different percussion instruments. In 1925 Spangenberg of Dresden brought out the 'kleine Tanzpauke' (little dance timpani) and the Gunther dance group immediately obtained a set. Orff's friend Oskar Lang purchased many exotic instruments, such as rattles and bells, from antique shops and second-hand fairs and, on one occasion, an African slit drum. Two Swedish dancers brought him an African xylophone. Orff saw the potential of this tuned percussion instrument, but replicas could not be built quickly and easily because of the calabash resonators. Orff needed a design which was simple and cheap to build.

The solution came in the form of the so-called 'Kaffir' piano: a simple instrument with tuned wooden keys using an old wooden nail-box as a resonator. This was the forerunner of the well-known Orff xylophones. The harpsichord maker Karl Maendler designed and built the prototypes. The Orff Instrumentarium was completed in 1932 with the addition of metallophones. John Paynter pays tribute to Orff's contribution to creative music-making, whilst at the same time pointing out the limitations of the Orff instruments:

> In schools up and down the country students are now creating music of their own. In much of the advanced work orchestral instruments are used. But probably most teachers rely on classroom instruments such as the Orff xylophones,

glockenspiels and metallophones. Useful as these instruments are, the range of sounds they offer – both in pitch and timbre – is extremely limited. In the circumstances there is much to be said for going beyond that range of sounds but without having to encounter the considerable technical difficulties of orchestral instruments (Paynter, 1982: 114).

But Orff was no respecter of the musical traditions from which these instruments came. His interest lay only in their potential for creating multi-timbral 'elemental' music. He did not welcome the non-western tuning of the African xylophone because it was difficult to combine with other western instruments such as the recorder and, in particular, the piano which was at the centre of his ensemble (Orff, 1978: 96).

Chris Small was one of the first to articulate the more open attitude expressed in *Striking a New Note*:

We should not, however, allow the brilliance of the western musical tradition to blind us to its limitations and even areas of downright impoverishment. We may be reluctant to think of our musical life, with its great symphony orchestras, its Bach, its Beethoven, its mighty concert halls and opera houses, as in any way impoverished, and yet we must admit that we have nothing to compare with the rhythmic sophistication of Indian, or what we are inclined to dismiss as 'primitive' African music, that our ears are deaf to the subtleties of pitch inflection of Indian raga or Byzantine church music, that the cultivation of bel canto as the ideal of the singing voice has shut us off from all but a very small part of the human voice's sound possibilities or expressive potential, such as are part of the everyday resources of a Balkan folk singer or an Eskimo, and that the smooth mellifluous sound of the romantic symphony orchestra drowns out the fascinating buzzes and distortions cultivated alike by African and medieval European musicians (Small, 1977: 1).

Echoing the sentiments of the 1982 Gulbenkian Report, *All Our Futures* emphasises how important it is 'to enable young people to embrace and understand cultural diversity by bringing them into contact with attitudes, values and traditions of other cultures' (Robinson, 1999: 188). The purpose of a multi-cultural approach to education was to 'Promote a sense of inclusion and respect between the different cultural communities and traditions in the school and the classroom' and to 'point to the contribution of different local and national cultures to global culture' (Robinson, 1999: 188).

I discussed Peter Wiegold's use of African drumming in the Guildhall PCS course in Chapter 2 (p. 90). Nigel Osborne, aware of the potential of drumming as a way of releasing feelings of anger and aggression, invited the South African percussionist Eugene Skeef to join his team of workshop leaders and music therapists working at the Pavarotti Centre in Mostar, Bosnia. Here, African drumming was used as part of a psychological healing process for war-damaged children caught up in the Balkan conflict.

Vibrant new musical forms have been born out of the fusion of European harmony and the rhythms and melodies of African or South American indigenous music. As organisations like Peter Gabriel's 'Real World' have shown, musical 'crossover' can be a rich and rewarding area of musical experience and progression. The fusion work of 'White, Green and Red' with Vai Doudoulay, was another example of crossover between different vernacular styles.

In my opera *Seven Stars* (1994) I took advantage of what Swanwick has called music's 'free standing cultural autonomy' (Swanwick, 1988: 107) by transforming the same melodic and harmonic material into eighteenth-century classical pastiche, dissonant expressionist and avant-garde idioms, sea shanties, hi-life, reggae, and African drumming rhythms, using them as stylistic leitmotifs to identify the different ethnic origins of the protagonists in the drama. Various stylistic fusions, and sometimes disintegration and parody, took on a symbolic function in this story of racial intolerance and enslavement.

'Rainbow over Bath' presented several education projects which used a variety of other rationales as the basis for an 'open' approach to 'classification'. *Rhythm of the Tides*, devised by Tony Haynes' 'Grand Union Orchestra', brought together musical styles from the former Portuguese colonies in Brazil, Macau, and West Africa. In 1998 the orchestra presented *Silk Road* with a fully fledged education programme, bringing together music from countries along the ancient Silk Road through the Middle East, India and China.

In October/November 1999 we worked with Ensemble Esoterica, directed by Tunde Jegede and Paul Gladstone Reid, to create an educational programme based on musical forms derived from the African diaspora which took as its stylistic starting points, music of the folk cultures of Afro-Caribbean communities which had migrated to this country only a few generations ago.

Example 36: Matrix analysis of Ensemble Esoterica's 'African Diaspora' project.

At the centre of this holistic project was Ensemble Esoterica's public concert in October 1999 which brought together a versatile team of instrumentalists and singers fluent in the language of gospel, opera, African, jazz, reggae and classical forms. The ensemble included a rap poetry artist, Andrew Ward, and the recent winner of a national Scratch DJ competition who went by the name of Cut Master Swift. 'Rainbow' commissioned two new works – *Cello Concerto Initiation* from Tunde Jegede, and *I am*, an oratorio by Paul Gladstone Reid – which, according to Jegede's programme note, were a response to 'the experiences of growing up in the sub-cultures of a pan-African world'.

There is an important difference between 'weak' uncritical cherry-picking of poorly understood stylistic elements, and well-informed 'open' integration based on full understanding and sensitivity to the 'soul' of the music. In a recent article in *Music Teacher*, Ian Burton carefully analysed the subtle nuances of *clavé* patterns which characterise different forms of Latin jazz such as salsa, mambo, rumba or cha-cha (Burton, 2001). Such differences are second nature to Afro-Cuban musicians. But the difficulties encountered by year-ten pupils at St. Mark's School, Bath, illustrate the many pitfalls of trying to recapture on their own, the reggae feel of a song accompaniment they had created the week before with the help of Jamaican musician Cleveland Watkiss as part of the Ensemble Esoterica project.

3. Peter Wiegold leading a session of Preparation at the Hogeschool, Alkmaar.

4. Hogeschool students exploring sounds with lecturer Bob Martens.

Chapter 6
Places and people

The 'Places' and 'People' axes deal with people, who they are and where they live, and with geographical location in relation to music.

Music and place

The concept of 'music and place' embraces music in which location of sound in space is a compositional parameter and music which is 'site-specific'.

The antiphonal works of Gabrieli written for St. Mark's Cathedral in Venice are famous early examples of both categories. My own interest in sound in space was awakened by studying works by Karlheinz Stockhausen. *Gruppen* and *Carré* used antiphonal placings of entire orchestras around the audience so that sounds and textures could be flung from one side of the concert hall to the other, or rotate with spectacular effect. Similar effects were achieved electro-acoustically in *Kontakte*.

But what interested me more was a metaphorical link between Stockhausen's theoretical model of musical time, based on groups, collectives and moments, and the physical division of regions of space. In my own compositions *Locations* (1969) and *4 Times 4* (1968), structure in time was precisely mirrored by structure in space. In *Locations* this resulted in an exhibition of sound sculptures, arranged in adjoining rooms, which could be played like musical instruments either by musicians or by members of the visiting public – an example of complete 'openness' in performance. This was the first time I used the concept of 'windows' in imitation of Stockhausen's *Microphonie II*. Stockhausen's 'windows' showed recorded glimpses of his past works such as *Momente* and *Carré*. Mine showed glimpses of sounds in another 'location', or recorded from the past history of each 'location'.

The following year, I devised *Metropolis* as part of the Midland Group contribution to the Nottingham Festival. The work was conceptual in nature with musical and sculptural manifestations in selected positions all over the city at precisely determined time intervals throughout a period of one week. This was the first time I had used widely spaced geographical location and extremely long time periods in a musical composition. The 'places' axis of the theoretical model is a natural development.

Unconventional approaches to time and space are a feature of the music of the last forty years of the twentieth century. Nyman quotes the reactions of Cornelius Cardew to La Monte Young's *Poem for Chairs, Tables and Benches, etc., or Other Sound Sources* (1960):

> The work developed into a kind of chamber opera in which any activity, not necessarily of a sound variety, could constitute one strand in the complex weave of the composition, which could last minutes or weeks, or aeons. In fact it was quickly realised that all being and happening from the very beginning of time had been nothing more than a single gigantic performance of *Poem* (Nyman, 1999: 82).

Such a 'gigantic performance' of *Poem* could be analysed as follows.

Example 37: Matrix analysis of La Monte Young's *Poem*.

However, most of those people who, according to Cardew, were, are or will be, taking part were, are, or will be unaware and, in all probability, entirely uninterested in the fact. *Poem* is not open at all, but fundamentally weak. To become open according to my definition, it has to be realised. A full realisation would have to involve the willing and conscious participation of all people 'from the beginning of time'. Clearly an unrealisable objective.

Cardew's *Schooltime Compositions* was another manifestation of what, by then, was becoming a new artistic genre when it was presented at the Institute of Contemporary Arts in 1971. The score is a collection of drawings, diagrams, and short enigmatic texts, each occupying a single page of a tiny pocket book. There is no indication of temporal sequence. Any number of participants each choose a page, and interpret it however they wish. There are no rules. The performance took place in Nash House, a building which had been only recently occupied by the ICA. None of the present internal walls had yet been constructed. Musicians and visual artists from all over the country took part, arranging themselves over the entire floor area of the semi-derelict space. They performed in specially erected cubicles with walls made of large sheets of brown paper. A year later, the first London performance of John Cage's *Musicircus* likewise made use of the entire space of the Round-House at Chalk Farm.

American composer Stephen Montague acknowledged his own debt to Cage by staging *Musicircus* in London in January 2001. Montague has continued to develop the genre with events such as *Boulder Beach Band*, created for the 1998 Aldeburgh Festival, which achieved 'openness' on the 'people' axis and a 'strong' geographical focus by inviting a large number of people to participate in a performance on Aldeburgh beach that included brass bands, holiday-makers equipped with transistor radios, vintage cars with klaxon horns, ice-cream vans, and cassette tape recorders.

Since the 1970s, Maurice Agis' Colourspace, a series of interlocking inflatables of enormous size, has provided an adaptable and mobile site for many composers and sound artists with an interest in music and space, particularly Stephen Montague, Lawrence Casserley, and Simon Desorgher. In November 2000, the Colourspace organisation commissioned the Spanish composer Llorenç Barber to compose a *Symphony of Bells and Brass* for the city of York. Barber has built his career as a composer out of the idea of 'sounding' more than a hundred and fifty cities throughout the world. His 'Urban Landscape Citizens' Concerts' have made use of church bells, drums, cannons, ships' sirens, fireworks, and spatially distributed brass bands and wind bands. The work created for York pales in comparison with *O Roma nobilis – Concierto de campanas para cien iglesias de la cuidad de Roma* (O Noble Rome – Concert of bells from a hundred churches of the city of Rome) documented in his recent book (Barber, 1999). This remarkable performance, which took place across the entire historic centre of Rome on 28 June 1999, formed part of the opening ceremony of the year-long festival to celebrate Jubilee 2000, the 40th Jubilee of the birth of Christ. The score includes a map of Rome showing the locations of the churches (Example 39).

Example 38: Matrix analysis of Barber's *O Roma nobilis*.

An extract from the score of another of Barber's 'Urban Landscape' concerts, *The Grand Design*, created for the London borough of Croydon, shows how material for various carillons is laid out in proportional notation (Example 40) (Barber, 1999: 68). Barber's CDs include *Glockenkonzert* recorded in the Westphalian town of Münster in May 1998 (Barber, 1998: Track 14).

Some of Barber's 'Urban Landscapes' operate at the very limits of perceptibility. In Rome, there was no single point in the city where all the bells could be heard at once. So we run into the same kind of problems I referred to in connection with other holistic projects: that the public may not be aware of the full holistic nature of the small parts which they perceive. This is why documentation such as Barber's books, videos and CDs become an essential part of his projects' holistic expression.

On 31 December 1999 an international link-up between television companies brought twenty four hours of continuous live coverage of millennium celebrations into billions of homes across the world. This remarkable technical feat showed that modern communication makes it possible for real-time musical performances to happen on a global scale. Will we see composers like Barber trying to persuade global television and radio networks to allow them to create musical scores which achieve this kind of maximum geographical 'openness'?

Example 39: Barber, L. (1999) *O Roma Nobilis* Map of Rome showing churches.

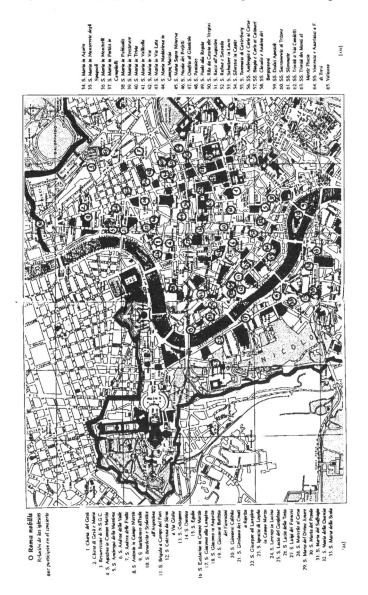

193

Example 40: Barber, L. (1996) *The Grand Design*
A City Symphony for the London Borough of Croydon.

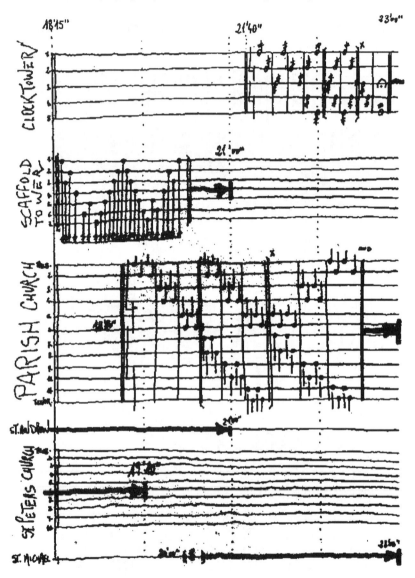

The conception and realisation of projects on this scale depend on creative imagination and resourcefulness in that part of the action/creativity matrix occupied by the producer/entrepreneur. As a composer, it is not enough to come up with the idea and write out the score. One needs qualities of personal charisma, persuasiveness, and tenacity, dogged determination in the face of institutional indifference – the ability to inspire many other people with enthusiasm for an idea, including local and national government officials and administrators, funding agencies, choir and orchestra conductors, teachers, and so on – all those qualities which seem to be implied in Cage's tongue-in-cheek remark in the score of *Variations V*: 'Changed function of composer to telephone to raise money' (Cage, 1968: 2).

Geographical location

In Chapter 4, I drew a distinction between qualitative, quantitative and categorical aspects of the axes of the theoretical model. The quantitative 'places and people' matrix measures the degree of 'openness' of a given project in terms of geographical spread and social inclusiveness. A categorical version of the 'places' axis could be based on administrative units of government from the smallest neighbourhood community up to the widest national, European or multinational level. In Great Britain the divisions are:

1. Parish, neighbourhood, street or village.
2. City, or District.
3. County – Somerset, Devon etc.
4. Region – the south-west peninsula, East Anglia and so on.
5. National groupings – England, Wales, Scotland, Ireland.
6. Country – The whole of Great Britain.
7. Continent of Europe.

Within each unit, defined crudely by size and population, there are more subtle distinctions, each characterised by a different social mix. A more detailed breakdown of different categories of 'neighbourhood' show the closeness of the relationship between 'Places' and 'People':

1. Place: inner city.   People: racially mixed community.
2. Place: housing estate.   People: social problems, high unemployment.
3. Place: outer suburbs.   People: relatively affluent.
4. Place: rural.   People: a wide mix of affluence and deprivation.
5. Place: tourist centre.   People: wide seasonal variations in population.

Some of the projects I shall look at have found inventive ways of defining their geographic focus and of dealing with the unique conditions encountered in specific localities. For instance, the aim of the Bristol-based 'Multi-A' organisation is to provide opportunities for the racially mixed populations of inner city areas around St. Paul's and Montpelier to encounter a wide range of artistic and cultural events. 'Multi-A', with its intimate knowledge of local conditions and its strong links with the community, can enable larger, nationally focused organisations such as Welsh National Opera or the Royal Ballet to discharge part of their artistic duty to be 'accessible'. 'Multi-A' made it possible for many thousands of primary school children of Jamaican or Pakistani origin to encounter the so-called 'élitist' experience of grand opera and ballet.

The *Confluence* project based at Shaftesbury in Dorset is entirely rural in its focus. This three-year creative music project, funded by the National Lottery 'Arts for Everyone Programme' (A4E), was initiated in 1998 by 'Common Ground', a pressure group which uses artistic activities to raise awareness of environmental issues. 'Common Ground' has initiated many events and programmes focusing on the renewal of disappearing rural traditions such as farmers' markets or the annual 'Apple Day' and 'Tree Dressing Day'.

'Common Ground' hit on the novel idea of using the Dorsetshire River Stour to define the geographical limits of the *Confluence* project. Not just the river itself but all its tributaries provided the geographical focus and a source of inspiration to the creative imagination. The project brought together communities in small towns and villages which lie within the river's watershed from Wincanton in the north to Wimbourne in the south, and from Sturminster Newton in the west to Gillingham in the east. A stylised diagram of the Stour system drawn

196

from a map of the district provided an eye-catching emblem for all publicity purposes (Example 41). I shall discuss 'Confluence', and the work of the featured composer, Karen Wimhurst, in more detail in Chapter 7 (p. 242).

Example 41: Common Ground *Confluence Project* River Stour emblem.

Other projects with a rural focus include Wingfield Arts, based in the tiny village of Wingfield near Bury St. Edmunds in Suffolk. Wingfield creative music projects supported by the National Lottery A4E Programme have included composer residencies by Edward Dudley Hughes, Lynne Plowman and Tunde Jegede, contextualised by concerts by the New Music Players, London Mozart Players String Trio and the African Classical Ensemble. Wingfield's Education Newsletter (Autumn 2000) shows a catchment area within a twenty mile radius of Wingfield village, extending as far as Stanton Village in the west, Bungay, Beccles and Lowestoft in the East, and Debenham in the south, with one far-flung event happening forty miles to the north at Fakenham in Norfolk.

Several of the most recent creative music projects supported by the Performing Right Society have shown a strong geographical focus. These include Hugh and Tony Williams' Valley Song-writing Project discussed in Chapter 5 (p. 180), the 'Musiko Musika' song-writing project with Chilean composer Mauricio Venegas-Astorga located on the Isle of Wight (p. 305), and Mark Hewitt's project on the Isle of Skye.

The education and community programme of 'Rainbow over Bath' included rural and urban projects. We defined more precise categories of rural community including:

4a. Villages at the centre of a scattered population of farms and hamlets; There is a strong sense of community, with many artistic activities of a traditional kind such as choral societies and amateur dramatic groups enthusiastically supported by local people. There are also wide divisions between affluent 'in-comers' and an indigenous farming community which suffers from rural isolation and poverty.

4b. Small conurbations of rural market towns lacking access to the artistic and cultural opportunities of larger centres of population.

Creative music projects co-ordinated by organisations based in a particular locality usually aim to involve the participation of people based in that local community. Larger organisations, including region-al opera and ballet companies such as Opera North, Northern Theatre Ballet, or Welsh National Opera, serve larger regions of the country and rely on the co-operation of organisations like 'Multi-A' to achieve a precise 'grass-roots' focus. National institutions, such as the London Sinfonietta or the Contemporary Music Network, also rely for the success of their education and community projects on the support of local arts centres, concert halls and education authorities in the locations they visit on tour.

Cultural diversity in Europe

A project which is located in a given geographical location will be 'open' on the 'people' axis if it seeks to involve a representative selection of people of both sexes from all social, ethnic or national groups living in that area. When the geographical focus of a project is widened in collaborations within Europe, the opportunities for 'openness' to people are increased.

The priorities of the EU Agenda 2000, such as the fostering of creativity and the preservation of cultural diversity through regional and folklore cultures, represent entirely laudable aims. It is difficult to find fault with the view that: 'Culture is increasingly emerging as a driving force in society, a source of vitality, dynamism and social development. Cultural creation should therefore be made a priority [...]' (European Commission, 1998b: 10). We can readily agree too about the problems of alienation and marginalisation of minority groups, and the threatened loss of diversity as a result of unification and the influence of global mass-media (European Commission, 1998b: 3).

All European countries contain, within their populations, different ethnic groups which can be categorised broadly as either indigenous or immigrant in origin. An analysis of the population of Europe along ethnic lines reveals an enormous richness of cultural forms. British immigrant communities include Afro-Caribbean, Indian, Pakistani and Chinese people. France has sizeable communities of North African people and in Germany there are many Turkish migrant workers. The Netherlands have long been home to Africans and Indonesians. The South American, African and Chinese links with Portugal have been mentioned in Chapter 5 (p. 186). More recent movements of refugees and asylum seekers have created growing communities of Kosovars in The Netherlands, or of Rumanians in Britain and Ireland. Indigenous populations include minority groups too, such as the French and Flemish populations of Belgium, the Catalans of Spain, and the Laps of Finland. Most eastern European countries have significant populations of Roma or gypsies whose traditional nomadic territories cut across modern political boundaries. Such diversity has both positive and negative consequences, as I discussed in Chapter 5 (p. 166). It is the celebration of these different cultures within each country, as well as differences between one country and another, which the EU has in mind when it talks of 'cultural diversity'.

But some forms of Western European culture are highly dominant. The situation is further complicated by American-influenced culture which includes jazz and rock music. Wherever these influences have spread, they have tended to be regarded as the mainstream culture, whether in the form of classical 'high art', or in the form of what the European Union calls 'global mass media'. As a result, folk cultures risk being marginalised, corrupted or destroyed. It is the 'must-have' mentality engendered by contemporary consumerist society which may destroy the multiplicity of cultural forms.

There has been a growing realisation on the part of the Arts Councils of England, Wales and Scotland, and the Regional Arts Boards, that they have a duty to support black and Asian artistic forms. This influenced the policies of the A4E Lottery funding programme. Such funding policies are widely reflected in other European countries. The awareness that cultural collaboration can be a positive force combating alienation and social exclusion between distinct ethnic and cultural groups both within the individual countries of the EU, as well as across national boundaries, is central to the agenda of the Culture 2000 programme.

Any programmes designed to rectify the lack of awareness of the cultures which make up Europe are a good thing. But is it possible to define what Europe actually is? How can we justify imposing geographical boundaries within which these programmes may take place, while what lies outside is none of our business?

Robin Guthrie has discussed the problem of European-ism at length in *The Good European's Dilemma* (Guthrie, 2000). Janet Mary Hoskyns too has attempted to define a 'European' in *Music Education and a European Dimension – A la recherche de L'Europe perdue...* (Hoskyns, 1996).

We could attempt to define 'Europe' according to a number of simple objective criteria such as race, language, religion or culture, but this is a complex issue and none of the resulting definitions are watertight. Europe as an administrative organism has only existed since the formation of the European Economic Community, but the European Union, as currently constituted, is not the same thing as Europe defined in cultural terms. Until the formation of the EEC, Europe had no boundaries like a nation-state. The Atlantic ocean forms a natural western boundary, but to the east and south, there is no compelling geographic justification for the present administrative boundaries.

The European Union has been seen as a kind of rich man's club. It is besieged by neighbouring nations eager to join. The original seven grew to nine, then to twelve, and so on. The collapse of Soviet-style communism led to applications for membership from former 'Warsaw Pact' countries and to the creation of a waiting list of accession countries who were permitted to negotiate 'Association Agreements' allowing them access to various cultural programmes but not all the economic benefits of full membership. A provisional timetable has now been set, and a first wave of accession countries joins the EU in 2004. There is a risk that, in their anxiety to take advantage of the material prosperity EU membership appears to offer, as an alternative to the poverty and economic stagnation which they once confronted, these 'accession countries' will reject and thus lose what they have which is of real and unique value. They are in vulnerable positions, and if any part of these unique cultures disappears, then the richness of the whole world's cultural heritage will be impoverished.

This then is the good European's dilemma. He wants to enter into a co-operative economic relationship with his immediate neighbours so that all may share equally in prosperity, without the risk of war and conflict engendered by rivalry and competition between independent states. He wants to pursue the interchange and celebration of cultural and artistic activities, believing that such cultural co-operation 'consolidates peace' (European Commission, 1998b: 10). But the creation of the super-state which may be the outcome of political union threatens to destroy that very cultural diversity he so much wants to preserve and celebrate. Moreover our 'good European' is the inheritor of a mainstream cultural tradition which has already been guilty of overbearing colonial influence all over the world, where it has destroyed or corrupted many of the indigenous cultures it has encountered. But if we cannot find humanitarian ideals and a commitment to cultural co-operation within the artistic community of Europe, where can we expect to find them? If steps are not taken to encourage the propagation of cultural values based on co-operation and mutual understanding, then we risk being overwhelmed by the dual forces of political power and competitive economics, where the motivation may be less idealistic, and more opportunistic, based on instincts of greed for wealth, power and influence.

This book is not about politics and economics, and I do not intend to discuss the economic and administrative merits or demerits of any future super-state. The pros and cons of membership of a common European currency, and the likely effects on the independence and sovereignty of individual nations within the Union are issues which fall outside the scope of this thesis. I concern myself only with its likely cultural effects, and in particular I propose ways in which artistic collaboration through music can help to maximise the benefits brought by cultural contact and understanding.

Such considerations were uppermost on the agenda of the recent conference 'Bigger, Better, Beautiful' convened in Budapest in February 2002 jointly by the British and Hungarian European Cultural Contact Points (EUCLID and Kulturpont Hungaria). Delegates from arts and cultural organisations in most of the accession countries and in several full EU member states especially UK, Ireland, France and Germany, as well as from European institutions such as the European Commission, the Council of Europe and CIRCLE (Cultural Information and Research Centres Liaison in Europe) met to discuss the cultural opportunities of EU enlargement.

There was general agreement that if co-operation on cultural projects was encouraged before full economic union, the EU would be getting its priorities in the right order. Art and culture could be ahead of the game, paving the way for full integration. During the first two years of 'Culture 2000', accession countries were unable to participate in its programmes as full 'co-organisers'. Only one small part of 'Culture 2000' was open to them, and then only through officially constituted governmental bodies such as the British Council. Delegates welcomed the fact that this policy had now been reversed and that accession countries would be able to participate fully for the remaining three years of Culture 2000.

202

Many problems would arise. There were misgivings about excessive levels of bureaucracy, and about the abstract nature of the language used in describing the various framework programmes and structural funds available through the EU, with resultant difficulty in converting them into real cultural activity. There would be financial problems because of the wide disparity in wealth between EU full members and accession countries. There was concern over the indifference towards European matters amongst ordinary people in both full-member states and accession countries. It was essential to emphasise that cultural co-operation was a matter of real co-operation between ordinary people of different nationalities working together at a grass-roots level.

How could any limit be put on the process of enlargement? If the EC gave in to pressures from all the applicant states, the concept of 'Europe', already difficult to define, would become even less meaningful. When the current candidate nations had succeeded in meeting the economic requirements, there would be another wave of nations eager to join this affluent club including Beloruss, Ukraine, the countries of former Yugoslavia, Moldova, Georgia and even Russia.

The population distribution across Europe, Western Asia and North Africa shows the significance of the real geographical boundaries represented by Siberia, the Ural Mountains, the central Asian steppe, the Caspian Sea, the highlands of Afghanistan, the Mediterranean Sea, and the deserts of Saudi Arabia and the Sahara. This vast area of land containing some fifty three countries is defined by where people actually live. Is it unrealistic to propose that it should be the proper field in which we should seek to create cultural co-operation projects in music, rather than limiting our field of operation to the narrow confines of the EU?

Beyond the boundaries of Europe

Remarkably, creative and educational music projects, some based on models developed in Britain have already taken place in twenty-three of these fifty-three countries. The list includes some of the most notorious trouble-spots in the world. Critics have asked how we can justify the expenditure of hard-earned aid money on apparent luxuries like musical activity, when the basic needs of food, clothing and shelter are barely being met. However the examples of Nigel Osbourne at the Pavarotti Centre in Bosnia, Laura Hassler's 'Musicians without Borders' project in Kosovo, the Armagh Music Week in Ulster, and the work of the Israel Philharmonic among Palestinian communities on the West Bank all testify to the power of music, and especially creative music projects, to help in the healing process across sectarian divides.

The Marseille-based *Orchestre des Jeunes de la Méditerranée* (OJM), under its conductor Roland Harabedian, brings together young people from countries on all sides of the Mediterranean rim. The cultures of the Arabic, African and Asian countries which fall within its frame of reference are demonstrably different from Europe, but it is this very difference which makes the need for cultural contact all the more compelling. Where more than here do we need the healing power of music? OJM's repertoire draws heavily on that culturally dominant European classical mainstream tradition. Its approach to 'classification' tends to be closed and its position on the 'creativity' axis is biased towards the 're-creative' end. However the orchestra has a policy of commissioning new works which integrate instruments and stylistic elements representing the different folk-music cultures of its multinational membership.

Example 42: Matrix analysis of the OJM.

The frame of reference of the Brussels-based Jeunesses Musicales International is set well outside the confines of Europe. JMI's title locates it immediately on three of the axes of the theoretical model:

Jeunesses:	Age:	—	Young people
Musicales:	Classification:	—	interested in music
Internationale:	Places:	—	throughout world.

According to its mission statement JMI 'Enables young people to develop through music across all boundaries' (Franzen, 1999). With the complete lack of geographical limits implied by this statement, the organisation lays itself open to accusations of tokenism. JMI's activities include the JM World Orchestra which brings together some one hundred young people aged between sixteen and twenty-five from many different countries in two annual tours. The Orchestra carries a message of world peace through cultural co-operation and has performed at many special events such as the United Nations International Youth Day in August 1999, and Concert of Reconciliation in Warsaw in September 1999 marking the sixtieth anniversary of the outbreak of World War II. The JM World Youth Choir of a hundred singers aged seventeen to twenty-six fulfils a similar function, touring as part of the UNESCO 'Artists for Peace' programme.

But how can a hundred musicians and a hundred singers represent the whole world? JMI's own publicity describes the members of both these groups as 'the most talented'. Necessarily these are privileged youngsters selected by audition because JMI and its associate organisations need to put on a polished show which will impress their audience of international delegates and draw attention to the message of world peace. Such events are powerfully symbolic but, although JMI's activities bring huge public-relations benefits, in reality projects like the World Orchestra are 'closed' in the 'ability' axis, geographically 'weak', and, like OJM, adopt a closed approach to 'classification' as shown by the following matrix analysis.

Example 43: Matrix analysis of the JMI World Orchestra.

JMI is not unaware of such criticisms, and has made strenuous efforts to become more truly 'open'. It has been bringing the children's opera *Brundibar* (BC1) by the Czech Jewish composer Hans Krasa into schools, music camps and conservatories in Germany, Poland and the Czech Republic since 1995. The aim is to introduce children to opera performance and 'to teach the values of tolerance, hope and solidarity'. In his foreword to JMI's *Brundibar* programme, Dag Franzen, Secretary General of JMI expresses his personal vision of peace and progress through cultural collaboration:

> The human being is a creature with a very short memory. Despite what our elders tell us, each generation feels obliged to act on its own experiences, often repeating the same mistakes as our parents and forefathers. However it is my belief that, with each generation, the human race is becoming a little wiser, adding emotional and social intelligence to our existing intellectual capacities (Franzen 1999).

A multinational tour in Autumn 2000, based on a school production with forty-eight children and seventeen members of JMI World Orchestra supported by the CONNECT program of the EU, took the work to Oslo, Lund, Copenhagen, Amsterdam, Barcelona, Paris, and Brussels, ending at the Bloomsbury Theatre in London.

The political message of this simple story, and the historical background of its creation in a Nazi concentration camp, make it an ideal focus for a JMI peace project. Krasa's accessible and tuneful musical idiom presents no aesthetic challenge, and the work offers no opportunity for creative compositional input by the participants. However the *Brundibar* CD (Krasa, 2000), a compilation of extracts from performances in different languages in the Czech Republic, France, Italy, Sweden, and Germany, manifests the geographical 'openness' of this international project, as shown in Example 44.

Example 44: Matrix analysis of JMI's *Brundibar* project.

JMI's remit is world-wide. The *Brundibar* project's geographical limitation to Europe was dictated by the rules of EU funding. JMI's 'Music Crossroads Southern Africa' programme (MCSA) brings the organisation closer to a practical realisation of its world-wide mission by harnessing individual musical creativity at a more inclusive level beyond the boundaries of Europe. Its three aims are stated as follows:

- To introduce young people to different musical genres.
- To promote live performance opportunities for young musicians.
- To enhance understanding of other people's cultures and music.

MCSA challenges my Euro-centric hypothesis. It was initiated in 1996 by the Swedish music animateur Stig Asp 'to empower young people through music' in countries of the Southern African Development Community (SADC) including Zimbabwe, Mozambique, Malawi, South Africa, Tanzania, Namibia, Zambia and Botswana (JMI, 2000). JMI's Executive Summary describes the project's long-term goal: 'to establish a self-sustainable cross-border youth music structure which could become a positive vehicle for cultural collaboration within the entire SADC region' (JMI, 2000).

JMI identified many urgent challenges including high youth unemployment, lack of motivation and positive role models for young people, high drugs misuse, high AIDS infection, disrupted communication between communities and generations, limited social participation of women, and poor organisational and educational infrastructure. Concerns for the disappearance of ethnic and traditional music cultures 'due to the globalisation of commercial music' (JMI, 2000), echo the agenda of the EU Culture 2000 programme.

MCSA is organised as a series of competitive festivals at national level, feeding into a regional final. In 1998 there were festivals in nine provinces of Zimbabwe, in Mozambique and in South Africa. MCSA aims to enhance skill development, to present all styles of music including stylistic fusion, to bring young African musicians together across cultural, social, ethnic, economic, linguistic and national boundaries, and to help them to realise their full potential in making a beneficial difference to their immediate environment. The scheme also aims to encourage existing networks to work towards a sustainable collaborative relationship serving as a model in areas other than music.

Example 45: Matrix analysis of 'Music Crossroads Southern Africa'.

JMI, working from its Brussels office with forty-one member sections all over the world, provides models of world-wide co-operation between organisations and funding agencies across national boundaries. The London performance of *Brundibar* was originally co-ordinated by Y&M (Youth and Music), but the organisation was abolished due to lack of funding just before the Bloomsbury performances, leaving JMI with no British partner. As far as I know, no other UK organisation has yet stepped in to fill the vacuum, yet I am certain that there is enormous potential for cross-fertilisation of UK methodologies in creative music making with JMI's world-wide network of youth music organisations.

Rainbow across Europe:
a creative response to European cultural policy

In 1996, I initiated a programme of European musical collaboration called 'Rainbow across Europe'. How did it match up to the EC's idealistic aspirations, and to the stated missions of some of the other international programmes I have been discussing? I believe 'Rainbow across Europe' was the first attempt to create a fully structured European network of creative music projects based on the holistic principle. The aims of 'Rainbow across Europe' were deliberately framed to conform to the aims of the Kaleidoscope Fund. Its formation was opportunistic in the best sense.

The idea was an imaginative response to a careful study of the conditions of funding laid down by the EU Kaleidoscope scheme, already discussed in Chapter 3 (p. 116). It called for 'experimental measures designed to encourage cultural co-operation between a minimum of three member states.' In particular the fund invited proposals which were innovative and exemplary in conception and designed to involve the participation of young people. Optionally, projects could also involve the participation of organisations based in one or more 'third countries' (European Commission, 1996b).

This set of conditions suggested a rationale for a possible choice of collaborators for a new European network to foster creative music projects based on the British model. The four cities represented in the original 'Rainbow across Europe' project were Bath and three of its twin cities, Aix en Provence in France, Alkmaar in The Netherlands and Kaposvár in Hungary.

The tradition of town twinning is an alternative structure to the European Union, though with much more limited objectives. It, too, grew out of a desire to propagate peace amongst the peoples of Europe, but at a grassroots level, rather than at a national and governmental level. It is argued that if we are united by bonds of friendship amongst towns and cities, then ordinary people are much less likely to agree to go to war with one-another. Town-twinning has its origins in a treaty of friendship between Bath and Alkmaar drawn up during the final months of the Second World War when Bath citizens sent aid shipments to the ravaged city in the wake of German retreat. The twinning with Aix en Provence is of later date. Bath and Aix are both ancient spa resorts of Roman origin famous for their eighteenth century architecture. Etymologically, both cities have the same name. The word 'Aix' derives from Latin 'Aquae Sextius', meaning 'Waters of Sextius', while Bath was called 'Aquae Sulis' by the Romans. The last partner in the network was Kaposvár, a small city in the south western Somogy region of Hungary, also a spa town.

The partnership between British, Dutch, French and Hungarian organisations conformed to all the Kaleidoscope conditions. The twinning relationship was important because the project immediately attracted the support of the respective civic offices in each city, and led to important 'symbolic' demonstrations of international partnership such as mayoral receptions and exchanges of civic letters.

However, the International Offices in each city had a wide remit embracing everything from gardening societies to fire brigades. They were not specialists in music. Essential information about contemporary music and contact with sympathetic individuals in each city was provided through the respective Music Information Centres, the Gaudeamus Foundation of The Netherlands, Le Centre de Documentation de la Musique Contemporaine, France, and the Hungarian Music Council.

I believed that the project needed key individual composers resident in each city to act as local co-ordinators. The choice of lead composers contributed significantly to the success of the project. There was an element of self-interest amongst the composers all of whom saw it as an opportunity to promote their own work in an international context.

We were able to locate composers in Aix and Alkmaar who became active and reliable supporters. Michel Pascal and Kees van Unen possessed essential qualities of commitment and leadership. The success that these two brought to the project, both in their own localities and in the other cities, supports my argument. Michel Pascal was Composition Professor at Nice University and Director of his own electro-acoustic ensemble 'Studio Instrumental'. He worked closely with the Director of Aix en Musique in the promotion of new music concerts. Kees van Unen was Theory Professor at the Hogeschool Alkmaar Conservatorium, Concert Organiser of the Provadja Theatre, and Secretary of Stichting Componisten Noord Holland (North Holland Composers Foundation).

The Hungarian programme, by contrast, suffered from the fact that no composer could be identified living and working in Kaposvár. A Budapest-based steering group consisting of representatives of the Hungarian Music Council, the InterArts Festival Centre, and the publishing house Edition Musica Budapest, nominated the composer

Lászlo Tihanyi, who was not based in Kaposvár and had no connections with the city. As a composer and as conductor of his own ensemble, Intermodulaçio, Tihanyi was an ideal choice in all respects except for his lack of connection with Kaposvár. He was Composition Professor at the Liszt Academy, Budapest, and assisted Peter Eötvös as Conducting Professor at the annual International Bartok Seminar in Szombathely.

The project was co-ordinated in Kaposvár by the Director of the Municipal Arts Centre. Lack of commitment, knowledge and understanding of the aims and objectives of the project at the grassroots level led to serious breakdowns of communication and to a failure to generate any significant local interest in the project. Percussion instruments were not provided, very little publicity was organised, and concert audiences failed to materialise.

The overall success of the project depended on effective overall co-ordination by the lead organisation, 'Rainbow over Bath', and on efficient and speedy communication with local co-ordinators. The problems in Kaposvár showed only too clearly the results of failings at the local level. 'Rainbow across Europe' needed local support to achieve its Europe-wide aims and objectives, just as organisations such as the Contemporary Music Network or the London Sinfonietta, working within the UK, need the support of locally based concert halls and local authorities.

The education programme which formed a central element to the whole project reflected a specifically British expertise. All workshops were led by Sean Gregory with only minimal input from the other composers, none of whom possessed the same level of skills in communication and leadership in relation to young people. Sean Gregory's work as an animateur in Great Britain was already well known at the time. In 1996 he was on the point of taking over from Peter Wiegold as Director of the Performance and Communication Skills Course at the Guildhall School, London.

The education project in Alkmaar involved the participation of five different school and community groups, totalling some one hundred and eighty young people in a memorable fifty minute performance. Louis Pirenne of the British Council invited a group of

Netherlands educationalists to attend the event as a showcase for British expertise in the field of creative music-making.

Ironically, 'Rainbow across Europe', which was so closely modelled on an interpretation of the EU Kaleidoscope terms and conditions, failed to secure Kaleidoscope funding. However, 'Rainbow over Bath' obtained grants from Kaleidoscope in 1997 and 1999. The structural grid (Example 46) shows a network of eight partners established over several years. It is a 'categorical' version of aspects of the theoretical model. The horizontal axis is a version of the 'places' axis focusing on particular cities and countries, while the vertical axis lists institutions and individuals in each city able to deliver aspects of the 'holistic model' and the 'community of learners'. The grid demonstrates how co-operation between similar institutions within Bath was echoed in each of the partner cities and countries. It also shows the response to individual composers to an invitation to compose new works for the project. Members of the ensembles from each country came together to form the Rainbow International Ensemble.

New partners in the 'Rainbow across Europe' network have included cities which are not officially twinned with Bath, but have other characteristics in common:

1. Similar population size.
2. Location within a similar kind of rural hinterland.
3. Provincial or non-metropolitan status.
4. Common architectural, cultural or historic features which may have a symbolic value, e.g. Roman origins, thermal spa, Georgian building style, seven hills, abbey or cathedral church.

For practical reasons it was important that the cities were all within a short fly-time of Bath, an expression of the 'near/far' qualitative aspect of the places axis which ensures that they are our geographical near-neighbours. The fact that they are also part of the European Union is irrelevant, except that it makes them eligible to benefit from EU funding. More significantly they are also near-neighbours in cultural terms, possessing cultures which are not so very far removed from our own, an expression of the 'near/far' qualitative aspect of the 'people' axis.

Example 46: Rainbow across Europe – Structural grid.
Underline indicates previous participation in 'Rainbow across Europe'.
Asterisk (*) indicates commissioned work.
Italics indicates provisional involvement.

Country:	Britain	France	Netherlands	Austria	Hungary	Finland	Eire	Bulgaria
City (all non-metropolitan):	Bath	Aix en Provence	Alkmaar Zwolle	Salzburg	Kaposvar	Joensuu	Cork	Plovdiv
Funding agencies:	SW Arts, British Council, ACE, EU	Alpes Maritimes, AFAA, ARCAM	Nord Holland, DCSVB	MICA	Budapest Spring Festival	Joensuu City		Obstina Plovdiv
International Office:	Bath & NE Somerset	Aix international office	Alkmaar inter-national office					Internationa l office
National Music Information Centres:	British Music Information Centre	CDMC	Gaudeamus Foundation	MICA	Hungarian Music Council	*Finnish Music Information Centre*	Irish Music Information Centre	*Bulgarian Music Information Centre*
Universities:	University of Bath	*Université d'Aix*		Mozarteum		University of Joensuu	*University College*	*University College*
Research programme:	Bath Spa U.C. & York University							

213

Country:	Britain	France	Netherlands	Austria	Hungary	Finland	Eire	Bulgaria
Conservatoire trains teachers, composers, & instrumental-ists:	Bath Spa UC	Conservatoire Darius Milhaud	Hogeschool, Alkmaar; Christian Huygens, Zwolle	Carl Orff Institute and Mozarteum	Franz Liszt School of Music		Cork School of Music	National Academy of Folk Music and Dance Art
Participating Ensembles:	Rainbow International Ensemble	Studio Instrumental	Asko Ensemble	Nouvelle Cuisine, Camerata Obscura	Intermodul-acio	Joensuu City Orchestra	Irish National Chamber Choir	White Green & Red, Vai, Doudoulai
Participating composers:	Peter Wiegold, Barry Russell, Deirdre Gribbin	Vinko Globokar, Michel Pascal,	Kees van Unen, Alex Manessen	Christoph Cech, Klaus Feßmann, Klaus Ager,	László Tihanyi	Kimmo Hakola	Ian Wilson, Colin Mawby	Nikolay Stoykov, Vesselin Koychev
Commissioned or featured works:	'In the Wake of the Child' *, 'A Feeling in Time'* 'Within this Body' *	'Szivarvany' *, 'Liens', 'Ram'	'Ab Rae' *, 'A Time and a Place'	Stone Instruments	'Serenade' *, 'Silence of Winds' 'Pylaios'	Piano Concerto		'Trio Sere-nade' 'Ala Bala Nica' 'Samba in 7/8'
Workshop programme:	Peter Wiegold, Barry Russell, Deirdre Gribbin	Sean Gregory, Deirdre Gribbin, Rob Smith	Sean Gregory, Peter Wiegold	Peter Wiegold Christoph Cech	Sean Gregory	Sean Gregory, Peter Wiegold	Evelyn Grant	Barry Russell

Within each city we sought out organisations with aims and objectives similar to 'Rainbow over Bath'. I list here the important characteristics:

1. A commitment to the promotion of contemporary music.
2. A commitment to training musicians at higher education or conservatoire level.
3. A commitment to music education at all levels, particularly the training of teachers, and community-music workers.

The symbolic value of cultural and historic features is exemplified by the collaborations with the Bulgarian city of Plovdiv. Both Bath and Plovdiv were formerly Roman towns and were said to have been loved by the Romans because of the seven hills which reminded them of home. Plovdiv's Roman remains include the spectacular ruins of a great outdoor amphitheatre which is still used for concerts and was made available for the final concert of the ten-day project organised there by 'Rainbow across Europe' in September 1999.

How should 'Rainbow across Europe' now develop? A matrix analysis is effective in revealing the potential. In principle, 'Rainbow across Europe' is geographically 'open', but this becomes 'weak' unless it is 'strengthened' by collaboration with locally based partnerships which can organise component parts of the project with a 'strong' geographical focus. The long term aim of 'Rainbow across Europe', as exemplified by the following matrix analysis, is to achieve 'openness' on the 'places' and 'people' axes at a pan-European level.

Example 47: Matrix analysis of 'Rainbow across Europe'.

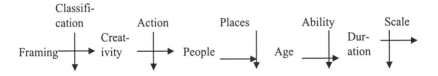

This was achieved to a limited extent when artists of different nationalities met together on tour. But such a degree of openness was not possible for the children and young people who participated in the workshop programme. Because of financial limitations, we could not arrange for children to travel to different countries, and so for them, a project which began with a 'strong' geographical focus, became 'closed' in comparison with the experience enjoyed by the professional musicians.

We achieved greater 'openness' with later phases of 'Rainbow across Europe' when the student orchestra from Aix en Provence visited Bath in 1997, and when students from Bath and Salzburg took part in mutual exchange visits to each other's institutions. Likewise regular annual exchanges between student composers and instrumentalists of Bath Spa University College and Hogeschool Alkmaar Conservatorium since 1997 achieved a degree of 'openness' for successive generations of students.

The Rainbow Foundation recently initiated a project designed deliberately to test the potential of creative music projects in a non-European context. This was *Mengjiang Weeping at the Wall* created in collaboration with Chinese musicians. It will be discussed in more detail in Part 3 (p. 255).

5. Junior school children before the final performance of the 'Rainbow over Bath' *Parents and Children* project 1997. Photo Nick Delves-Broughton.

Chapter 7
Age and Ability

Music can play different roles in different stages of people's lives. The creative workshop leader needs to be aware of this and to apply appropriate methodologies in each case.

'Ability' presents a complex picture, already touched on in discussion of the 'skill-gap'. The qualitative 'age/ability' matrix was a simplified analysis confined to the consideration of a single activity such as piano playing. We have to ask: 'ability in what?', thinking about how 'ability' intersects with 'classification' (What style of music are they good at?), or with 'creativity' (Are they good at writing or playing music?). We have to make predictions about latent ability in the 'could-do-better' zone between manifest skill and potential ability.

Formal graded music examinations define musical standards in the classical tradition independently of age, but they are poor indicators of wider skills of musicianship, originality in composition, or skill in traditional or popular styles. A comprehensive ability axis must extend from people with learning difficulties, through different degrees of 'normal' intelligence, to gifted people. There will always be exceptions, for example so-called autistic savants whose minds are closed to normal communication with other human beings but who possess extra-ordinary gifts as musical performers or visual artists.

The National Curriculum with its four key-stages is a product of mass education. It sets a minimum level of attainment for each age-group, progressing in incremental steps. The danger of a generalised minimum requirement is that it may come to represent an average, offering little room for deviation, whereas a matrix analysis draws attention to the extremes of ability.

The nature of the skill-gap

Any philosophy which seeks to democratise the act of musical creation, or re-creation must come to terms with this 'skill-gap'. Paynter, Cardew and Rzewski all sought their own solutions to the problem. In adult life, the skill-gap shows up in the difference between amateur and professional. In 1921 Holst said: 'We all begin our education by being amateurs, and in a real sense of the word we must remain amateurs' (Holst; cited in Short, 1990: 70). He is said to have strongly disapproved of the way some musicians talked-down to amateur performers, and insisted that everyone who wished to do so should take part in music-making, regardless of their own level of ability.

In 'Past and Future' Orff states: 'My experience has taught me that completely unmusical children are very rare and that nearly every child is at some point accessible and educable'. In creating his Schulwerk he seeks to make musical education available across the whole ability range: 'I do not think of an education only for specially gifted children but of one on the broadest foundation in which moderately and less gifted children could also take part' (Orff, 1978).

But there is an essential difference in the notion of 'music for all' between the approaches of Cardew and Rzewski on the one hand, and Orff and Kodály on the other. The former were looking for ways in which a creative musical experience could be made directly available to all people, without the need to acquire even a basic level of musical literacy. Orff and Kodály saw the acquisition of those basic musical skills of reading, writing and performance as a primary aim of their teaching programmes.

It is clear from two assertions made in the 1982 *Report on Artists in Schools*: that the Gulbenkian is on the side of Orff and Kodály:

a. Creativity is not a special faculty with which some children are endowed and others are not, but that it is a form of intelligence and as such can be developed and trained like any other mode of thinking.
b. Creativity is something which requires discipline, previous experience and a firm grounding in knowledge (Gulbenkian, 1982: 29).

The musically gifted

In tackling the question of musically gifted children, the CGF favoured an unashamedly two-tier approach, with a combination of specialist training for the gifted and a more general approach for the less musically gifted:

> We do not accept the charge of élitism in this context, because we are not postulating the gifted versus the non-gifted. All children may have gifts of some kind. These need to be discovered and developed to the best of their and our ability' (Gulbenkian, 1982: 100).

The development of particular gifts and talents required 'time and effort, specialised tuition under well qualified teachers, a sympathetic school environment, and the facilities to develop the gifts in question' (Gulbenkian, 1982: 100 ¶162). Some schools denied that such special provision was required, or were simply prevented from making it available by lack of funds. Pupils were obliged to seek private tuition outside the school, an option denied to those from economically deprived backgrounds. Even those parents who could afford it might find their children coming into conflict with the school over time for homework, or time off for special exams. Such conflicts are symptomatic of a general non-acceptance of the importance of the arts in society.

The report summarised some of the pros and cons of special provision: it offered opportunities for the gifted to succeed, removing frustration, and ensuring that potential was not wasted. On the other hand, it could impoverish the rest of the school by diminishing the value and achievements of the less gifted, and depriving them of access to the best teachers who were concentrating their time and energy on a small minority. It could be socially divisive, encouraging élitist attitudes. Children who received special coaching might be socially ostracised. However many of these problems could be diminished if there was adequate provision of good teachers at all levels (Gulbenkian, 1982: 99).

While the CGF came down on the side of creating an élite tier of specialist music schools, Paynter advocated mixed-ability teaching.

But how mixed? In Paynter's model, mixed-ability teaching only takes place within the year-group to which the children belong. Contrast this with the situation in most out-of-school music centres and school orchestras where children are grouped according to ability (junior, intermediate and advanced) resulting in mixed-age-group teaching.

Music and disability

To label the opposite extreme of the 'ability' axis with the word 'disability', brings us perilously close to a mine-field of political correctness. Successive waves of euphemisms such as 'challenged', 'different' and 'learning difficulties' have been introduced to describe degrees of physical and mental disability. A home for adults with learning difficulties is a community defined by a shared level of mental or physical disability. It is the extreme nature of the disability which unites them as a community, and sets them apart from people of 'normal' ability.

To narrow the gap between 'manifest achieved skill' and 'maximum potential ability' in the qualitative age/ability matrix is a challenge for all of us. For people of disability, physical and mental impairment sets a low limit on 'maximum potential ability', but today, we are constantly hearing of individuals who have successfully challenged what were previously thought of as the limits of achievement, forcing us to revise upwards our notion of where this 'maximum potential ability' lies. New approaches to teaching and learning, supported by new technologies, have increased enormously the opportunities to transcend physical and mental obstacles to learning.

Such detail is outside the scope of my book but it is important to acknowledge two points. Firstly the principle of maximum openness in the 'ability' axis implies that we should make serious efforts to be inclusive of people who are disadvantaged either by physical or mental incapacity. Secondly, just as different age-groups require different approaches to workshop methodology, so too do different forms of

220

mental and physical incapacity. Specialist knowledge and skill in techniques of music-therapy may be required beyond the scope of the more generalised skills of the music animateur.

This is not to say that some composer/animateurs do not possess such skills. Barry Russell worked with a wide range of young people with disabilities including Downes syndrome, cerebral palsy, and spina bifida during his composer-in-the-community programme in Bristol in 1988. During the Music Now conference at 'New Music '98 Manchester', Paul Wright and Duncan Chapman from Sonic Arts Network demonstrated how severely disabled children could take part in an electro-acoustic music improvisation using sensing devices which responded to minute residual movements of their paralysed and contorted bodies.

The use of electronic technology to enable the disabled to create music is the starting point of the London-based Drake Project, founded and directed by Adèle Drake. The Spring 1998 edition of the organisation's quarterly newsletter describes how the project helped composer Stephen Wade, a stroke victim in 1993, to write a work for string quartet using the CuBase system. The piece was then performed as part of a workshop with members of the City of London Sinfonia at the Barbican Hall.

The Drake Project is 'open' as to age and style, but there is an emphasis on contemporary idioms susceptible to the use of electronic technology such as rock, R&B, and contemporary folk music. The specialist nature of its work is recognised by a one-year tutor training programme leading to a BTEC Advanced Award. No-one is immune from the possibility of the unexpected onset of mental or physical disability, and the recognition that advanced musicians can also become disabled was reflected in the formation of an Advanced Musicians Group in 1998. Drake seeks a wide geographical spread with the formation of regional cells in Coventry, Manchester, Milton Keynes, Edinburgh, and Ireland.

Bridging the skill-gap

Socialist-inspired principles of openness demand access to musical experience as a fundamental right of all people, regardless of age and ability. My theoretical model advocates 'openness' in the age and ability axes as an ideal characteristic in creative music projects. To realise this ideal represents a great challenge to the workshop leader. The greater the 'openness', the greater the challenge. The problem is to devise a project which contains enough of a technical, creative and artistic challenge to advanced musicians, but at the same time is not beyond the capabilities and understanding of younger or less advanced participants. Get this wrong and the advanced players will be bored and dissatisfied, and the beginners baffled, discouraged and frustrated.

Such problems beset adult and community projects and evening institute classes, and represent a fundamental difficulty for organisations such as COMA. Cardew and Rzewski encountered the same problems in the late 1960s. Rzewski's solution in *Sound Pool* was to define a new role for the strong musician working alongside the musical innocent:

> [*Sound Pool*] [...] gives the specialist musician a new role [...] it contains the instruction: 'if you are a strong musician mostly do accompanying work, that is, help weaker players to sound better. Seek out areas where the music is flagging, and organise groups' (Nyman, 1999: 131).

Recent years have seen the rise in popularity of 'all-comers-orchestras' choosing their repertoire from the classical/romantic past, or commissioning new compositions. Here there is a requirement that everyone possesses at least some minimal level of instrumental skill and can read music. Players with little skill can be successfully integrated into large ensemble performances by practical approaches. Sectional rehearsals are preceded by 'plotting sessions' when difficult passages are broken down by agreement into shorter manageable fragments. The rule is: 'If you can't play all the notes, then play every other note, or every fourth note but, whatever you do, play only correct notes.'

All-comers orchestras are often associated with COMA, or with Sound Sense, the Suffolk-based organisation for community music and social inclusion. The title of their conference *Music for a changing world* in June 2000 is a pre-echo of the title of my thesis. If the role of music in the modern world is changing, as the conference agenda implies, then composers must change with it.

In Chapter 1, I discussed how Britten, David Bedford and George Odam were able to integrate material of different degrees of technical difficulty to achieve 'openness' in age and ability. The degree of 'openness' which can be achieved depends on a project's duration and scale. A given situation will present its own limits and set its own challenges: a class of thirty mixed-ability year-six juniors; a dozen evening institute students of widely separated age and musical ability; a group of learning-difficulties adults. In all such situations, a degree of 'openness' is built in. In projects organised by 'Rainbow over Bath' we preferred in principle to work with such intrinsically 'mixed-ability' groups rather than a group of music specialists hand-picked from various classes within a school.

In larger scale projects we were able to plan more strategically, for instance working with an entire year group within one school ('closed' in age; 'openness' in ability), or selecting one complete class-group from each year ('openness' in age and ability). *Bladud* (Laycock, 1985), involved all ninety children in Bathampton Primary School, an example of maximum 'openness' within a self-limiting context. Greater 'openness' could be achieved when more than one school took part in a larger scale project. A favourite format involved several year-groups from a secondary school working alongside classes from feeder primaries in the same geographical area.

Although we felt entitled to regard our projects as 'exemplary', 'Rainbow over Bath', as a small organisation without substantial and consistent financial backing from local district councils, could never hope to see the propagation of its structural model as standard practice throughout the entire Bristol and Bath area. In spite of our best efforts a policy which can claim only to be 'exemplary' emerges as 'weak' rather than 'open'.

The 'exemplary' nature of Rainbow projects can be seen in Barry Russell's *Opening Doors* devised for the re-opening of the Michael

Tippett Centre in June 1999. This strove to achieve 'openness' in age and ability by involving adults with learning difficulties working alongside junior, secondary, 'A' level and BA music students. Russell's skill at working with people with learning difficulties showed up in the way their contribution was incorporated into the larger project. Given the extrovert personality of the Downes syndrome youngsters, their mock opening ceremony outside the main doors of the Tippett Centre was conspicuous and entertaining.

In the autumn of the same year, by exploiting a range of specialisms across a team of workshop leaders associated with Ensemble Esoterica including Tunde Jegede, Paul Gladstone Reid and Eugene Skeef, we were able to involve an even wider range of participants. With his charismatic personality and highly skilled approach to severe learning difficulties, Skeef's sessions at Lime Grove School, creating a musical procession of percussion players, some of them in wheelchairs, were greatly valued by the staff and by those participants who were capable of expressing their enjoyment. However, this aspect of the project's 'holism' could not be demonstrated publicly during the final concert of the education project. I was forced to acknowledge that some very extreme forms of disability can present very real practical obstacles to full involvement in a holistic scheme.

Conditions of openness

Picking up brownie points for widening the age and ability range is all very well, but quantity is no substitute for quality of experience. The issue highlights the difference between 'weak' and 'open'. Project reports full of pictures of small children grinning behind metallophones, Downes Syndrome teenagers enthusiastically beating African drums, and elderly ladies pinging self-consciously on triangles may look impressive to the regional arts board which is being asked to cough up some cash, but we must ensure that this is more than just window dressing. To show genuine openness in age and ability a pro-ject must level up to an exacting set of conditions. It must:

1. Contain material at appropriate levels of difficulty for the different abilities of the participants.
2. Present an appropriate level of challenge to each participant so that he or she can achieve a degree of progression in musical understanding, technical ability, creativity, personal self-confidence and interpersonal relationships.
3. Engage all participants in some aspect of the creative process in a way which is meaningful to them, and makes a significant and conspicuous contribution to the project as a whole, allowing them to take personal pride and satis-faction from it.
4. Ensure that all participants are aware of the nature and significance of other participants' contributions to the project.
5. Provide opportunities for more advanced musicians to support, encourage and help the creative work of less skilled participants.
6. Focus on an appropriate non-musical theme or idea which can engage all participants at an intellectual and emotional level.
7. Leave a memorable and lasting impression with all those who took part.
8. Make a significant contribution to the on-going programme of music-education, or community work of each of the participating schools or organisations.
9. Employ workshop leaders with skills and experience appropriate to the range of ages and abilities of the participants.

The London Symphony Orchestra 'Discovery' programme

I now want to evaluate the approach of a number of different projects to 'age' and 'ability', beginning with the LSO's 'Discovery' pro-gramme.

When sixty or so young people trooped onto the narrow apron stage at the Barbican Hall in June 2001 to perform their own material for the 'score windows' of Rachel Leach's *Hector and Harriet*, I was not convinced that they were fully engaged by the project. There was barely room to sit down with their Orff percussion instruments in front of the assembled might of the LSO. The contrast between the professional polish of the orchestral and chamber sounds in the composed sections of the work only emphasised the gulf between them.

I do not say that the concept of score windows is unsatisfactory, only that their function must be considered carefully and sensitively. Score windows should flow naturally and seamlessly as part of the discourse of the work, or take on a convincing dramatic function within the design. The score windows in *Hector and Harriet* seemed artificially imposed.

The project touches all the right buttons of educational methodology. It was commissioned as part of the LSO Discovery Programme in October 2000 in relation to LSO performances of Berlioz' *Romeo and Juliet*. It is educational in the broadest sense as defined by Paynter and Odam in that it provides many opportunities for cross-curricular links. It is carefully targeted at particular key-stages. It involves children at key-stage 2 in creative composition work, and at key-stage 3 & 4 up to A-level as members of a school orchestra. Professional players from the LSO are involved as workshop assistants.

Of the work's seven movements, all odd-numbered ones are score-windows while even-numbered ones are played either by full orchestra or by the LSO professionals as a chamber group. The score windows invite the children to respond to episodes in the story of the love affair between Hector Berlioz and Harriet Smithson. Children are introduced to various compositional devices such as the transformation of a motto theme, as exemplified in Berlioz' own technique. They use ciphers to create themes based on the names 'Harriet' or 'Hector' or 'Romeo and Juliet'. In the sixth movement, they are invited to distort the 'Harriet' theme to represent her insanity (Example 48).

On paper at least the project is difficult to fault and appears to conform to all of my conditions of openness. Comments from participating schools are full of praise: 'It's hard to imagine ways the project could have been improved' said the Head of Music at Gloucester Primary School. Thomas Fairchild School children were 'inspired and motivated' by the energy and dedication of the LSO musicians, while the Head of Music at Camden Girls School, for whom the orchestral score was written, described it as 'an enhancing experience' and 'something exceptional'.

226

Example 48: Leach, R. (2001) *Hector and Harriet* Creative window section.

The Fall of Harriet - project (in brief)

Using Harriet's theme (see over) and the French horn accompaniment your task is to create music to describe the end of her life. Harriet was penniless when she finally married Hector and she began to lose her mind. Hector had to put her away in a mental hospital where slowly and tragically she died.

1.   Learn to play Harriet's theme. Listen to the French horn accompaniment. Can you describe the mood of it and of Harriet? Can you play Harriet's theme along with the French horn.

2.   Split into small groups. Can you create an accompaniment for the theme to describe Harriet before things start going wrong. She is a young, happily married, beautiful woman. Will your music be fast or slow, loud or soft?

3.   When you are happy with your group's version of the theme try to distort it. What do you think Harriet was like in the hospital? Do you think she realised that Hector had put her away? Was she angry or just very sad? Can you alter your music to describe Harriet's changing feelings.

4.   Towards the very end of her life Harriet didn't recognise anyone or even know who she was. Can you distort your music so much that it sounds completely different to the beautiful Harriet you created at the start.

5.   Now work on making one piece out of all your separate pieces. Think about the shape of the piece, its structure and how it relates to Harriet's story. Where does the French horn fit in? Can you still tell it is Harriet at the end? Think really carefully about the last few moments of your music when you describe Harriet's death.

6.   Finally, practise your piece really well so that it is the same every time and exactly how you want it to be.

Part VI - The fall of Harriet
composition project

RACHEL LEACH

However, the performance I attended was a disappointment. The work lacked overall cohesion. The Camden School Orchestra which took part in the première in October 2000 was replaced by the full LSO whose members appeared to lack emotional involvement and enthusiasm. The work failed to achieve any strong cathartic feeling in the closing bars of 'Hector Alone', and I doubted if, on this occasion, the experience was likely to leave a lasting impression (7th condition of openness).

I hesitate to level too much criticism against the LSO Discovery programme. It is a model of best practice based on the strong and visionary leadership of Richard McNicol who brings to it a lifetime of practical experience in many educational contexts through the Apollo Trust. The programme is accurately targeted at the different key-stages (conditions 1 & 2), and adds considerable value to the on-going class-teaching programmes of many schools in the London area (condition 8). *Hector and Harriet* exemplifies McNicol's admirable policy of giving young composers and musicians such as Rachel Leach and, more recently, Hannah Conway, an opportunity to develop their 'performance and communication skills' through the Edward Heath Assistant Animateur Scheme – an excellent example of practical steps being taken to educate a new generation of composers (condition 5).

The performance of Leach's work was part of an event which followed in the tradition of the children's music-appreciation concert. The atmosphere was patronising, typified by the uncomfortable and restless silences which greeted McNicol's carefully placed but ineffectual jokes. Mercifully the music itself won the day. The roar of applause which followed the final chord of Berlioz' *Witches' Sabbath* had that quality of exuberance which only five hundred school children can achieve. They clapped, cheered, stamped and – horror of horrors – whistled! My sense of horror was not provoked by the whistlers themselves, but by McNicol's attitude towards them. Apparently whistling was 'against the rules in a classical concert hall', and he told them so. I wondered who had made up these rules. Was there a bye-law I didn't know about? Perhaps McNicol had read Chris Small but missed the irony:

The listener himself is not involved in any way in the creative process; his task is merely to contemplate the finished product of the artist's efforts, to respond to it inwardly, without any outward show or physical reaction (even to tap one's foot in time to the music is to invite condemnation as an ignoramus or a boor) (Small, 1977: 29).

Measuring *Hector and Harriet* against the exacting standards of the nine conditions of openness and the Theoretical Model shows where some of its deficiencies lie. Leach's work is an example of Bedford Category 3: 'written score with creative windows'. However, the fact that these windows constitute single movements puts them into BC5: 'fully creative project'. The odd-numbered movements are BC1: 'fully written score'. Only the key-stage 2 children take part in the score windows, and, but for one short section at the end of the seventh movement, only the school orchestra children take part in the fully-scored sections.

The result is a hybrid project. Not all children in the project have an equivalent experience (condition 3). The orchestral players' experience is 'esthesic', while the junior's experience is 'poietic'. In that sense, *Hector and Harriet* is not a fully holistic concept. Its holistic potential can only be realised when it is integrated into a larger strategically planned programme which gives the school-orchestra players other creative opportunities, or the juniors other re-creative opportunities. This could be through another part of the Discovery programme, or as part of a larger programme organised within each school of which Discovery forms only a part.

What Leach gets right in *Hector and Harriet* is the provision of musical material of an appropriate level of difficulty (condition 1), and the focus on a non-musical narrative theme which can engage all participants (condition 6). The question of the appropriateness of musical style and idiom is where 'age' and 'ability' intersect with 'classification'. In principle *Hector and Harriet* need not be specifically style-centred since its primary aim is to build an educational experience around the music of Berlioz. McNicol is inviting school students to respond creatively, in their own musical language, to some of the concepts in Berlioz' music (e.g. thematic transformation, telling stories in music etc.), and not simply to try and imitate the music of Berlioz.

He is offering the work of a young protegé, Rachel Leach, by way of example – to quote Paynter again: '[…] "here is another composer making music like yours". It is confirmation and enrichment' (Paynter & Aston 1970: 12).

Example 49: Matrix analysis of *Hector and Harriett* project.

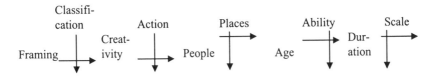

Chamber Music 2000

The dual question of appropriate difficulty and appropriateness of style continue to pre-occupy composers who write for educational and amateur performance. I discussed musical style in Chapter 5. Degree of difficulty is the other side of the same coin. This has been the motivation behind several recent projects including Chamber Music 2000, initiated by William Howard and the Schubert Ensemble, and two collections commissioned by Thalia Myers, Chamber Music Exchange, and the Associated Board *Spectrum* collection of solo piano pieces. Such pre-occupations also lie behind the repertoire of COMA, and the C4K programme run by the SPNM. All these programmes produce repertoire typical of BC1. The music must be in a style typical of the composer's normal output, but lie within the technical capabilities of a given group of performers – defined according to the AB examination boards, or a set of objective criteria for COMA.

The aims of Chamber Music 2000 are stated in its February 2001 press release:

> [...] to commission a large number of works for piano and strings from leading composers, suitable for playing by young and amateur musicians [...] to encourage chamber music playing, especially among students, and also to give young musicians and amateur players the opportunity to experience at first hand the works of living composers.

The all-important principle is expressed as follows:

> Composers are invited to write short pieces for piano and strings, pitched at the easiest technical level for which they feel able to write, while still preserving the integrity and individuality of their own musical language (Chamber Music 2000 press release).

The small selection of pieces I heard at the official launch at Steinway Hall in February 2001, and the seven pieces I heard at the Wigmore Hall in March, showed a widely eclectic range of musical styles. None could be described as easy to play. Music for junior strings often uses open strings to give complete beginners an early experience of ensemble playing, but Piers Hellawell's open strings at the start of *White Room* required a degree of sensitivity to bowing and articulation far beyond the beginner (conditions of openness 1 & 2).

For this public show-case, young instrumentalists from Mill Hill School, Bromley Youth Music Trust, and from Trinity College Junior Department had been hand-picked for their high level of instrumental skill. I was not convinced, either, whether all the composers had really 'preserved the integrity and individuality of their musical language'. Avant-garde idioms or new-complexity were not on the menu. Resonant tonal harmonies and singing melodies were, as well as descriptive titles like Martin Butler's *Spring Rounds*, or Peter Sculthorpe's *From the River*. Only Alwynne Pritchard's *Barbara Allen: Fragments of a Lament* challenged the players on a conceptual level by presenting a series of musical fragments to be freely assembled within a time frame so that they were obliged to make some creative compositional input (BC2 and conditions 2 & 3). The event showed some of the characteristics of a holistic project in that the early evening showcase preceded an evening concert by the Schubert

Ensemble which set Martin Butler's *American Rounds* alongside Schumann and Elgar.

In spite of claims in the marketing copy, projects like Chamber Music 2000 are nothing new, but their contribution is much to be valued. They require composers to modify their attitude to what they write, and think more carefully about its purpose. Instead of writing for specific instrumentalists with uniquely developed skills (Stockhausen for the Kontarsky brothers, Gorecki for Elizabeth Cojnacka, Cage for David Tudor and so on) they are asked to aim their music at a range of specific ability groups. Thus they are taking practical steps to remove some of the exclusive and 'closed' mystique which surrounds contemporary music and to encourage ordinary amateur instrumentalists to become more interested in it, giving new life to the European classical tradition. In terms of the 'ability' axis, this repertoire is not more 'open' but 'stronger' in the sense that it is precisely targeted. In as much as its aims and objectives are to remind composers what their relationship to those who play their music ought to be, rather than to define a new role, Chamber Music 2000 is only peripheral to my discussion.

Example 50: Matric analysis of Chamber Music 2000.

Society for the Promotion of New Music
'Composing for Kids'

The C4K project of the SPNM comes closer to redefining the composer's role. Here, as in Chamber Music 2000, composers are invited to write music for young people to perform. But in this case 'kids' means 'school children'. The project is aimed at ordinary school classes rather than at music specialists. There is also a difference in the status of the composers. They are young professionals at the beginning of their careers, and the project is intended to be educative for them as well. Each composer is guided by a more established mentor.

The C4K concert I attended at the Purcell Room in July 2001 contained one salutary lesson on how not to write appropriate material for a particular ability group. The children from Selwyn Primary School could not sing in tune. Their singing of Maud Hodson's *Songs for Selwyn* was so un-tuneful that I wondered if the children had any concept of what 'in-tune' meant. They delivered the words in a sort of rhythmic sprechstimme. Possibly the piece was badly conceived for this school. They needed something with fewer notes, set at a level which would allow them to accept the challenge of achieving a degree of progression in technical ability (condition 2). The poems were written by the children, and Hodson set them to music (BC1 with a BC4 approach to words).

David Charles Martin's C4K contribution was *Bug, Better, Beast*, an attractive and entertaining treatment of green issues and the survival of species such as the cockroaches, the sharks, the dinosaurs, tigers and man. These pieces were technically well written in a chromatic idiom, but sing-able and very practical in conception. The composer used two-part rounds to get the already very confident children of Camden Junior School singing in parts in antiphonal groups. All vocal phrases were pre-echoed in the piano accompaniment to help them find their notes. In conversation the composer defined this as BC1, but an element of BC4 was involved in that the subject of the poems was based on preliminary discussions with the children.

Example 51: Matrix analysis of SPNM 'Composing for Kids'.

'Rainbow over Bath' 'Parents and Children' project

Literary, poetic, historical or pictorial subjects which provide some kind of narrative framework are often the key to making a project coherent for different ranges of age and ability (condition 6). The *Hector and Harriet* theme was well-chosen because it provided a narrative framework and suggested ideas and technical devices at a specifically musical level such as transformation of motto themes.

An example from the 1997 Rainbow project with Deirdre Gribbin and Rob Smith illustrates how important it is to treat a poetic theme in a manner which is appropriate to the age-range of the participants. A hundred and sixty children took part, drawn from primary and secondary schools in the Bath and Bristol area, supported by BA Music students from the University College. The project was constructed on holistic lines including professional concerts organised in collaboration with European partners in the 'Rainbow across Europe' network. Parallel projects were mounted in The Netherlands and France, using the same literary and poetic theme. Deirdre Gribbin was featured composer, and the final education concert included the British premiere of her new work for soprano and clarinet entitled *In the Wake of the Child*, especially commissioned by 'Rainbow over Bath'.

Over a two-month period, children took part in a song-writing project led by Deirdre Gribbin and Mary Wiegold, based on the theme of 'Parents and Children' using techniques similar to *Say it till a song comes* (Davies, 1986). Gribbin's new work was written in response to the same theme of 'parents and children' as the education project. I believed that children should not just encounter Gribbin as a workshop leader, but also experience some of her own work as a composer. We took a realistic attitude. Rather than programming the première as part of a separate professional evening event, with the almost inevitable outcome that most of the children would never hear it, we decided it should be performed during the education concert along with music by Rob Smith and other composers played by the Roger Heaton Ensemble.

Gribbin's work, though fine in its own terms, failed to connect with the audience, and in particular with the participating children. It was met with a mixture of incomprehension and indifference – an unwelcome and irrelevant intrusion into the sequence of children's creative work (condition 7). Gribbin's own response to the subject was so intensely personal that, had the children and the audience really understood the narrative justification behind the histrionic nature of her music, this might have engendered a level of emotional distress quite out of keeping with the celebratory nature of the project as a whole. Here was an example of the application of Paynter's stage D – encounter with the musical model – which did not work.

My point is made by the third of three poems set by Gribbin, Seamus Heaney's *Limbo*. It tells a harrowing tale of a baby drowned in the sea by its desperate mother, later to be pulled out by fishermen (Heaney, 1990: 37).

Fishermen at Ballyshannon
Netted an infant last night
Along with the salmon.
An illegitimate spawning,

A small one thrown back
To the waters. But I'm sure
As she stood in the shallows
Ducking him tenderly

Till the small knobs of her wrists
Were dead as the gravel,
He was a minnow with hooks
Tearing her open.

She waded in under
The sign of her cross.
He was hauled in with the fish.
Now Limbo will be

All cold glitter of souls
Through some far briny zone.
Even Christ's palms, unhealed,
Smart and cannot fish there.

We should not underestimate the capacity of children to appreciate a tragic story of this nature, but the content of the poems should have been introduced to the children at a much earlier stage so that they had an opportunity to come to terms with it. The theme which the children were actually asked to respond to was much more generalised than the very specific set of circumstances expressed in Heaney's poem with its background in Irish Catholicism (condition 6).

The meaning of the words was to some extent obscured in performance by Gribbin's fractured musical style. The texts were not provided with the programme notes. All three poems contained many contemporary resonances in relation to one-parent families and issues of child abuse. But the project failed to pick up on the potential to engage the older children on such an important emotional level. Measured against the 6th condition of openness, the project had fundamental failings. There was no discussion with the children's class teachers at which agreement might have been reached in advance as to whether such sensitive subject matter was appropriate to all ages of children in the project, and how it should be dealt with.

The 'Parents and Children' project was also presented in Aix en Provence and the Dutch town of Zwolle as part of *Rainbow across Europe* during Autumn 1997. Any possible unsuitability of the subject matter of Heaney's *Limbo* was masked by differences of language. Problems of a different kind arose at the Ecole Sellier in Aix because of expectations aroused in the teachers following their experience in 1996 of Sean Gregory's high-energy approach, based on repetitive rhythms and African drumming patterns. The teachers were unprepared for the more detailed, individual approach to composition of Deirdre Gribbin and Rob Smith. Here, failures of communication at the introductory briefing stage – Paynter's phase A, and Asher's 'specification' (p.162) – led to misunderstandings aggravated by language differences.

The Dutch however, had little previous experience of creative music projects. The whole process took place intensively in only two days. Teachers and pupils from three schools across age ranges of 10–11, 13–14 and 15–18 years approached the project with well-focused commitment and enthusiasm.

Two recorded examples illustrate the well-focused commitment of the young people from Greydanus College. The first is a lilting composition for recorders, folk harp and piano (rainbow: Track 10), the second a rollicking and joyful pastiche samba (rainbow: Track 11). An audience of parents and friends listened to In the Wake of the Child with considerably more attention and appreciation than the Bath audience.

Example 52: Matrix analysis of 'Parents and Children' project.

'Rainbow over Bath' 'Igor's Boogie'

In view of the difficulties of reconciling the needs of different age and ability groups, Peter Wiegold's approach in such projects as *Igor's Boogie* is to keep activities separate. It is his aim to encourage participants to progress in their creative work on an individual basis rather than to go for an impressive large-scale final performance like Russell or Gregory. As a result, attention to detail is more important than the achievement of a climax or catharsis. The timetable of *Igor's Boogie* contained two completely separate but parallel workshop programmes with separate outcomes. The junior project was based on group work, while GCSE students were asked to compose individual pieces for the Composers Ensemble. Both sets of workshops followed the same theme of treatment of a favourite piece of popular music, but no attempt was made to bring together the results of these parallel processes (see Example 35, p.178 for a matrix analysis of 'Igor's Boogie').

St. George's, Bristol 'Perform'

An even more 'strongly' defined project in terms of age and ability was St. George's Music Trust *Perform*. Here, too, primary and secondary were kept completely separate. The primary school element was contracted out to Jane Pountney's Children's Music Workshop, which works almost exclusively at key-stage 2, but occasionally involving younger children. The CMW workshops at St. George's allowed me to observe the outstanding work of Andy Baker, double bass player and education officer for the Bournemouth Symphony Orchestra, supported by Chris Glynn of Artwork in Cardiff. The focus for this project was a concert at St. George's by the Boyan vocal ensemble from Kiev, although it is unclear whether the project led to any real encounter between the children and the visiting Ukrainians or their music. It thus failed one of the tests of holism.

However the project was precisely and skilfully targeted at the chosen age-group (condition 1). The fifty year-four children each painted a 'Russian icon' – a self portrait incorporating an image of something they were good at, such as playing football. There were two different musical elements: improvisations based on ostinato patterns generated from verbal phrases, and songs invented in Russian style. The principle of the 'community of learners' prevailed here. There was no chance that I would be allowed just to watch. I got dragged in as a group leader and later recognised my group's contribution to one of the pieces in the final concert (rainbow: Track 12). Other riffs built out of such everyday words and phrases accumulated towards a final tutti in which four groups competed enthusiastically to make the biggest sound (rainbow: Track 13).

The children made up a simple tune in a very Russian-sounding phrygian mode and created fake-Russian words to go with it:

Szitoya moojaya szitoya moojaya
Stookoshaya shewmaea stookoshaya shewmaea
Bonakata zum bonakata zum
Zigalu ordinoshta zigalu ordinoshta

The melody was sung in call-and-response patterns, or in close canon at two beats (rainbow: Track 14).

Example 53: Matrix analysis Children's Music Workshop, St. George's, Bristol.

Children's Music Workshop works as an 'arts-in-education' agency with several large opera companies and national orchestras such as the English National Opera Bayliss Programme, Glynebourne, the LSO, the Orchestra of the Age of Enlightenment, and the City of London Sinfonia. The aim of CMW projects is to encourage children to compose music, but they are led by a variety of artists, not all of them composers. Pountney prefers to collaborate with opera companies because of the opportunities for multi-disciplinary work. Among CMW's most prominent recent projects have been the Verdi Requiem project forming part of ENOs contribution to the *Reseo* programme (p. 117), and Rachel Leach's *Rigoletto* workshops. Issues of freedom and redemption in Glynebourne's production of Beethoven's *Fidelio* were the focus of a project in isolated rural primaries in Crowborough which took place just after the destruction of the New York World Trade Centre on 11 September 2001, and gave children the opportunity to externalise their own feelings about the tragedy.

The primary and secondary school elements of 'Perform' were kept separate. During the three years of the secondary project, led by cellist Matthew Barley, a group of only twenty or so young people from three Bristol schools took part. Participants were not selected for high musical ability, but because they were the first to volunteer. The project leaders justified such exclusivity because this was seen as a pilot project, testing a model which could be applied more generally when more cash was available. The selected students encountered a variety of models such as the Orchestra of the Age of Enlightenment, Jazz pianist Julian Joseph, Joanna MacGregor, and Ensemble Bash. Thus at each of the individual stages, classification was entirely 'style-based' and therefore 'strong', whereas, by offering a carefully chosen and representative range, the project was relatively 'open' as a whole.

'Perform' was precisely targeted at this small group of students over an extended period, allowing them to make very considerable progress as creative musical personalities during a formative phase of their lives. Quality and depth of educational experience were set well above social inclusiveness. My conversations with young people who took part in the final concert in January 2002 indicated that they had derived enormous personal benefit. Recorded extracts made at the final concert with Matthew Barley's own ensemble *Between the Notes* reveal a serious-minded pre-occupation with personal self-discovery and fulfilment, typical amongst participants in this age-group, expressed through original poetry and song lyrics (rainbow: Track 15).

Classification at this final phase was not 'strong'. The young people, supported by Barley and the other members of *Between the Notes,* were given the opportunity to 'speak' through their own personal style. The rock-inspired musical vernacular of the final song, with its climax building over a repeated chord sequence, was a characteristic outcome of a project with an 'open' approach to classification in this particular age-group (rainbow: Track 16). Thus, as a whole, the project offered more than one approach to 'classification', deliberately progressing from 'strong' to 'open', a reversal of the process followed by Richard McNicol's Janacek project with students from Royal Holloway College discussed in Chapter 4 (p. 157).

In terms of the scale and duration matrix, 'Perform' was of long duration and small scale. It was supported by a three-year National Lottery grant from the Arts Council. The lack of financial resources and appropriate teaching skills within the school sector means that such experiences are a rarity. No one can doubt the value of this project to those lucky enough to take part, but we are forced to question whether expenditure of public funds to benefit such a small group of young people can be justified, while thousands of others in the Bristol area go without.

'Perform' succeeded in finding a balance between detailed individual creative work and focus on large-scale group performance. For instance the final concert to the secondary-school programme achieved an effective climax, was coherently planned, and gave full prominence to individual creative work. But the organisers did not bring the junior and secondary school aspects together, thus missing any opportunity for a more 'open' encounter within the wider 'Community of Learners'.

Example 54: Matrix analysis of 'Perform' secondary school project.

Common Ground 'Confluence' project

Common Ground's 'Confluence' project achieved an almost ideal balance by running parallel programmes of workshops with separate outcomes leading to small concerts of individual compositions, as well as a final concert presenting group creative work. This visionary project succeeded in bringing together several hundreds of people of many ages and abilities living in the Stour valley. A substantial part of the three-year programme consisted of regular workshops with many different community and school groups. Several were formed in response to the project including the Cutwater Band, the Confluence Choir and Ensemble, the 'Scattered Shower Sisters' *a capella* group, and the hilarious 'Pipeworks' Band, a variant of the junk-band using instruments made and played by plumbers using all manner of copper tubing, joints, accessories and so on. There were frequent public performances by these and other groups to provide a focus for creative work. With a team of workshop leaders including music animateur Helen Porter, composer in residence Karen Wimhurst (literally in residence because she lived in a river-side cottage for the duration), and folk singer Tim Laycock (no relation), the project's stylistic range was eclectic including folk ballades as well as avant-garde idioms.

The final concert in June 2001 brought these disparate strands together in a show-case for the project and a celebration of three years' work. The first half consisted of a selection of songs and compositions created during the workshops. The second half was given over to the performance of *Silver Messenger*, a fifty-minute choral and ensemble work by Karen Wimhurst to a libretto by James Crowden, featuring many of the groups and individuals from the first half.

'Confluence' propagated a message of good management and conservation of water resources. The theme was an excellent stimulus to the imagination of local participants. It was well-chosen in terms of age and ability, since all members of this disparate community could respond to it, regardless of their level of musical ability (condition 6). The results of using music to promote a political or social message in this way can often appear contrived and rather 'worthy'. However any misgivings about the polemics of water-evangelism were dispelled by the sheer poetic force of words and music in *Silver Messenger*. This was not only an artistic triumph, but a feat of organisation, bringing together soloists, amateur and professional musicians, the combined voices of the Candlelight Singers, the Confluence Singers and the Priory Choristers, the Christchurch Wind Band, Dorset Youth Percussion, and young people from a local School.

The libretto drew on many elements: the purely descriptive ('Between open sky and curved water, Tall stands of black poplar, Clumps of alder skewed, Speckled with willow shade [...]'), guide-book prose ('The Stour rises on chalk and green sands, flows sweetly from magnificent gardens at Stourhead [...]') and a litany of tributary names. The musical style transformed seamlessly between funky jazz riffs and massive dissonant choral and orchestral textures. The composer never fell into the trap of 'writing down' for amateur performers. She made no stylistic compromises. With *In Time of Flood*, she achieved spectacular antiphonal effects held together with two conductors directing the Confluence Choir and Ensemble at the Eastern end of the nave and the Christchurch Wind Band at the West.

Beautifully evocative were the distant voices of the priory choristers, hidden from view in the sanctuary, or the ethereal counterpoint of four female singers in *Source*, standing high on the top of the rood screen. But the mood was rescued skilfully from over-seriousness by the verbal wit of poems like *The Blandford Fly*, or the theatre-of-the-absurd finale *Nothing to declare*, dominated by the larger-than-life stage presence of soprano Frances Lynch, half-drunk bottle of illicit contraband concealed inside her black oil-skin coat, peering out from beneath her sou'wester to parody Nelson's Trafalgar speech: 'Christchurch Expects Every Man to Evade his Duty And every woman to hide the evidence under her skirts.' (Crowden; quoted in Clifford and King, 2001: 16 [Author's upper case]) Then just as suddenly the mood switched to rapt nature mysticism in the ecstatic closing bars: 'Nothing to declare but the curlew calling... Nothing to declare but the sea's chasm yawning.' *Silver Messenger* ended as it began – with nature's own music: the wing-beats of a flight of swans, mingling distantly with recordings of bell-buoy and foghorn at Hengistbury Head.

In terms of the theoretical model, 'Confluence' scored highly in openness of 'age' and 'ability', as well as being strongly and imaginatively focused as to 'places' and 'people'. The workshop programme gave participants an opportunity to progress through a good balance of instruction and encounter. In terms of classification it was sufficiently open to provide appropriate starting points for a wide variety of people through jazz, folk and classical idioms, but offered a strong style-centred focus of the highest quality through the music of Karen Wimhurst. The organisers recognised the importance of publicity and public relations. They organised many special community events and activities, and published a regular news letter called *Confluence*, as well as several one-off publications of poetry and ballades, and CDs such as the compilation of songs and other material called *Otter – Lutra, Lutra on the Stour*. As a result the project and its aims and objectives were conspicuous throughout the region, so that its holistic nature was widely known about and understood. As a celebration and a culmination of all that had been achieved during this three-year project, the final performance was a memorable event. The 7th condition of openness was brilliantly fulfilled.

Example 55: Matrix analysis of Common Ground 'Confluence' project.

Part 3
The theoretical model in action

Chapter 8
Before the project starts

So far my discussion has focused on fixed matrix positions describing either the conception of a whole project, or its aspect at a particular moment in time. The time has come to discuss how the three-stage structure described in chapter 4 (p. 162), and the four-phase model which forms its central element, can be used as the basis of the timetable for a creative music project.

All 'Rainbow over Bath' projects were preceded by a period of preparation encapsulating Asher's sequence of preparation, specification, contact, and planning. Typically at 'Rainbow over Bath', we followed a timetable of five phases:

1. Consultation.
2. Project conception.
3. Strategic planning.
4. Introductory meeting.
5. Inset or training day.

Consultation

The importance of local consultation cannot be emphasised enough. Paynter and Aston asserted that 'Education [...] should be child-centred and start from the needs of the individual' (Paynter & Aston, 1970: 2). This has become the guiding principle of many recent theories of music education. For George Odam it was synonymous with 'weak classification' in the Bernstein sense: musical style left to the choice of the child (Odam, 1995: 56).

I have already discussed Tippett's reference to what he saw as Kodály's dilemma. How can the contemporary composer really make a valid contribution to an education process which is seen as 'child-centred' without compromising what Tippett saw as the composer's mandate 'to reach down into the depths of the human psyche and bring forth the tremendous images of things to come' (Tippett 1974: 129)?

The desire to draw over-rigid lines of demarcation between 'composing-in-education' and 'composers-in-education' is an example of the tendency towards specialisation typical of what Chris Small called the 'schizoid culture' (Small 1977: 70). 'composing-in-education' is seen as an essentially 'child-centred' approach to the teaching of composition in which the professional composer may have only an incidental part to play, if at all. The teaching of 'composing-in-education', or 'Composing-in-the-classroom', is seen as a job for the trained professional teacher. Composers may be ill-equipped for the rough-and-tumble of everyday classroom life, lacking specific knowledge of up-to-date teaching and learning strategies, and of modern educational psychology. If they set foot in the classroom, it is at the risk of doing damage to the education of the young people they have come to help.

Resistance from teachers to the idea of 'artists-in-schools' is not unfounded, hence the need for the handbook of Sharp & Dust (1992). Mistakes have been made when composers and other artists have entered the classroom, or other community-based situations, ill-equipped for what they find there and unable to put across their message effectively. But they can learn, and some of them have become very good at it. As a result the situation is not so clear-cut as it was even ten years ago. It is part of the aim of this study to put forward strategies to resolve this dichotomy, so that young people in schools and, more generally, people in the wider community can benefit from the particular skills and knowledge which the professional composer has to offer.

'Top down' versus 'bottom up'

Community-based projects can also suffer from a parallel demarcation between 'community-music' and 'musicians in the community'. Here, the child-centred learning approach is replaced by an insistence that community-based projects should build on an expressed need within the community; that projects should be 'community-led' or, as it is sometimes expressed, organised 'from the bottom up'. The opposite approach which is seen as 'patronising' is a project built 'from the top down', where outside experts who think they know what is best impose their doctrinaire ideas from outside.

Some of the many benefits which come from involving professional musicians and composers in community-based creative music projects include:

- Increased skill base (raising the action/creativity plane).
- Exposure to a wider range of ideas and approaches (open framing).
- Opportunities to try new and unfamiliar repertoire leading to widening of artistic horizons (open classification).
- Increased financial support from funding bodies.
- Increased public and media interest.

Whether these benefits can be fully realised depends on the approach of project organisers. There are positive and negative arguments for both the 'top down' and the 'bottom up' approach. Project organisers and workshop leaders must discover a middle way. The level of diplomacy that this implies is itself one of the qualities of leadership so essential to a successful project. In Examples 56 and 57, I tabulate some of the pros and cons of the two approaches in terms of the 'giving/receiving; offering/taking' framework discussed in Chapter 4 (Example 16c).

Example 56: The organiser's viewpoint.

Top down:
Giving:
- Strategic planning:
Organisers can be pro-active in relation to a wider strategic plan.
- Identification of needs:
Organisers respond sensitively to perceived community needs.
- Increased funding opportunities:
Access to funding schemes at regional, national, or European level.
- Media interest:
Press & media interest at national level.
- Recognition:
Projects achieve national credibility.

Bottom up:
Offering:
- Lack of strategic planning:
Organisers only respond to specific ideas expressed within the community.
- Recognition of desires:
Organisers only try to give the community what it wants.
- Poor funding:
Funding may only come from limited local sources.
- Media indifference:
Interest only from local press and media.
- Oblivion:
Projects ignored and quickly forgotten.

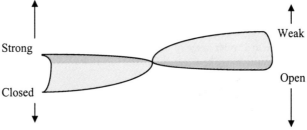

Strong

Weak

Closed

Open

- Arrogance:
Organisers claim to know what is best for the community.
- Ignorance:
Lack of community consultation leads to poor decision-making.
- False assumptions:
Organisers ignore community needs, or make incorrect assumptions.
- Remoteness:
Project organisers take little interest in the project's progress, & see participants as just a statistic in the final report.
- Deception:
Project organisers falsify project reports in order to make a convincing case for future funding of their work.

- Humility:
Organisers are prepared to listen to members of the community.
- Knowledge:
Full consultation and discussion leads to informed advice.
- Responsiveness:
Organisers take an informed and critical view of community desires.
- Involvement:
Organisers take a close interest in the project, and take steps to monitor and evaluate sensitively and realistically.
- Honesty:
Project reports and evaluations are based on verifiable facts and local testimony and therefore have full legitimacy.

250

Example 57: The participants' viewpoint.

Top Down:
Receiving:
• Responsiveness:
Participants welcome exposure to a wider range of ideas and approaches.
• Increased skill base:
Wider range of expertise is welcomed.
• Courage:
Opportunities to try new repertoire lead to widening of artistic horizons.
• Professional expertise:
Access to highest quality expertise.
• Excellence:
High artistic quality of final outcome.
• Gratitude:
Acknowledgement of benefits.

Bottom up:
Taking:
• Limitations:
Lack of any wide awareness of contemporary musical forms.
• Complacency:
Unaware of need to widen skill-base.
• Conservatism:
They are content to go on working on the same familiar repertoire.
• Mistakes:
Badly informed choice of animateur.
• Mediocrity:
Poor artistic quality of outcome.
• A flawed success:
Artistic imperfections are overlooked.

Open

Weak

Closed

Strong

• Lack of motivation:
No advantage taken of national schemes.
• Excuses:
Community blames lack of central provision for its own lack of initiative.
• Resentment:
'We have been trying to raise funds for years. Now outsiders get all the support.'
• Defensiveness:
'We don't need outside interference.'
• Scepticism:
Outsiders seen as 'arty-farty', ignoring the community's real needs and desires.
• Indifference:
Hardly anyone turns up to the project sessions, or to the final performance.
• Failure:
The project flops or is cancelled.

• Good motivation:
Participants will be fully committed to the success of the project.
• Requests:
Community members, aware of their own limitations, request specific help.
• Ownership:
Community asserts ownership of the project & works hard to raise funds.
• Expertise:
Project exploits and benefits from local expertise and knowledge.
• Adulation:
Audience swelled by friends and family.
• Support:
Project fully supported by community.
• Local media interest:
Increased likelihood of local coverage.

The 'top down' approach is sometimes seen as 'cultural colonialism' by analogy with a situation in which a 'superior' invading culture imposes its own patterns on another society which is viewed as more primitive and therefore of less worth. The community artist who 'comes down from London' is seen as a representative of a centralised metropolitan culture imposing its 'superior' standards on a provincial and therefore more 'backward' local culture.

Hand in hand with this attitude goes the presumption that there is a distinction to be drawn between high and low art. Even the socialist-inspired approaches of Holst or Tippett imply the acceptance of this distinction. Enlightened paternalism of this kind lay behind the Workers Education movement for which Morley College was such an important powerhouse, and which found its expression in widespread university extra-mural departments, nowadays replaced by more 'politically correct' community education programmes, partly in order to counter such accusations of 'paternalism'.

The former extra-mural departments were, and the new Community Education Programmes still are, useful organisations with well-established communications in the community which can help to facilitate creative music projects. For example, Arnolfini Music collaborated with the Extra-mural Department of Bristol University to run the Arnolfini Music Workshop as an 'evening institute' from 1982 to 1988. The collaboration required a flexible attitude from both institutions in order to accommodate the University's academic requirements alongside the Arnolfini's commitment to contemporary musical forms involving experiment, improvisation and performance.

The distinctions between high and low art, between the 'top down' and the 'bottom up' approaches, or between projects which are 'community led' (weak or open) and 'music-style led' (closed or strong) continue to present dilemmas for the composer in education or the community. Many composers working in the field of community music who come from a background in classical contemporary western music regard it as part of their mission to foster the appreciation of that genre. Any institution or group of like-minded individuals adopting an evangelistic approach to a particular kind of music, and seeking to propagate it within society at large, risks attracting the 'paternalist' tag.

The composer or musician in the community may arrive in that role through a variety of routes: by invitation because of a reputation in the field; because of personal fame; by responding to an advertisement for the job; or because of a desire to make a contribution to the community in which he or she lives. But whichever is the case, it is an essential part of leadership to mediate between two aims:

1. To respond to, and interpret creatively, the musical needs and desires of the host community in relation to their chosen form of music.
2. To educate the members of that community and open their ears and minds to forms of music which lie beyond their previous experience.

To see why it is that both of these aims are important, let us consider the case that a community musician adopts only one of them, taking the hypothetical example of a male voice choir who manage to raise several thousand pounds from a National Lottery scheme.

There is a difference between needs and desires. The word 'desires' implies areas of musical activity where improvements can be made which the choir has already identified for itself. 'Needs' implies aspects of musicianship which the choir may not be aware of. A community musician who takes a 'creative' approach to these 'needs and desires' is already beginning to move towards the second aim and, by identifying 'needs' as well as 'desires', has already introduced an element of paternalism into the situation.

If the choir decided to invite a renowned barbershop conductor to work with them for a week of intensive workshops, they would probably improve their intonation, tone, diction, presentation and other qualities of ensemble singing and would perhaps go on to win competitions. But the weak approach to classification of the funding organisations would have allowed the choir to come up with a project with extremely closed classification and framing, and no exposure to any form of poietic experience. The participants would be unlikely to expand their musical horizons either as individuals or as a group. In view of the Lottery guidelines, I would question whether this was a legitimate use of public subsidy.

If, on the other hand, prompted by the persuasive powers of an over-zealous Regional Arts Music Officer, they hired the services of an 'avant-garde' composer who then took no interest in barbershop singing styles and subjected the choir to exercises in extended vocal technique without explanation or any attempt to establish common ground, the result would be bafflement and alienation. The project might match up to the Lottery guidelines on paper, but it would have failed to meet its own objectives. In this case the closed attitude to classification of the funding organisation would have resulted in a project of weak classification and framing, offering no opportunity for esthesic experience. It would have done more harm than good. Members of the choir would probably never take part in a creative music project ever again.

How then should this hypothetical project proceed? Certainly the workshop leader would need to be skilled and knowledgeable in the techniques and repertoire of barbershop singing already familiar to the choir. But he must be broad enough in his wider experience of music to be able to help them progress towards a more open realisation of the musical potential of their corporate vocal sound. The project should adopt a balanced approach to framing, action and creativity by offering both instruction and encounter, participation and listening, and creation and recreation. Taking elements of the 'closed' technique of barbershop singing as a starting point, it should progress towards open classification.

Project conception

The need to strike the right balance between the top-down and bottom-up approach was therefore a central pre-occupation in planning the education programme of 'Rainbow over Bath'. Each year we had several projects to propose. These were devised at the 'project conception' stage in discussion with composers, and with orchestral or ensemble directors or their education co-ordinators. We consulted with individual teachers and with the director of the LEA music service. In European collaborations I called a meeting of partners at an agreed central location, or undertook individual meetings with partners in their own countries, asking them for an overview of their forthcoming plans to assess the potential for integration into a larger collaborative programme.

It was at this stage that we made strategic decisions about musical styles, people and places, age and ability, or duration and scale. Project themes might be discussed without necessarily reaching a decision. The right moment to choose a project theme depends on its aims and objectives. In the Williams brothers' song-writing project choice of themes within broad guidelines was left to the individual children as an important part of the creative process. Grand Union's *Silk Road* came as a ready-made package with a project theme laid down in advance.

Practical aspects such as drafting project timetables to show availability of artists, and proposed dates for Inset days and final performance came up at this stage. We also took decisions about the educational focus: whether a project was to be repertoire-centred or concept-led; whether the outcome would be a group-performance, or individual compositions; which of the Bedford Categories the project belonged to and so on. A period of several months could elapse before we were ready to begin active work on a project, taken up with budgeting, and applications to grant-giving bodies. Projects featuring a newly commissioned work (BC1, 2 or 3) required a longer gestation period because the composer needed time to complete the work.

Exact costings vary widely with variations in duration and scale. The budget for *Mengjiang Dream River Great Wall*, mentioned in Chapter 6 (p. 216), included an ensemble of twenty-four European and Chinese musicians, with lead composer/workshop-director, and small workshop team. Presenting the project in several different venues would achieve economies of scale. At each venue a two or three month programme was undertaken consisting of the following elements:

- Creative workshops in four schools or community centres.
- Composers' workshop and final concert performance of workshop pieces.
- Demonstration workshop by UK Chinese Ensemble.
- Professional concert of contemporary pieces including performance of *Mengjiang Weeping at the Wall* with professional musicians, local choral society and children's creative music group.

Between 2002 and 2004, the project received five performances, each time involving different groups of between eighty and a hundred and twenty primary school children in Corsham, York, Bristol, Midsomer Norton and Bath. Allowing for initial set-up costs including composer commission, the project cost some £33,000, and secured grant aid from the National Youth Music Foundation, the Paul Hamlyn Foundation, Arts Council England and the Performing Right Society.

Strategic planning

Following a successful campaign to raise funds, a range of creative music projects would be offered, either to specific targeted organisations to achieve a strategic balance across the region, or on a first-come-first-served basis by sending open letters to many schools, community centres and other organisations within our geographical catchment area. European partners used their own equivalent networks of contacts. Certain schools which were enthusiastic about creative music projects could be relied on to respond every year, and used 'Rainbow' projects as part of their own educational programme, but 'openness' is an essential principle at this stage, and it was also important to try and reach new communities. The timing of these approaches is crucial. Most schools are planning cultural projects during the summer term before the start of the next school year.

Introductory meeting

Organisations which responded positively were invited to an introductory meeting with project leaders, composers, musicians, education co-ordinators and other representatives of each ensemble. The meeting served four purposes:

1. Description – To describe in broad outlines the aims and objectives of each project, what sectors of the community they were aimed at, and how they were to be run.
2. Consultation – Discussion of how the projects fitted into the context of music teaching and learning strategies in each school, or of how they could benefit participating amateur or community groups.
3. Selection – To select schools and participating organisations.
4. Scheduling – To draw up a skeleton timetable for each project.

We made a presentation of each project, with sound-recordings, slide-projections, video, and printed dossiers. At the beginning of the meeting we did not expect delegates to be committed to participation, although clearly they were interested enough to attend the meeting. However, by the end, we expected them either to have made that commitment, or to arrive at a decision within a few days. In practice, interest was usually converted into commitment immediately. We speedily moved on to time-tabling, dealt with very practically by a kind of 'date-auction', filling up vacant slots on a pre-prepared time-table as bidders called out things like 'I take GCSE Music with year 10 on a Wednesday afternoon'. For this reason we asked teachers to come with term-dates, and a teaching time-table.

Inset or Training day

The next step was the Inset or training day. Normally there would be a separate day for each project in our annual programme, taking place only a week or two before the start of the appropriate project. Before the training day, we would confirm the time-table and exchange formal letters of agreement with each participating school or organisation.

In nearly all 'Rainbow' projects, we relied crucially on the support of teachers. Although it might be seen as a wonderful opportunity for a school to have the full-time attendance of a composer-in-residence throughout an entire three-month period, financial constraints rule this out. The fair allocation of scarce resources is a constant issue. There is a temptation, which must be avoided, for the teacher to attend to other administrative duties, leaving the visiting composer to get on with the job single-handedly. The provision of training for teachers and community leaders is an obvious way in which practical workshop skills can be passed on to a wider group of people. It is more effective than spending money on expensive placements because it leaves a lasting resource of skills within the community. If music students are involved as workshop assistants, they too should attend the training day.

European projects encountered the added obstacle of language differences. I have made claims for music's power to unite people across linguistic boundaries, but creative music projects which operate on a European or international basis cannot side-step the question of language. It is part of the richness of cultural life opened up by such collaborations. Aspects of language, literature, local myths and legends, and indigenous music and dance, become available as sources of inspiration in a multi-national project.

In general, British people are resistant to learning foreign languages. On the other hand, English has become the dominant language for international communication. It has been an important principle in international exchange projects organised by 'Rainbow over Bath' that British participants should not be too ready to rely on their hosts' ability to speak English. Although almost all Dutch adults speak good English, we could not rely on teachers in the South of France or Bulgaria to do so. It was essential to have interpreters who could participate fully as part of the creative team. But we also encouraged our musicians and composers to acquire some basic acquaintance with the language of any host country. We regarded it as a basic courtesy, and found that it paid dividends in hospitality and willingness to co-operate in our projects. This was particularly important with minority languages such as Dutch, Finnish, Bulgarian or Hungarian. The learning of technical terms used in music was particularly useful, a process aided by the recent publication of an international glossary by the European Music Council (European Music Council, 2001).

It needs a good turn-out for the training day to go with a swing. Optimum numbers generate and sustain enthusiasm and commitment. If, for example, five or six schools, two community groups, and a Saturday morning music centre all send two representatives and there is group of ten or a dozen music students, including language specialists if appropriate, as well as the composer/workshop leader and two or three professional musicians of the visiting ensemble, we will have between twenty and thirty participants – the ingredients for an inspiring day! It may seem an obvious point, though apparently not to some schools, that the teachers attending the training day should be the same ones who will be running the project in their schools.

It is here that the leadership qualities of the composer/workshop leader first come to the fore. The training day has many purposes:

1. To instruct teachers and students in general workshop skills, and in any specific techniques required for this project;
2. To ensure that all teachers and students have the clearest possible understanding of the aims of the project, its chosen theme and the final objectives;
3. To allocate each of the students acting as workshop assistants to a school, and give them an opportunity to meet and work alongside the teacher from that school;
4. To ensure that all participants are aware of their role in the project, and to clarify the relationship between the students and the schools to which they are allocated;
5. To allow participants to get to know one another as individuals;
6. To build the confidence of teachers and students in their own creative abilities, and their ability to see the project through to its conclusion (This is especially important in the case of those who are not music specialists such as primary school teachers, staff at special schools and community leaders);
7. To enable the workshop leader to assess the strengths and weaknesses of individual teachers and students, and of the participating schools;
8. To build this disparate group of teachers, students and others into a coherent local team;
9. To answer any queries, discuss and resolve any practical problems, and reach final agreement of the project timetable.

The best way to instruct people in new techniques is by direct experience. The training day followed the intended format of the project itself. It was run as an intensive project-in-miniature. Participants were introduced step by step to the four-phase model. By the end of the day delegates acquired a small repertoire of preparatory games and warm-up exercises and an understanding of their purpose. They gained experience of how musical processes can grow and develop through improvisation. They saw how sounds can be organised into larger structures, and gained insight into modal, melodic and rhythmic processes. They experienced at first hand what it feels like to respond to the challenge of being asked to create musical ideas and other material against a deadline – challenges which they would shortly be setting their own pupils. They worked with others in the group to co-ordinate and rehearse a final performance of their work. Even for experienced teachers the training day was a valuable refresher course, as well as an introduction to the specific concepts of a particular project.

The relationship between artists and teachers in the workshop team

Delegates should finish the training day with the clearest possible understanding of their function in the workshop team. *Artists in Schools* (Sharp & Dust, 1992) provides much practical advice on this subject, but almost entirely from a 'child-centred' perspective. A discussion of the book's recommendations throws interesting light on the dichotomy between composing-in-education and composers-in-education. Missing is the refreshing attitude expressed in Schafer's maxim: 'Teach on the edge of peril' (Schafer, 1975: 132–133).

According to Sharp and Dust, a common complaint from artists is of lack of support from the school. Artists complain of being used as supply teachers, that they are asked to carry projects alone, or that they are seen as a prop for failing and therefore resentful teachers. *Artists in Schools* advises that schools should be carefully chosen, rejecting those where such problems are judged likely to happen, but if schools are chosen only on the basis of likelihood of success, we will never make any impact on those failing schools which most need the input of creative artists. Our projects would not be truly 'open'. The training day is especially important for schools which fall into this category.

Unprofessional behaviour from artists is sometimes blamed for lack of success. Misdemeanours such as turning up late, cancelling at short notice or being poorly prepared are all cited in Sharp and Dust.

But what about frustration at lack of progress or the effects of emotional involvement in the subject-matter of the project? Artistic creation is a volatile process. There must be room for deviation, lateral processes, adventure, and exploration. In practice, misunderstandings between artists and teachers about what a project is aiming to achieve are fairly common. Sharp and Dust declare that: 'It is important to have a clearly expressed set of aims and objectives', but they do not point out that it is also important to avoid the opposite extreme – being too prescriptive so that spontaneity is ruled out. This is one very important way that creative/artistic projects differ from the normal school curriculum.

It is essential to minimise misunderstandings, but it is rare that they are clear-cut. They can never be avoided completely. Uncertainty is central to the nature of the artist/teacher/pupil relationship. It is impossible to convey the precise nature of the outcome of a creative process using verbal descriptions alone, even if that outcome can be precisely formulated in the first place. It is important to make it clear that 'uncertainty' is a key element of the process, that the outcome is unknown except within loosely defined parameters, and that we are all travelling together on a voyage of discovery. What distinguishes the skilled composer/workshop leader from fellow travellers is that he or she knows how to deal with the unexpected, and is the one equipped with survival skills in uncharted seas.

Sharp and Dust advise that 'Teachers and artists should check that they have a common understanding' (ibid., 1992: 13), but how can they? However much they 'Check', there is always room for doubt. Do artists and teachers both 'mean' the same thing when they use a particular word or phrase? The teacher's ability to understand is limited by his or her own knowledge or experience of the arts, or of previous projects. Here is another reason why the training day is so important. It instructs by direct example, avoiding the ambiguity of words. By definition the artist is setting out to do something new. It would be an unusual teacher who could grasp immediately, or foresee the likely outcome of such a process. What is required from teachers is courage and openness, and an ability to encourage their classes to have confidence in the artist to lead them to an interesting and exciting conclusion.

According to Sharp and Dust, artists frequently complain of lack of pupil commitment. There can be many reasons for this. Not being informed in advance is only one of them. They might have been informed but were not listening, or didn't understand what was being said to them, again because of simple things like a misunderstanding about what particular words 'mean'. Later this would be converted in their minds into a perception that they had not been informed of the outcome because they did not understand the significance of the verbal descriptions given to them. Misunderstandings will inevitably emerge at every stage. A good teacher, and a good artist employed as animateur, will be constantly alert to this situation, and will know how to get maximum educational benefit from it.

At 'Rainbow' we learnt the value of regular project meetings as the exact nature of project outcomes became clearer with time. The full team of teachers and students, supported by the local director of the music service and the lead composer, needs to meet at regular intervals as a steering committee, optimally at the end of each stage in the process.

Sometimes teachers' resentment of artists is a problem. Again this focuses on irreconcilable expectations. Maybe the GCSE syllabus is wrong if it only allows room for 'acceptable' work. Artists need space for free experimentation. The schools which cannot cope with this fundamental principle are the ones which most need the experience of creative projects. But how do you persuade them in the first place? If schools are only able, or ready, to cope with a completely predetermined path, then they will be unable to derive much of the real benefit which comes from the encounter with a creative artist.

It is important, however, for artists to be sensitive to teachers' status and methods. It is therefore essential to train artists and musicians to do this type of work. If lack of practical experience is an issue, particularly in the case of young composers, a more experienced project mentor can be appointed, a strategy adopted recently by the SPNM for its C4K and 'Adopt-a-Composer' schemes, and by the PRS Composer-in-Education programme.

The function of students in the workshop team

Students, too, need to be clear about their role in a project. Since they are 'learning on the job', care needs to be taken in briefing them about their role, and discussing this with them throughout the project. Verbal briefings at the start of the project are not enough. Workshop leaders need to be alert at all times to the way student assistants are relating to workshop participants. We found that students varied widely in resourcefulness, initiative and self-confidence, and even in basic musicianship. We could suggest ways in which students might support a workshop programme but it was impossible to lay down hard-and-fast guidelines. Students have to find for themselves the level at which they feel capable of making a contribution, progressing from that towards a position of greater responsibility as the following list indicates:

1. Operating the tape recorder when something needs recording.
2. Joining in as a participant alongside everyone else.
3. Helping individual, less skilled participants to keep a rhythmic pattern or pulse going.
4. Keeping an up-to-date journal of the workshop in progress: what activities took place, what outcomes were achieved and what tasks were set before the next session.
5. Writing down musical ideas in staff notation and keeping them as part of the written journal.
6. Using their own instrumental skills to strengthen the overall sound of the music.
7. Supporting the work of the class teacher or community leader when the lead composer is absent.
8. Acting as a group leader during group-work sessions; Taking over the running of a full workshop session.

We normally allocated students in teams of two to each school. This was better for the students' self-confidence, and provided companionship when they went into a strange school for the first time. They functioned better as a team in the classroom situation. Students in 'Rainbow' projects, such as Grand Union's *Silk Road* and Ensemble Esoterica, were asked to compile their own project reports which were then marked as a piece of course-work. We therefore had two ways of assessing students' response to the module: by observation of their practical involvement in workshops, and by their ability to analyse the experience systematically in project reports.

During the period between the training day, and the start of the project, the teacher's task is to secure the commitment of the school, to motivate the children taking part, and to ensure that all are fully aware of the timetable and the degree of commitment required. The same tasks apply to community leaders, directors of amateur choirs and en-sembles, and so on – a process which is greatly enhanced if the artist can be asked to come and talk to all the participants in advance.

Chapter 9
Project themes

I have referred several times to the importance of project themes. The topic appears amongst the eight 'conditions of openness' in Chapter 7 (p. 225). Over an eight-year period, 'Rainbow over Bath' initiated and managed creative projects which took a wide variety of starting points and project themes. Outcomes and means of achieving them were defined in different ways:

Example 58: 'Rainbow over Bath' list of projects.

Year	Project Leader(s)	Age range	No. taking part	Location	Stylistic starting point	Theme, Model or Title	Objective
1996	Sean Gregory	8–25	170	Bath, Aix Alkmaar Kaposvár	Contemporary minimalist	*A Feeling in Time*	Group compositions
1997	Deirdre Gribbin Mary Wiegold Rob Smith	8–18	120	Bath Zwolle (N) Aix (F)	Voice & clarinet; Electronics	Parents & Children, Small sounds	small group compositions
1998	Alistair King	16–18	12	Bath	Chamber orchestra	Skempton *Lento*	Individual compositions
1998	Ros Davis Grand Union Orchestra members	8–40	120	Bath	Ethnic musical forms	*A journey along the Silk Road*	Group composition
1999	Peter Wiegold Phil Sheppard Phil Cashian	8–11	120	Bath	Favourite popular song	*Igor's Boogie*	KS 2: small group compositions

Year	Project Leader(s)	Age range	No. taking part	Location	Stylistic starting point	Theme, Model or Title	Objective
1999	Peter Wiegold, Phil Cashian, Deirdre Gribbin	15–18	60	Bath	Favourite popular song	*Igor's Boogie*	KS 4: Individual compositions
1999	Nikolay Stoykov	18–50	90	Bath	Contemp. folk, jazz	*Bridge to Bulgaria*	Adult participatory
1999	Barry Russell & Cardew Ensemble	8–80	200	Bath	Contemp. styles	*Opening Doors*	Large group composition
1999	Barry Russell, & Cardew Ensemble	8–20	200	Plovdiv (Bulgaria)	Contemp. & folk	*Rituals for Orpheus*	Large group composition
1999	Eugene Skeef, Paul Gladstone Reid, Tunde Jegede	15–40	150	Bath & rural areas	Afro-Caribbean styles	*African diaspora*	Small group composition
1999	Klaus Feßmann, Margarida Pinto do Amaral	18–22	20	Bath	Music, Dance & Set design	*Change of Para-digms*	Individual compositions with dance
1999	Peter Wiegold	18–22	20	Salzburg (Austria)	Contemp. neo-romantic	*Sufi* texts	Group compositions with dance
1999	Peter Wiegold	15–22	20	Alkmaar (Holland)	Contemp. neo-romantic	*Sufi* texts	Group compositions
2000	Peter Wiegold, Mary Wiegold, Duncan Prescott	15–18	40	Bath & rural areas	Writing for voices & instruments	Various themes	Individual compositions

During my wider research I encountered a wealth of different themes. Broad categories can be defined, but they are not hard and fast, and particular projects may exemplify more than one category. I divide them between musical and non-musical, and between those which provide their own time structure or narrative, and those in which time structure is a separate abstract concept.

Categories of project themes:

1. Musical concepts:

    a. Musical model – particular work by a composer, or his or her style in general.
    b. Musical concept – e.g. 'imitation', 'improvisation', 'silence', 'only 4 notes'.
    c. Exploration of a musical form – e.g. blues, song or fugue.
    d. Exploration of a particular type of musical instrument or variety of sound.

2. Non-musical concepts without a narrative component:

    a. Abstract ideas expressed as a verbal phrase or image.
    b. Pictorial themes.
    c. Experiences drawn from life.
    d. Political or social themes.

3. Non-musical concepts with built-in narrative component:

    a. Telling a story, relating historical events etc.
    b. Poem or piece of descriptive prose.
    c. Geographical journey described in music.
    d. Myth or legend associated with a particular place.

(These categories will be referred to as Theme Categories – TC)

Musical concepts (TC1)

I discussed some examples of the use of a musical model (TC1a) in previous chapters. Repertoire-based starting points are typical of education teams attached to orchestras and opera companies where there is an obligation to focus on works in the concert repertoire such as LSO's Berlioz season and the *Hector and Harriet* project which simultaneously belongs in the 'telling a story in music' category (TC1a+3a).

Gamelan instruments are used widely in creative music projects because musical novices can produce an immediately attractive and resonant sound. The instruments themselves become the main project theme (TC1d), but Lynne Plowman's choice of an additional imaginative theme as a focus for her Norfolk Gamelan project for Wingfield Arts in 2001 emphasises the importance of making an appropriate choice. She chose the frequently used theme of 'Earth, Air, Fire and Water' (TC2a), but to ask children to discover dry crackling sounds of a forest fire in the resonant sonorities of gamelan instruments is stretching their imagination to the limit (rainbow: Track 18).

Non-musical concepts without a narrative component

Abstract idea expressed as a verbal phrase or image (TC2a)

'Rainbow' presented two projects based on an abstract idea expressed as a verbal phrase (TC2a): Sean Gregory's *A Feeling in Time*, and Barry Russell's *Opening Doors*. Gregory drew his title from a beautifully evocative, and expertly crafted work for soprano and small ensemble by Netherlands composer Kees van Unen called *A Time and a Place*. The title was taken from a poem by Philip Larkin which formed part of Van Unen's trilogy of settings of English poets, so the theme also belonged indirectly to the 'poetic text' category (TC3b).

During the workshop programmes in four European cities, Gregory took the theme of 'Time' as a starting point for creative work with young people across a wide age-range.

Example 59: Matrix analysis of Sean Gregory's 'Time' project.

He took the many disparate musical responses to the rather generalised theme and welded them together into a convincing large-scale musical structure (BC4). The result was successful in achieving a strong cathartic climax. Gregory was commissioned to write a work for the quartet of clarinets 'No Strings Attached', and incorporated into it melodic material from the educational project. Such thematic unity emphasised the holistic nature of the project.

Gregory used musical material from the opening bars of his clarinet quartet *A Feeling in Time* (rainbow: Track 19) at the beginning of the creative music project *A Rainbow at the End of Time* (rainbow: Track 20; Example 60).

Example 60: Gregory, S. (1996) *A Feeling in Time*, bars 1–15.

Later in the creative project he took an ostinato pattern from *A Feeling in Time* associated with the passing of time (rainbow: Track 21) and asked the young musicians to create their own variations (rainbow: Track 22; Example 61).

Example 61: Gregory, S. (1996) *A Feeling in Time*, bars 51–68.

The quartet and the creative project both ended with the same 'End of time' riff played by the bass clarinet (rainbow: Track 23; Example 62).

Example 62: Gregory, S. *A Feeling in Time*, bars 69–82.

In the creative project, for maximum dramatic effect, the quiet coda was approached by an extended build-up in which several of Gregory's hall-mark workshop techniques appear including accumulating riffs and chord sequences involving the entire orchestra of two hundred young musicians. At one point, musical tension is built through sudden silences of progressively decreasing length. Gregory's own improvisation on piccolo can be heard clearly in the closing moments of the tutti (ibid.: Track 24). The same 'End of Time' motive is heard in the closing bars of *A Feeling in Time* (rainbow: Track 25).

Pictorial themes (TC2b)

Barry Russell has made considerable use of pictorial themes, though not in 'Rainbow' projects. An example devised for key-stage 4 children which I saw at Dean Clough East Mill Gallery in Halifax in October 2000 was called *Gone to Play at Mr. Escher's House* (TC2b+1b). It was based on the idea of subjecting musical material to transformations which are 'like' the ones in Escher's prints such as *Other World* in which staircases climb in different directions, provoking the question 'Which way is up?' The theme suggested musical concepts such as inversions and retrogrades and other kinds of serial transformation. Another example was *Metamorphose* in which interlocking patterns and tessellations are subjected to gradual trans-

270

formation. A Teacher's pack provided musical ideas for starting points (Example 63).

Example 63: Russell, B. (2001) extract from *Gone to play at Mr. Escher's house.*

The project was prepared intensively with only two sessions in each of four schools, and a final session in the gallery at Dean Clough during the final afternoon – one fewer sessions than advocated in the Wiegold model – with the result that the performance lacked the polish and assurance that Wiegold's final session of 'rehearsal and performance' brings.

This was a theme which did not suggest its own temporal structure. Russell linked the otherwise disparate material in a kind of rondo form. Five episodes of creative work (each school in turn plus a section in which they all played together) were interspersed with instrumental sections played by the 'orchestra' of nine members of Northern Opera Education Link (NOEL). The result was a composed work with creative windows (BC3). The orchestral players had not been involved in the creative workshops, and I detected a lack of commitment from them, unlike the instrumentalists of Russell's own 'Cardew Ensemble' who were so closely involved in *Rituals for Orpheus*.

Experiences drawn from life (TC2c)
Political and social themes (TC2d)

Experiences drawn from everyday life were used as a non-musical stimulus in The Valleys Song Writing project in Caerphilly. Huw and Tony Williams asked children to write songs on a subject of their own choice. According to the teachers' pack 'the children will be encouraged to look at their own surroundings (where they live, for example, and its surroundings) for suitable ideas.' The children came up with lyrics about everyday life such as shopping, television programmes, holidays, and parties (2c), or songs with a social conscience on war, drugs or cruelty to animals (2d).

The timetable mapped out in the teachers' pack follows the classic four-phase pattern, taking place intensively over only five days:

Day 1:
Session 1 (morning) is concerned with the sounds of instruments. The Williams brothers play some of their instruments, and the children get a chance to try them out for themselves (Equivalent to Swanwick's 'mastery through manipulation of materials' or elements of Wiegold's 'Preparation').

Session 2 (late morning) is concerned with thinking about what a song is, and why people write them. The Williams brothers play and sing songs from their own repertoire, and ask the children to think about and discuss the lyrics (Equivalent to Swanwick's 'imitation of vernacular', or Wiegold's 'Presentation' but also Paynter stage 'D' brought to the beginning of the process, therefore 'instruction' rather than 'encounter').

Session 3 (afternoon) explores suitable ideas for songs and simple song-writing techniques. At the end of the day, the children are given the task of thinking up their own subject before the next session (Equivalent to the introduction of an idea or concept at the end of Wiegold's 'Presentation' phase).

Day 2:
Session 1 (morning) is concerned with making up lyrics about their chosen subject.

In Session 2 (late morning) they create a simple melody, and by Session 3 (afternoon) they get as far as trying to invent a simple chordal accompaniment helped by the Williams brothers on guitar or keyboard.

Day 3:
Concerned with rehearsing the songs for performance, and recording them (Equivalent to Wiegold's 'Rehearsal and performance').

The children visit the Williams' professional studio, an educative experience in its own right, although I discussed in Chapter 5 (p. 181) my misgivings about the degree of intervention required from the brothers to produce the highly polished results on CD or cassette which are one of the outcomes of the project.

Project themes based on everyday life (TC2c) are often chosen because they are seen as 'more relevant' to children's experience, but expert and visionary leadership is needed to prevent these subjects from becoming merely mundane. The English Chamber Orchestra's *Supermarket Symphonies* project performed at a Primary School in south Bristol in July 2001 fell into this trap. Supermarket products do not make good sounds unless they are very carefully selected. These were not. At the 'manipulation of materials' stage there had been too little attention to details. Baked-bean tins with the beans still inside are not especially resonant. Packets of pulses and dried peas don't make good rattles unless the contents are removed and put into other, more carefully chosen, containers as an example of a rhythmic call-and-response game shows (rainbow: Track 26). The project fell down on the second, third and fourth 'conditions of openness': the children were not sufficiently challenged, their contributions were not meaningful, and they could not take pride in the result.

The project-leaders managed to generate some level of pupil enthusiasm by resorting to well-tried traditional formats such as a variant of *She'll be Coming Round the Mountain* (rainbow: Track 27). A round based on the chanted words 'A shopping list, a shopping list, a supermarket trolley and a shopping list' introduced an element of part singing, but barely rose above the banal (rainbow: Track 28).

The concert was badly co-ordinated. What looked on paper like a coherently put together programme of fifty minutes duration, alternating the results of creative workshops with professional performances by members of the ECO, lasted over two hours. Vital stage-management issues which are essential at phase four (rehearsal and performance) had not been resolved.

This concert presented work at an intermediate stage in a longer holistic project featuring a new symphony by David Bedford to be performed by the ECO in Bristol during Spring 2002. Although Bedford was not directly involved in the July performance at the school, I was surprised to find a project with which he was associated falling down on basic principles of good practice. It is my own view that the imaginations of most people, children included, are more likely to be stimulated by a challenging and poetic idea, than by being asked to respond to the mundane everyday world around them (Laycock, 2002: 285–286 and rainbow: Tracks 32–34).

Non-musical themes with built-in narrative component

Telling a story (TC3a)

Opera companies have a ready-made source of stories for their educational projects. Ruth Byrchmore's opera *Katerina*, commissioned by
WNO and performed in June 2001, grew out of workshops with young
people which paralleled WNO's production of Janacek's *Katya
Kabanova* (TC3a+1a). It was written for nine WNO principles and
chamber ensemble of six, with a gigantic chorus of two hundred and
twenty primary-school children. With so many youngsters on stage at
the Rhydcar Leisure Centre in Mythyr Tydfil, the director ducked the
challenge of choreographing them and, instead, seated them in large
raked seating, making synchronised arm and body movements to
underline the narrative.

Poem or piece of descriptive prose (TC3b)

Peter Wiegold took Sufi religious and philosophical texts as his starting point for a project entitled *Creative Mind, Creative Body*, created
during collaborative workshops with music students and adults in
Alkmaar and Salzburg during November and December 1999. These
programmes showed how Wiegold's four-phase model can form the
basis of an intensive five-day project. They were also examples of how
a composer can use creative workshops as a source of musical material
for his own compositional work (BC4).

Example 64 is a matrix analysis of the prototype performance at
the Provadja Theatre in Alkmaar, created collaboratively by a group of
adults, students and lecturers from the music Conservatorium. Thematic and harmonic elements from this performance found their way
into Wiegold's commissioned work *Within this Body,* performed by
the Composers Ensemble in a concert at Bath University in March
2000. A jam session at the Conservatorium was the origin of a chord
sequence and a set of rhythmic and melodic riffs which were inte-

grated into the opening movement of the work. In a recorded extract from the session, Wiegold's voice can be heard calling out chord changes and other instructions (rainbow: Track 29).

Mary Wiegold was the singer at the first performance of the completed work in Bath. I prefer the untutored simplicity of tone of the two original performers, with their tinge of Dutch accent and hissed sibilants as they sing the slow introduction, 'Listen my friend! listen!' at the Provadja concert (rainbow: Track 30) in comparison with the sophistication of Mary Wiegold's trained and mature soprano voice (rainbow: Track 31).

An infectious jazz-rock idiom in the original Dutch performance (rainbow: Track 32) converts into strange and other-worldly textures with repeated pulsing high cello notes and wailing soprano melismas in the Composers' Ensemble performance (rainbow: Track 33).

Example 64: Matrix analysis of *Creative Mind, Creative Body.*

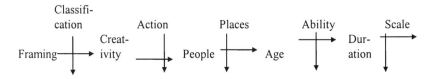

Geographical journey in music (TC3c)

Some of the most stimulating themes used during 'Rainbow' projects were geographical, relating them to the 'places' axis. We can distinguish between themes based on geographical features (TC3c), and the use of stories uniquely associated with a specific geographical location (TC3d). I touched on George Odam's use of geographical maps inspired by Bruce Chatwin's *Songlines* in Chapter 2 (p. 82). Many composers have been influenced by the Australian Aborigines' concept of the Songline. Tony Haynes in a project for the 'Grand Union Orchestra', and Barry Russell in *Songlines and Longlines* (1997) have both responded imaginatively to this theme. My own *Hetty Pegler's Tump* (1988) was based on the idea of Songlines applied to the Cotswold countryside near Uley in Gloucestershire.

Bladud (Laycock, 1985) and *Woden's Dyke* (Laycock, 1988) both used specific landscapes as a means of generating musical material through conceptual processes, as opposed to being vaguely 'inspired'.

Geographical location expressed in music provided project themes for 'Rainbow' projects featuring the Grand Union Orchestra and Ensemble Esoterica. The theme of Grand Union's *Silk Road* provided a non-musical rationale for what was in reality a musical concept: that of stylistic 'fusion' (TC1b+3c). This was a fully holistic project, with a project theme which grew naturally out of the Orchestra's performance of Tony Haynes' work *Now Comes the Dragon's Hour*, itself a skilfully assembled sequence of multi-cultural fusions. The work was scored for five singers, each representing a different ethnic style including a Beijing Opera singer, black soul music, Bangladeshi music, Chilean folk music, and a western operatic tenor. Example 65 is a matrix analysis of the educational project:

Example 65: Matrix analysis of *Now Comes the Dragon's Hour.*

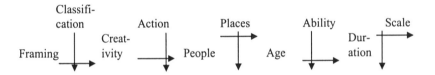

The strong commitment of the Grand Union musicians to education work and the importance that Haynes himself attaches to it were essential ingredients in the success of this project. All the professional paraphernalia of the orchestra's public concert staging, including sound system and lighting effects, were put at the disposal of the education concert. Roz Davis' skill in stage-managing a complicated sequence of group-performances by children and adult groups meant that the concert ran smoothly and to time, with a cathartic climax in which all joined in the singing of a song composed by children from St. George's Community School. Moreover the Orchestra took a realistic attitude to the likelihood of large numbers of the children turning up for an evening performance of *Now Comes the Dragon's Hour* by performing the whole piece as part of a separate schools matinee.

Myth or legend associated with a particular place (TC3d)

Geographical location can provide a rich source of narrative subjects in the form of local myths or legends associated with a particular place (TC3d). I have already referred to projects with such starting points in this country. Collaboration with organisations in other countries, for instance through 'Rainbow across Europe', opens up enriched possibilities. The choice of subject can draw attention to, and celebrate, the international nature of the partnership.

The Alkmaar collaboration began in 1995 with an education project based on a legendary theme. It was my intention to introduce a story of Bathonian origin to our Dutch partners. I chose King Bladud's attempt to fly from the roof of the Temple of Apollo, a story which parallels that of Daedulus and Icarus, except that, in Bladud's case, it is the inventor himself who dies. The theme expressed itself in a creative music-theatre project with twenty students at the Hogeschool Alkmaar Conservatorium, and my own twenty-minute work for eight instruments, *A Dream of Flying*.

A couple of projects not part of the Rainbow programme illustrate other approaches to historical and mythological subject matter. In David Blake's *The Fabulous Adventures of Alexander the Great* (1996) a story taken from the history of the host country provided the narrative. This semi-staged opera for children and students (BC1), on a libretto by John Birtwistle, became the focus for a European exchange project co-ordinated by Miranda Caldi of Korfu University. It was performed at the castle of Mitelene on Lesbos by Finchley Children's Choir, the Radio Children's Choir of Berlin and the University of York Orchestra with funds contributed by the EU Kaleidoscope fund.

On a visit to Dublin and Cork I encountered the primary school education programme of the Irish National Chamber Choir (NCC), based entirely around an opera for young people by the choir's director, the English composer Colin Mawby. *The Torc of Gold,* with libretto by Maeve Ingoldsby, is based on a kind of synthetic Irish myth – a fantasy tale in which a group of children must perform various heroic feats to win the ultimate prize of a golden neck torc. I saw two performances of this piece, one by a junior school, and the other in an abridged form by children with learning difficulties. It is intended to be a piece in which young people can take part with a small element of percussion improvisation (BC2). Most of the musical material is sung by the NCC itself as an off-stage chorus with piano accompaniment, completely un-involved in the dramatic action. The children's creative input is primarily dramatic, with opportunities for acting, set-design and construction, and costume making. Their musical contribution is confined to a small number of solo songs, and two unison choruses, one of them the finale. The score invites schools to provide a percussion band and, at one point, to perform a percussion impro-visation of two minutes duration, but these are described as optional. In the productions I saw, they were dispensed with entirely.

Extra-ordinarily, *The Torc of Gold*, written in 1996, has been performed repeatedly several times a year by different primary schools all over the Republic up to May 2000, usually with great commitment and excitement, and a high level of polish and professionalism by the participants. The work is published in a well-produced multiple edition in glossy covers. Yet it falls well short of several of my 'conditions of openness' and requires little musical creativity from the children. It seems strange too, given the richness of true Irish mythology – heroic stories of Finn Mac Cumal and Cú Chulain amongst them – that the *Torc of Gold* is based on an artificial assemblage of quasi-mythical elements. The work also makes no attempt to draw on the rich instru-mental or vocal traditions of Irish music.

Barry Russell's *Rituali za Orfeii (Rituals for Orpheus)*, with the Cornelius Cardew Ensemble, which took place in Plovdiv, Bulgaria in September 1999 as part of the 'Rainbow across Europe' programme, is an excellent example of a project theme based on the mythology of a host country (TC3d). With its coherent four-phase structure, its holistic nature, its strong geographical focus, its balanced approach to 'creativity' and 'action', and its integration of many different levels of ability in the 'community of learners', the project came close to being an ideal example of the theoretical model. Plovdiv, described in the tourist brochures as Bulgaria's 'second city', is the capital of Thrace, said to be the birth-place of Orpheus. What better subject could we have for a creative music project? The story of Orpheus and Euridice provided a ready-made narrative to link together the disparate musical and choreographic elements. It was a story all the participants knew well, and regarded as their local legend. The composer remarks in his report: '[…] here the sense of ownership of the myth led to a sense of shared ownership of the performance' (Russell 1999: 7). The project will be discussed in more detail in Chapter 11 (p. 311).

The success of the 'Rainbow across Europe' Bulgarian project and the potency of the Orpheus story as a thematic basis suggested the possibility of future projects built on similar lines using stories associated with the geographical locations of existing and new partners in 'Rainbow across Europe'. During visits to Salzburg, I discovered a rich store of legends associated with the Untersberg mountain. Predictions about the resurrection of the legendary Emperor Karl, who is said to sleep on the Untersberg, cry out for dramatic portrayal in music. It is said that when his beard has grown three times round the summit, the ravens no longer circle the mountain and the withered pear tree of Walserfeld sprouts, the trumpets of doom will sound and the battle of Walserfeld will begin. The mountain is supposed to be the haunt of wild women in white gowns – the Wildfrauen – who can become mortal only through the love of a man, but mortals who dare to visit the legendary Great Hall deep in the mountain should beware. Like Rip Van Winkle, they risk being kept there in thrall for a generation. Every Christmas the Wildejagd (Wild Hunt) crosses the mountain in ghostly baying tumult, but go and look for it at your peril! If you are caught by the hunt you are doomed to follow it until doomsday.

Exploratory visits to potential new partners in 'Rainbow across Europe' revealed many sources of suitable themes. Discussions with Joensuu City Orchestra in Finland prompted my research into the Finnish epic the Kalevala, especially for stories associated with Karelia. Vainamoinen's fight with Giant Antero to get the secret spell to finish building his ship, and the story of Lemminkainen and the killing of the Swan of Tuonela are shamanistic in origin, and hinge on the magical uses of music.

Projects in Austria, Ireland and Finland, built on similar lines to *Rituals for Orpheus*, based on local myths or legends, integrating contemporary musical techniques with traditional or folk idioms and instruments, and with full involvement in the creative process from all

280

participants now stand as a future objective for 'Rainbow across Europe'.

My visit to the Podewil Arts Centre in former East Berlin suggested subjects of a more contemporary historical relevance. I already discussed how *Confluence* avoided the worst pitfalls of self-conscious contemporary relevance. Berlin, a city which has been the focus of some of the most violent political divisions of twentieth century Europe, is still haunted by the spectre of its recent history and cries out for the healing effects of artistic catharsis achieved through a sensitive and imaginative treatment. I was aware of the symbolism of walls when I wrote *Woden's Dyke*, seeing this story of ancient political division between Celts and Saxons in Dark-Ages Wessex as symbolic of 'the political division of Berlin, Korea, Cyprus and Ireland' (Laycock, 1988). Although little remains physically of the Berlin Wall, it is still a potent symbol of division between peoples – the very opposite of the cultural integration which the EU seeks to achieve through programmes like 'Culture 2000'. Berlin reminds us forcibly of the historical background against which present-day European moves towards the consolidation of peace through cultural exchange and dialogue are taking place.

Recent contact with members of the UK Chinese Ensemble, and the revelation of plans by the city of Bristol to forge a twinning link with the Chinese city of Guang Zhou (Canton) led me to begin re-searching the viability of the Theoretical Model in a non-European context. I looked for a suitable story to form the basis of a work for education and community performance involving Chinese and Euro-pean musicians which would embody the holistic principles of the theoretical model and could be performed in UK and China. The result was *Mengjiang Weeping at the Wall* (2001).

This two-thousand year old story from the Qin dynasty tells of Mengjiang's epic search for her husband who has been conscripted into a work-gang to build the Great Wall. It dramatises the individual suffering of ordinary people caught up in an authoritarian nightmare. The contemporary relevance is unmistakable. The piece, scored for soprano soloist, community choir, chamber orchestra, and Chinese classical orchestra, contains improvisational windows for interpretation by school groups, and material for a drumming group using huge

Chinese temple drums. A frieze depicting the rising and falling profile of the Great Wall as it crosses the northern provinces of China, forms a back-drop to the performance, and provides a 'conceptual score' for improvisation, an idea borrowed from *Hetty Peglers Tump* (Laycock: 1988). The piece ends with a section of music describing the journey of Mengjiang from west to east along the entire length of the wall. (TC3c+3d).

8. Final performance of Barry Russell's *Gone to play at Mr. Escher's House*.
Dean Clough, Halifax, October 2000.

Chapter 10
The project in action

I turn now to discussion of the stage described by Asher as 'the project'. It is here that the four-phase model comes fully into action. If the model is a good one, it should work equally well for one-off workshops of ninety minutes duration, three-year projects like 'Perform' or 'Confluence', or as a description of the learning process of a child spread over fifteen years. In the Swanwick spiral the progression is achieved through a balanced alternation between 'instruction' by a teacher, and personal 'encounter' by the pupil. As a metaphor for a fifteen-year process, this is a simplification. Clearly there is much more contact time between teacher and pupil than the diagram implies. However, it describes very well the progress of creative music projects of the kind organised by 'Rainbow over Bath'.

The project timetable

The Swanwick Spiral can be used to describe the process by which participants make progress along the 'ability' axis from 'beginner' to 'advanced'. A synthesis of elements borrowed from the Wiegold and Paynter models, with the creativity and framing axes of the theoretical model illustrates the point (Example 66). The diagram could describe a BC3 project in which rehearsal work on composed sections of the piece takes place concurrently with creative composition work on the score windows which becomes more 'instructional' as the project proceeds. The introduction, final rehearsal and performance are located midway along the 'creativity' axis because they combine esthesic and poietic elements.

Example 66.

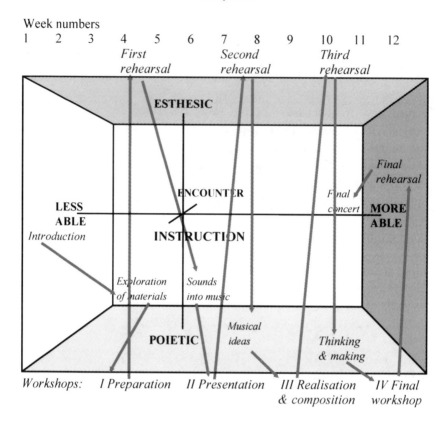

Week numbers
1   2   3   4   5   6   7   8   9   10 11 12
            First   *Second*   *Third*
            rehearsal   *rehearsal*   *rehearsal*

ESTHESIC

Final
rehearsal

ENCOUNTER   F*inal*
LESS   c*oncert*   **MORE**
ABLE   **ABLE**
Introduction   INSTRUCTION

Exploration   *Sounds*
of materials *into music*

                Musical
        POIETIC *ideas*   *Thinking*
                              & making

Workshops: *I Preparation*   *II Presentation*   *III Realisation*   *IV Final*
                                                     & composition   *workshop*

Week numbers are given as for a school term, but the same model can be adapted to many different time-scales. It can form the basis in microcosm for single workshops of ninety minutes duration, for a teachers' Inset day, for an intensive weekend school, or for a twelve-week educational project. The timetable for the 'Composing in Education' project during the Spring term 2000 with Peter Wiegold and Composers Ensemble shows how the four-phase model works in practice for a typical three-month project. In this context the word 'phase' is not synonymous with 'workshop'. Each of the 'phases' encompasses a number of different activities, including workshops, rehearsals, individual group work and classroom sessions with a teacher. The beginnings and endings of the phases are not clear cut.

The workshops stand out like nodal points in a continuous process. Each school receives four workshops, one during each phase of the project.

Example 67: Composers Ensemble project timetable – Spring term 2000.

	Morning	Afternoon	Evening
Inset day			
Fri. 14 Jan.	Inset day: Bath Spa University College; Peter Wiegold, Duncan Prescott		
Phase 1			
Tue. 25 Jan.	Broadlands School, Keynsham; year 10; 10.15–12.15; Duncan Prescott, Mary Wiegold	Somervale School, Midsomer Norton; 13.30–15.15; Duncan Prescott, Mary Wiegold	
Wed. 26			
Thur. 27	Kingdown School, Warminster; year 10; 09.05–10.50; Duncan Prescott, Mary Wiegold		
Phase 2			
Tue. 8 Feb.	Broadlands School, Keynsham; year 10; 10.15–12.15; Mary Wiegold, Phil Sheppard	Somervale School, Midsomer Norton; 13.30–15.15; Mary Wiegold, Phil Sheppard	
Wed. 16	Kingdown School, Warminster; year 10; 09.05–10.50; Peter Wiegold, Duncan Prescott	St. Augustine's School, Trowbridge; 13.30–15.30; Peter Wiegold, Duncan Prescott	University Orchestra; 17.15–19.00; Peter Wiegold, Duncan Prescott

285

Phase 3

Tue. 29 Feb.	Broadlands School, Keynsham; year 10; 10.15–12.15; Mary Wiegold, Tansy Davies	Somervale School, Midsomer Norton; 13.30–15.15; Mary Wiegold, Tansy Davies
Wed. 1 Mar.	Kingdown School, Warminster; year 10; 09.05–10.50; Duncan Prescott, Tansy Davies	St. Augustine's School, Trowbridge; 13.30–15.30pm; Duncan Prescott, Tansy Davies

Phase 4

Tue. 14 Mar.	Broadlands School, Keynsham; year 10; 10.15–12.15; Mary Wiegold, Tansy Davies	Somervale School, Midsomer Norton; 13.30–15.15; Mary Wiegold, Tansy Davies	
Wed. 15	Kingdown School, Warminster; year 10; 09.05–10.50; Duncan Prescott, Tansy Davies	St. Augustine's School, Trowbridge; 13.30–15.30; Tansy Davies, Jolyon Laycock	
Thur. 16	Workshop & recording at Kingdown; clarinet and voice 09.05–11.00; Duncan Prescott, Mary Wiegold, Peter Wiegold	Workshop & recording at Broadlands: 13.30–15.30; Duncan Prescott – clarinet, Sue Knight – viola, Phil Sheppard – cello	Evening rehearsal 18.00 – 21.00 with Tom Kerstens – guitar
Fri. 17	Composers workshop; University of Bath; 10.00–13.00 A level students from Somervale School – full ensemble	Rehearsals for evening concert	Evening concert Arts lecture Theatre; University of Bath 19.30 *Composers Ensemble* plus Tom Kerstens
Sat. 18		Rehearsals: Windows Arts Centre; also music by Ed Zhao and two students from St. Augustine's School	Mid-Somerset Festival concert; 17.00pm; Windows Arts Centre; Adjudication and prize giving

286

Each workshop visit corresponds to one of Swanwick's 'instructional' phases (manipulative, vernacular, idiomatic and systematic). In between visits, participants work on their own, or in collaborative groups, in response to tasks set by the workshop leader, exploring in turn 'materials', 'expression' and 'form' equivalent to Swanwick's 'encounter' phases. The teachers' role is to support and guide the pupils through these encounter periods and to share in the creative process. Music students at Bath Spa, studying on the 'Composing in Education' half-module, participated as workshop assistants, again reinforcing the principle of Schafer's 'Community of learners'.

Phase one

The first workshop is the lead composer's opportunity to establish a rapport with all the participants. This session is equivalent to Wiegold's 'Preparation', a time when warm-up games come into their own. Games imply 'fun': an emphasis on the enjoyment of working together as a group to make sounds. The title of Wishart's *Sounds Fun*, implies as much (Wishart, 1975).

Wiegold has warned against the un-critical use of workshop games. They should never become an end in themselves. If they do, we invite the scepticism of participants. As Paynter once heard a teacher protest: 'Our children are not enthralled by experimenting with sound. They dismiss it as "kid's stuff" […] do not want to play games, but to take part in real tunes and real songs' (Paynter, 1982: 51). The workshop leader must always have a clear idea of the purpose of a musical game, and be able to explain it convincingly to the participants. The following is a progressive list of the purposes of workshop games:

- Awakening mind and body for action.
- Getting to know each other – names and faces.
- Losing inhibitions, encouraging spontaneity.
- Developing concentration and alertness to sound and visual signals.
- Listening to qualities of sound.

- Learning to imitate accurately.
- Developing memory.
- Developing awareness of rhythm, pitch and melody.
- Developing musical invention.
- Developing team-work and ensemble awareness.
- Developing awareness of relationships between sound and body movements.

The sequence of games can be directed in a logical progression towards a planned objective. For instance, song-writing workshops can grow out of getting-to-know-you games in which participants speak or sing their own names. Passing spoken names round in a circle is an undemanding, low-key way to start a workshop on a cold winter morning and helps strangers, including workshop directors, to memorise them. But the process soon develops into more stimulating activities perhaps using different styles of vocal delivery (operatic, sergeant-major, bossy teacher etc.). With responsive students, the process can turn into full-scale vocal improvisation: a process which is moving towards exploration of the raw material of sound, the other aspect of Wiegold's 'Preparation'.

We kept the multi-cultural aims of the Ensemble Esoterica project firmly in mind when we played 'call-and-response' games designed to encourage the accurate imitation of rhythmic patterns. 'Accuracy' in this case meant not only getting note values correct, but also 'getting into the groove' of the rhythms so that they 'felt' like Reggae or Blues and so on.

As Sean Gregory showed in his 'Feeling in Time' workshops, rhythmic impetus is an important ingredient. When all participants are swaying to the same compelling pulse, treading from side to side in synchronised bodily movement, inhibitions fade and even the shyest find personal expression in sound without thinking about it. This is the atmosphere in which spontaneous music begins to happen. It will be the job of later project phases to fix and notate some of these fleeting images and organise them systematically into a formal composition.

Many originators of creative composition work have stressed the value of improvisation as a generator of musical material, but it is not the only way to begin. Many ingenious devices have been evolved to cope with that moment of paralysis when the composer is confronted with the 'full horror' of an empty sheet of manuscript paper. Games

288

which use observable features in the surrounding environment to create musical patterns were the starting point for a GCSE composition project with the Composers Ensemble in 2000. The idea originated from a clapping game in which children in a circle clapped once for a girl, twice for a boy, and three times for someone with a pair of glasses. The result was an iso-rhythm which could be clothed in melody. Asking people to start several waves of the rhythm in canon, perform it backwards and forwards at the same time, or suddenly mix up the order of the circle, creating a completely new and unpredictable rhythm, kept them on their toes.

Faced with a group of youngsters with rudimentary music-reading skills at the start of a GCSE composition project, we asked them each to write down a random sequence of noughts and crosses. Clarinettist Duncan Prescott 'interpreted' these 'scores', playing noughts as high notes and crosses as low notes, or vice-versa. Children quickly caught on to the idea of making up simple two-note compositions for clarinet, a task which could be readily set for them in the intervening weeks before our next visit. The final objective was the composition of individual pieces for clarinet and voice. The 'noughts and crosses' game served as an introduction to the sounds of the clarinet, showing how the words 'high' and 'low' have different meanings relative to the compass of the instrument – anything from notes a minor third apart, to sounds at the extreme ends of the register.

This was an example of a project which needed a dual starting point. It was inadequate to set the task of writing just anything for clarinet and voice. The voice needed words to sing. This was a school in a semi-rural location, so we asked children to compose their own short lyrics about the contrast between city and country life – two tasks to complete before our next visit, and something the class teacher was well-equipped to help them with (rainbow: Track 34).

For them, the second phase of the project was concerned with how to find melodic shapes for the verbal texts they had created, a process which continued after the second workshop. They were expected to turn up to the third workshop with sketches for complete songs.

The first 'Preparation' workshop is likely to conform to the four-phase model in microcosm. In other words it will be a complete self-contained project in miniature. Participants will work individually or in small groups on ideas which have emerged during games, or as part of the exploration of sounds. We might ask instrumentalists working in small groups to find as many unconventionally produced sounds on their instruments as they can. They will also listen to musical examples which may later be used as a model, for instance a performance of short songs for clarinet and voice, but the emphasis will be on the sound of the instruments and their technical capabilities. The groups will come together at the end of the workshop to 'show and share' the results of individual work.

Likewise, all later workshops can conform to the four-phase model in microcosm. They will begin with some preparation in the form of games, but the emphasis will be less on their use as a source of creative ideas, and more on awakening mind and body for action, removal of inhibitions which will certainly have re-asserted themselves in the intervening weeks, and re-establishment of an attitude of concentration and alertness, becoming more focused with each succeeding phase. There will be a move 'to deepen the tone of the workshop' as Wiegold has put it (Wiegold, 1997: 1–2).

Phase two

The second-phase workshop, described by Wiegold as 'Presentation', is concerned with a higher-order of musical organisation – with forms and processes. This phase is equivalent to Swanwick's 'Imitation of vernaculars' (Swanwick 1988: 78). Grand Union, during the 'Silk Road' project, introduced examples of different forms of eastern music at this stage such as sitar improvisations by Baluji Shrivasta, or Miao Xiao Yun playing the Chinese pipa. Music for the pipa is particularly useful because it is nearly always programmatic, telling stories of heroic battles with sword strokes or the clamour of hand-to-hand fighting depicted by spectacular 'rasguado' effects. But it is also very simple in its musical means, achieving optimum expressivity with

290

only five notes. The value of the pentatonic scale was well understood by Kodály and Orff, and its potential as a harmonic and melodic framework for improvisation in creative music work is widely recognised (Orff, 1978: 66).

The second workshop is also the time to introduce more elaborate modes. A feature of Barry Russell's projects have been his invented modes, often based on modules other than an octave. It is during this phase that participants begin to become familiar with their particular colours, and to work with them in an improvisational way. Russell has developed a large repertoire of practical devices, and he is able to work with large groups of instrumentalists to create, with surprising rapidity, dense orchestral and choral textures which are musically convincing and harmonically rich. Such reservoirs of notes are used as the basis of improvisational work in *Symphony for large ensemble* (Example 68).

Russell's projects for 'Rainbow' have been open as to age and ability, but strong as to musical classification in that they have been based on stylistic features typical of his wider compositional work. At this second phase he introduces processes and forms based on improvisation within defined parameters to create dense masses of sound which move and change, or contrast dramatically. Examples used in *Rituals for Orpheus* included the concept of a 'musical labyrinth'. Instrumentalists walk slowly in straight lines across the stage, playing long held single notes. Every time they change direction, as if at a corner in an imaginary labyrinth, they also change the note they are playing. Such a device underlines Russell's debt to Cardew, in particular Paragraph VII of *The Great Learning* (Cardew, 1968). In *Symphony for Large Ensemble*, the same approach is applied to groups of notes arranged in a matrix of boxes (Example 69).

Example 68: Russell, B. (1999) Symphony for Large Ensemble, p.19.

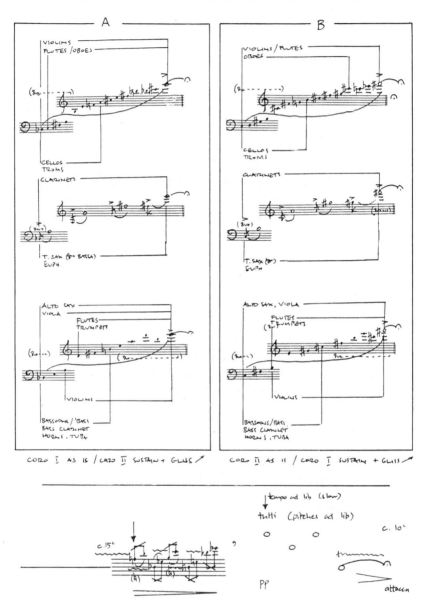

Example 69: Russell, B. (1999) Symphony for Large Ensemble, p.17.

labyrinth (iv)

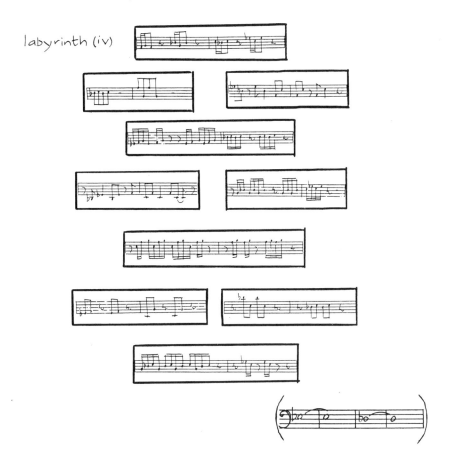

Mid-project meeting

The period between the second and third phases of the project is the time when ideas begin to take on a tangible form and to be written down or recorded in some way. Song melodies take shape, melodic and rhythmic ostinati emerge from improvisational work, and modal structures are agreed on. We will not see finished compositions but, rather, the musical ideas out of which they will be built. In a project led by Rob Smith in 1997 whose aim was to experiment with amplified small sounds to produce sound-scapes, the pre-third-phase activity consisted of developing and perfecting the technical production of sounds which had been discovered by experiment during the second phase.

This also seems to be a moment when problems are beginning to surface, including misunderstandings about aims and objectives which may have been latent from the start. Russell, in his report on *Rituals for Orpheus*, refers to 'The usual second workshop syndrome' (Russell, 1999: 7). It is essential to confront such problems and discover viable solutions before disagreements become entrenched. I discussed in Chapter 8 (p. 261) how uncertainties inherent in the creative process make it impossible to pre-determine the final outcome. By the time we reach the third phase things should start to become clearer, and it is an important moment to take stock.

Frequent meetings of the project team are valuable at any time but we found that a mid-project meeting, before the phase-three workshops, was essential. Continuing assessment should be an integral part of the creative process, feeding back into the workshops at every stage. Students can help with this process by keeping minutes, and producing their own reports. In Bulgaria, the Cardew team met every morning before starting the day's work. During the Ensemble Esoterica project, weekly seminars with the student workshop assistants provided a valuable forum for problem analysis and diagnosis.

The project may be losing focus for a variety of reasons. Participants are bound up in individual creative processes with no awareness of the general picture. Different groups and individuals will be responding to the project in different ways, and there is a need to compare these differences. Ideas may turn out to be too ambitious. Participants may be responding badly and require remedial action. Teachers or students may be losing confidence in their own abilities because of apparent lack of progress. They may be losing confidence in the project because of problems in motivating children to take it seriously. There may be failures of communication, disagreements about working methods, problems of discipline and control of unruly classes, failure of the workshop leaders or visiting professional team to

294

understand children's levels of ability, arguments about lack of professionalism or breakdowns in inter-personal relationships. There may be practical problems with timetabling, availability of musical instruments, practice rooms and so on, sometimes caused by unforeseen developments of a creative and artistic nature which ideally we want to encourage. Considerable powers of leadership and diplomacy are required of the workshop leader to keep the project on course.

It is instructive to examine some of the problems which arose during this phase with the Grand Union *Silk Road* project. The project was targeted at a strategic and geographically 'open' selection of primary, secondary and tertiary educational establishments. Two of the schools, St. George's Community School and Cabot Primary, are racially mixed with a high proportion of children from Afro-Caribbean, Indian and Pakistani backgrounds. Although the children from both of these schools participated enthusiastically in workshops on their own school promises, it proved difficult to persuade all of them to leave their familiar home ground for the final rehearsal and performance at the University of Bath. Prompt identification of the problem meant we had time to lay on emergency transportation.

This highlights the problems which can arise in creative projects which aim to be socially inclusive. Project organisers have to be sensitive towards the different cultural attitudes towards out-of-school activities, particularly within Afro-Caribbean communities. Unwillingness of members of such communities to venture into what can be seen by them as alien white-dominated environments such as Arts Centres or Universities is a real issue with a bearing on wider questions of cultural integration. Collaboration with locally-based organisations, such as Multi-A, dedicated to fostering social inclusion through the arts can be crucial. They were prepared to find the money to remove as many practical obstacles as possible, such as helping with coach hire.

Remedial intervention from Multi-A failed to prevent one of the schools dropping out of the project altogether. This was a primary school unfortunately typical of many in the Bristol/Bath area in that there was no teacher qualified in music. The class teacher confessed to a lack of musical training during the preliminary inset day. The school failed its Ofsted inspection a year before and was 'statemented' for a year. Members of our workshop team agreed to make a special effort to support the teacher. Student project assistants made extra visits, and did more than enough to make up for any deficiencies of the class teacher.

The school's fundamental lack of internal leadership, and refusal to accept responsibility for its participation in the project was expressed first of all by the last-minute cancellation of a crucial penultimate workshop. They had just heard the good news that they had passed their Ofsted, and wanted to give the children an impromptu celebratory party. We could understand their elation, but their decision to cancel the workshop was taken on the spur of the moment when our workshop team could not be contacted.

The school finally withdrew altogether, claiming that parents had not given the necessary permission for the children to take part. We felt great disappointment, not only because of the loss of one of the schools in what turned out otherwise to be a most stimulating and successful project, but because we knew that the children themselves had derived enormous enjoyment form the workshops, and had been extremely committed. Many had responded through dance rather than music, creating dance sequences in response to the sitar improvisations of Baluji Shrivastav. In line with the principles of inclusiveness expressed in this book, we should not give up on this school, but seek opportunities to involve them in future projects, applying the lessons learnt from this setback.

The 1999 Ensemble Esoterica project was beset by organisational problems from its inception, many of them springing from cultural differences between communities. This project was to have been a major part of the second year of the 'Composing in the Community' programme funded by 'Arts for Everyone' in Autumn 1998. Even a year's postponement was not enough to solve all the many problems of this ambitious undertaking, originally styled as two one-act operas: Paul Gladstone Reid *One Day We Will No Longer Sing the Blues* and Tunde Jegede *The Return*. Escalating production costs including unforeseen requests for costume hire, additional lighting, and extra rehearsals compelled a drastic reduction in size and complexity. Some problems seemed to be related to lack of organisation on the part of the ensemble, probably due to over-work since both composers were involved in at least two other major productions at the same time.

296

The extensive educational project began on 28 September and culminated in a final concert at the Michael Tippett Centre on 1 December. The dates are significant because they show a timetable which deviates to some extent from the four-phase model. Although the deviation was forced on us for practical reasons (availability of artists and so on), it provided useful lessons about the loss of focus which occurs when the climax of an educational project (Paynter stage C) becomes disassociated from its musical model (Paynter stage D). As I discussed in Chapter 4 (p. 157), placing stage D earlier in the process strengthens 'framing' by making it more instructional. But this pre-supposes that participants in the educational project can be persuaded actually to attend the performance (Example 70).

Example 70: Ensemble Esoterica – Project timetable – Autumn 1999.

	Morning	Afternoon	Evening
Fri. 10 Sept.	Inset day – teachers	Inset day	
Phase 1 Tue. 28 Sept.		Chew Valley School Eugene Skeef; 13.30	University Samba club Eugene Skeef; 19.00
Wed. 29	St. Marks; year 10; Eugene Skeef; 09.00	Lime Grove Special Eugene Skeef; 13.40	
Thur. 30		Ralph Allen School Cleveland Watkiss; 13.30–15.30	Percy Boys Club after school club Cleveland Watkiss
Fri. 1 Oct.	St. Marks – year 10 Cleveland Watkiss; 10.00	Hartcliffe School Cleveland Watkiss; 13.15–15.30	
Wed. 6 Oct.	BSUC students; Paul Gladstone Reid; 09.00	PGCE talk	

Phase 2

Tue. 12 Oct.		Chew Valley School Diane Charlemagne, Paul G.R.; 13.30	University Samba Diane Charlemagne, Paul G.R.; 19.00
Wed. 13	BSUC students Diane Charlemagne, Paul G. R.; 09.00	Ralph Allen School Diane Charlemagne, Paul Gladstone Reid	
Thur. 14		Clarendon, Trow-bridge; Eugene Skeef; 13.45	Riverside group 16.30
Fri. 15	St. Marks; year 10; Eugene Skeef; 10.15	Hartcliffe School Eugene Skeef; 13.15	

Sat. 30 Oct.	Get-in	Rehearsals	Ensemble Esoterica professional concert

Phase 3

Tue. 9 Nov.		Chew Valley School Paul Gladstone Reid, Tunde Jegede; 13.30	
Wed. 10	BSUC students; Paul Gladstone Reid Tunde Jegede; 09.00	Lime Grove Special Paul Gladstone Reid, Tunde Jegede; 13.40	
Thur. 11		Clarendon, Trow-bridge; Jan Hendrikse, Tunde Jegede; 13.45	
Fri. 12	St. Marks School Jan Hendrikse, Tunde Jegede; 10.15	Harcliffe School Jan Hendrikse, Tunde Jegede	

298

Phase 4

Tue. 23 Nov.		Chew Valley School Diane Charlemagne, Paul G.R.; 13.30
Wed. 24	BSUC students Diane Charlemage, Paul Gladstone Reid	Ralph Allen School Diane Charlemagne, Paul Gladstone Reid
Thur. 25		Clarendon, Trowbridge; Eugene Skeef
Fri. 26	St. Mark's School Eugene Skeef	Hartcliffe School Eugene Skeef; 13.15

Wed. 1 Dec. Final workshop day:

Time	Compton Room 112 own material	Compton G01 Group material; Gospel	Lunch
09.45–10.30	Ralph Allen; rehearsal		
10.30–11.15	Chew Valley Rehearsal	St. Mark's School	
11.30–12.15	Clarendon; rehearsal	Harcliffe	
12.15–13.00	St. Marks; rehearsal	Chew Valley Ralph Allen Clarendon	Clarendon School Hartcliffe School St. Mark's, Chew Valley, Ralph Allen
13.00–13.45	Hartcliffe; rehearsal		
14.00–15.30	Group rehearsals in Tippett Centre; Gospel songs		
15.30–17.30	Full dress rehearsal		
17.30–18.30	Break for tea		
18.30–19.00	Assemble for performance		
19.00–20.30	Public Performance		

During this project, young people from secondary schools in Bristol and Bath created their own music in response to the theme of music with its roots in Africa. Additional workshops took place at Lime Grove Special School, with the University Samba Band, and a newly formed group of singers which subsequently consolidated itself as the University of Bath Gospel, A-capella, Soul and Pop Choir (GASP).

An important difference between the Esoterica and Grand Union education programmes was the absence of a dedicated workshop co-ordinator. In the case of Ensemble Esoterica, although Orchestra members led individual workshops, none, including the two composers, were able to undertake an overall co-ordinating role. I was obliged to make up for these deficiencies even though I, as local organiser, was neither closely involved with the ensemble and its work, nor skilled in any of its musical idioms.

In spite of these problems, I welcomed Rainbow's involvement in this genuine creative engagement with issues of multi-culturalism through music, a subject which was central to the aims and objectives of the Arts Council Lottery programme, and the EU 'Agenda 2000' programme. The volatility of the artistic content introduced an element of uncertainty and adventure which is to be welcomed in any creative music project. Part of the teaching and learning value lies in the stimulation of discovering creative solutions.

Phase three

Third-phase workshops are a time for detailed work. Wiegold suggests that the workshop leader may now need to adopt a more 'instructive' approach. Participants will have work to show, either written, or in performance. There will be an atmosphere of critical discussion about the effectiveness of musical ideas. The workshop will be concerned with problems of notation and finally how individual musical ideas can be put together to create larger structures.

Before the fourth-phase workshops, participants will work individually or in groups to create the larger structures of their compositions, or, in the case of a large communal project, their own individual sections of the final performance.

Works in BC4 may need a longer period while composers incorporate material generated during workshops into their own compositions.

Phase four

The fourth phase (Wiegold's rehearsal and performance) can be a more complex undertaking spread over several days. In all 'Rainbow' projects, with the exception of Ensemble Esoterica, phase four included an element representing Paynter stage D: either a separate professional concert, or performances by professional musicians as part of the final concert of the creative project. During phase four, the workshop leader will visit each school or group to hear finished group-pieces, and to discuss and implement final adjustments and modifications. This will also be the time to learn material which is to form the basis of large-scale tuttis when all participants join forces such as the Gospel songs in the Esoterica project. In spite of earlier problems, the final concert of this project was well structured and well-organised, and achieved the level of cathartic climax which is an essential ingredient of a successful project.

The smooth running of the event was due to Ian Burton, the tutor for the BA Composing in Education module, in holding together the group of nearly a hundred young people. On an individual level, children of often rather indifferent musical abilities surprised themselves with the emotional and atmospheric power of their own creative work. The cathartic outcome of the project as a whole depended on the personal charisma of Paul Gladstone Reid, and particularly his prowess as a Gospel singer and pianist. His inspirational leadership of the massed choral singing of *I hope to see you there* in the two group-climaxes gave shape to the concert. However, it was disappointing that these were Gospel classics, and not songs created by the young people themselves.

Individual composition projects need a different approach at the fourth phase. Ideally a professional ensemble plays the students' works in a composition workshop during which any necessary modifications are suggested and put in place. It is important that completed scores and parts are ready for this phase. A project led by Tansy Davies and mentored by John Woolrich, which I observed at North Kesteven School Lincoln in April 2001, had failed to solve notation problems in one of the two schools involved. Scores and parts were badly presented. These key-stage 4 and A level students had been working for six months on the composition of short pieces for the Schidlof Quartet, and in that time should have been able to produce material to a much better standard.

The students from Guthlaxton School had used computer notation software, but basic computer errors were not corrected. The scores showed all the signs of last-minute production, using technology which was not well understood. Although one piece, *The Question*, was passionate and expressionistic, the written score gave the players many problems in understanding its unnecessary rhythmic complexities (rainbow: Track 35). Students attended a performance of Woolrich's 2nd Quartet the previous October, at the very beginning of the project – an example of Paynter stage D in its most instructional position. Apart from that, there was no other encounter between the young composers and even one string player in a practical session of idiomatic string writing at close quarters. Final scores and parts had not been submitted and checked before the final workshop, an illustration of how detrimental the omission of such vital phases in a project can be.

Students, for whom the opportunity to write music for string quartet and hear it played by leading professionals should have been a valuable and unique educational experience, failed to derive anything like the full benefit. This was remarkable in view of the considerable reputation of the Schidlof Quartet in the field of education, and the fact that Guthlaxton School was a participant in Odam and Paterson's *A Creative Dream* (Odam & Paterson, 2000). Pupils at the same school produced exceptionally good work for the Philharmonia Orchestra *Antarctic Waves* project related to the world première of

Peter Maxwell Davies' Symphony a few weeks later, alongside pupils from Norwood School, Leicester (rainbow: Track 36).

The importance of a final performance has been widely discussed. Paynter and Aston saw performance as a way in which pupils could experience each other's response to the same musical concept (Paynter's stage C). Sharp and Dust question whether a final performance is always a desirable outcome, suggesting that it can apply too much pressure on pupils. They admit however that in most cases it does provide a useful goal (Sharp & Dust, 1992: 15). I believe it provides an essential challenge, and brings that sense of catharsis which is its own reward. There is pressure to have the composition ready, but learning to cope with deadlines is one of life's lessons, and knowing how to help participants manage the pressure is part a workshop leader's job. We want to give participants a chance to experience 'the thrill of going before an audience and risking all' (Wiegold, 1997), to rise to the challenge and surpass what they previously thought was the limit of their ability. Otherwise they will not have progressed.

The timetables for Ensemble Esoterica and Grand Union show how the final rehearsal and performance was managed in 'Rainbow' projects. The final group rehearsal is a co-ordination session, bringing all the disparate elements together and running through the concert from beginning to end. Before this can happen, the workshop leader must plan the order of events and the disposition of participants on the stage.

The Gribbin/Smith *Parents and Children* project in 1997 showed how badly things can go wrong if anything is left to chance. The vital co-ordination meeting failed to take place due to late arrivals by professional musicians from London. Problems were compounded because we were overwhelmed by the size of the audience. The concert turned out to be too long because of stage-management problems. It was only because Rob Smith, realising the need for a continuity announcer, jumped in at the last minute to provide verbal links that any sense of overall coherence was achieved. This final concert failed to achieve an effective climax, leaving the audience bored and restless, and the participating children unfulfilled, in spite of the high quality of much of the material. The seventh condition of openness remained unfulfilled.

The four-phase model in projects of long duration

This chapter has concentrated on the application of the four-phase model to projects of around twelve weeks duration. Projects of longer duration which develop over periods ranging from many months to several years may conform to more complex timetables applying the four-phase model in a variety of different ways. As I discussed in Chapter 2 (p. 84), each of the three Merseyside Boroughs in the ground-breaking 1985 Gemini Project followed a different pattern over the seven months of the residency. Other programmes of long duration might consist of a sequence of self-contained projects, each conforming to the four-phase model. This was true of three-year projects such as the 'Rainbow over Bath' 'Composing in Education' programme, and St. George's 'Perform'.

'Perform' gave the same small group of students the opportunity to progress as individuals through the series of self-contained projects. Although individual projects in 'Rainbow' and 'Perform' each achieved their own climax through a final performance, there was no overall celebration at the close of the three years.

Confluence was planned strategically over three years towards a final climax. Specific strands developed during the programme, and were celebrated in the final performance. The River Stour was a potent metaphor for progression in time, and the siting of this final concert in Christchurch Priory at the mouth of the river was powerfully symbolic: the end of the river's journey; the end of the project in time.

Chapter 11
The final performance

I have referred repeatedly to the all-important moment of catharsis of a final performance. It is the ability to evoke, unify and support corporate human emotion without the use of the spoken word which contributes to music's special qualities among the arts. The emotional catharsis which can overwhelm both performers and audience at the final performance of a creative music project is what gives such experiences their unique social and cultural value. With this quality, it will be an experience which they remember for the rest of their lives. Without it, the memory will soon fade.

This is not to say that an uplifting final performance can make up for the deficiencies of a badly conceived and badly run project. Overlooking artistic imperfections in the euphoria of the final performance was listed as an example of a 'closed' attitude to the 'bottom-up' approach to project conception in Chapter 8 (pp. 250–251). Very few things in life, and particularly in the arts, are ever perfect, but if all participants in a well-conceived creative project have aspired, to the best of their ability, to attain all the requirements of the theoretical model, the final performance will become a celebration of something achieved. It is one of the most important ways that a creative project can achieve the third and fourth 'conditions of openness' – an opportunity for participants to take personal pride and satisfaction from their creative contribution.

Such emotional engagement comes across loud and clear in the full-throated singing of a procession of two hundred small pirates who trooped out at the end of the final concert of the *Pirates and Heroes* song-writing project run by the Musiko-Musika team of Mauricio Venegas-Astorga and Rachel Pantin at Newport, Isle of Wight, in July 2001 (rainbow: Track 37).

The nature of emotional catharsis

The rather generalised phrase 'emotional catharsis' embraces a wide range of emotional states. John Paynter has discussed more precise definitions of the nature of this overwhelming 'power' (Paynter, 1997b). Our contemporary Western European culture finds difficulty in the precise expression of personal feelings and emotions, in contrast to the classical music of India where the nine states of emotion, or 'rasa', are precisely defined. Even without a precise vocabulary of this kind, music can help to make the expression, or rather the evocation of many nuances of feeling and emotion much more precise. Such an emotional involvement with the creative outcome operates on both a group, and individual level.

The ability to achieve this charge of emotion is not dependent on musical style. As Carl Orff discovered, it has more to do with the most primitive elements of music: pulse, repetition, the building of climaxes through the accumulation of repeated elements: features shared among many styles. It is a quality achieved in various 'Rainbow' projects by the dynamic creative energy of composers as diverse as Sean Gregory whose idiom is essentially experimental and improvisational, or Paul Gladstone Reid, whose music relies on the ecstatic repetitions of Revivalist gospel singing. Such projects have resulted in many different emotional states which, following the example of the nine Indian Rasas, could attract labels such as 'Triumphal', 'Tragic', 'Ecstatic', 'Tranquil', 'Mystical', 'Joyful', 'Frenzied' and so on. This power is not necessarily a force for good when it is used to provoke feelings of destructive anger, leading to violent social disorder, or to inspire and support feelings of extreme nationalism leading to political fanaticism and intolerance, but with enlightened and inspirational leadership, music's power can be wholly positive.

The twentieth century was a time of debate about the emotional power of music. Kodály's view of a good musician emphasised four areas of training of equal importance, of which one was concerned specifically with the emotions: 1. Trained ear; 2. Trained intellect; 3. A trained heart; 4. Trained hands (Kodály; cited in Szönyi, 1961: 25).

The Hadow Report recognised the importance of emotional expression in music: '[...] in no subject is there so much scope for the disciplined and corporate expression of the emotions' (Hadow, 1931).

Some composers of the twentieth century have rejected emotional expression in music. Writing in 1957 Cage exhorts us: 'to let sounds be themselves rather than vehicles for man-made theories, or expression of human sentiments' (Cage, 1967: 10), echoing Boulez' similar desire 'to eliminate from my vocabulary absolutely all trace of heritage' (Boulez, 1952; cited in Nyman, 1974: 60). Such philosophy gave rise to genres of music dissonant in sonority, dis-continuous in syntactical development, aggressive, fractured and histrionic in gesture. Far from being devoid of emotion, untutored listeners might find such music expressive of anguished and tortured human reactions to a cruel and alienating industrial world. Yet those who created it denied vehemently that what they were writing contained any emotional expression at all, but was an exploration and development of abstract forms and shapes, or of sounds in their own right.

Stravinsky's attempts to write music which was devoid of emotional expression resulted in the creation of stage works such as 'Oedipus Rex' where the stylisation and objectivity of the music leads to a sense of heightened emotion. As Chris Small has commented:

> Stravinsky's music generally lacks any form of outward emotional display. It presents, like an African ritual mask, a deadpan face, with all the impassivity of a priest performing the mass, and just as, for a Christian believer, the ceremony can be a powerful emotional experience, so can the music (Small, 1977: 110).

The writers of *All our Futures* detected a renaissance in the idea of emotional expression in the arts:

> In recent years there has been a new recognition of the vital importance of what David Goleman (1996) calls emotional intelligence: the ability to understand, express and use our feelings and intuition... There are many ways in schools of enabling young people to discuss and express their feelings and emotions. Among the most important are the arts (Robinson, 1999: 39).

But there was a difference between giving direct vent to feelings, as in a cry of pain or jump for joy, and the creative processes of the arts: 'Composing and playing music, writing poetry, making a dance may all be driven by powerful emotional impulses; but the process is not simply one of discharging feelings [...] but of giving them form and meaning' (ibid.: 121). This section of the report reaches a climax with an impassioned statement of belief:

> The arts are concerned with understanding and expressing, the qualities of human experiences. Through music, dance, visual arts, drama and the rest, we try to give forms to the feeling and perceptions that move us most as human beings: our experiences of love, grief, belonging, and isolation, and all the currents of feeling that constitute our experience of ourselves and of others. It is through the arts in all their forms that young people experiment with and try to articulate their deepest feelings and their own sense of cultural identity and belonging. A balanced arts education has essential roles in the creative and cultural development of young people (Robinson, 1999: 121).

The importance of emotional engagement

Our judgement of the quality of the work of individual pupils and students during 'Rainbow' projects stresses emotional engagement. We look for the creation of an effective atmosphere, something which can often be achieved by the simplest of means.

When a pupil's work has grown out of real emotional engagement with the material, he or she is likely to develop a feeling of ownership over the work. Conversely a lack of 'ownership' is at the root of the kind of scepticism alluded to in this study. Scraps of manuscript left lying around unclaimed in the classroom are symptomatic of a lack of ownership. When teachers or workshop leaders are too ready to praise a student's merest insignificant dottings simply because he or she has created them, it is hardly surprising if the student is inclined to regard both the teacher and the work with contempt.

On the other hand, a young composer can be taken by surprise by the degree of emotional charge contained within a simple melodic phrase he or she has written when it is played by skilled musicians. A revelatory experience of this kind it just what is needed to inspire the self confidence a pupil or student needs to carry on work as a composer.

The April 2000 'Rainbow' project with the Composers Ensemble led by Peter Wiegold, which I discussed in Chapter 10 (p. 284), provided a boost to the confidence of a range of pupils at both GCSE and A level by showing how much emotional charge could be contained in a simple melodic phrase. Previously, these students had access, at best, only to their own in-expert skill on musical instruments, or at worst, only to poor quality electronic keyboards and headphones. As a result of a 'Rainbow' project, they heard their compositional attempts brought vividly to life by expert professional musicians who accorded the work as much seriousness of attention as they gave to an established composer.

Not all the work produced by the pupils in this project was of a high quality, but some at least showed potential, and when there was any special quality, it was manifested for all to hear. Amongst the GCSE group were two young composers whose work, when written down, or played imperfectly on electric keyboards, seemed unremarkable in comparison with that of their class-mates. Of these, one boy was so severely disabled by partial sightedness, that he found it almost impossible to write his music down. The class teacher and I acted as his amanuensis. What he produced was a melodic line for solo viola of such grace and melancholic beauty that few who heard it at the final concert were unmoved (rainbow: Track 38).

The second boy wrote a brief trio for clarinet, viola and cello which, when written out, looked clumsy and ill-conceived. His central focus was a melodic line in the Lydian mode of sinuous beauty, surrounded by a luminous colouristic halo. The composer himself can only have been able dimly to guess at the effectiveness of this before the workshop performance. Again, all who heard the piece were convinced by its sense of colour and atmosphere (rainbow: Track 39).

With such a project, it was important to do everything we could to encourage the pupils' sense of emotional commitment and ownership of their own work. We produced a compilation CD of the results of the whole project (some forty minutes of music in all), and gave a copy to each pupil who took part.

Listeners might appreciate such qualities of grace, melancholic beauty, or luminosity by listening to these compositions in the rehearsal room or on their CD players at home, but the sense of occasion present at a public concert heightens the emotional response. The intensity of the performer's interpretation of the piece is influenced by the mood of attentive corporate listening. The appreciative applause which follows celebrates the creative achievement and gives it greater value.

The emotional charge present in the final performance may be increased for those who know something of the creative struggle behind the achievement. The partially sighted boy at one stage lost the written score of his piece, not realising the importance of this visual record for sighted teachers and musicians. The lad himself relied almost completely on his own memory which, though already well developed, was far from accurate. He created musical material of an effective kind on an electric keyboard, but when asked to repeat it could usually only manage a version which resembled the first attempt in very general terms. He was incapable of recreating his first attempt without introducing variations. It was our task to help him move towards a definitive written-down version of his ideas which could be presented to a performing musician.

Unfortunately, he lost the first draft during a half-term break and, being unable to recognise the difference between one piece of paper and another, had no means of searching for it amongst his other papers. The whole piece had to be reconstructed with the help of his teacher. From this experience he learnt an important lesson about relating to, and communicating with, the sighted world around him. For those of us who knew of this incident, the final performance was all the more moving.

Barry Russell and the Cardew Ensemble:
Rituals for Orpheus

Rituals for Orpheus was an outstanding example of how a high level of cathartic climax can be achieved. Our team worked in Plovdiv for ten days with two youth choirs, two folk bands, a wind orchestra, an accordion orchestra and children from an institution for abandoned street children – a total of a hundred and eighty children and young people – to produce a public performance in the city's magnificent open-air Roman amphitheatre, attended by over two thousand people and filmed by Bulgarian National TV. Two students from Bath Spa University College accompanied us as trainee project assistants. The English language school in Plovdiv provided some of their senior students to act as interpreters thus giving them valuable practical experience in the English language.

Involvement of the street children from the Rada Kirkovitch Institute was an important symbolic gesture. Such 'openness' is an accepted part of many creative projects in Britain, but to the Bulgarians it was a new idea. Russell ensured that these socially underprivileged children played an important and conspicuous role in the final performance of *Rituals for Orpheus*, singing the 'Creeping Song' of fearful souls entering the underworld which opened the performance (Example 71). However these six-to-nine-year-olds were by no means musical novices. In his report, Russell remarks: 'I was struck by their sheer delight in performance and their strong performance skills' (Russell, 1999: 6).

Our collaborators were the 'White, Green and Red' Jazz Formation and the National Academy of Folk Music and Dance Art, Plovdiv. Though not officially a twin town of Bath, Plovdiv was adopted by 'Rainbow' after I met representatives of 'White, Green and Red' at an international jazz conference in Bath in 1997 and discovered that both cities were settled by the Romans and boast of legendary 'seven hills'. I made an exploratory visit to Plovdiv in April 1998. This was to be a bipartite project with an exchange of artists and ensembles between our two cities, beginning with *A Bridge to*

311

Bulgaria in Bath in March 1999. In April 1999 we held preliminary sessions with Bulgarian teachers and group leaders – the equivalent of a UK teachers' Inset day. We returned to Plovdiv again in September with the full 'Cardew' team to work with the young people themselves.

Example 71: Russell, B. (1999) Extract from *Rituals for Orpheus.*

Creeping Song

Example 72: *Rituals for Orpheus* – organisations and groups taking part.

Organisation	Group	Ages	No.	Instruments, repertoire etc.
Luben Caravelov School	Folk Orchestra	14–17	20	Kaval, rebek, gadulka, tambura.
(Teachers: Sasha Sterva and Todor Todorov)				
Cyril Metodi School	Folk Orchestra	14–17	20	Kaval, rebek, gadulka, tambura
	Girls choir	14–17	40	Classical and folk repertoire
(Teachers: Vitchka Nikolova and Radiana Dimitrova)				
Plovdiv Boys Choir		9–11	30	Bulgarian music, folk songs
(Teacher: Lili Slavova)				
Plovdiv Music School	Wind Orchestra	14–17	45	Orchestral woodwind & brass
(Teacher: Stravka Andreiva)				
	Accordion Group	14–17	12	Piano accordions
Rada Kirkovitch	Childen's Choir	6–9	25	Mixed voices of all abilities
(Institution for abandoned children)				
Cornelius Cardew Ensemble		adult	6	Flute, trumpet, cello, piano, percussion, voice

Example 73: Matrix analysis of *Rituals for Orpheus.*

It is useful to analyse how the four-phase model was applied in a relatively distant east European country. All organisations concerned gave the project their full commitment. They were willing to re-schedule normal school timetables, and even agreed to work on a national public holiday. The timetable (Example 74) shows how most participants enjoyed four full workshop sessions. Those who did not, such as the Wind Orchestra and the Accordion Orchestra, were given extended sessions as part of the final rehearsal and co-ordination session in the Amphitheatre on the day of the performance. Plovdiv

Children's Choir persuaded us to offer them an extra workshop, making a total of five. The timetable shows the importance of strategic deployment of members of the Cardew Ensemble, all of whom were skilled workshop leaders with several years experience of working as a team with Barry Russell. With such a large group of young people working intensively over ten days, it was impossible for Russell himself to lead all the workshops.

An analysis of the elements – some musical and some extra-musical – which contributed to the emotional content of *Rituals for Orpheus* demonstrates the many added benefits of international projects. The early involvement of teachers and group leaders six months before the start of the project led to a high level of anticipation and excitement, and to their full commitment and emotional engagement throughout.

Part of this excitement was due to the fact that we were a group from outside the country, imbued with exotic curiosity value. Bulgaria suffered enormous economic deprivation during the closing years of the communist administration, and continues to do so during the difficult and protracted process of reconstruction. We were seen as representatives of a self-confident and successful western social and economic system in which they were anxious to participate. They wanted to learn as much as possible of the secrets of our success in order to apply this in their own institutions.

We were also seen as a means of escape for those artists and musicians looking for a way to present their own cultural traditions to the wider European world. Pupils and students saw clearly that the success of their own futures lay in seeking opportunities to travel outside Bulgaria, and in becoming citizens of a larger pan-European society. Britain was seen as a source of cutting-edge theories and practice in music-education from which the Bulgarian teachers wished to learn. These factors pre-disposed our hosts to work hard to make the project a success.

All participants were stimulated and inspired by the idea of a fusion between contemporary classical sounds and procedures and their own Bulgarian folk idioms. This was expressed through specific encounters with folk melodies, such as the English folk song *The Lark in the clear Air*, or between equivalent instruments from the two cultures, expressed through a drum improvisation duet between Bulgarian Tambura and Irish Bodhran, or a quartet of three Bulgarian kavals and one orchestral flute (Laycock, 2002: 333).

The story of Orpheus and Euridice was seen as Plovdiv's own local myth, and the project enabled the participants to create a unique expression of it. The story itself, with its strong dramatic shape and familiar dénouement, helped to give a convincing form to the disparate musical elements. My conversations with the participants after the concert testified to the emotional high which all experienced during the final moments when Orpheus 'looks back' only to see Euridice drawn away for ever into the swaying arms of the spirits of the underworld. This was vividly and movingly portrayed as a dance sequence by the girls of the Cyril Metodi choir.

Bulgarians are a naturally demonstrative people and, as visitors to the country, we responded to the exceptionally generous and warm friendship and hospitality shown by our hosts. This was repaid in the high degree of commitment our own team gave to the project, and spilled over into the lively and agreeable social aspect of the project, with many meetings in restaurants and bars after busy days of rehearsals and workshops. Several social events were sandwiched into the schedule including an official evening reception, and visits to local beauty spots such as Bachkovo Monastery and the Rhodop mountains, the legendary birthplace of Orpheus, the theme of our project.

We were impressed by the level of instrumental and vocal skill of the Bulgarian children and students, most of whom were fluent in the folk-idioms of their country. At one school, whenever members of the school's folk band had a break in their rehearsal timetable, they filled it, not by running out in the playground to kick a ball but by organising impromptu jam sessions on traditional gadulkas, rebecs, kavals and timbura in any convenient corner of the school they could find.

Barry Russell called on his own large repertoire of well-tried compositional devices designed to generate impressive and effective-sounding musical textures with simple means, while still allowing maximum flexibility for the display of individual skill and virtuosity on the part of the participants. The Cardew Ensemble is a team of musicians who are well used to working together on creative projects of this kind, and although we were working with young people who

315

spoke a completely unfamiliar foreign language, the truth of the assertion that music is a universal language, able to transcend cultural and international boundaries, was abundantly demonstrated. All members of our team made some attempt to learn Bulgarian, a gesture which was appreciated by our hosts, and helped further to cement the 'entente cordiale'.

Rituals for Orpheus was covered by Bulgarian National Television and broadcast as a forty-five minute documentary later that month. I am sure that the presence of the television cameras at the final performance was a further encouragement to the participants to give it their best shot, but even if the cameras had not been there, the presence of an audience of over two thousand people in the wonderful setting of the ancient ruins of the open-air Roman amphitheatre would have assured the same level of commitment.

Philip Craig, one of the Bath students who assisted the project summed up the experience in his own report:

> [...] the whole project was without doubt a huge success. [...] it was a pioneering and ambitious project and in my opinion accomplished everything that was in the original plan. [...] The enjoyment was there to be seen in everyone involved (Craig, 1999: 12).

Rituals for Orpheus was an example of BC4: a work created by the composer using material generated in creative workshops, but it constituted only one half of the final concert. The holistic aspect of the project was expressed through performances by the Cardew Ensemble of pieces from their own repertoire, including new pieces by Barry Russell. However, for unavoidable practical reasons, this formed the second half of the concert.

With such a major climax in the first half, the smaller-scale Cardew Ensemble performances were severely over-shadowed. Many of the audience left after the interval, as did the television crew and most of the young people who took part in the performance. Those who remained were politely appreciative, but the music of the second half made little impact on them. The holistic nature of the project was thus compromised. A comparison with the final concert of the *Confluence* project would suggest a reversal of the programme order: a first half consisting of short items by groups taking part in the project, interspersed with a smaller number of repertoire pieces from the Cardew Ensemble followed by *Rituals for Orpheus* in the second half.

Example 74: Rituals for Orpheus – project timetable.

Date	Time	Event
16 April	All day	Inset day: all teachers & group leaders plus Barry & Jolyon.
Thu. 16 Sep.	4.00pm	Cardew Ensemble Rehearsal.
	6.00pm	Plovdiv Children's Choir: workshop at Culture Centre (1).
Fri. 17 Sep.	12 noon	Workshop with Luben Caravelov School: folk band (1).
	2.00pm	Workshops with Cyril Metodi folk orchestra and choir (1).
	6.00pm	Plovdiv Children's Choir: workshop at Culture Centre (2).
Sat. 18 Sep.	10.00am	Cardew Ensemble Rehearsal at School of Music.
Sun. 19 Sep.	all day	Visit to Bachkovo Monastery.
Mon. 20 Sep.	9.00am	Interview on Radio Darik: Barry and Jolyon.
	10.00am	Interview on Bulgarian State Radio: Barry and Jolyon with Vitchka Nikolova.
	10.00am	Cardew Ensemble rehearsal: School of Music.
	12 noon	Workshop with Luben Caravelov: folk band (2).
	2.00pm	Workshop with Cyril Metodi folk orchestra and choir (2).
	4.00pm	Workshops with Music school wind orchestra (1).
	6.00pm	Plovdiv Children's Choir: workshop at Culture Centre (3).
Tue. 21 Sep.	12 noon	Workshop with Luben Caravelov: folk band (3).
	2.00pm	Workshops with Cyril Metodi folk orchestra & choir (3): all Cardews.
	4.00pm	Workshop with Plovdiv Accordion Orchestra (1): Barry.
	4.00pm	Music School Wind Orchestra (2): Jos and Steve.
	6.00pm	Plovdiv Children's Choir: workshop at Culture Centre (4): Susan and Damien.
	6.00pm	Workshop at Rada Kirkovitch Institution for Abandoned Children (1): Barry and Jolyon.

Wed. 22 Sep.	10.00am	Interview for Bulgarian National TV: Barry and Jolyon.
	12 noon	Workshop with Luben Caravelov School: folk band (4) (covered by Bulgarian National TV).
	2.00pm	Workshops with Cyril Metodi folk orchestra and choir (4): All Cardews.
	4.00pm	Workshop with Plovdiv Accordion Orchestra (2): Barry.
	4.00pm	Music School Wind Orchestra (3): Jos and Steve.
	6.00pm	Plovdiv Children's Choir: workshop at Culture Centre (5): Susan and Damien.
	6.00pm	Workshop at Rada Kirkovitch Institution for Abandoned Children (2): Barry and Jolyon.
Thu. 23 Sep.	12 noon	Rehearsals in Roman Amphitheatre.
	5.30pm	Break.
	8.00pm	Final Concert, filmed by Bulgarian National TV. Programme: *Rituals for Orpheus* 50 minutes. Pause The Cornelius Cardew Ensemble: Four pieces by Frank Zappa: *Little House I used to live in; Oh No! I don't believe it!; The Black Page; Uncle Meat.* Cornelius Cardew *The Tiger's Mind.* Barry Russell *Songs…Not Love Songs.* Stephen Montague *Paramell VI.*

Chapter 12
Project outcomes

If a project has culminated in a performance which was truly memorable in the ways I have discussed above, so that it becomes a 'life-altering' experience for both participants and audience, is this enough in itself? Are the members of the project team now entitled to pack up and move on to the next venue, congratulating themselves on a job well done? The answer is an emphatic 'No!' If attitudes to music and personal creativity have truly been opened up – if ordinary people have been inspired by a memorable experience, and are left with a strong desire to repeat and build on the experience – we who have helped to awaken such desires in them must take some responsibility for what comes after. We have a duty to take account of the legacy that a project leaves behind. In the three-stage structure (Example 30, p. 162) only Asher, from her education officer's viewpoint, takes account of the project's long-term legacy.

Continuity and project legacy

Schools and local community groups can be left feeling let down and disappointed if no new opportunities come their way at the end of a successful project. Orchestras, ensembles, opera companies, concert halls and arts centres with well-run educational programmes, and close links with surrounding communities, are in an ideal position to provide the essential year-on-year continuity which helps to avoid such an outcome, thus fulfilling the eighth 'condition of openness'.

The Arts Council National Lottery and the EU Culture 2000 programme tried to alleviate some of the problems of one-off project funding by offering three-year funding contracts. Although this was a

319

great improvement, allowing initiatives to grow and develop to a much larger extent, the evil hour was bound to arrive eventually, leaving an even larger gulf in people's lives since expectations had been raised that much higher.

This has been the fate of many of the major three-year programmes funded from the *Arts for Everyone* scheme such as 'Rainbow over Bath' and the Confluence Project. Enforcement of the principle of 'additionality', which meant that Lottery money could not be used to bolster up core funding, dictated that projects had to be seen to be new and different from the organisation's normal programme. At the end of three-year funding of 'Confluence', directors Sue Clifford and Angela King were reduced to expressions of pious hopes in the preface to the final concert at Christchurch Priory:

> Well the three years have gone. What have we achieved? We know the experience has passed many people by, affected some people deeply, changed all of us – much like the river really. And we feel we have just begun [...]. The challenge now is to encourage people to continue in the valley in whatever appropriate way. [...] Our role will be to pass the experience on, to give people ideas and courage to be as creative for other catchments, to demonstrate in all kinds of ways what we have done as an example for others to build upon (Clifford & King, 2001: 3).

At least they can point to some tangible evidence that their ideas have caught on elsewhere: 'Already in corners of Australia and North America people are building on the things we have been learning here' (Clifford & King, 2001: 3). But without the input of professional workshop leaders such as Helen Porter or Karen Wimhurst, will groups like the Confluence Performing Club or 'Pipeworks' be able to survive and develop?

This is why so many projects are conceived of as 'pilot schemes', or, as the EU Department DGX calls them 'experimental measures', set up for limited periods on limited funding with the idea of putting forward examples of best practice, hoping that in the not too distant future it will be possible to establish a permanent programme. But as I have argued, a project which can only claim to be exemplary is 'weak', not 'open'. The 'Composing in the Community' programme of 'Rainbow over Bath' was seen as just such a pilot project. When it ended, it left a vacuum. Conceived as a form of practical action-based research, at least the findings of its final report have fed into a PhD thesis and this book which both form part of the project's legacy.

The legacy of a creative music project takes different forms, falling into two categories, the intangible and the tangible.

The intangible legacy – activities and skills:

> Performance groups and choirs, formed as a result of the project, which go on to have an independent life.

> Skills and knowledge left behind – Local class teachers, and community leaders use the project as a form of in-service training. They should now be able to carry on working more effectively at a local level.

> Skills and knowledge dispersed – Students acting as workshop assistants will have gained much useful knowledge and skills, and will take this on into their professional life.

> Wider propagation of skills and knowledge – In the case of projects outside UK, skills and knowledge will have been imparted to teachers and arts professionals in other countries.

The tangible legacy – documentary resources:

> Scores of newly commissioned works which can be used as the basis of future projects and performances.

> Evaluation reports and other documentation.

Musical scores

A musical score formed part of the legacy of several of the projects I have already discussed. Colin Mawby's *Torc of Gold*, David Bedford's *Timepiece*, Rachel Leach's *Hector and Harriet* and Nicola

LeFanu's *The Green Children* all resulted in published scores which could be performed again and used as the basis for other creative projects.

Another LSO 'Discovery' project, Judith Bingham's *Red Hot Nail*, has been particularly successful in this respect. This work, commissioned in 1994, is an excellent example of BC3, and achieves better integration between creative windows and fully scored material than Leach's work.

The theme comes from a folk tale of Serbian Gypsies who believe their forbears forged the nails of the Crucifixion. Four were manufactured, but only three were used. The fourth, red-hot from the furnace, still pursues them, forcing them forever to move on. The work depicts a journey through Romania, Transylvania and Serbia (TC3c + 3d – see Chapter 9, p. 267).

Bingham chose the theme because Bosnian refugees attended one of the Hackney schools involved in the original project. She wanted to find a way of treating displacement and intolerance. The theme provides a narrative thread to support the work's time structure, and a geographical connection for some of the participants. An extract from the score shows how an instrumental section entitled 'Romania' ends with atmospheric bird-song effects leading into the first creative window 'In the forest' followed by 'Travelling music' which recurs throughout the piece like a ritornello (Example 75).

Lloyds TSB sponsored a tour which took *The Red Hot Nail* to twelve different schools widely spaced across the country during May, June and July 1999, with a further performance at the Barbican in November.

Example 75: Bingham, J. *The Red Hot Nail*
2nd creative window & 'Travelling Music'.

Project reports and evaluations

Projects in BC5 specific to a particular group of participants do not always result in a written score which can be re-created by others. Exceptionally, Musiko-Musika published a booklet of all the songs produced during *Pirates and Heroes* (Chapter 11, p. 305), an excellent souvenir for all children and their parents. More often the tangible legacy of BC5 projects rests entirely in reports and evaluations compiled from a number of different sources:

- Questionnaires completed by participants (children, adults and so on).
- Participants' project journals.
- Project journals and reports compiled by student workshop assistants.
- Verbal reactions of participants recorded on tape or taken down by dictation.
- Teachers' and community leaders' written reports.
- Lead composer's written report.
- Musical scores produced during the project.
- Sound recordings of workshops and final concerts.
- Photographic archive.
- Video recordings.
- Report compiled by a mentor.
- Report or evaluation conducted by an independent observer.

Many projects which are successful in other ways fall down on evaluation, an aspect which too often gets pushed to the bottom of the priorities list. Many models for questionnaires have been proposed. In order to complete her evaluations of PRS 'Composer in Education' projects, Gillian Perkins required reports from lead composers, project organisers, teachers and from children taking part. She provided a list of what she called 'pick and mix questions' (Example 77). She expected the most detailed report to come from the project leader, and provided notes detailing the points to be covered (Example 78).

Perkins wanted reports which were candid and detailed. Her 'pick and mix' format looks rather unsystematic on paper, but left maximum freedom to her respondents to construct their own response forms, giving as much or as little emphasis to each point as they saw fit. Her questions were designed to find out whether the project met its aims and objectives, how well it related to the requirements of the school curriculum, whether participants enjoyed the experience, whether it brought about change, and whether it left a lasting legacy. Strangely, project organisers were not asked if they would make changes, whereas teachers were. Questions such as 'What was really good about the project?', or 'What did you like most?' suggest an emphasis on positive and enjoyable aspects. Negative comments, on the other hand, are to be dressed up in the more positive form of suggestions about change: 'What changes would you make to the structure of the project to make it more effective?'

The sample questionnaires compiled by Sharp and Dust are much more systematic. They begin by explaining the purpose of the evaluation in a way which makes the participants feel that their response is valued (Example 79). The happy, neutral and sad faces make the school-pupil's task easy. Ideally one might wish to modify some of the questions to make them positive in tone. It is confusing to indicate agreement with a negative question by marking a happy face, for example, 'It was too difficult'. If it was, I would want to mark the unhappy face to show I was unhappy about this aspect, not the happy one to show I agreed with the statement.

The authors seem aware that this multiple-choice format leaves less scope for individual responses, and the questionnaire ends with an invitation to pupils to respond to four questions in their own words. Unfortunately, pre-literate or learning-difficulties children cannot respond so directly to these final questions as they can to the happy and sad faces.

The Sharp and Dust Teacher Response sheet, like Perkins, asks teachers to assess how the project met its aims and objectives, how enjoyable it was, and what lasting impact it made. Mindful of the problems of hard-pressed teachers, it sets a series of multiple-choice questions, this time replacing the sad and happy faces with a more adult format of numbers one to five indicating degrees of agreement and disagreement (Example 80).

The artists' response sheet uses the same format, but epitomises the child-centred focus of the handbook. In spite of earlier chapters which encourage artists to scrutinise their own motivation for taking on educational work, none of the questions asks them to comment on the impact of an educational project on their own creative work (Example 81).

It is important to be clear about who benefits from evaluation. Participants will readily agree about the value of thinking about how they have benefited from a project, and of making some sort of permanent record of their response, but in practice, hard-pressed teachers with piles of marking, or children who would rather be out in the playground letting off steam, will put the task off until the memory has faded.

A number of inducements have been used to encourage the completion of evaluation reports. Appeals to altruism such as reminders that evaluations will help other people to organise better projects in future – 'This will contribute to our evaluation report and help us in planning new developments' – or vague promises that a favourable evaluation may lead to the possibility of future projects in their school may not be enough to overcome the inertia. Funding bodies like the Arts Council National Lottery, or the European department DGX, use an unashamedly stick-and-carrot approach by offering substantial project funding up-front, but withholding a crucial small percentage unless a full evaluation and financial report is received by a certain deadline.

The multiple-choice format certainly helps by making the process easy and quick. Teachers can circle numbers and tick boxes over a quick cup of staff-room coffee. Pictorial response-forms devised by the London Sinfonietta got round the problem with young children by providing space for them to illustrate their response in pictorial form, making the process into an enjoyable and creative activity in its own right.

A pupil self-evaluation session was built into the timetable of the *Pirates and Heroes* song-writing project of Musiko-Musika. Pupils talked about their experience of the project in a discussion on the penultimate day before the final rehearsal and performance, and put down their thoughts in a short paragraph of writing. A small selection then read out their evaluation as part of the final performance.

A comparison with the wide-ranging requirements of the theoretical model shows up the sketchiness of the response forms of Sharp and Dust, and of Gillian Perkins. In an attempt to keep things simple and straightforward, they only ask a minimum of questions. The questionnaires are cold and objective in tone. Words such as 'excitement', 'commitment', 'feelings' or 'emotional engagement', which dominated my discussion in Chapter 11, are missing. A compilation of completed response forms on their own does not add up to a full evaluation. For Perkins, the purpose of the forms was to elicit feedback from teachers, pupils and composers so that their views could be set alongside her own well-informed judgement of a project.

A more holistic picture is expressed in Perkins' 'Pick and Mix list of possible objectives for a Composer in Education Project' where phrases such as 'Provide an enjoyable and memorable experience', 'Give opportunities for social and/or emotional development', and 'Provide opportunities for integration between different schools/ ages/abilities' appear. In line with the commitment of PRS to the interests and rights of composers, Perkins gives some thought to what they might get out of a project such as 'Give fresh impetus to my own composition', 'Help improve my presentation/teaching skills', and, in a pre-echo of the subject of this book: 'Stimulate better understanding of a modern composer's value to society'.

Three types of evaluation

Sharp and Dust distinguish between two types of evaluation: formative and summative. Formative evaluation is a continuous process which takes place during the project. It feeds back into the project, asking how it is shaping up against the original aims and objectives, and proposing modifications to structure or content. It is here that a project demonstrates its flexibility and its ability to respond spontaneously and positively to creative accidents. The response forms of Perkins, and of Sharp and Dust, are part of a process of summative evaluation taking place after the project. The aim is to establish how successful a project has been in meeting its aims and objectives.

I propose to distinguish a third form of evaluation, and to call it 'consequent'. The response forms of Sharp and Dust do not ask teachers to comment on how the project related to the pupils' normal class-work in music, or in other subjects, or on more general outcomes such as the development of communication skills, improvement of social attitudes, general discipline, or benefits to the school as a whole. As we saw, the artist's response form does not ask about the impact of educational projects on the artist's own creative work. An assessment of the social, educational and creative impact of the project on the future lives of the participants belong to what I call 'consequent' evaluation.

All evaluation is comparative. Formative evaluation takes a snap-shot in time, asks 'how does the project at this moment compare with the original objectives?' and suggests modifications. Summative evaluation compares the final outcome with the original aims and objectives, and judges the degree of success in achieving them. Consequent evaluation compares levels of skill, knowledge and understanding before and after the project and assesses what lasting impact it has made. An analysis of the development of a composer's work in education and the community over a number of years, a survey of a programme of out-reach projects undertaken by a particular orchestra or arts organisation, an examination of the impact of a series of creative music projects within a particular school, or studies tracking the progress of a sample of individual pupils, are all examples of consequent evaluation.

Formative evaluation is an essential tool helping the composer to achieve a successful outcome for a creative project. Summative evaluation allows us to judge how successful the composer has been in that particular project. Formative and summative evaluations both contribute to consequent evaluation which seeks to provide an assessment of the long-term social and cultural impact of the composer's work. Consequent evaluation is therefore central to the search for a re-definition of the role of the composer in society.

Apart from Winterson's *An Evaluation of the Effects of London Sinfonietta Education Projects on their Participants* (Winterson, 1994), and some aspects of *Arts Education in Secondary Schools:*

Effects and Effectiveness (NFER, 2000), there have been few thorough-going and effective examples of consequent evaluation.

Consequent evaluation is crucial also in European and international projects if they are to yield maximum benefit, especially in countries such as Bulgaria where there is no established tradition of creative music projects. Barry Russell comments on such a shortcoming in his report on *Rituals for Orpheus*, blaming it on the lack of time available in this intensive project: 'There was no chance to debrief with groups and group leaders and talk about the product and project with them and suggest how to move ideas forward' (Russell, 1999: 7).

Anonymity and confidentiality

In the response forms discussed above, issues of anonymity and confidentiality arise. Both have a bearing on the usefulness of evaluation reports. Perkins encouraged a frank expression of views by assuring her respondents that, if they wished, confidentiality would be protected, and their remarks would be read only by the PRS committee. Both the pupil and teacher response forms of Sharp & Dust state that respondents need not give their names if they wish their identity to be protected. Sharp and Dust imply that evaluation is the job of the project organiser and that the results feed back in the form of improvements in future projects. 'Decide how to capitalise on what has been learned from the evaluation in planning what to do next' reads one of the points in their 'evaluation checklist'. But they also exhort project organisers to 'report your findings'. How can we report our findings and preserve confidentiality at the same time?

No benefit can be drawn from these reports unless they are read and their lessons noted and acted upon. Most funding bodies ask for evaluation reports as a condition of funding. The PRS appointed Perkins, and more recently other professional evaluators, for the purpose of obtaining independent evaluations of the projects being supported. Others, including the Arts Council, the EU Department DGX, and other private trusts and foundations, have been content to accept reports compiled by project organisers themselves. The objectivity and, therefore, the true value of such reports is debatable. We all try to be objective, but the temptation to show everything in the best light is almost irresistible when the future continuation of grant aid may depend on the result. It is therefore important to distinguish between objectively verifiable facts such as workshop timetables, dates and times of concerts, numbers of participants, published documentary material in the form of publicity and press reviews, and budgetary statements on the one hand, and subjective evaluations on the other.

Evaluation reports which do not preserve anonymity often remain confidential for a variety of reasons:

- Reports always contain an element of subjectivity on the part of the writer. Other people may disagree with the evaluation in respect of specific individuals or organisations.
- Reports may contain negative criticism of organisations which could harm future funding prospects.
- They may contain negative criticism of individuals who could suffer in their professional life as a result – either workshop leaders, composers, teachers, or arts professionals, etc.
- If individuals or organisations are singled out for particular praise, this can give them an unfair advantage over others, giving rise to professional jealousy.

For the same reasons, those reports which are published try to maintain a level of anonymity in an attempt to protect reputations, but if specific organisations and individuals are not named, this severely limits the value of the report since it can only deal in generalisations. Nobody else will be in a position to check the accuracy of the report, or to compare its findings with the views of people who were directly involved. It may make an assertion about the failure of a particular activity to capture the interest of a group of children, but provide no clue as to the identity of the school, teacher, workshop leader or project which could enable other researchers to seek alternative views from those involved. Anonymity also makes it impossible to conduct any form of consequent evaluation such as follow-up research investigating the response of a particular community organisation to a suc-

330

cession of different projects, comparative studies of the responses of different organisations to the same project, or studying the work of a particular composer involved in a variety of projects.

I encountered several examples of evaluation reports which were unhelpful in this respect. They include Andrew Peggie's report on the London Arts Board/Yamaha Kemble project, *Musicians Go to School*, which contains much sound wisdom. It would offer several opportunities for consequent evaluation if it were not forced, by the need for anonymity, to make unsubstantiated generalisations.

The seven case studies to be found in the appendices to Odie and Allen *Artists in Schools – a review* (Odie & Allen, 1998) could also form the basis for consequent evaluations, but are similarly sanitised. There are two case studies of music projects. Unfortunately, because no details are given allowing them to be identified, their usefulness for a thesis based on the study of the methodologies of particular composers and workshop animateurs is limited. The following is typical in its anonymity:

> The train draws into the capital. *A young composer and orchestral education officer* recollect the progress of a unique music project spanning three years. An *arts venue with a national focus and significance* had negotiated a music project with *six inner city schools* which involved one class from each school. [...] The project had been conceived by *the education department of the arts venue* working in collaboration with *the local University's Institute of Education* (Odie & Allen, 1998: 56–57) (my italics).

And later, avoiding even any implication as to the gender of the composer: 'With the help of other musicians the pupils then studied the style of *the composer* and created their own compositions based on *this* style, which were later performed at *the centre*' (Odie & Allen, 1998: 56–57) (my italics).

Some of us in the profession may deduce from the list of acknowledgements at the back of the book that the composer concerned was Fraser Trainer, and that the orchestra was the London Sinfonietta, although even here, Trainer is referred to only as 'an artist'. Since no other composer is listed in the acknowledgements, it seems a fair bet! Unless someone is prepared to spill the beans, I cannot follow up with my own researches. Which were the six schools? Have they undertaken other projects of a similar nature? If so, how do they integrate such activities into their music curriculum? What other work has the orchestra undertaken? Is this project part of an on-going programme of educational work? This case study raises many more questions than it answers and provides no clues which would help us to get at the answers.

In the second example there is some hint of geographical location: 'Our journey ends with two folk musicians in the South West and a comprehensive school, with a large proportion of pupils in the lower ability range, on an outer-city estate'. The Wren Trust is the only folk-music agency mentioned in the acknowledgements, and it is based in the south west, but it is impossible to be sure. The comments in this study are somewhat critical. Were the writers afraid of upsetting the Wren Trust, or protecting themselves against any accusation that they had compromised the Trust's future funding prospects (Odie & Allen, 1998: 70–71)?

Composing in the Classroom - The Creative Dream (Odam & Paterson, 2000), the two-year research project sponsored by the National Association of Music Educators, and based in a number of secondary schools up and down the country, is similarly non-specific about the location of its case-studies. Even the photographic illustrations carry no captions, although an appendix gives a list of schools and LEAs which participated showing an impressively wide geographical spread ('openness' on the 'places' axis). The booklet, containing much practical advice based on observation of what teachers actually do, sets out to 'develop teachers' practice through a set of principles, methodologies and case studies drawn from detailed qualitative and quantitative research' (Odam & Paterson, 2000: 5). This sounds like a form of consequent evaluation, but its usefulness is again limited by anonymity. It is difficult to see why identities needed to be protected. The book is almost completely positive in tone, offering excellent examples of good practice based on approaches which were judged by the researchers to be successful. There can have been little risk of upsetting individuals who thought their work had been misrepresented.

The *Creative Dream* is about 'composing in education', as opposed to 'composers in education'. Inexplicably it does not even refer to the existence of composers in education, let alone attempt to assess their value as an adjunct to professional class teachers' work. Instead, in a chapter about the composing process, it tries to summarise in four paragraphs what composers do, falling back on such sweeping generalisations as 'the majority of composers work for most of their time on pieces commissioned by, or limited by constraints put on their work by others'. This is surprising for two reasons. Firstly the research programme was based at Bath Spa University College where many of the projects analysed in my thesis took place, often within the context of the department's own B.A. module 'Composing in Education'. Secondly at least one of the schools which took part in the *Creative Dream* research programme, Guthlaxton College, Leicester, has also participated extensively in 'composer in education' programmes funded by the PRS, or as part of the Philharmonia Orchestra's Antarctic Symphony project with Peter Maxwell Davies in May 2001 (Chapter 10, p. 302).

Attitudes to confidentiality have hardened over the years, influenced partly by the Data Protection Act. The PRS Composing in Education programme took evaluation very seriously, and still does. Gillian Perkins monitored the projects every year from 1989 when they started, until 1999, producing a full set of reports. They are not anonymous. Perkins was openly critical of individuals and organisations, or lavish with her praise when she thought appropriate, although she does assure project leaders of confidentiality if they request it. PRS intended to make the reports freely available as an archive and encouraged project organisers to let local education establishments have access to them (Example 79, point 6 'Future'). Other project organisers could consult the reports in order to learn from the experiences they contained, both positive and negative.

Over the years I assembled a more-or-less full set of the reports for my own reference. However my recent attempts to plug some of the gaps met with resistance from the administrators of the PRS Foundation who were at first reluctant to release what was now apparently regarded as confidential information. I subject the entire archive of Perkins' PRS reports to detailed scrutiny in Chapter 13.

The PRS is just one example. I encountered similar reluctance from the SPNM when I asked to see reports of C4K and *Adopt a*

Composer projects. Conversely other organisations have been completely open. Spitalfields Festival gave me full access to a file of project reports, and Ian Mitchell of Gemini compiled a collection of reports and documentation stretching back many years.

I have also been refused opportunities to watch projects in action from organisations including SPNM, PRS and Welsh National Opera, although I was always made welcome at final performances. Two principal reasons were usually given:

1. My presence might inhibit the spontaneity of the workshop.
2. The organisers already had their own evaluation procedures in place.

I suspected the possibility that there were other reasons including:

1. Organisers feared that I would catch the project on a bad day.
2. They feared that I would witness activities which were inconsistent with project publicity, for instance the rehearsal of fully composed music during a project which claimed to represent children's own creative work.
3. I might spot serious skill and personality deficiencies in a visiting composer who claimed extensive skill and experience in this field.

I have to respect the right of project organisers to decide who can and who cannot observe creative workshops, or read confidential reports, but it is a sad indictment of the present highly competitive nature of arts funding if it prevents a free exchange of theory and methodology which could benefit current and future practice. Openness has been a recurrent theme of this thesis. The methodologies of composing in education and in the community can only grow and develop if practitioners are prepared to engage in a free exchange of ideas and experiences, drawing lessons from the failures as well as celebrating the successes. When things go wrong, remembering Schafer's 2nd maxim (Schafer, 1975: 132–133), we must be able to admit mistakes in an atmosphere of open and constructive debate.

Children's Music Workshop

A number of organisations have taken seriously their duty to share their experience of music education and community work, among them Children's Music Workshop. Co-Director Jane Pountney made herself available to answer my questions and welcomed my presence as observer at workshops in two Bristol primary schools, and at the final rehearsal and performance at St. George's, Bristol. Far from inhibiting the children's response, I was able to make a positive contribution (Chapter 7, p. 239).

One lasting legacy of Children's Music Workshop is its 'qualitative study' of *Arts Projects in Primary Schools* (Hedges, 2000). It preserves the anonymity of all the fifteen schools which contributed, revealing only that they were in London and Norfolk. The study was based on conversations with heads of schools which had experience of working with artists and arts organisations. Since none of the arts projects are identified or described in any way, the study can only draw the broadest of conclusions. It lists the familiar Gulbenkian-inspired benefits including gain in confidence and self-esteem, access to cultural excellence, development of concentration, unlocking of creativity, fostering of social skills, personal growth and so on, which are discussed in *All Our Futures*, but more concisely. No school heads reported any negative effects of arts projects in their schools. Negative comments all focused on excessive government bureaucracy, the difficulty of raising funds, the prescriptive view of the DFEE, and occasionally pressure from parents who saw the arts as an optional extra.

Spitalfields Festival education programme

A sixty-page evaluation report on the 1999–2000 Education and Community programme of Spitalfields sent to me by Philip Flood is detailed and specific, and neither confidential nor anonymous. When Flood took over from Simon Foxley, he seemed to favour a radical change of policy away from Gemini's 'deep-toned', Wiegold-influenced emphasis on individual creativity, towards a wider variety of style and idiom which took in workshops by jazz-singer Brenda Rattray and folk singer Vivien Ellis, composers Ian McQueen and Glyn Evans, Indian musicians Sanju Sahai and Sajata Banerjee, and ensembles such as Saxploitation, and the Duke Quartet.

The report is preceded by an introduction which outlines the Festival's educational policy and lists six priorities. The emphasis on long-term partnerships, the use of evaluation to influence improvements in service, and the introduction of mentoring schemes indicate an awareness of the importance of consequent evaluation:

- Establishment of long-term partnerships with schools, community groups and other organisations.
- Working closely with teachers, head teachers and community workers to ensure projects are planned effectively.
- Rigorously monitoring and evaluating projects in order to constantly improve the level of service.
- Employing artists with national and international reputation in the field who have particular skills in working in an inner city environment.
- Developing the skills of young animateurs through a scheme of mentoring and apprenticeships.
- Giving adults and young people the opportunity to develop musical and social skills through creative exploration and discovery (Flood & Haines, 2000: 4).

Each of twenty-two separate projects which took place during the season (four in autumn, eight in spring, and ten in summer) are subjected to the same systematic analysis under seven headings:

- Outline of project.
- Aims and how the project worked towards achieving them.

336

- Learning outcomes.
- Good practice.
- Issues.
- Considerations for future projects.
- Comments.

The format allows both good and bad aspects to be aired frankly, with negative comments categorised euphemistically as 'issues'. It also invites discussion of future developments. Factual information and statistics are given in a set of appendices showing clearly how many people took part or attended, and providing statistics for gender and racial origin. The claim made in the introduction that three thousand five hundred individuals participated is substantiated. The list of schools includes fourteen primaries, six secondaries, and two special schools. Over nine hundred children and four hundred adults took part in workshops. As the following matrix analysis shows (Example 76), the whole adds up to a programme which has a strong geographical focus, is as open as possible within budgetary constraints, as to people, age and ability, and takes a fully open approach to musical style and idiom. The need to train for the future through artists' apprenticeships and teacher Inset is taken seriously (Flood & Haines, 2000: 59).

Example 76: Spitalfields Festival education programme 2000.

The candid nature of the report also allows me to delve beneath the bland superlatives of the introduction and tease out the less than satisfactory aspects of some of the projects, including Ian McQueen's *Compose 2000* at St. Paul's Community and Swanlea Secondary Schools. The project was built on a lasting partnership with the two schools, and formed part of long-term GCSE composition project for year ten and eleven. It was holistic in that it involved four members of Jane's Minstrels, including composer/percussionist Simon Limbrick, and singer Denise Mulholland, as well as the input of two other composers, Jonathan Dove and Diana Burrell whose work *Barrow* featured in the final June concert (Flood & Haines, 2000: 526).

The timetable differed from my four-phase model in that, following the preliminary planning meeting, and teachers' Inset, each school enjoyed the luxury of ten workshops with Ian McQueen over a period of five months. This implies that McQueen adopted a more direct teaching approach and relied less on the support of class teachers. Involvement of professional musicians allowed the students to hear the results of their compositional work, and a selection of the completed pieces was included in the final evening concert.

Remarks made in the context of 'issues' and 'considerations for future projects' echo some of our own experience at 'Rainbow over Bath'. Problems created by examination timetables seems to imply less than full support from schools. Disappointing attendance at the Inset day indicates lack of teacher commitment, and poor attendance at the final performance by some pupils suggests failure to motivate them effectively (Flood & Haines, 2000: 28). This negative slant is contradicted by the report's remarks under 'good practice' about 'strong support from heads of music and senior staff' and 'obvious student understanding, appreciation and enjoyment of Jane's Minstrels concert', suggesting some variation between the two schools. The year-10 pupils at Swanlea seemed to be getting more out of this project than the year-11 pupils at St. Paul's.

The fact that some of the professional musicians cancelled workshop sessions with inadequate warning and that some expressed 'a need for more guidance as to the needs and abilities of students' leads the report to conclude that: 'there needs to be careful thought as to musicians/ensemble chosen to be part of this project' (ibid., 2000: 29). The report's conclusion that 'There should be a formal interim monitoring meeting, attended by the whole team built into the project in the future' (Flood & Haines, 2000: 29) implies that the organisers were not already aware of the importance of 'formative evaluation'.

The Association of British Orchestras

The Association of British Orchestras (Penny, 2000) is an excellent example of an organisation which takes seriously its duty to pass on its experience in music education. The ABO has so far brought out two volumes of Workbooks containing essays and project evaluations based on the education programmes of its member orchestras. With contributions from Gillian Moore of the London Sinfonietta, Ann Tennant at the CBSO, Richard McNicol at LSO, Stephen Carpenter of the City of London Sinfonia and others, this represents a valuable corporate legacy of shared experience. Volume two contains an article by Mark Withers – 'Composers: are they worth it?' – in which he concludes that they are. Mark Withers is now working for Fundaçio 'La Caixa' in Barcelona on a new programme of performances and workshops – yet another example of British methodologies exported to Europe (Withers, 2000: 12–13).

Example 77: PRS Composers in Education monitoring form.

Pick and Mix questions to help evaluation for project organisers (Perkins, 1989)

1. What were the outcomes?
2. What was really good about this project?
3. What has developed since the project?
4. To what extent were the aims of this project already being met?
5. Will the project change:
   – future relationships with arts providers?
   – future relationships with other educational institutions?
   – curriculum attitudes?
   – curriculum content/issues?
   – teaching and learning strategies?
6. What are the specific outcomes for:
   – art professionals?
   – teachers?
   – pupils as individuals, or as groups?
   – others involved?
7. What has been good about the impact of the project?
8. What has been difficult in realising the significance of the project?

Example 78: PRS Composers in Education.

Points to be covered in Project Leaders' reports: (Perkins, 1989)

Factual history – planning, agreed objectives, and summary of events.
Finance – expenditure and income including all partnership funding.
Media coverage.
Value – an estimate of the value of the scheme to schools and other host groups; were objectives achieved?
Recordings.
Future – what follow-up has been planned? Plans to invite the composer back, or to invite other composers; availability of your report to other organisations.
Problems – A frank response is requested. Controversial comments will not be made public except to the PRS which would like to know if it can improve on the project.

Example 79: Pupil response sheet (Sharp and Dust, 1982: 1990–1991).

We would like to find out what you thought about working with

....(enter name of artists).

This will help us to plan other facilities in future.
Please spare a few minutes to give us your views. No need to give your name.

Are you learning to play an instrument?   yes   no

Indicate which instrument:

About the pre-concert talk: agree   not   don't
                                                          sure   agree

The talk was interesting.   ☺   😐   ☹

It helped me to appreciate the music.   ☺   😐   ☹

I would have liked more information.   ☺   😐   ☹

About the concert: agree   not   don't
                                                          sure   agree

I enjoyed the music.   ☺   😐   ☹

I thought they played well.   ☺   😐   ☹

They were enthusiastic.   ☺   😐   ☹

It went on too long.   ☺   😐   ☹

341

About the group work:	agree	not sure	don't agree
I liked working with musicians.	☺	☺	☹
I found out what it was like to play in an orchestra.	☺	☺	☹
I learned a lot about ....(type of) music.	☺	☺	☹
They explained clearly what we were supposed to do.	☺	☺	☹
I found it hard to concentrate.	☺	☺	☹
We could try our own ideas.	☺	☺	☹
It was too difficult.	☺	☺	☹
There wasn't enough time.	☺	☺	☹

General impression:	agree	not sure	don't agree
I enjoyed this project.	☺	☺	☹
I found it interesting.	☺	☺	☹
It was a good way to learn.	☺	☺	☹
I would like to do something like this again.	☺	☺	☹

What did you like most about the musicians' visit to your school?
What did you like least about their visit?
If we were planning to do this again, is there anything we should change?
Any other comments on this project, or on what you would like us to arrange in future?

Thank you for answering these questions, and telling us what you thought about the visit etc.

Example 80: Teacher response sheet: (Sharp and Dust, 1982: 1992–1993).

We would like to find out what you thought about our involvement with the players from ....
This will contribute to our evaluation report and help us in planning new developments. Please spare a few minutes to give us your views. You need not give your name.

1. This project had three main aims. Please indicate how far you think each of these was realised by circling a number, and adding a brief comment.

a. To enable pupils to respond to and evaluate a high quality live-music performance.

Not at all				Fully achieved
1	2	3	4	5

Comment: ....

b. To help pupils to develop an understanding of .... music

Not at all				Fully achieved
1	2	3	4	5

Comment: ....

c. To produce a group composition taking .... as a starting point.

Not at all				Fully achieved
1	2	3	4	5

Comment: ....

2. a. How were you involved in the musicians' visit to the school?
    b. Would you have preferred a different role?
3. What did your pupils learn from the experience as a whole?

4. a. What did you like most about the musicians' input?
    b. What did you like least about the musicians' input?
5. Is there anything you would suggest the musicians change next time they visit the school?
6. Do you plan to follow up this project in any way? If so, how?

7. Do you have any comments on the project or suggestions about what you would like the school to arrange in future?

Thank you very much for giving your time to answer these questions.

Example 81: Artist response sheet (Sharp & Dust, 1982: 1994–1995).

We would like to find out what you thought about your involvement with
…………………………………………………………….………….. school.

This will contribute to our evaluation report and help us in planning new developments. Please spare a few minutes to give us your views.

1. Please circle one number in each row etc.

The school provided sufficient information to help us plan the visit.
We felt welcome in the school.
The pupils spoke enthusiastically about the concert.
The pupils were well prepared.
The pupils were well behaved.
There wasn't enough time.
The teachers supported our work in the classroom.
The pupils worked well in groups.
Too many pupils were involved in the group work.

What do you feel the pupils gained from:
The concert?

Your visit to the school?

Please comment on the teachers' involvement with your work.

If we were planning a similar project in the future, is there anything you would suggest we change?

Any other comments on the visit?

344

Chapter 13
The PRS scheme – a case study

The Performing Right Society Composing-in-Education Scheme was launched in 1987 to commemorate the seventy fifth anniversary of the PRS. Its aims and objectives were related to the introduction of the new GCSE syllabus in 1985 which attached a high priority to creativity. The PRS Donations Committee wanted to put the resource of PRS composer/members at the disposal of teachers, and to encourage composers and teachers to work together. Based on the advice of the Music Advisers' National Association they co-opted two music advisers, Keith Sedegbeer (Wolverhampton) and Hamish Preston (Reading), and the Deputy Head of Eastern Arts Association to join the advisory panel. In the first year, the panel was overwhelmed with ninety applications which they whittled down to nine, a number which they have continued to support to the present. The PRS insisted that its contribution should be matched with funds from other sources. The new PRS Foundation with David Bedford as its Chair took over the Composer-in-Education Scheme in 1998, and now gives half a million pounds a year, a fourfold increase.

Gillian Perkins, then Music Officer for Eastern Arts, was asked to compile evaluation reports. The advisory panel needed someone 'to help navigate': to provide a set of guiding principles and leave a legacy of documentation as blueprints for other project organisers. Over a nine-year period Perkins provided summative evaluations of a total of eighty-two projects and summarised each year's achievement in a form of consequent evaluation. This chapter is given over entirely to an evaluation of the whole scheme and discussion of issues arising from Perkins' reports under headings which relate to various aspects of the theoretical model.

The primary mission of the PRS is the collection of performance royalties due to its composer-members. It follows that the work of the donations committee, and its successor the PRS Foundation, is geared towards the creation of schemes to support the work of the Society's composer-members. The Composing-in-Education scheme therefore has dual objectives:

1. To encourage the creation of Composing-in-Education schemes throughout the UK.
2. To create opportunities for employment in such schemes for PRS composer-members.

Framing, action and creativity

The primary aim of the scheme is to encourage young people to become actively involved in the composition of music. According to Perkins, the emphasis is on 'demystification' of the creative process:

> [...] almost without exception, the composers on the PRS scheme have raised the profile of composition dramatically by the enthusiasm and enjoyment they have engendered in the classroom, and by exemplifying a professional use of music in the Real World. Composition becomes Fun, Purposeful and Achievable. Composers become Real People; modern music becomes something to be re-considered (Perkins, 1990: 41 (author's upper-case)).

PRS projects tended to polarise into child-centred (coming from education authorities and schools) and repertoire-based (coming from arts organisations). The most successful ought to be those in which a balance between 'strong' and 'open' framing is achieved through real and close partnership, but these projects also turn out to be the most problematic because of the difficulties of reconciling the different aims and objectives of the two sectors.

Andrew Potter, Chairman of the PRS, has drawn attention to the way in which the initiation of projects has changed over the years. In the first few years, initiatives came predominantly from local authorities. Music Advisers encouraged consortia of schools to apply. Later the focus shifted to Arts-in-Education agencies and promoters. This shift may be the result of increasing workload on advisers, the break-up of advisory services following Local Management of Schools, increasing confidence among advisers about setting up their own schemes, or even loss of confidence in the scheme itself. John Stephens, a member of the PRS Advisory panel, has suggested that there is now a serious lack of leadership at advisory level.

Classification

Composers are the central ingredient of all PRS Composer-in-Education projects. The selection of projects shows a great range of stylistic allegiances, reflecting the catholic nature of the PRS which represents all copyright music, regardless of idiom, including popular music, jazz, folk song, dance music, educational music and many other categories. The PRS scheme is well placed to achieve open classification.

The following chart is an estimate of the number of projects which fall into each stylistic category based on the lead composer's normal style. It is difficult to provide a precise stylistic categorisation of the projects themselves since many were 'open' as to musical style. The lead composer's style cannot necessarily be taken as an indication of the stylistic focus of the project which may be more concerned with developing children's creativity in music using their own musical vernacular. Projects featuring Huw and Tony Williams in Caerphilli in 1997, and John Woolrich at Walton on Thames in 1991 shared the same objective of encouraging children to write songs, though clearly from an entirely different stylistic focus.

Contemporary classical	47
Commercial styles including rock	10
Experimental and improvisation	8
Non-European ethnic forms	7
Jazz	6
European folk	5
Electro-acoustic	2

The view that most of the expertise and ideological commitment to creative-music-making is to be found in the 'Contemporary Classical' sector is supported by the fact that 55% of the projects were led by composers whose work falls into this category, although this may also represent a bias on the part of the PRS selection panel.

Many familiar names are found amongst the forty-seven 'contemporary classical' projects. Perkins' reports provide snap-shots of moments in the careers of various composers who were already leading figures in British musical life, or were about to become so. Some have already been discussed elsewhere in this book. Nicola LeFanu, Mervyn Burtch, Alec Roth, Diana Burrell, Alan Belk, Brian Bedford, Simon Limbrick, Roxanne Panufnik, David Bedford, Jeni Roditti, John Hardy, Avril Sutton Anderson, Jane Wells, Duncan Chapman, Javier Alvarez, and Ian Dearden all took part in one PRS project. The names Sean Gregory, Bill Sweeney, Alistair Anderson, David Sutton-Anderson, Deirdre Gribbin and Bill Martin appear twice. Graham Fitkin holds the record with three projects. In many cases, composers were taking part in such projects for the first time. Some never tried the experience again. For Simon Limbrick, Philip Cashian, Daryl Runswick, Stephen Montague, Gary Carpenter and Deirdre Gribbin, community and education work became an important element, while for Sean Gregory, Alec Roth, Duncan Chapman, Hugh Nankivell and Bill Martin it came to dominate their musical careers.

The scheme carries some commitment to women composers. Seventeen female names appear amongst the total of eighty-two projects, a ratio of 20%. Only one project, a song-writing programme led by folk artist Al Bell at Buddle Arts Centre in North Tyneside in 1991, carried a specifically 'Women in Music' banner.

The statistic of seven projects in non-European ethnic styles is misleading. Three are Gamelan projects led by white British artists such as Janet Sherbourne and Mark Lockett, and one, a world-music project led by Peter Stacey. The representation of composers from truly non-European ethnic minorities includes only John Mayer's Indo-Jazz Fusions in Birmingham in 1989, Mexican composer Javier Alvarez and Korean musician Inok Paek in Newcastle in 1991, and black woman composer Errollyn Wallen at Allerton Grange Festival in Leeds as part of *Music without Frontiers* in 1993. I suspect this reflects an imbalance in applications rather than a bias against minority ethnic work from the selection committee, although there is little evidence that the PRS actively encouraged such applications.

It is important to distinguish between projects led by non-European artists, and those in which non-European ethnic minorities were specifically targeted as part of a socially inclusive programme – openness on the 'people' axis. Of these there are several good examples. The following are only a selection:

1989 – Bill Martin and Rob Worby in twenty-one Leicestershire schools.
1989 – John Mayer working with the Indian Community in Birmingham.
1993 – Simon Limbrick in Blackheath schools.
1995 – David Bedford in Spitalfields.
1997 – David and Avril Sutton Anderson with Colourscape in Croydon.

Over the years Perkins formed a view of what constituted the right composer for the job, drawing attention to qualities of self-motivation and personal charisma:

The more I see of these solo projects, the more I realise that the composers have to be rather special people. The most successful have a certain inner strength which carries them through, coupled with an outward charisma which endears them to those who meet them. My ideal composer would positively want to be part of the planning of these projects, sharing its aims and its development (Perkins, 1998: 22).

She is aware that not all composers possess such qualities, suggesting that those who 'are not so robust should perhaps be part of a team, which may have orchestral members, singers or any other performing musicians working alongside' (Perkins, 1998: 22). John Foster, Music Officer for Devon County Council enumerates some of the most important qualities in his glowing evaluation of Graham Fitkin's work in Ivybridge and Teignmouth in 1997:

Undoubtedly the luckiest things in this whole project was identifying Graham as the composer to bring on board [...] (Commenting too on Andy Baker, double bass, and Matthew Griffiths, percussion) [...] there could have been few better role models when it came to absolute respect for students and their work, motivating by encouragement, communicating easily, setting high personal and musical examples and pitching challenges just right to be achievable (Forster; cited in Perkins, 1998: 5).

Perkins' remarks about composers' methodologies in the classroom echo Paynter's views about flexibility of approach (Paynter, 1982: 51–52):

> Most education workers have ideas on how composers work. Most are surprised that composers seldom provide instant schemes of work, or solutions to students' demands. Watching composers at work, one is struck again and again how responsive they are rather than pro-active. One commented to me recently that he did not care what ideas came forward, so long as there was something to begin asking questions with, evaluating the answers, and developing and extending the material into something else (Perkins, 1992: 35).

However some teachers found this laid-back, 'open-framing' approach frightening or considered it wasteful of valuable curriculum time. Some students felt let off by the apparent lack of pressure, and became bored, especially if they did not understand the structure of the session.

The community of learners

What do the composers themselves get out of the scheme? Perkins quotes many of their remarks. John Cooney's are typical:

> I feel my composing has always benefited from my involvement in education work because the continual need to find ways to express often very complex and subtle musical concepts in a clear and meaningful way forces me to address the issue of music and communication (Cooney; cited in Perkins, 1993: 22).

One benefit many composers might have enjoyed was the opportunity to attend the annual training weekend, once considered an essential element in the scheme. In 1990, Perkins took the view that 'the majority of the composers on the scheme were, and will be, out of touch with current educational practice' (Perkins, 1990: 43). If this were true, it could be seen as an indictment of the whole scheme. Could the PRS really justify sending inexperienced composers into the classroom with only as much training as they could get in an intensive weekend course? Luckily, in many cases, the composers who took part in the scheme were rather better equipped than Perkin's remarks indicate.

The training weekend should have been an ideal opportunity to compare the different approaches of various projects, and to make all grant recipients aware of the wider holistic nature of the scheme. The purpose of the weekend was to draw project co-ordinators' attention to possible failings in their schemes, to emphasise the need for good planning, and awareness of the practical constraints of working in schools. As Andrew Potter put it:

> The idea of the PRS Training weekend is to challenge the composers and organisers. It is also a gathering point for ideas, as well as people. It is useful for composers and project directors to learn about the education side of things. The training weekend could usually spot a dud project even if it had got through on paper. Some were ditched as a result (Potter & Laycock, 2000: interview notes).

Unfortunately PRS was not always able to compel attendance at the weekend, and projects were sometimes not represented at all, or sent only a token participant. Composers in particular were remarkably unwilling to subject themselves to the rigours of a grilling by the selection committee. Either they thought themselves above such scrutiny, or simply did not have the time. Even 'Rainbow over Bath' was unable to persuade Sean Gregory, Deirdre Gribbin or Rob Smith, supported by the PRS in 1996 and 1997, to attend the training weekends. Sadly, in 2000, the PRS appeared to have abandoned the idea altogether.

Perkins also recommended the incorporation of in-service training for teachers before the start of each residency, and this quickly became an obligatory element. However the level of teacher-training and higher education involvement in the projects themselves is disappointing, indicating little awareness of the principle of the 'community of learners'. Two of the nine examples are provided by the involvement of students on the Bath Spa University College Composing-in-Education module in 'Rainbow over Bath' projects. Very few other projects seem to have realised the potential for involving trainee teachers or providing work-experience placements in 'performance and communication skills'.

Age and ability

The PRS scheme is primarily re-active and can only respond to those organisations which are motivated enough to apply. However, by strategic selection of project submissions the PRS can be 'open' in its approach to 'age' and 'ability', and also to 'people', creating a wide mix of social background and ability across the whole scheme. However this does not mean that all individual projects achieve such a balance at a local level. Some are better than others.

The following table shows the total number of groups which participated over the nine years. By 'groups' I mean whole class-groups of children, out-of-school music centres, youth centres, or other community organisations. Unfortunately, the reports are poor on statistical information and although Perkins gives details of all schools and groups which took part in each project, she does not give numbers of participants in each group, and only estimates the total numbers of participants in four of the years:

1989/90	1662 children	100 teachers
1990/95	no data provided	
1995/96	2060 children	126 teachers
1996/97	765 children	49 teachers
1997/98	1803 children	60 teachers

My figures are based on an estimated average of thirty people per workshop-group, producing figures consistent with Perkin's own estimates. She admits that, as a proportion of the entire national school population, this is minute, a reminder that projects funded from private foundations can only ever hope to be 'exemplary' in nature, and therefore never truly 'open'. As she points out: 'The only way to reach more is to spend more'.

Number of workshop groups per age or ability range between 1989 and 1998:

KS1	KS2	KS3	KS4	A level	Higher education	Adults	Special needs	Music centres	Youth groups	Total
12	145	56	173	62	9	16	29	18	9	529

Estimated numbers of participants at each age range:

360	4350	1680	5190	1860	270	480	870	540	270	15870

The PRS scheme defines 'education' primarily as 'education for school-age children'. The small number of adult groups (16) are represented by members of various community choirs and orchestras which took part in larger-scale projects such as Jeni Roditti's *Gift of Angels* at Dorchester Abbey in October 1996, when PRS was one of a number of funding partners. Keith Morris' project for Gateshead Borough Council during the 1991 Gateshead Music Week achieved an ideal balance by integrating children from five schools, students from Gateshead College, a folk choir, a children's street band, and a community bus project into one performance.

Sometimes projects appear 'open' on paper as to age and ability in that they are targeted at a range of disparate groups, but miss out on the opportunity for social mixing and encounter implied by the fourth condition of openness. Paul Griffiths' project in Suffolk in Spring 1996 grasped firmly the issue of social mixing by stipulating that groups from Bungay, Debenham, Eye and Framlingham High Schools should each write for another local organisation or centre such as a feeder middle school, a feeder primary, an old people's home or an amateur choir. The project however fell down holistically in that there was no opportunity for participants to encounter Griffiths' own work as a composer.

Projects show a marked concentration at the GCSE and upper junior levels, reflecting the priorities set by the schools. A recurrent pattern of secondary schools linked with feeder primaries emerges. Music projects formed part of the secondary school's wider agenda of familiarising top juniors with the more attractive aspects of life in the big school. Bill Martin's project for the Forest Arts Centre in New Milton in 1994/1995 brought together children of mixed abilities and ages from four comprehensives and four primary schools in the New Forest, chosen because they might benefit socially rather than for musical ability.

Conversely, Bill Connor's project *Bridging the Gap* for the Hallé Concerts Society in 1996/1997 certainly bridged no social gaps by targeting five high-flying grammar schools from socially privileged areas in Sale, Oldham, Bury, Tameside and Manchester. The project's title referred to the role of the musical score as a bridge for the composer's intentions. Perkins rated this ambitious project highly because of the polished results it achieved. Ten musicians from the Hallé Orchestra performed students' group compositions at the end of two days of intensive workshops, as well as scores by Bill Connor and Camden Reeves, a pattern which conforms well to the holistic model. Perkins drew attention to its public relations value for the PRS. This was the Hallé's first major project in schools led by an outside composer, and its success was crucial to the orchestra's growing educational work.

The phrase 'special needs' necessarily lumps together a wide spectrum of very different categories including 'severe learning difficulties', 'behavioural problems' or 'hearing impaired'. The chart on page 353 suggests a clear commitment from many of the projects to the integration of some form of 'special needs' provision into a larger project. Bob Peacock's project in 1994/1995 as Composer in Residence at the Dovecot Arts Centre in Cleveland was unusual in targeting exclusively six local special-needs schools.

By focusing on specific age/ability groups were these projects 'strong' or merely 'closed'? The answer depends on whether the local organisers saw them either as a strongly and coherently focused part of their own more 'open' strategy, or as part of an agreed collaborative 'open' strategy with other organisations in the same region.

The statistic of eighteen out-of-school music centres is poor. It includes the one shining example of Gary Carpenter's project for Wirral Borough Council in 1998 when 283 young instrumentalists from six different music centres participated. Perkin's critical remarks of this brave undertaking are symptomatic of the scepticism which creative music projects engender in both staff and students at this level

– a problem I have already discussed under the heading of the 'skill gap'. Remarks such as 'they could not accept the sounds they created as real music' (Perkins, 1998: 3) typify the problem.

Of the other dozen examples of work in music centres, three are accounted for by 'Rainbow' projects with Bath Society of Young Musicians and the Mendip Music Centre. The remaining nine show clearly how this sector has fought shy of becoming involved in creative music-making. Young players who took part in the project led by Stuart Bruce and Sean Gregory with the Cambridge Youth Orchestra in 1994/1995 were 'very dubious of creative workshops which first of all demanded that they put their instruments away' (Perkins, 1995: 7). They saw little point in using orchestral sessions for vocal and rhythmic games. By the end, some players were won over and acknowledged benefits such as freeing up their improvisation, development of memory; aural training and the challenge of creating a piece of music in three two-hour sessions.

The small involvement of out-of-school youth groups echoes the experience of Gemini's Merseyside residency when youth clubs turned out to be a very unpromising context for creative projects. Almost all the PRS examples took place in the first two years of the scheme and, apart from Amanda Stuart who worked with youth theatre and dance groups at Peterborough Arts Centre in 1989, are oddly concentrated in the North East of England. They include Keith Morris' work with a children's street band at Gateshead Music Week, and Al Bell's young women's song writing project at the Buddle Arts Centre in Tyneside, both in 1991. John Kefala Kerr worked with unemployed adults at the Theatre Station and Blyth Resource and Initiative Centre as part of his Blyth Valley project *The Apprentice Composer* in summer 1992. Many regard this as a difficult or disorganised environment but Kefala Kerr himself described his experience as 'a very fruitful liaison with the community-based groups [...] that often harbour gifted and enthusiastic attenders' (Kefala Kerr; cited in Perkins, 1993: 26).

It was not until Frankie Armstrong's *Let your voice be heard* organised by 'Voices (Powys)' and 'Community Music Wales' in 1995 and 1996, that PRS supported a project again covering not only the youth sector (Mid-Powys Youth Theatre) but people of all ages 'from four to eighty'. The almost complete openness in the 'age' axis implied by this statement speaks of ideological fervour. Perkins' report indicates how successfully it was converted into reality: 'Some members of the choir, both men and women, began with open scepticism of approach; their eventual enjoyment of the evening was self evident, and I recall a seventy-six-year-old dancing in sheer delight' (Perkins, 1996: 7). Here was an excellent example of the power of personal charisma in a creative music project. Perkins expressed doubt as to whether improvisational singing met the PRS definition of musical composition, but my 'community of learners', and my discussion of Wiegold's use of improvisation both show that it can be an integral part of a holistic scheme. The remarks of the Head of Music at Gwernyfed High School sum up the level of enthusiasm:

> From its first moments when Frankie Armstrong introduced herself to an understandably apprehensive year 10 group, it was clearly not a singing project as they had imagined it. Whatever we sang was a veritable act of group creation, the whole of the learning process underscored by an intensely participatory feeling. So where there was prepared performance it was performance freed from the rigours of note learning and concentrated on natural expression and free-ranging improvisation (Paul Shallcross; cited in Perkins, 1996: 7).

Example 82: Matrix analysis of *Let your voice be heard.*

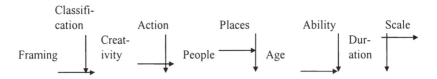

Frankie Armstrong's project is one of the few which covered key-stage 1. The poor statistic for participation at this level probably represents a real lack of knowledge, skill and confidence on the part of workshop leaders.

Places and people

The PRS scheme is available in all parts of the UK and Northern Ireland. However, it was difficult in practice for the PRS to operate a geographically 'open' strategy. This said, the scheme has done a good job in selecting projects in many parts of the country including Scotland, Wales and Ulster, and has avoided being too London-centric. However projects in England have tended to cluster around Tyneside and Northumberland, East Anglia, Liverpool and the Wirrall, South Wales and Yorkshire, reflecting the enthusiasms of organisers in those localities. We can see how certain organisations have shown consistent development, benefiting from previous experience, and integrating the PRS scheme into a wider educational and social context.

A large number of composers directed projects in their own locality, reflecting PRS' own commitment to fostering local relationships. Several categories are discernible. John Kefala Kerr, a music lecturer at Northumbria University, directed two projects in Newcastle on Tyne and Blyth in 1990 and 1992. The Gamelan projects of Janet Sherbourne and Mark Lockett in Derbyshire, the work of Keith Morris in Gateshead and Newcastle, John Maxwell Geddes in Dumfries and Galloway, Jane Wells in Norfolk, and Robin Grant in Wolverhampton are all examples of composers working in their own communities. The Song-writing workshops led by the Williams brothers (Chapter 5, p. 180) have become a regular annual project as part of a strategically-planned programme in Blackwood and Caerphilly.

Some PRS projects formed part of larger composer-in-residence schemes, a pattern which constitutes an excellent model of local collaboration and partnership. Reports indicate that Graham Fitkin's residency with the Royal Liverpool Philharmonic Orchestra was one of the most successful examples of a composer working in many different contexts in schools and the community as well as establishing an excellent relationship with the hosting orchestra. Fitkin has also been supported by the PRS in projects in Devon, and in Cornwall where he lives.

Relationships with a place were important in Sean Gregory's project in Bath because of the aspect of town-twinning discussed in Chapter 6 (p. 211). Likewise Deirdre Gribbin and Rob Smith were currently teaching part-time on the staff at Bath Spa (p. 235). These two 'Rainbow over Bath' projects were unique in the PRS scheme in that they involved real creative collaboration outside the UK.

Only two other PRS projects pretended to have any kind of European focus. Alan Belk's 'Moves Abroad' in Wolverhampton in 1992 took Europe – its diverse and idiosyncratic qualities – as its project theme, but there was no actual European collaboration.

Daryl Runswick's 'Blueprint for Orchestra' was written to celebrate the fiftieth anniversary of the twinning between Enfield and Courbevoie near Paris in September 1993. This was part of a larger cultural collaboration involving dancer Kay Beach, designer Dean Blunkell and six members of London Sinfonietta, organised by Gillian Moore. Its aim was 'to explore and reflect the diversity of cultural heritage and performing arts across all national and ability barriers, and further to explore the arts through multi-disciplined activities' (Perkins, 1994: 12). But no children from Courbevoie were involved, neither did the Sinfonietta team do any work in Courbevoie.

Perkins had much detailed condemnation for this project. It involved the participation of children from infants, junior, secondary and special needs schools, but Perkins found that some of the musicians had little experience of such a wide ability range, thus infringing my ninth condition of openness. The final performance in a marquee surrounded by dog shows and discos did little to enhance the enjoyment of the music.

The project left a legacy in the form of *Blueprint for Orchestra*, an example of a window structure consisting of what the composer called 'empty rooms' (BC3). Runswick has since written other pieces with 'empty rooms' such as *Blueprint II* (1995) written for the London branch of COMA (Example 82). Each 'room' provided a musical framework of chordal, and rhythmic material into which members of the orchestra incorporate their own material. The piece exists as a do-it-yourself composition pack in the form of sheets of instructions including a sheet of modes built out of ciphers of the names of people associated with COMA.

Example 83: Runswick, D. (1997) *Blueprint for Ensemble.*

Gillian Perkins' glowing accolade for the first European collaboration of 'Rainbow over Bath' is flattering indeed:

> This project broke new ground, taking creative music making into European classrooms in several countries at once. The energy of Jolyon Laycock and Sean Gregory is unstoppable (Perkins, 1996: 11).

However, as this thesis shows, as yet there are very few examples of other projects which have followed our lead. The PRS could not of course support the European element of these 'Rainbow' initiatives, but it could be worth exploring the potential of cross-border partnership funding with its sister performing rights organisations in other parts of the world.

The four-phase model

The PRS scheme has thrown up a wide variety of timetables, many of them variants on the four-phase model. Perkins herself advocates a kind of four-phase pattern as a minimum requirement. In her 1991/1992 report she asserts that 'two sessions are never enough' (Perkins, 1992: 34). In 1994/1995 she draws a general principle out of her critique of the Gamelan project of Mark Lockett and Janet Sherbourne in Chesterfield when she says 'I hesitate to commend a scheme with only three sessions of a double period each', concluding that:

> To be effective composers need a certain amount of time with pupils. They are strangers to each class they meet, and to expect them to have a long-lasting impact, to provide something the teachers themselves cannot, in less than four sessions is over-optimistic. [...] To be effective the minimum of four sessions depends on at least a double period each time and there should also be time for follow-up work in between (Perkins, 1995: 23).

John Hardy's project with the BBC Welsh in 1995 at Wyeside Arts Centre, Builth Wells, followed the classic pattern with teachers'

Inset followed by four half-day visits to each school and a final joint rehearsal. John Cooney's project in Chatham Grammar School with the Capricorn Ensemble, based on Messiaen's *Quartet for the end of Time*, began with a half-day joint session; then five double periods in the school followed by final rehearsal and performance.

The four-phase model depends on the active involvement of class teachers working with pupils during the weeks between the composer's visits. Graham Fitkin spent ten sessions in each school in his two projects in Sefton, organised by Merseyside Education Authority and the Royal Liverpool Philharmonic, implying that he undertook a much heavier share of the teaching load than the four-phase model implies.

Bill Martin's Forest Arts Centre project at New Milton in 1995 followed a rather complex timetable with an introductory-day, a three-day residential course, two follow-up sessions and a final performance. This extended timetable reflects the composer's well developed and intensive method of presentation. His approach, which is the basis of his pioneering work with CODA, emphasises the value of the composition process not only in releasing musical inspiration but also in developing team-building, management, communication and inter-personal skills.

Projects in 1997/1998 led by Lucas Goss with Community Music Wales, and by Tim Fleming and Elaine Whitewood in Calderdale, show the practical advantages of locally-based composers when travel and accommodation costs become negligible. Both these projects were spread over an entire year. Fleming and Whitewood created their *Song Book for the year in Calderdale* by visiting the three schools once a month. Each visit resulted in one song form each school – a pattern which deviates completely from the four-phase model. Fleming concentrated on a different approach to song writing in each session, using words, rhymes, rhythm, soundscapes, storytelling or games as starting points. Thus the complete creative process from 'preparation' to 'final performance' was re-enacted at each workshop.

Final concerts

Most projects culminated in some kind of final concert or showcase. During the early years of the scheme Gillian Perkins took a cautious view of them:

> Undoubtedly they can be a great boost to the music department of a school [...]. Such a target can result in enormous increase in self-confidence by the participants. The danger of show-cases is the obvious one of panic during those all-too-short sessions with the composer in the classroom, and the tendency to regard them as the end rather than merely a statement of 'here's how far we got'. [...] I have come to the conclusion that given a sufficiently generous residency, a small-scale showcase does give a target worth having. A small degree of panic can work wonders at oiling the musical decisions that will have to be taken eventually. But if the residency is too short, avoid the word Showcase, let alone Concert, and have a Work in Progress session instead, very privately to the other participants in the project only (Perkins, 1991 5.1.8).

Hugh Nankivell expresses an even more sceptical view, developed at greater length in his thesis on the subject of 'Process and Product', following his Composer in Residence project with schools in culturally deprived areas of North Kirklees in 1997/1998:

> [...] one of the things to realise is that at the start of school, especially key-stage 1, children are not aware of the difference between process and product. It is all making music, it is exciting and **it is now** (author's emphasis). This is important to promote, even at older levels as otherwise the whole purpose of a class session can seem only to be relevant to some future performance/recording and not pertinent to here and now (Nankivell; cited in Perkins, 1998: 25).

Instead of a final concert, this project led to the production of a cassette and teachers' pack featuring musicians from English Northern Philharmonia (the orchestra of Opera North) as well as exotic instruments such as Chinese reed organ, Japanese banjo, Korean gong, mbira, cello and percussion in a recorded performance of *Bustling Bands Rhythmic Town*.

Nankivell is however in a minority amongst PRS project leaders, most of whom acknowledge the cathartic value of a final concert.

Most, like Wiegold, see the preparation and performance of the final concert as an essential part of 'process'. The word 'product' is distasteful in this context. It carries a negative 'consumerist' connotation, equating final concerts with a commercially oriented outcome – something which can be sold to the public. Just like Nankivell's hypothetical key-stage 1 pupil, we should refuse to see the difference between 'process' and 'product'. If the composer is unable to develop the work of participating students or children beyond the excitement of the 'now' towards the more distant goal of a final concert, then this may point to a failing in inspirational leadership, even at key-stage 1. We should emphasise process and product in balanced measure as part of a continuum. Wiegold's four-phase process does this by concentrating on exploration and play in the early phases, leading to refinement and deeper focus later on. All phases can and must be 'exciting' and 'now'.

Perkins' own view of final performances shifted noticeably over the nine years of her involvement with the PRS scheme. In 1995 she was forced to admit that: 'Virtually every composer this year has told me how important they thought the end performance was in stimulating the classroom work which preceded it' (Perkins, 1995: 74). By 1996/1997 she was acknowledging that 'people have complained that I am critical of performances as part of these projects'. For her, only one reservation remained. The composer may find that there is 'insufficient creative time because people start worrying about performance standards before they are ready to take them on board' (Perkins, 1997: 26). In what amounts to a complete climb-down, she admits that this is no more than a planning issue, and not a denial in principle of the value of a final concert.

Only twelve PRS projects were without a final showcase of some kind, most of these in the earlier years of the scheme before 1993. Some, like John Cooney's work at Bexhill on Sea in 1992/1993 which tended to peter out towards the end, suffered from serious lack of focus as a result.

A wide variety of formats for final performances were tried including incorporation into a festival or other local event such as the twinning celebrations at Enfield. Alec Roth's project with ten London Borough schools, both primary and secondary, in 1991, organised by

Trinity College, suffered from too little preparation time and plumped for a less pressured 'Final Gathering Day'. In some cases final concerts were inappropriate because the project had specific aims such as John Kefala Kerr's project for Blyth in Northumberland which created occasional music for all sorts of different contexts such as telephone answering-machine jingles, the Mayoress' tea party, and dances for a Ceilidh. All the music created in the Folkworks 1991 project in Cumbria with Freeland Barbour, Robin Dunn, & John Kirkpatrick was performed in Ceilidhs.

David Bedford's *The Old House* for Christchurch Spitalfields, only merited a lunch-time concert as part of the 1995 Spitafields Festival resulting in a small audience. This excellent project was not given a high enough profile. Perhaps at the planning stage, the festival organisers were unconfident about the outcome. They should have been more willing to take a risk. Simon Foxley's comments make it clear why:

> [...] unusual among education projects mounted at Spitalfields for an end product to be so clearly defined in advance [...] pupils took responsibility for the content and, therefore, the final performance truly reflected their own ideas. This was an important feature of the project since the end product was 'owned' by the pupils, who were helped by the artists to present them in the most appropriate fashion (Foxley; cited in Perkins, 1995: 74).

Bedford brought together a large team of collaborators including storyteller Virgine Gulbenkian, singers Linda Hirst and Sarah Goldfarb, and Theatre Director Edward Kemp for *The Old House*. The project was based on a simple idea, guaranteed to stimulate children's fertile imaginations: 'Goings on in on in a derelict warehouse'. Groups of children in years 5, 6, 7 and 8 from six different schools were each responsible for a different scene in the story of a group of children trying to escape the clutches of a sequence of scary ghosts.

The Old House was one of a small number of multi-arts projects supported by PRS. Two, including Paul Robinson at Bradford with the Harmonie Band in 1991 and Pete Rosser at Guildhall Arts Centre in 1997, involved film. Adrian Lee with the story-teller Tim Ward Jones and the Obelon Art and Puppetry Company in 1991 was one of the first of many projects organised by Pauline Allan using the Norfolk

Gamelan. Perkins praises highly Chris Burn's work with dancer Cecilia Macfarlane and ceramic artist Val Toft in Ipswich in 1992, singling out the important personal qualities of all the workshop leaders in this multi-arts team:

> Projects in Ipswich and Conisborough succeeded largely because both composers and, in the case of Ipswich, other artists involved, were resourceful, patient and educationally skilled *and able to offer workshops which were valuable and relevant to everyday music teaching*, rather than being geared exclusively to the final show (Perkins, 1993: 25; [author's italics]).

Sometimes, music ran the risk of being overshadowed by other aspects in multi-arts projects. This was a problem with Rob Godman's project in rural schools in Bedfordshire involving visual art, poetry, drama, video and instrument design, even though it involved percussionist Evelyn Glennie.

Perkins praises the guts, courage and hard work which went into what was perhaps the most spectacular event sponsored by the PRS scheme, a community production of *The Gift of the Angels* by Jeni Roditti mounted by Coral Arts at Dorchester Abbey. This told the story of the seventh century Anglo-Saxon princess Cyneburga. The performance consisted of tableaux incorporating puppets, dancing, flags, masks, and video in which, according to Perkins, music was the weakest link.

The holistic model

One obvious benefit for the composer in a PRS scheme could be that of getting paid to write a new piece of music. One of the 'tests' for holism is the focus on new commissioned works, but in this respect, most PRS projects do not score well. Those initiated by education authorities tended not to focus on the composer's own creative work. This is to lose a major part of the educational benefit. It turns the composer into a teacher, usurping the class-teacher's role. The composer should be used by class teachers as a role model. This is part of the composer's inspirational or catalytic function. His or her experience of life, the sound of his or her music, insight into how it was made, and an awareness of the tradition to which it belongs are all important parts of the educational process. Education which is entirely child-centred is seriously unbalanced.

Only fourteen projects incorporated commissioned works by a lead composer. It is likely that this reflects a failure of the scheme to attract the right projects rather than a lack of willingness of the selection committee to choose them. The committee was keen to encourage new commissions, but the rules did not allow PRS money to subsidise the costs. Applicants were encouraged to raise cash from other sources such as Regional Arts Boards or the Arts Council which both had budgets for commissions.

An interesting case of a failure in the commissioning process concerns John Cooney's project featuring the Capricorn Ensemble with six Medway Grammar schools based at Chatham Grammar School in 1995. Messiaen's *Quartet for the End of Time* was used as a model for this advanced composition project. The organisers failed to raise funds for the planned commission of a work by Cooney using the same instrumentation. The report indicates the importance he attached to this aspect of the project, and the disappointment he felt that the project organisers were unable to respond:

> Cooney was very keen to have a commissioned work. [...] He has argued a powerful case, comparing the use of a violinist in school, who does not actually play the instruments in front of the pupils, with the case of the composer whose work is never encountered by those with whom he works (Perkins, 1995: 8).

The danger is that the composer appears only as a musical anima-teur, focusing on the work of another, more established figure, while his own creative work is ignored.

Two approaches to commissions are discernible:

Type 1:
Commissioned piece for professional ensemble, not involving children or community participants (Paynter stage D). Only seven projects included professional performance of a commissioned work:

1990: Sean Gregory – String Quartet for the McCapra, and Carols for Stamford Choral Society.
1993: Rob Godman – work for percussion and tape premiered by Evelyn Glennie as part of a multi-media project for rural schools in Bedfordshire.
1994: John Maxwell – Geddes *Dances at Threaves* for the BBC Scottish project in Dumfries and Galloway Regional Council.
1995: Graham Fitkin – new composition for the RLPO in connection with his work in Southport Arts Centre, under the auspices of Sefton Leisure Services.
1996: Sean Gregory – *A Feeling in Time* commissioned for 'No Strings Attached' by 'Rainbow over Bath'.
1997: Deirdre Gribbin – *In the Wake of the Child* commissioned for Mary Wiegold and Roger Heaton by 'Rainbow over Bath'.
1997: New works by Camden Reeves & Bill Connor performed by ten musicians of the Hallé Orchestra as part of Bridging the Gap with six high schools in the Manchester area.

Type 2:
Commissioned piece for performance by amateurs and children (Variants of Bedford Categories 1, 2 or 3); Again, the scheme is disappointing with only seven examples:

1990: Nicola Lefanu – *The Green Children* commissioned by St. George's Guildhall for the King's Lynn Festival, in association with the ENO Baylis programme (BC3).
1991: Bill Sweeney – *A Set for the Kingdom* for the Fife Regional String Orchestra (BC1).
1991: Elaine Agnew – *Tir na Nog* for East Ulster Youth Orchestra (BC1).
1992: Alan Belk – *Moves Abroad* for Wolverhampton Borough Council. Score with aleatoric sections, extended vocal techniques; composed for school orchestra and two soloists (BC2).
1993: Tim Fleming – Oratorio with community musician Ian Heywood on a theme related to post-industrial regeneration. Performed in Conisborough Castle, Doncaster (BC1).
1994: Daryl Runswick – *Blueprint for Orchestra* for the Enfield/Courbevoie twinning celebrations (BC3).
1996: Robin Grant – *Owd Jonah's Ghosts* for Wolverhampton Education Festival (BC1).

Some of these have since become repertoire pieces, available for use in other projects. Nicola Lefanu's *The Green Children*, published by Novello in 1997 in a revised edition, had the distinction of being the very first project of the PRS scheme. It suffered the teething problems of all ground-breaking initiatives. It was also the first to be evaluated by Gillian Perkins. The project team included the Gemini Ensemble. The project was set up by Irene Macdonald, then the General Manager of the King's Lynn Arts Centre. Macdonald's comments on the differences of attitude between artists and educationalists echo the views she had expressed ten years earlier as Education Officer for the Arts Council Contemporary Music Network:

> To my mind almost all the artists (except Gemini) were concerned more with the opera than with the project i.e. with the product rather than the process. The event did not arise sufficiently out of the work with the schools (Macdonald; cited in Perkins, 1990: 6).

The opera, based on a story written down by the twelfth century chronicler Ralph de Coggeshall, calls for five professional musicians. In the score five windows, described as 'project scenes', are intended 'to involve a whole class in cross curriculum work (poetry, music, art craft and design, drama and movement, history)' (BC3). Elements such as traditional singing games, dramatic depictions of life in the country, or the market at Bury St. Edmunds are suggested but the published score gives no starting points for musical invention. The realisation of the project scenes depended on the leadership of Ian Mitchell and Nicola LeFanu, supported by librettist and director.

Perkins' report suggests that the project was beset by the kind of misunderstandings about expectations and outcomes I discussed in Chapter 8 (p. 261). In its original conception, the project had been described as a 'framework', but Irene Macdonald's remark that 'the framework was far more than I expected it to be' (MacDonald; cited in Perkins, 1990: 6) indicates that the Festival got more than it bargained for. The work grew into a full-length children's opera in two acts and nine scenes. Within this scheme, the creative 'project scenes' formed only a small part.

The comments of Derek Paice, the project manager, underline the need for some form of formative evaluation. He suggests a structure of regular briefing meetings:

> What tended to happen was the artists for the most part plied their crafts out of sight of everyone and the teachers tried to make sense of the conflicting demands which came with each visit. [...] Each artist came into school with little apparent knowledge of what had happened previously (Paice; cited in Perkins, 1990: 6).

Perkins' report reveals the many negative aspects of this undertaking. The scale of the libretto and opera were much greater than expected. There was insufficient contact between creators and festival organisers during the composition phase. Costs escalated beyond budgetary provision as a result of the loose management structure, and the composer and others did more work than they were paid for. Insufficient resources were allocated to In-Service work and the parameters of the teachers' input were not clearly defined.

None of this should detract from the work itself, nor from the artistic achievement and value of the four high-profile public performances which Perkins describes as 'incalculable'. The attractive story touches on green issues appropriate to the countryside environment of the six rural primary schools which, with Downham Market Junior School Choir, took part in the performances. The music is written in an attractive, lilting diatonic style, delicately and transparently scored so as not to overwhelm young voices. There are occasional moments of aleatoric working such as the instrumental 'mobiles' (Example 84) which accompany the final procession when the composer uses the familiar device of a round, this time in seven parts, to get all the children singing in harmony. Critical comments about project management pale in contrast to the composer's enthusiastic reactions to the final performances:

> One of the things that was very moving in the performances of the opera was to see those children taking part who had learning difficulties; [...] I think that educationalists who stress process over final performance can never have taken part in such performances, and therefore do not fully comprehend the delicate balance and necessary complementation between process and performance (LeFanu; cited in Perkins 1990: 7).

Example 84: Lefanu, N. (1989) *The Green Children* Instrumental mobile from p.182.

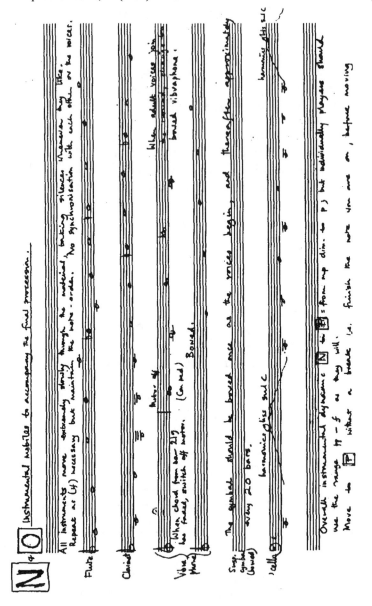

Evaluation

Gillian Perkins acknowledges the need for long term evaluation of the PRS scheme in the conclusion to her first report in 1990: 'It is impossible to evaluate the effect of this scheme after only one year' (Perkins, 1990: 47). After nine years, her reports add up to a unique record of an evolving scheme. I know of no other consistent and unbroken record of reports over such a long period of time. There are many opportunities for consequent evaluation of organisations, composers and other individuals whose names recur repeatedly over the years, and a full consequent evaluation of the whole scheme is overdue. In view of my discussion of issues of confidentiality and anonymity in Chapter 12 (p.329), it is important to emphasise that, at the time, it was the stated aim of the PRS to make the reports freely and publicly available. There is no anonymity, and the accompanying commentaries make it clear that the reports were not intended to be confidential.

Perkin's association with the scheme ended in 1998, and since then projects have been evaluated by a panel of assessors. There is no longer one single individual able to give a comparative overview. My own partial evaluations of aspects of three of the 2000/2001 projects appear in other chapters of this book. They are the Williams brothers song-writing project in Caerphilly (pp. 180 and 272), the Schidlof Quartet with Tansy Davis and John Woolrich in Lincoln (p. 302), and the 'Pirates and Heroes' project of Musiko-Musika in the Isle of Wight (pp. 305 and 324).

9. The author addressing the audience at the final performance of the *Parents and Children* project, Bath Spa University College 1997. Photo Nick Delves-Broughton.

10. Duncan Prescott and Mary Wiegold, Rainbow over Bath 'Composing in Education' project, Kingdown School 2000.

Part 4
Conclusions, proposals and recommendations

Chapter 14
Conclusions and recommendations

The central message of this thesis is one of hope and optimism. I am arguing for the power of music to build bridges between people, bringing about international understanding through cultural exchange. The fulfilment of such a vision requires positive commitment from individuals and institutions at many levels. Loss of contact with a wider audience is not just a crisis for the composers themselves, but for the whole 'schizoid culture' (Small, 1977: 70) in which we live. Getting back on track must be a two-way process.

Education today is dominated by modular programmes. Modules break everything into bite-sized pieces with defined direction of progression and outcome, and sharp subject boundaries. There is only one direction to go in, and only one possible outcome. The multi-dimensional matrices of my theoretical model emphasise the inter-connectedness of all things. They offer an infinity of possible routes, and allow for going off at a tangent in pursuit of an interesting idea. There are no boundaries.

The division in Chris Small's 'schizoid culture' was between two branches of learning: science and art. The rush towards specialisation has continued unabated. The schizoid tendency has led to more and more divisions so that now the separation is even between different approaches to the same subject, exemplified by the dichotomy between the 'child-centred' approach of 'composing in education' and the 'repertoire-based' approach of 'composers in education'. Modularization encourages this type of thinking.

Reconciliation of opposites: the five dichotomies

The theoretical model shows that these opposites are part of the same continuum. The reconciliation of the 'child-centre/repertoire-based' approach requires collaboration between teacher and composer. The teacher must be clear about how he or she can exploit the full potential of the composer's essentially style-centred approach, using it as a model within a wider child-centred teaching programme. A similar level of collaboration can resolve the related dichotomy between the 'top down' and 'bottom up' approach in community projects.

My research revealed four other dichotomies. The conflict between the Wiegold-influenced deep-toned small-group approach which focuses on individual creativity, and large-scale prestigious projects involving impressively large numbers of people, is highlighted by the 'duration and scale' matrix. Arts Centres, orchestras and other organisations looking for impressive prestige events can resolve this dichotomy by giving sufficient space and time during the early stages of the creative process for essential detailed small-group working so that individual participants feel that their contributions are fully valued. Discussion of the 'framing' axis focused on the dichotomy between free creative work and disciplined instruction in the rudiments of music. I discussed questions of cultural unity and diversity in relation to 'classification' and 'people' in the context of the aims and objectives of the European Commission Culture 2000 programme. Finally, in discussion of 'age' and 'ability', I offered practical solutions to the 'skill-gap', relating them to Schafer's 'community of learners'.

The search for a middle way through reconciliation of these five dichotomies is my recurrent theme. It was the extremism of Maoist/Leninist doctrines which caused the break-up of the Scratch Orchestra, but Socialism of a less doctrinaire kind, with its assertion of humanitarian ideals of equality, freedom and human rights, has often been embraced by composers and educators devoted to the democratisation of creativity which is the guiding principle of creative music-making. A middle-way in political terms compliments the middle way between freedom and control advocated by Wiegold in his workshop techniques.

Examples and case studies

I have used the work of many different organisations, as well as projects which I devised and ran as part of 'Rainbow over Bath', to exemplify the theoretical model. There are many more examples of organisations which have not been discussed in this thesis, both in the UK, in Europe, and in other parts of the world. In some cases documentation was not available, either because of a failure to keep systematic archives, or because of problems of confidentiality. New initiatives are constantly springing up such as the creation of Education Action Zones, Music Action Zones and the Arts Council of England's Creative Partnerships scheme. In many cases there has simply not been enough space to discuss all the many projects which exemplified some aspect of the theoretical model.

Lack of systematic archival material prevented me from discussing Gillian Moore's education work with the London Sinfonietta during the 1980s and early 1990s. I discussed the SPNM C4K programme, but not the parallel Adopt-a-Composer scheme in collaboration with 'Making Music' (formerly National Federation of Music Societies) which has given rise to several new compositions of BC4. I discussed none of the work of Sound Sense, the organisation based in East Anglia which acts as a focus for many of the community music activities happening in this country.

Many festivals apart from Spitalfields have well-developed music education programmes which incorporate elements of the theoretical model such as those in the Bath, Huddersfield, Cambridge and Aldeburgh but lack of space has prevented more detailed discussion.

The spread of UK methodologies abroad is exemplified by John Paynter's work in Italy and Scandinavia, the input of Peter Renshaw, Peter Wiegold and Sean Gregory into the educational programme of the Finnish Joensuu City Orchestra and its Rhombus Education group, or the adoption of an education programme based on the UK model by Orquestra Filharmonica de Gran Canaria. The educational work of the LSO's *Discovery* programme in Sapporo, Japan, in July 1997, and the London Sinfonietta's residency at the Athens Concert Hall relating to its performances there of Marc Anthony Turnage's opera *Greek* in November 2000 were two other pioneering initiatives.

My discussion of educational work in Eire centred on the National Chamber Choir, but also prominent in the Republic is Evelyn Grant's 'Children's Music Hour' and her work with the Cork Pops Orchestra, a programme influenced directly by a period of study with Bruce Cole on the MA course in Community Music at York.

Everywhere I looked, in UK and in Europe, I encountered new and interesting projects and activities. I suspect that my research so far has revealed only a small proportion of the wider international picture, although it has tended to support the theoretical model. The importance of sharing this expertise across national boundaries cannot be stressed enough, but examples such as the 'Reseo' project are few and far between and the full potential is yet to be realised.

The value of creative music-making: a struggle for recognition

This expertise is just as much part of the 'artistic capital' of the developed nations as are the 'great works of art' Tippett was referring to (Tippett, 1974: 129). So are the minority cultures and folk traditions which are under threat from globalisation and commercialisation. So much today is judged by its monetary value. We must ensure that the non-monetary value of this 'artistic capital' is recognised, especially since those communities which most need the benefits of creative music-making are those least able to pay for it and are, at the same time, amongst those who have the greatest contribution to make in the form of their own unique folk cultures.

Part of the problem in Britain is that, in spite of so much persuasive discussion on the subject during the twentieth century, many remain unconvinced of the value of creative work in the arts. Unless successive generations of theorists and practitioners maintain a constant pressure by argument and example, a host of irresistible counter claims from the scientific and technological lobby for ever more resources and financial investment will threaten to overwhelm the arts.

The apparent benefits of scientific and technological research are so much more tangible and therefore more beguiling in a materialistic world. That the world needs hard-headed, practical people, such as mathematicians, scientists, engineers, doctors, lawyers, accountants, manufacturers, computer programmers and so on, to create the material necessities of life, is so much easier to demonstrate than that it needs dreamers, thinkers, creators of beauty, poets, musicians, painters and so on. Faced with a world of global mass-media, computer games, pop-videos, twenty-four-hour TV and the like, those who advocate active participation in creative music-making, or any other form of hands-on artistic activity, find it difficult to make themselves heard. *Striking a New Note* painted a gloomy picture:

> In this highly competitive world, new music of all sorts may struggle to maintain its live appeal. Some forms – such as contemporary Western classical music – already find it difficult to reach out beyond small bands of enthusiasts (Gowrie, 1996: 72).

The history of educational reform in the twentieth century is littered with reports whose well-reasoned recommendations concerning the arts have been ignored, or resulted in only partial implementation for a short period. The Hadow Report asserted that: 'The educative value of music has often been overlooked in the past. It has been sometimes mistakenly regarded as a soft relaxation' (Hadow, 1931). In spite of the Hadow recommendations, it was still necessary in 1963 for the Newsom Report to note that more than half the schools in its survey had no provision for music, and that 'music is the subject most frequently dropped from the curriculum' (Newsom, 1963: 140).

In 1967 The Plowden Report was still finding 'the present position unsatisfactory'.

The 1982 Gulbenkian report found that issues highlighted in reports like Newsom and Plowden did not seem to carry forward into proposals for the core-curriculum in 1981, suggesting that the government was ignoring its own recommendations. The Foundation was open in its condemnation of the way the arts were taught in schools. The good sense of what it proposed as an alternative cannot be denied, but lack of financial resources will always limit what can be achieved. This is as true now as it was in 1982 and it is depressing to note how little of this report has been acted upon. The GCSE syllabus, with its emphasis on musical composition, encourages the kind of creativity recommended by the Gulbenkian but the imposition of the National Curriculum appears to militate against the kind of freedom and flexibility which is needed if this level of artistic creativity is to be developed to the full.

All Our Futures found that promotion of creative and cultural education in schools was being increasingly restricted 'by the cumulative effects of successive changes in structure, organisation and assessment of the National Curriculum' (Robinson, 1999: 110). It suggests that 'the existing distinction between the core and foundation subjects [...] appears to have reduced the status of the arts and humanities and their effective impact in the school curriculum' (Robinson, 1999: 131). Such remarks imply a return to a situation perilously close to that which Blackham described forty-five years ago: 'We believe that neither the contribution of the arts to general education, nor the place of general education in the national life has yet been recognised' (Blackham, 1957).

The principal solution put forward by *All Our Futures* is the development of creative partnerships in schools. Such partnerships, it asserts, do not yet have a high enough priority in many schools. All children are entitled to opportunities to encounter working artists. Schools should be required to make explicit provision and the work should receive public recognition (Robinson, 1999: 230).

The government appeared at first to be dragging its feet over the implementation of *All Our Futures* even though it was prefaced by glowing introductions from both the Culture and Heritage Secretary,

380

and the Secretary for Education. However the establishment of Youth Music Action Zones in 2001, administered by National Youth Music Foundation, and the Creative Partnership Programme in 2002 gives some room for optimism.

Why is there so much scepticism?

As Paynter has pointed out, past and present failures in creative music projects have contributed to a level of scepticism:

> There is no doubt that, from time to time, creative music-making has got itself into disrepute by being badly organised. Teachers have not planned clearly enough, nor thought through beforehand the kind of results they would expect to see coming through the work (Paynter, 1982: 81).

There will of course be failures – failures of schools to recognise the value of opportunities; failures of workshop leaders to engage with children at a meaningful level; failures of individual teachers to take advantage of the creative possibilities open to them; failures of whole projects due to lack of adequate funding. Failures can result from lack of knowledge of the contemporary arts on the part of teachers, lack of teaching skills on the part of visiting composers and musicians, lack of good project management on the part of organisers or administrators, and lack of vision at all levels, but let us not forget Schafer's second maxim: 'In education, failures are more important than successes' (Schafer, 1975: 133).

Twenty years ago Paynter reported that pupils dismissed creative music-making projects because:

> [...] they have come to expect or have been brought up to expect exactly the kind of things they are given – they expect to be taught skills, music history, to listen to records, to make notes, to be disciplined, and above all to be led. Understandably for these students any kind of experimental activity with sounds appeared to be 'messing about' (Paynter, 1982: 88).

In spite of several years of the inclusion of composition and im-provisation as part of the GCSE music syllabus, such prejudices against creative work still exist. Although teacher-training and in-service courses have ensured that more and more teachers are provided with the tools to enable them to teach composition effectively in the classroom, few authorities recognise the importance of wider provision of creative music by giving it a central role in the teaching programme for all children. The geographical clustering of PRS Composer-in-Education projects discussed in Chapter 13 (p. 357) underlines this patchiness of provision.

Scepticism about creative music-making is also to be found in higher education institutions. Departments of Education, too, tend to sideline '*composers*-in-education' in favour of the more 'child-centred' study of '*composing*-in-education'. Fragmentation of methodologies increases, fuelled perhaps by incomplete knowledge of the historical background. In the foreword to *Composing in the Classroom* Anice Paterson states that such work 'began in the 1960s' (Odam & Patterson, 2000: 5). This is to ignore the pioneering influence of earlier practitioners mentioned in Part 1 of this book, and contributes to the misconceptions about the origins of composing in education.

Only a handful of universities are prepared to recognise the validity of creative music-making as an area of legitimate academic study within departments of music, alongside composition, musical analysis, or historical musicology. My offer to speak at the Goldsmiths College *Second Biennial International Conference on Twentieth-Century Music* in 2001 was rejected in favour of areas of music research which the organisers regarded as more mainstream. The decision of the University of Bath and Bath Spa University College to abolish 'Rainbow over Bath' in June 2000 can be seen as symptomatic of their unwillingness to acknowledge the research value of this holistic model of a contemporary concert programme incorporating educational and community work in a cultural collaboration with European partners.

Creative music-making is a rapidly expanding and developing field. One of the original motivations for my research as discussed in Chapter 3 (p. 97) was that there appeared to be no overview. This is still the case, a fact exemplified by the recent announcement of a

Composers-in-Residence Conference at Bedford School, sponsored by 'The Music Teacher' in May 2002. In an article in SPNM 'New Notes' Alan Charlton, Composer-in-Residence at Bedford School, described the aim of the conference: 'to give composers an insight into what can be achieved by composers in residence', and to arrive at 'some sort of consensus on how to draw on a composer's skills in a way that is most mutually beneficial to school and composer' (Charlton, 2002). I am certain that the conference will have turned out to be very beneficial as an opportunity to share ideas, but Charlton also makes the extraordinary claim that this is 'the first ever conference about school composers-in-residence', while an advertising feature about the conference in 'Music Teacher' claims that this is 'the first conference in the UK to be devoted to the work of composers in schools' (Morris, 2002: i). Are we now to draw distinctions not only between 'composing-in-education', and 'composers-in-education', but also between both of these and a separate field called 'composers-in-residence'? School pupils may enjoy all the many benefits of increased contact time with composers as a result of such 'composer-in-residence' schemes, but they still belong to the same continuum of creative music projects, as shown by my discussions of 'classification', 'framing', the role of composers in the 'community of learners', and the different formats of the 'holistic model'.

What I have called 'creative music-making' is a vital manifestation of a living tradition of music, an essential means of artistic and cultural contact between people from different social, ethnic and national backgrounds, and a search for ways in which a truly creative approach to music can survive in a world increasingly dominated by electronic means of mass communication and entertainment. This is not to say that technology is to be rejected, but to emphasise that it is an aid to creativity, and not a substitute for it. We can use all the technical equipment we like, but without musical ideas and an awareness of the musical qualities of what is produced, the result will be artistically worthless. Creative music-making looks forward to the future by seeking to ensure that our children – all our children – are brought to a point where they too are convinced of the essential importance of creativity in music in a modern peace-loving society.

What is so special about composers? Defining a new role

Where scepticism about creative music-making is concerned, experience at 'Rainbow over Bath' has been that the issue is partly one of confidence in the workshop leader. My thesis asserts the importance of charismatic leadership. Few commentators disagree with this hypothesis but far fewer have attempted to define in detail what these qualities are. Here I bring together all the qualities required of this new kind of composer.

I am concerned with the issue of creativity in music as expressed through musical composition or improvisation. In Chapter 3 I suggested that all of us are to some extent capable of musical creation. Several examples have arisen of musical animateurs such as Andy Baker and Matthew Barley who are not primarily composers, but who clearly possess skills of musical creation of a high order. Since it is the development of musical creativity which is looked for in my thesis, those who lead the process must themselves possess such skills, as well as a systematic understanding of the process and an ability to inspire creativity in others.

Skill and originality as a composer, together with musicianship of the highest order, must therefore be the first priorities, followed by a high level of skill on an instrument, or ability as a conductor. The level of originality must be equivalent to the third category: 'historical originality' as defined in *All Our Futures* (Robinson, 1999: 30). All these skills have an obvious practical application but they also add to the composer's charisma. The ability to conjure up musical material out of nowhere like a magician, or to hear a melody or phrase a couple of times and then write it down in staff notation, strikes many ordinary people as miraculous. Skill on a musical instrument attracts admiration and respect from those who do not possess it.

This new kind of composer, however, cannot get away with simply being a good all-round musician, but must be a good communicator, educator, and inspirational leader as well. As Rwzeski once said 'we are all creators', but now there a is new role for the musician and composer 'as organiser and redistributor of other people's energies' (Rzewski; cited in Nyman, 1999: 130).

A good composer/project director must have a clear intellectual grasp of the function of the composer as creative catalyst and a strong and convinced philosophy of the purpose of creative musicians in society. It is necessary, as Paynter insisted, to recognise an educational as well as a musical duty (Paynter, 1982: 90). The composer must be aware of the different needs of opposing child-centred and repertoire-based approaches, and be able to balance the two. Knowledge and understanding of the different approaches is needed at different age-groups and with different social groups, or with different kinds of mental and physical disability. There must be respect for pupils, students and adults and their work, motivating by encouragement, setting high standards but pitching challenges just right to be achievable.

There must be a degree of humility on the part of the composer who is first amongst this 'community of learners'. There will be a recognition that we all have something to learn and something to teach, and a desire to help others to progress, seeking the best balance between instruction and encounter. At the same time there must be courage to take risks 'on the verge of peril' (Schafer, 1975: 133) leading to the opening of new creative horizons.

Understanding and sympathy for other cultural traditions, modes of behaviour, etiquette, language and so on, are essential, particularly in working outside the UK or with minority ethnic communities in this country. There must be a willingness to learn and practice 'correct behaviour' in all situations without appearing to take either a paternalistic or condescending attitude.

The composer must be an expert diplomat in order to mediate between the 'top down' and 'bottom up' approach, responding to, and interpreting creatively, the musical needs and desires of the host community, educating its members and opening their ears and minds to new forms of music.

There will be an element of self interest, but the composer must, like Holst, be 'kind and full of deep feeling' or, like Cage, 'blessed with a sunny disposition', possessing virtues of infinite patience, self-effacement, and an ability to keep a cool head in a crisis. 'Il n'y a pas de problèmes, que de solutions' ('There are no problems, only solutions') memorably said Marylène Lequesne, the P.A. of Gerard le Berre, Director of Aix en Musique, during just such a crisis. An inexhaustible supply of jokes is a huge asset.

In his eighth maxim, Schafer declared that 'the teacher and the student should first discover one another' (Schafer, 1975: 133). Getting to know workshop participants as people is a key element of leadership. School break-times with children and teachers, or an hour in the pub after a rehearsal with adults are the best places to do it. What are their interests? What do they do in life or after school? Why is music important to them? What do they hope to get out of this project? Asking questions like these will show care about them as people, and will encourage them to give full commitment in return.

Leadership involves listening as well instructing. There must be an ability to accept and respond to constructive criticism, listening to what other participants are saying in a creative debate, knowing how to reject diplomatically and sensitively without causing discouragement, and incorporating good ideas whenever they occur. There will be times when participants' motivation slips. The lead composer must know how to keep the project on course, giving encouragement and inspiration, and reconciling conflicts in interpersonal relationships.

There must be an ability to write and speak persuasively about ideas, methodologies and philosophical rationale, and an ability to evaluate the work objectively, compiling it in convincing project reports. There must be persuasiveness, tenacity and dogged determination in the face of institutional indifference or hostility.

Leadership skills first come to the fore during a training day when the object is to communicate enthusiasm and excitement for the project, building a cohesive creative team, making sure everyone understands their place within it, delegating responsibilities to dependable, resourceful and experienced teachers, and less responsible functions to project assistants.

The composer must know and understand the purpose of all stages in the creative process, be able to convince everyone of the rationale for warm-up games and other preparatory work, keeping the momentum of the project going, knowing when to drive the work forward and when to hold a peaceful moment, ensuring unanimity of purpose at the final performance, and taking responsibility for leaving an effective legacy.

A final speech, striking just the right note of triumph and informality, expressing thanks for hard work, praise for achievement, and appreciation of people behind the scenes like school caretakers who often get forgotten, helps to focus the most positive energies. In a foreign country, a speech given in the host language will help to increase bonds of affection. Quaint accents, bad grammar and mistakes of vocabulary will all be forgiven.

Can all this be learned? The need for training

This list of qualities required of composers who would, in Kodály's phrase, become 'benefactors of humanity' by rendering their art 'accessible to as many people as possible' (Kodály, 1974: 185) is long and daunting. They need inner strength to carry them through, and an outward charisma which endears them to all who meet them. I have spoken often about the need for training courses, but many of these qualities cannot be taught. We can list them, and spell them out to our students, but a real understanding of their importance comes only with years of direct experience.

However, we must begin somewhere. There must therefore be an expansion of the range of training opportunities to develop workshop skills and to train teachers as composers, and composers as teachers. PGCE and QTS courses are already helping teachers to develop skills of teaching composition in response to the inclusion of composition in GCSE and 'A' level, but they need also to learn how to make use of the full potential of visiting or resident composers and musicians coming into their schools. Many composers and musicians need to develop their communication and workshop skills in classroom and community situations. MA courses at the Guildhall School and the Universities of York, and Edinburgh, or in professional development programmes such as the Musicians Union GNVQ are already taking a lead.

However, if a full realisation is to be achieved of the potential for creative music-making to support cultural collaboration across international borders, such courses must develop a wider international focus. The following is a list of possible measures:

- Recruit internationally, attracting student-composers from abroad to acquire knowledge of UK methodologies.
- Seek regular collaboration with similar institutions outside UK.
- Establish reciprocal work-experience programmes on an annual basis, allowing students to undertake placements outside their home country.
- Set up collaborative creative projects conforming to the theoretical model in which students visit institutions in partner countries and work alongside one another as workshop assistants, supporting professional workshop leaders and composers.

That courses must contain practical training in workshop technique is self-evident, but it is also clear that a study of the historical and philosophical background as set out in Part 1 of this book is essential to a full understanding of the origins of current methodologies. None of us can claim to be lone pioneers.

Who will be the advocate?
The need for specialised agencies

It is easy to recommend all these laudable measures in a written thesis but who, in practice, will be the advocate? There are two tasks in hand. One is to propagate the idea of creative music projects based on the theoretical model, the other to encourage its application in a European and international context. It may be possible to persuade existing organisations to take on these roles. There is already some commitment among art education agencies and other music organisations to creative music-making, but only a very few have explored the potential of European collaboration. The involvement of Chard Festival of

Women in Music, Community Music Wales and the ISCM British Section in projects funded by the EU was discussed in Chapter 3 (p. 117).

Most local authorities have an international office and, in some cases, international officers with specific responsibility for education or for town twinning. At national level the Cultural Contact Points in each EU country, such as EUCLID, provide important information about funding schemes. However, none of these organisations specialises in music. They have a much too generalised commitment to a wide variety of artistic and cultural forms.

The propagation of creative music-making in a European and international context requires the formation of specialised agencies. Such an agency can have a variety of constitutional formats:

1. Independently funded fully constituted limited company with charitable status.
2. As a project within an existing organisation such as a music information centre, or a national organisation such as the SPNM or Sound Sense, or their equivalent in other countries.
3. As part of a department of music within a university or college of higher education.
4. As a section within a local authority department of education, or leisure and tourism.

Plans for the formation of the Rainbow Foundation already offer a model for an independently constituted agency. It develops and extends work in the field of creative music previously undertaken by 'Rainbow over Bath' which, as part of the University of Bath, represented the third category of organisation. Its functions can be summarised under six headings:

1. Initiation and management of creative music projects.
2. Co-ordination of a network of European and international partners similar to the model in chapter 6 (pp. 213–14).
3. Fund-raising either independently or in collaboration with partner organisations to support creative music projects.
4. Research, documentation and evaluation of work in the field of creative music in UK, Europe, and internationally, leading to the establishment of a data-base of information about composers, workshop-leaders and projects.

5. Propagation and advocacy of the value, ideas and methodologies of creative music through teaching, lecturing, broadcasting, publication, attendance at conferences and political lobbying.
6. Organisation of an annual international conference of creative music-making in education and the community.

There is an immense amount of persuasion to be undertaken by agencies of this kind. It will be necessary to target international conferences, national, regional and international organisations, orchestras, ensembles and artists, and educational institutions at all levels, speaking up for the benefits of international partnerships in creative music-making.

Music conferences can provide a platform for advocacy provided that the organisers can themselves be persuaded. The 'Bigger Better Beautiful' conference (BBB) on the cultural effects of EU enlargement in January 2002 (see Chapter 6) should have been an ideal context in which to present the benefits of cultural collaboration through music, but the organisers decided on a format which focused exclusively on EU Framework Programmes such as Culture 2000, or on various EU Structural Funds, rather than on examples of the artistic and cultural activities which these funds might be intended to support. An opportunity was lost.

However, amongst delegates who attended were several from organisations dedicated to music. Informal networking made up for the lack of opportunities to make a public presentation. The presence of the Chairman of 'Making Music' (formerly the National Federation of Music Societies) showed that this UK organisation is actively seeking collaborative links with organisations in Europe, in this case with choirs.

COMA is another example of a UK organisation well placed to develop collaborative international links which can involve encounters between contemporary composers and un-skilled or community-based music groups.

National UK organisations such as the National Association for Music Education (NAME), in setting their own conference agendas based on the interests of subscribing members, will not necessarily set a high priority on international issues. The theme of the annual NAME conference in July 2000 was 'composing in education', but this did not include *'composers* in education'. Conference papers focused on methodologies of composition teaching which would be of use to class teachers in this country, and there was no consideration of the possibilities of international collaboration.

The interests of many other organisations including the Musicians Union, the International Society for Music Education (ISME), the British Academy of Composers and Songwriters, and the Incorporated Society of Musicians overlap in the field of creative music-making. It is clear that a greater openness to free discussion and exchange of methodologies would bring great benefit, but a closed membership by subscription, though this is a financial necessity, can militate against such sharing of ideas.

Certain international organisations are prime targets for advocacy. Among them the International Society for Contemporary Music (ISCM), the European Conference of Promoters of New Music (ECPNM), the International Association of Music Information Centres (IAMIC), Jeunesses Musicales International (JMI) and the European Arts Festivals Association.

The signs are that the ISCM is already moving in the right direction with projects such as Children's Future 2001 in Yokohama, Japan in October as part of *Dou Gaku* organised by the ISCM Japanese section and aimed at school age children from 6–14, or the 'Mass Participation' carnival and concert at the Hong Kong World Music Days in October 2002.

Through its membership of the ECPNM, the Rainbow Foundation, successor to 'Rainbow over Bath', is in a position to influence the policy of a number of contemporary music organisations within Europe, many of which are willing to follow a British lead in the initiation of holistic projects in cross-border collaboration.

The International Association of Music Information Centres (IAMIC), with its forty-three members world-wide, is ideally placed to facilitate collaborative projects beyond the boundaries of the European Union by providing information about composers and music promotion organisations with real or potential interest in creative music projects. Jeunesses Musicales International could be approached with a proposal to establish an international creative music programme for young people linked to a network of ECPNM members, and other non-European contemporary music promoters identified on the basis of information and contacts supplied by the IAMIC.

More UK-based ensembles, artists and composers should be encouraged to follow the example of the London Sinfonietta or the LSO by seeking opportunities to work in creative projects whenever they accept European and other overseas engagements, avoiding the fly-in-give-concert-fly-out-again pattern. Conversely, UK promoters should encourage visiting overseas artists and composers to become involved in education work when they visit this country, allowing a trained musical animateur to guide the project if the visiting composer lacks the necessary skills. In this case the visiting composer submits to the régime of the theoretical model, voluntarily becoming part of the 'community of learners' as did Dutch and French composers in 'Rainbow across Europe'.

Schools, too, should be encouraged to set up new international exchange programmes, particularly through existing town-twinning relationships. Music exchange programmes are nothing new but, traditionally, they involve youth orchestras and choirs. Creative music projects which are 'open' as to musical ability would allow children who are not music specialists to take advantage of all the social and cultural benefits.

Where will the money come from?

Creative projects take time to organise, can be expensive to run, and therefore require an enormous effort of fund-raising. Yet, at any one time, we can never reach more than a small proportion of the people in a given area, and within a given age or social group. Experienced leaders such as Sean Gregory or Peter Wiegold may well be able to win over a sceptical group of teenage musicians within minutes, and leave them begging for more next week, but lack of financial resources means that 'more next week' is not affordable. The group's regular leader or conductor will, in all probability, lack the workshop skills, and be unable to repeat, let alone build on the success achieved by the visiting workshop leader. The experience quickly becomes a distant memory as the orchestra lapses back into weekly rehearsals of well-tried and familiar printed repertoire. When resources are limited, priorities must be defined, otherwise we run the risk of trying to do everything rather badly, and doing nothing very well. We lay ourselves open to criticisms not of élitism, but of tokenism. If resources prevent 'openness', it is better to be 'strong' than 'weak'.

The Gulbenkian Report (Calouste Gulbenkian Foundation, 1982) recommended grants and awards, but made no specific suggestions about where these should come from. In spite of many funding pro-grammes including the relative abundance of funds through Lottery programmes and EU schemes, funds are still limited, and schemes short-lived, with the result that provision is patchy. It is rare to find a consistent policy of ongoing partnership between arts organisations, education and community sectors in a given area which really succeeds in making opportunities for creative music-making available to all young people throughout their school life.

'Rainbow over Bath' initiated the projects discussed in this book with money from Arts Council Lottery Schemes, the European Union Kaleidoscope Fund and many other smaller trusts and foundations. It made available the expertise of some of the leading practitioners of techniques of 'composing in education' to young people in Bath and the surrounding areas, as well as to European partners. But every child we reached was part of a privileged minority, not for any reason of social or economic good fortune, but because they happened to be attending one of the schools who joined the project. For every child who took part, there are a hundred in the region who did not.

The best we could claim was that our programme was in some way exemplary, a model for others to emulate and build upon, an attitude I have already defined as 'weak'. My research revealed many others who believed their work to be ground-breaking and important. We have seen too many 'pilot programmes' and not enough of intro-ducing these models into the mainstream teaching curriculum. The situation should not be so hit and miss. Our work should be part of a planned and integrated system which allows all young people in all schools to reap the benefits of working directly with professional composers and musicians as part of an on-going teaching and learning strategy in music.

All our Futures exemplifies the holistic vision of the theoretical model when it concludes that arts organisations do not need two separate policies of public presentation versus education, but 'one co-ordinated and unified cultural policy' (Robinson, 1999: ¶240). Educational institutions involved in music must develop a commitment to the provision of opportunities for creative music-making by allocating the necessary financial and staffing resources in partnership with music-promoting organisations, orchestras, choirs and so on.

In creative music projects based on the theoretical model, organised as part of a planned strategic programme, all participants become part of Schafer's 'community of learners'. Such projects can become a training ground for all teachers, students and children who take part. The expertise gained at all levels should benefit the whole community. It should be the 'seed-corn' of the future.

It is easy to diagnose some of the reasons why this does not always happen. Leaving aside the problem of lack of commitment on the part of heads of music, or of local authority directors of music, there is a problem of finance. As discussed in Chapter 9 the total cost of a typical project could be as much as £20,000.

One reason why daily fees are so high is that the life of the professional musician can be so precarious. The establishment of a full-time workshop team large enough to serve all the schools and some of the community organisations and amateur groups within a given region could bring about economies of scale. Such a scheme would also bring a welcome level of job security to musicians and composers, and would persuade them to accept lower fees. It is also true that musicians and composers with a high level of expertise in this field are scarce. Increased opportunities for the training of professional musicians and composers in the skills of creative music-making, linked to work-experience programmes as project assistants on existing projects would, in a few years time, increase the pool of expertise in this vital area.

Since part of this book was motivated by the pronouncements of the European Commission, logically it is to the European Union with its enormously well-endowed Structural Funds that we should turn in our search for financial support to bring about something which is so close to the European cultural vision.

However EU funding programmes are not yet sufficiently widespread in their influence to provide all the necessary cash for the resulting expansion of international collaboration. Neither are they sufficiently flexible to allow EU money to benefit collaborative projects which extend beyond the boundaries of Europe. Until 2002, the EU was unable even to support the participation of accession countries. At present they cannot support more than a handful of exemplary programmes and, as yet, seem unable to command enough influence over arts-funding agencies in member states to bring about a significant change in attitudes.

As a result there is very little flexibility in national funding systems to facilitate cross-border collaborations. Pan-European tours are not currently recognised as 'tours' by the Arts Council if only one concert takes place in the UK. Nationally based overseas funding programmes such as the British Council, or the French AFAA, exist primarily to propagate the work of their own national artists in foreign countries. Their official policies, while not actually discouraging reciprocal arrangements, can do little to facilitate return visits by foreign artists. Greater flexibility in the funding of creative music projects within UK is also needed, including a relaxation of the National Foundation for Youth Music condition which limits its ability to support school-based projects.

However, as 'Rainbow' showed, it is possible to obtain funding from a wide range of national sources within each partner country. A greater willingness on the part of national and regional funding bodies to collaborate on joint initiatives across national boundaries would facilitate this process, adding value to the seeding money which the EU can provide.

Cultural contact and collaboration through creative music-making

Because of its abilities as a means of non-verbal artistic expression through live performance, music can play a crucial role in the process of European cultural integration. However the concept of Europe cannot be satisfactorily defined. The European Union as an administrative entity is not the same thing as a Europe defined in cultural and social terms. This affluent club of rich nations must accept a duty to use its material richness in support of the development of cultural co-operation of the kind advocated in the EU Culture 2000 programme beyond the arbitrary administrative boundaries of Europe. Music can bridge cultural gaps within Europe, but it can also do this outside Europe. It refuses to be limited by administrative boundaries.

Great benefits in terms of self-confidence, personal achievement and self-expression can come from a creative as opposed to a re-creative approach to music. It is music's 'free-standing cultural autonomy' (Swanwick, 1988: 107) which creates the possibility of experiment and innovation in stylistic fusion. It is the universality of the musical instinct which make it possible for people from a wide range of national, regional, linguistic, age, and social groupings to come together in an atmosphere of creative collaboration and exploration.

Creativity in music is the business of composers and improvisers. It follows that they are the people most likely to possess the knowledge and experience required to lead processes of creative collaboration through music. But to be leaders, they have to become versatile in a great many more skills than simply inventing sounds, writing them down and performing them. If music is to meet the challenge of those new social and global imperatives, then composers, in partnership with other individuals and organisations, must be willing to make far-reaching adjustments to their traditional role. As Gillian Perkins wrote (Perkins, 1998: 22) 'composers have to be rather special people'.

Appendix
Chronological chart of projects since 1960 discussed in this book

Date Scheme	Composer (Classification)	Title/Subject Categories	Place/Location Organisation	page
1960	Peter Maxwell Davies (Contemp.)	*O Magnum Mysterium* **BC2**	Cirencester Grammar School	47
September 1965 Fluxus	La Monte Young (Experimental)	*Fluxorchestra*	New York	37
1966	Harrison Birwistle (Contemporary)	*The Mark of the Goat* **TC3a BC1**	BBC Schools programme	45
1966, 1969	David Bedford	*Whitefield Music*		48
1968 Experiment	Jolyon Laycock (Experimental)	*Locations* sound sculptures **TC1d**	Nottingham Midland Group	53, 189
1971	Cornelius Cardew (Experimental)	*Schooltime Compositions* **BC4**	ICA, London	38, 39, 40, 191
June 1971	Jolyon Laycock (Experimental)	*Super Spectacular Symmetry Show* **TC2a BC4**	Birmingham Arts Laboratory	53
Autumn 1972	John Cage (Experimental)	*Musicircus* **BC4**	The Round House, London	191
1976–1979 Arnolfini	Peter Wiegold (Contemporary)	Gemini Ensemble project **BC5**	Bristol; Arnolfini Music Workshops	54, 82
March 1982 CMN	Peter Maxwell Davies (Contemporary)	*5 Klee Pictures, Kirkwall Shopping Songs* **TC2b+2c**	Arnolfini, Bristol	54

Date Scheme	Composer (Classification)	Title/Subject Categories	Place/Location Organisation	page
March 1983 CMN	David Bedford (Contemporary)	*The Rime of the* *Ancient Mariner* **TC3a BC2**	Arnolfini, Bristol	49–50
February 1985 CMN	Harrison Birtwistle (Contemporary)	*The Mark of the* *Goat* **TC3a BC1**	Arnolfini, Bristol	46, 54
Autumn 1985	Jolyon Laycock (Contemporary)	*Bladud*, Local legend **TC3d BC3**	Bathampton, Bath	55–59, 276
February 1986 CMN	Steve Reich (Minimalist)	Minimal processes **TC1a BC2**	Arnolfini, Bristol	55
November 1985	Peter Wiegold (Contemporary classical)	Several themes inc. portrait of River Mersey **TC3c BC5**	Merseyside schools and youth centres	83–89
February 1988	Jolyon Laycock (Contemporary)	*Woden's Dyke* Local myth **TC3d**	Rural areas near Bristol & Bath	55–57, 60, 276
Spring 1988 Prema	Jolyon Laycock (Contemporary)	*Hetty Pegler's* *Tump* **TC3c BC4**	Rural area of Uley, Cotswolds	55–56 276, 282
1987–1997 Gemini Ensemble	Variety of composers e.g. Bruce Cole	Themes include 'Radio Project' Music & movement	London boroughs inc. Barnet & Enfield	89
Summer 1990 PRS & ENO Bayliss	Nicola Lefanu (Contemporary); Libretto: Kevin Crossley Holland,	*The Green* *Children* **TC3a BC3**	Kings Lynn Festival, Norfolk	89, 322, 367, 368–370
July 1990 PRS	John Kefala Kerr (Experimental sound)		Projects UK, Newcastle on Tyne	355, 364
1989–1990 PRS	Mervyn Burtch (Contemporary)	Opera project	South Glamorgan EA	348
1989–1990 PRS	Digby Fairweather (Jazz)	Jazz project with Stan Barker **TC1a**	South Glamorgan EA	

Date Scheme	Composer (Classification)	Title/Subject Categories	Place/Location Organisation	page
1989–1990 PRS	Peter Stacey (World musics)	World Musics **Tc1a**	South Glamorgan EA	348
January 1990 PRS	Sean Gregory (Contemporary)		Stamford Arts Centre, Firebird Trust	367
Summer 1990 PRS	Stephen Pratt (Experimental)		Wirrall Education Authority	
September 1989–1991 PRS	Sandy Lowenthal (Experimental)		Richmond on Thames	
1989–1990 PRS	Bill Martin, Nigel Morgan, Rob Worby (Rock)	Rock music, songs writing, technology **TC1a BC5**	Leicestershire County Council	349
1989–1990 PRS	Amanda Stuart (Contemporary & world music)		Peterborough Arts Council, & Arts Centre	355
1989–1990 PRS	John Mayer (Multicultural; Indo-jazz fusions)	Indian music fusions	Birmingham Polytechnic Faculty of Education	348, 349
Autumn 1990 PRS	Mark Lockett & Janet Sherbourne	Javanese Gamelan **TC1d**	Derbyshire County Council	348, 356, 360
November 1990–April 1991 PRS	Bill Sweeney (Contemporay classical)	*A Set for the Kingdom*	Fife Regional Council	371, 392
1990–1991 PRS	Javier Alvarez & Inok Paek (World musics)	Electronic work, plus Korean Kayagum **TC1d**	Projects UK Newcastle on Tyne	348
1990–1991 PRS	Mal Eltringham (Rock)	Electric guitars etc. **TC1d**	as above	

Date Scheme	Composer (Classification)	Title/Subject Categories	Place/Location Organisation	page
1990–1991 PRS	Sylvia Hallett & Paul Burwell (Experimental)	Percussion with junk **TC1d**	Projects UK Newcastle on Tyne	
1990–1991 PRS	Hugh Nankivell & Alistair Anderson (Contemporary)	Rhythm games plus concertina **TC1b+1d**	as above	
1990–1991 PRS	Kevin O'Connell, Elaine Agnew (Contemporary)	Modeled on Reich, Stravinsky, Pärt, & O'Suillabhain **TC1a**	Down Arts Centre, Northern Ireland	367
1991–1993 PRS	Keith Morris (Jazz and improvisation)	Community project focused on Gateshead	Gateshead Borough Council	353, 355, 357
1991 PRS	Paul Robinson (Minimalism)	Silent film project **TC2b**	Bradford MBC	364
1991–1992 PRS	Paul Mitchell-Davidson (Contemporary)	'Earth Rites' **TC2a**	Burnley BC, Mechanics Arts Centre	
1991 PRS	Alec Roth (Contemporary)	Gamelan **TC1d**	South Cambridgeshire TVEI	348
Spring 1992 PRS	Andrew Taylor-Maskrey (Local) (Contemporary)		South East Derbyshire College	
1991 PRS	Ian Dearden (Electro-acoustic)	Space Journey Electro-acoustic **TC3c+1d**	Lea Valley, Hertfordshire & Sonic Arts Network	348
1991 PRS	Diana Burrell, replaced by Alec Roth (Contemp.)		Trinity College London	348

Date Scheme	Composer (Classification)	Title/Subject Categories	Place/Location Organisation	page
1991 PRS	Adrian Lee (Folk)	Gamelan project Homer's Odyssey **TC1d+3c BC4**	Norfolk County Council	364
1991 PRS	Freeland Barbour, Robin Dunn, & John Kirkpatrick (folk)	Ceilidh Bands **TC1d**	Folkworks	364
1991 PRS	Nicky Rushton replaced by Al Bell (folk)	Women in music; Folk style songs **TC1a BC5**	N Tyneside MBC, Buddle Arts Centre	348
June 1991 PRS	Stan Barker & Nick Ingman (jazz, commercial)	Commercial music course, plus jazz composition **TC1a**	Welsh College of Music and Drama	
1991–1992 PRS	Stan Barker (Jazz)	Jazz composition **TC1a BC2**	South East Wales Arts	
April 1991 PRS	John Woolrich & Mary Wiegold, (contemporary)	Song writing sub-jects from every-day life **TC1c BC5**	Riverhouse Barn, Walton on Thames	347
June 1992 PRS	Alan Belk (Contemporary)	Europe, *Moves Abroad* **TC2e**	Wolverhampton Borough Council Civic Centre	348, 358
1991–1993 PRS	John Maxwell Geddes (Contemporary)		Dumfries and Galloway Regional Council	
1992–1993 PRS	Brian Bedford (Contemporary classical)	Folk song writing 'Thinking out loud' **TC1a+2d**	Rotherham MBC, Rotherham Arts Centre	348
Spring 1992 PRS	Chris Burn (Contemporary)	Journey: Snape to Ipswich **TC3c**	Suffolk County Council, Ipswich	364

Date Scheme	Composer (Classification)	Title/Subject Categories	Place/Location Organisation	page
1992–1993 PRS	John Cooney (Contemporary classical)	Texture, dynamic, layering, non-west- ern modes **TC1b**	East Sussex Council, Bexhill on Sea	363
1992–1993 PRS	Tim Fleming (Contemporary classical)	Oratorio – Local history, post-in- dustrial regenera- tion **TC2d BC1**	Doncaster Arts Project, Conisborough Castle	367
Summer 1992 PRS	John Kefala-Kerr (Experimental)		Northumberland CC and Blyth Valley DC	355, 357, 364
1992–1993 PRS	Simon Limbrick (Contemporary classical)	Percussion and electronics; **TC1d+2b BC5**	Blackheath Concert Halls & The Drake Project	348, 349
1992–1993 PRS	Jez Lowe (Folk)	Folk style music **TC1a BC5**	Easington District Council	
Autumn 1992 PRS	Colin Riley (Contemporary classical)	'Energy' variation, repetition, ostinato etc. **TC2a+1b**	Crosby & Sefton MBC	
1992–1993 PRS	Errollyn Wallen (Multi ethnic)	'Music without Frontiers' **TC2a+1a BC5**	Centenary Office, Leeds CC	348
Spring 1994 PRS	Phil Cashian (Contemporary classical)	Highwayman Brockley Jack, Henry VIII, Anne of Cleaves **TC3a**	Blackheath Concert Halls, London plus Drake Project	348
1993–1994 PRS	Rob Godman (Experimental sound)	Multimedia: drama, video, percussion instrument design; **TC2b+1d BC5**	Bedfordshire CC	365, 367

Date Scheme	Composer (Classification)	Title/Subject Categories	Place/Location Organisation	page
1991–1994 cf previous entry PRS	John Maxwell Geddes (Contemporary)	'Dances at Threave' **TC2e**	Dumfries and Galloway Regional Council	357, 367
Summer term 1994 PRS	Eddie Parker (Jazz & improvisation)	Frameworks for development: **TC1b+1a BC4**	Cheltenham Festival	
1993–1994 PRS	Daryl Runswick (Contemporary classical)	Twinning cele- brations Enfield & Courbevoie **TC2e BC4**	Enfield EAS, Artswork Centre, London Sinfonietta	348, 358, 359, 376
1993–1994 PRS	Bill Martin (Contemporary classical)	Sense of purpose and community identity **TC2d BC5**	Forest Arts Centre, New Milton	354
June 1995 PRS	David Bedford (Contemporary classical), Edward Kemp – direction	*The Old House* goings on in a derelict warehouse **TC3a+1c BC4**	Spitalfields Festival	364, 365
1994–1995 PRS	Stuart Bruce & Sean Gregory (Contemporary classical)	Lost children in Milton Country park; Music and video **TC3c BC4**	Cambridgeshire CC	355
1994–1995 PRS	John Cooney (Contemporary classical)	Messiaen *Quartet for the End of Time* **TC1a BC5**	St. George's Centre, Chatham	350, 360 366
Spring 1995 PRS	Graham Fitkin (Contemporary)	'Celebration' **TC2a BC5**	Sefton EA, Royal Liverpool Phil.	348, 357, 361, 367
Spring 1995 Rainbow	Jolyon Laycock	*A Dream of Flying* Bladud of Bath **TC3c BC5**	Hogeschool Alkmaar Conservatorium	278

Date Scheme	Composer (Classification)	Title/Subject Categories	Place/Location Organisation	page
May 1994 and spring 1995 PRS	John Hardy (Contemporary classical)	*Tilting at Windmills in Powys* Wind farms in Wales **TC2b BC5**	Wyeside Arts Centre, Builth Wells; BBC Nat. Orch. of Wales,	348, 360
1994–1995 PRS	Andy Jackson (Commercial music) with Writer – Sue Kane,	Creation of a musical: *Something is happening* **TC2a BC5**	Durham City Arts	
1994–1995 PRS	Steve King (Contemporary classical)	Song writing, percussion, home-made instruments **TC1c+1d BC5**	Grampian Regional Council	
1993–1995 PRS	Bill Martin (Contemporary)	**TC1b+1c+1d BC5**	Forest Arts Centre, New Milton	354, 361
1994–1995 PRS	Bob Peacock, Composer in Residence (Contemporary)	'Seasons of the Year' **TC2b BC5**	Dovecot Arts Centre, Stockton on Tees	
1995–1996 PRS	Alistair Anderson & Katrina Porteus (Folk)	*Retelling Morpeth in Flood 1963* traditional music, dialects **TC2e**	Mid-Northumberland Arts Group, 2000 Voices	348
1995–1996 PRS	Frankie Armstrong (Experimental music) with African music, Welsh harp.	*Let your voice be heard* **TC2a+1d BC5**	Voices' network and Community Music Wales, Builth Wells	355
1995–1996 PRS	Robin Grant with Neil Beddoes librettist (Commercial)	*Owd Jonah's Ghosts* the iniquities of new roads **TC3a BC3**	Wolverhampton Music Service	357, 367
Feb–Mar 1996 RAE, PRS	Sean Gregory (Contemporary minimalist)	'Time' *A Feeling in Time* **TC1a+2a BC4**	Rainbow over Bath	210–214, 265, 269–270

404

Date Scheme	Composer (Classification)	Title/Subject Categories	Place/Location Organisation	page
Feb–Mar 1996 RAE	Sean Gregory	'Time': **TC1a+2a** *Arc en Ciel pour le fin de temps*	Project repeated Aix en Provence 'Aix en Musique'	210–214, 265
Feb–Mar 1996 RAE	Sean Gregory	Theme as above	Alkmaar: Stichting Componisten Noord Holland	210–214 265
Feb–Mar 1996 RAE	Sean Gregory	Theme as above	Kaposvar, Hungary	210–214 265
1995–1996 PRS	Deirdre Gribbin (Contemporary) Composer in Residence	Repertoire models: Ligeti, Reich etc. Aztec art theme. **TC1a+2b BC5**	Hertforshire Music Service, Stevenage	348
July 1995 PRS	Mark Lockett & Janet Sherbourne (Multi ethnic)	Gamelan **TC1d**	Derbyshire County Council, Chesterfield	348, 357, 360
1995–1996 PRS, 'More Music in Morecambe'	Pete Moser, Composer in residence since 1993 (Commercial)	*Music on More- cambe Streets* Songs about the locality. **TC1c+2e**	Lancaster City Council, Morecambe	
1995–1996 PRS	Roxanna Panufnik (Contemporary classical) Mentor: Bill Martin	River Thames theme **TC3c BC5**	Berkshire CC, Windsor	348
1995–1996 PRS	David Sutton- Anderson (Contemporary classical)	The Four Seasons, War and peace, Seven deadly Sins, Rituals. **TC2b**	West Sussex CC	348
1996–1997 PRS	Bill Connor (Contemporary classical) plus Camden Reeves	'Bridging the Gap' Score as a 'bridge' for composer's intentions **TC2a**	Halle Concerts Society, Manchester	354, 367

Date Scheme	Composer (Classification)	Title/Subject Categories	Place/Location Organisation	page
Spring 1996, PRS	Paul Griffiths (Jazz)	Improvisation **TC1b BC2**	Suffolk County Council, Bungay	353
April 1996 Rainbow, Bishop Ken	Jolyon Laycock (Contemporary)	*Edgar the King* Anglo-Saxon texts **TC3d BC2**	Bath Abbey, Diocese of Bath & Wells	
September 1996 PRS	Graham Fitkin (Contemporary classical)	Various themes: *The Owl who was afraid of the dark*, 'Transport' **TC2b**	Sefton Music Support Service, Merseyside	348, 357, 361, 367
1996–1997 PRS	Lewis Riley (Jazz)	Performance and improvisation **TC1a+1b BC2**	South West Jazz, Cornwall	
October 1996 PRS	Jenni Roditi (Contemporary classical)	*The Gift of the Angels* – story of Cyneburga, 7th century; **TC3d**	Coral Arts, Dorchester Abbey	
1996–1997 PRS	Pete Rosser (Commercial)	Silent Films: Felix the cat, Laurel & Hardy etc. **TC3a**	Guildhall Arts Centre, Gloucester	364
1996–1997 PRS	David & Avril Sutton-Anderson (Contemporary)	Colour **TC2a BC5**	Colourscape Festival, Croydon	348, 349
July 1996 PRS	Bill Sweeney (Contemporary classical)	Composer models: **TC1a;** or History of gallery building **TC2e** (SN group)	Paragon Ensemble, Glasgow	348
Spring 1997 'State of the Nation'	Fraser Trainer (Contemporary classical)	*True to Life* words Sue Butler based on nursery rhymes.	South Bank, London	

Date Scheme	Composer (Classification)	Title/Subject Categories	Place/Location Organisation	page
Spring 1997 PRS	Jane Wells and Duncan Chapman (double project) (Contemporary)	*Sounds Unusual* – electro-acoustic sounds etc. **TC1d+3a BC5**	South Kesteven DC Centre, Grantham, Fulbeck Hall	348, 357
1996–1997 PRS	Jim Woodland (Folk singer & writer), Pete Moser	*Mosaic* **TC2a+3b BC5**	Wyndham School, Egremont	
1997/1998 PRS	Gary Carpenter (Contemporary classical)	'Making Music', folio of compositions **TC1a+1c**	Wirrall Borough Council	
Jan–Feb 1997	Graham Fitkin (Contemporary classical)	'Opposites' & 'Ever Increasing Circles' **TC2a**	Devon County Council, Ivybridge	349
1997–1998 PRS	Tim Fleming (local) (Commercial) assisted by Heather Sharpe	A Song Book for the year in Calderdale **TC3a+3b BC5**	Whitewood and Fleming Theatre and Music, Calderdale	361, 367
1997–1998 Community Music Wales, PRS	Luke Goss (local) (Commercial) plus Storyteller, Dancer, Designers	*Gold* The Celtic Year, . **TC3a**	Cardiff Bay; high unemployment, social deprivation.	361
Nov 1997 PRS Rainbow	Deirdre Gribbin, Rob Smith plus Mary Wiegold (Contemporary)	*Parents and Children* and *Sounds through the magnifying glass*	Rainbow over Bath, Michael Tippett Centre	235–237 265, 303, 358, 367
Dec 1997 Rainbow	Deirdre Gribbin (Contemporary) plus Mary Wiegold	As above **TC1d BC5**	Zwolle: Conservatoire Christian Huygens	237, 265
1997–1998 PRS	Robert Jarvis (Commercial)	*Adventures in Sound:* Songs Rain, transport etc. **TCb2 BC5**	Canterbury	

Date Scheme	Composer (Classification)	Title/Subject Categories	Place/Location Organisation	page
1997–1998 PRS	Stephen Montague (Contemporary classical) with Cameron Sinclair	Ghosts (The Lady Grey of the Theatre Royal) **TC3d BC5**	Northants. EA Orchestra of St. Johns, Derngate Centre	348
1997–1998 PRS	Hugh Nankivell (Contemporary classical)	Exotic instruments: *Bustling Bands, Rhythmic Town* **TC1d+2c BC5**	Deprived areas of North Kirklees MC	362
1997–1998 PRS	Huw and Tony Williams (local)) (Commercial)	Song writing; **BC5** Isolation in the valleys. **TC1c+2c**	Caerphilly CBC Miners' Institute, Blackwood	180, 272, 347, 371
Spring 1998 Rainbow over Bath	Alistair King (Commercial)	Skempton's *Lento* as model. **TC1a BC5**	Bath & Chew Valley; rural area;	265
June 1998 Aldeburgh	Stephen Montague (Experimental)	*Boulder Beach Band* **BC2**	The beach at Aldeburgh	191
October 1998 Barbican	Stephen Montague (Experimental)	Performance of John Cage *Musicircus* **BC4**	Barbican Centre, London	
November 1998 NESA & ACTA	Robin Grant (Commercial) Neil Beddoes (writer)	*People of Nothing* Keynsham work- house **TC2e+3a**	Keynsham, Bristol	
November 1998	Tunde Jegede & Paul Gladstone Reid (Contempor- ary, African)	*Hidden Routes* **TC3c** about black Cornish composer **BC4**	Truro, St. Austell, Cornwall	
Autumn 1998 Rainbow	Tony Haynes (Jazz & multi- ethnic) Project led by Roz Davis	Journey along the Silk Road, Indian, Chinese music etc. **TC3c BC5**	Bath, Bristol, & rural Somerset; Grand Union Orchestra	186, 255, 264, 265, 277, 290, 295, 300

408

Date Scheme	Composer (Classification)	Title/Subject Categories	Place/Location Organisation	page
1998	Stephen Montague (Contemporary experimental)	*Horn Concerto* for claxon horn & orchestra of cars **BC2**	Various venues: London & Houston	
February 1999 SPNM	Brian Inglis (Contemporary) Diana Burrell mentor	*Songs of Sorrow and Joy* Settings of poems **TC3b BC1**	Bath; part of Adopt-a-Composer	
March 1999 Rainbow & Arts Council	Peter Wiegold, Philip Cashian, Deirdre Gribbin	*Igor's Boogie* treatments of popular songs **TC1a BC5**	University of Bath and local schools	177–178, 238
May 1999 Rainbow and Bath Spa UC	Barry Russell (Contemporary) chosen by competitive tender	*Opening Doors* To celebrate reopening of Tippett Centre **TC2a BC4**	Bath, Michael Tippett Centre, SPNM, Bath Festival	221, 223, 224, 265
7 & 8 June 1999 'Make Music Live'	Rachel Leach (Contemporary classical)	Inoh' Pokak (Cacophony backwards) **TC2a**	London LSO 'Discovery'	
June 2000 Jubilee year	Lorenc Barber (Experimental)	*O Roma Nobilis* – Concert of bells of 100 Rome churches	The City of Rome	191–194
September 1999 RAE	Barry Russell (Contemporary classical) with Cardew Ensemble	*Rituals for Orpheus* Myth of Orpheus and Euridice **TC3d BC4**	Plovdiv, Bulgaria 'White Green and Red' Jazz Formation	266, 270, 272, 279, 280, 294, 311–318
November 1999 Rainbow	Tunde Jegede & Paul Gladstone Reid (Contemporary African) plus Eugene Skeef	Music of African diasporo: Reggae, Hi-Life, Salsa, Gospel, Blues, DJ **TC1c+2e BC4**	Bath, Chew Valley, Bristol;	186, 187, 224, 264, 265, 277, 288, 294, 296–303

Date Scheme	Composer (Classification)	Title/Subject Categories	Place/Location Organisation	page
11 Nov 1999 LSO	Judith Bingham (Contemporary classical)	*Red Hot Nail* Serbian Gypsy tale **TC3d BC3**	LSO Discovery, Barbican Hall, London	322–323
November 1999 RAE	Klaus Feßmann (Experimental) Margarida Pinto do Amaral (dancer)	*Change of Para-digms* **TC2a BC5** Dance–Music–Design all equal	Bath, Michael Tippett Centre	213, 216, 266
December 1999 RAE	Peter Wiegold (Contemporary classical)	*Creative Mind Creative Body* Sufi texts **TC2a+3b**	Orff Institute, Mozarteum, Salzburg	266, 275, 276
December 1999 RAE	Peter Wiegold (Contemporary classical)	*Within this Body* work using Sufi texts **TC2a+3b**	Hogeschool Alkmaar Conservatorium	266, 275, 276
Feb/Apr 2000	Ian McQueen (Contemporary classical)	Fanfares, arrivals and the Tudors **TC2a+1a BC5**	Spitalfields Festival Brady Arts & Com-munity Centre	
Spring 2000 Rainbow over Bath	Peter Wiegold & Tansy Davis (Contemporary)	Various themes: City & Country **TC1a+2b BC5**	Bath, Keynsham & Wiltshire	213, 266, 284–286, 309–10
May 2000 NCC	Colin Mawby (Contemporary) Maeve Ingolds-by libretto	*The Torc of Gold* Original story like a folk tale **TC3d BC2**	Rep. of Ireland, Irish National Chamber Choir	278–279
Summer 2000	David Blake (Contemporary classical), John Birtwistle (libretto)	*The Fabulous Adventures of Alexander the Great* **TC3d BC1**	Castle of Mitelene, Lesbos, Greece; University of Corfu & York	278
Jan–June 2000	Ian McQueen (Contemporary), Diana Burrell & Jonathan Dove	Various models: J.S.Bach, Cable Street riots **TC1a+3a BC5**	Tower Hamlets, London, Spitalfields Festival	337–338

410

Date Scheme	Composer (Classification)	Title/Subject Categories	Place/Location Organisation	page
June 2000	Margaret Lucy Wilkins (Contemporary)	*Revelation of Seven Angels* **TC3b BC1**	Timosuara, Rumania, Garboni Foundation	
July 2000 SPNM C4K	Gary Carpenter, Alec Roth, Nittim Sawhney, Peter McGarr (Contemporary)	SCRY **BC1**	Promenade concerts, London; Asian Music Circuit	
Summer 2000 Florida	Led by Richard McNicol	*Barbar the Elephant* **TC3a**	Florida State, USA	
October 2000 Jeunesses Musicales International	Hans Krasa 1899–1944 (Contemporary classical)	*Brundibar* Children's opera **TC3a BC1**	Tour Oslo, Lundt, Paris, Barcelona, Copenhagen, Amsterdam, Brussels, London.	206–207
2000/2001 JMI	Stig Asp (World music animateur) all styles – ethnic, pop, rock, hip-hop or new mergers	*Music Crossroads Southern Africa* **TC2e BC5**	Zimbabwe Zambia Mozambique, Malawi, S. Africa, Tanzania Namibia Botswana	207
October 2000	Hans van Zijp (Experimental) and others	*Klankspeeltuin* creative electro-acoustic sound devices **TC1d+2b**	University of Lueneberg; with Klankspeeltuin, Amsterdam	
October 2000 London Sinfonietta	John Tavener (Contemporary classical)	*One Single Moment* redemption of the thief on the cross **TC2a+3a**	Pentonville prison	151–154
12,13 October 2000	Barry Russell (Contemporary classical)	*Gone to play at Mr. Escher's House.* **TC2e BC4**	Halifax; Northern Opera Education Liason	270–272

411

Date Scheme	Composer (Classification)	Title/Subject Categories	Place/Location Organisation	page
4 Nov 2000 London Sinfonietta	Fraser Trainer (Contemporary classical)	Based on opera *Greek* & Oedipus myth. **TC3d+1a**	Turner Sims Hall, Southampton	
November 2000 Cambridge Festival	Stephen Montague (Experimental) featured composer for 'Year of the Artist'	'Sounds & Spaces' *Urban Strawberry* *Lunch*; *Bells of* *Remembrance*; **TC1d+2e**	Venues included Cambridge Regional College, Parish Church, Corn Exchange.	
7, 8, 21, 22 November 2000	Lynne Plowman (Contemporary classical)	*Earth, Air, Fire,* *Water* Norfolk Gamalen **TC2b+1d**	Suffolk Rural schools; Wingfield	268
Nov 2000 London Sinfinietta	Fraser Trainer (Contemporary classical)	*It's All Greek to* *Me* based on Oedipus myth **TC3d+1a BC4**	Huddersfield Festival	
Nov 2000 London Sinfonietta	Fraser Trainer (Contemporary classical)	Based on opera *Greek* & Oedipus myth **TC3d+1a**	*Athens; Pellini* *Experimental* *Music School*	378
November 2000	Colin Riley, John Cooney (Contemporary)	*Banging and* *Bowing* **TC1d BC5**	Huddersfield Contemporary Music Festival	
Dec 2000 Bayliss	Howard Moody (Contemporary)	Verdi centenary **TC1a**	ENO Bayliss Prog. London Coliseum	240
January 2001 Perform	Fraser Trainer & others, led by Matthew Barley	Many themes: e.g. Self-discovery, Hope for the future	Bristol, inner-city comprehensives	240–242 283,
Feb 2001 Adopt-a- composer	Rachel Leach (Contemporary classical)	*The Amortisation* *of Intangible* *Fixed Assets*	Leicester	

Date Scheme	Composer (Classification)	Title/Subject Categories	Place/Location Organisation	page
March 2001 LSO Explore	Richard McNicoll Philip Cashian (Contemporary)	Janácek *Intimate Letters* **TC1a BC5**	Barbican, London	157, 241
March 2001 Timepiece	David Bedford (Contemporary) directed by Sarah Tenant-Flowers	*Timepiece* Ideas & texts about time by many writers; focus on singing	Harlow Choral Society, Essex	51
20 March 2001 PRSF	Hugh & Tony Williams (Commercial)	Song writing Experiences from life **TC1c+2c**	Blackwood Miners' Institute, Caerphilly	180–181, 272–73
23 March 2001	Many composers (Contemporary Classical)	'Chamber Music 2000', new music for young people	Wigmore Hall (Official launch of scheme)	231–233
April 2001 PRSF	Tansy Davies (Contemporary), Mentor – John Woolrich	Writing for string quartet **BC5**	Leicester & Lincoln, Schidlof Quartet	302
6 May 2001 Philharmonia Orchestra	Peter Maxwell Davies (Contemporary)	*Antarctic Waves* Maxwell Davies Antarctic Symphony as model	Queen Elizabeth Hall, before premiere in Royal Festival Hall	302
3 June 2001 Bath Festival	Orlando Gough, Richard Chew (Minimalist)	*As Dark as Light* Community project **TC2a+3b**	Laura Place, Bath	
14 June 2001 WNO	Ruth Byrchmore (Contemporary)	*Katerina* Opera based on Jancek *Katya Kabanova* **TC1a+3a BC3**	Rhydycar Leisure Centre, Mythyr Tydfil	275
20 June 2001 LSO	Rachel Leach (Contemporary classical), Mentor– Richard McNicol	*Hector & Harriet* based on Berlioz model **TC1a+3a BC3**	LSO Discovery, London	225–231

413

Date Scheme	Composer (Classification)	Title/Subject Categories	Place/Location Organisation	page
5 July 2001 ECO	David Bedford (Contemporary) assisted by Marilyn Groves	*Supermarket* *Symphonies* sounds in a super- market **TC1d+2c**	Bristol housing estates, co- ordinated by Multi-A	273–274
12 July 2001 SPNM C4K	Maud Hodson David Chas. Martin Sally J. Davies	C4K Summer Showcase; various themes **TC3b**	London Boroughs	233–234
July 2001 PRSF	Maricio Venegas & Rachel Pantin (Folk/commercial)	*Pirates & Heroes* Jigs & shanties **TC1c+2b BC5**	Isle of Wight	305, 324, 371
July 2001 Confluence	Karen Wimhurst (Contemporary classical)	*Silver Messenger* The river Stour **TC3c BC3**	River Stour, Dorset; Common Ground	196, 242–244, 283, 337–338
14 Nov 2001 St. George's	Andy Baker (music animateur)	Ukrainian Boyar Ensemble **TC1d+2e BC5**	Bristol; Children's Music Workshop	238–239 335
24 June 2002 Corsham	Jolyon Laycock (Contemporary & Chinese classical)	*Mengjiang Weep-* *ing at the Wall* **TC3a+3c+3d BC3** Chinese legend	Corsham Festival	255–256

Key to abbreviations used in the chart:

ACTA – Avon Community Theatre Ass-ociation.

BC – Bedford Category.

CMN – Contemporary Music Network of the Arts Council.

ECO – English Chamber Orchestra.

ENO – English National Opera.

JMI – Jeunesses Musicals International.

LSO – London Symphony Orchestra.

NCC – National Chamber Choir of Ire-land.

NESA – North East Somerset Arts.

PRS – Performing Right Society.

PRSF – Performing Right Society Foundation.

RAE – Rainbow across Europe.

TC – Theme category, see p. 267.

UC – University College.

WNO – Welsh National Opera.

414

Bibliography

Allen, Graham, et al. (1998) *Birmingham Arts Laboratory*, exhibition catalogue. Birmingham: Museum and Art Gallery.

Anglani, Monika (1994) *beQuadro* 14. Fiesoli: Centro di Ricercara e di Sperimentazione per la Didattica Musicale.

Arts Council of England (1996) *Creating New Notes*. London: Arts Council of England.

Arts Council of England (1997) *Leading Through Learning*. London: Arts Council of England.

Asher, Rosalyn (1983) *Artists in Residence – A framework for schools*. London Borough of Enfield.

Barber, Lorenç (1999) *O Roma Nobilis – Concierto da campanas para cien iglesias de la ciudad de Roma*. Valencia: Apoyo Cultural Iberia.

Bedford, David (1963) *Piece for Mo*. London: Universal Edition.

—— (1965) *Music for Albion Moonlight*. London: Universal Edition.

—— (1966 & 1967) *Whitefield Music I & II*. London: Universal Edition.

—— (1969) *An exciting new game for children of all ages*. London: Universal Edition.

—— (1973) *Balloon Music*. London: Universal Edition.

—— (1970) *Some Bright Stars for Queens College*. London: Universal Edition.

—— (1971) *With a Hundred Kazoos*. London: Universal Edition.

—— (1979) *The Rime of the Ancient Mariner*. London: Universal Edition.

—— (1999) *Hetty Pegler's Tump*.

—— (2001) *From Clocks to Stars*.

Bergen, Jolande van (1986) 'Under Gemini's Influence' *Music Advisers National Association Magazine*. 3, 8.

Bernstein, Basil (1971) *Class, Codes & Control* vol. 1. London: Routledge Kegan & Paul.

Bingham, Judith (1994) *The Red Hot Nail*. Kenley, Surrey: Maecenas Music.

Birtwistle, Harrison (1966) *The Mark of the Goat*. London: Universal Edition.

Blackham, H.J. (1957) *A consideration of Humanity, Technology and Education*. London: RFH.

Blake, David (1996) *The Fabulous Adventures of Alexander the Great*. York: University Music Press.

Bolton, Eric (2000) *Arts Education in Secondary Schools: Effects and Effectiveness*. London: NFER.

Boulez, Pierre (1952) *Éventuellement*. Revue Musicale, Paris.

Braden, Sue (1978) *Artists and People*. London: Routledge.

Britten, Benjamin (1949) *The Little Sweep*. London: Faber.

—— (1958) *Noyes Flood*. London: Faber.

Bryars, Gavin (1975) *The Experimental Music Catalogue*. London.

Burton, Ian (2001) *Music Teacher* 80: 10; 29–30. London.

Cage, John (1960) *Theatre Piece*. New York: Peters Edition.

—— (1967) *Musicircus*. New York: Peters Edition.

—— (1967) *Silence*. Cambridge, Massachusetts: MIT Press.

—— (1968) *Variations V*. New York: Peters Edition.

Calouste Gulbenkian Foundation (1978) *Training Professional Musicians*. London: CGF.

—— (1982) *The Arts in Schools, Principles, Practice and Provision*. London: CGF.

Cardew, Cornelius (1960) *Autumn 60*. London: Universal Edition.

—— (1961) *Octet 61*. London: Universal Edition.

—— (1967) *Treatise*. London: Universal Edition.

—— (1968) *The Tiger's Mind*. London: Universal Edition.

—— (1968) *Schooltime Compositions*. London.

—— (1969) *A Scratch Orchestra*. London: Musical Times, June 1969.

—— (1971) *The Great Learning*. London.

—— et al (1974) *Stockhausen Serves Imperialism*. London: Latimer.

Charlton, Alan (2002) *Newnotes*. April 2002, London: SPNM.

Chatburn, Thomas Edward (1986) 'European Musicians in Conference, Strasbourg 1985'. *BJME*, 3, 91–100.

Chatwin, Bruce (1987) *Songlines*. London: Jonathan Cape.

Clifford, Sue and King, Angela (2001) *The Confluence – New Music for the River Stour*. Shaftesbury: Common Ground.

Conquer, Alistair (2000) *David Bedford Web Pages* http://www.jeffgower.com/bedford.html.

Craig, Philip (1999) *Rituals for Orpheus – report*. Bristol: Rainbow.

Davies, Coral (1986) 'Say it Till a Song Comes'. *BJME* 3; 279–293.

Davies, Peter Maxwell (1960) *O Magnum Mysterium*. London: Schott.

Davies, P. M. (1960) *Five Klée Pictures*. London: Boosey & Hawkes.

—— (1963) 'Music composition by children' in Colston Research Society *Music in Education – Proceedings of the 14th Symposium of the Colston Research Society,* ed. Lewis Grant, 108–115. Bristol: Butterworths.

—— (1978) *The Two Fiddlers*. London: Boosey and Hawkes.

—— (1979) *Cinderella.* London: Chester.

—— (1981) *The Rainbow*. London: Boosey and Hawkes.

Eley, Robert (1974) 'A History of the Scratch Orchestra – 1969–1972' in Cardew, C. *Stockhausen Serves Imperialism*, 11–32. London: Latimer.

Elkin, Susan (2000) 'Government accused of ignoring Robinson creativity report' *Music Teacher* 2, 13.

Eohrle, Elizabeth (1993) 'Education Through Music: Towards A South African Approach'. *BJME* 10; 255–261.

European Commission (1996a) Kaleidoscope press release 19 April, Brussels: European Commission.

—— (1996b) 'European Union Support for Culture – 1996 Kaleidoscope programme – information and call for applications'. *Official Journal of the European Communities*. 39, 5–12, Brussels: EC.

—— (1998a) *Kaleidoscope Programme Report 1996–1998*. Brussels: EC.

—— (1998b) *First European Community Framework Programme in Support of Culture (2000–2004)*. Brussels: EC.

—— (2001) 'Culture 2000 – List of successful projects January 2001' Brussels: EC.

European Music Council (2001) *International Music Directory of basic words translated into 25 languages*. London: Schotts.

Everitt, Anthony (1997) *Joining In – an investigation into participatory music*. London: Calouste Gulbenkian Foundation.

Evers, Steven, et al. (1999) 'The cerebral haemodynamics of music perception; A transcranial Doppler sonography study'. *Brain:* 122; 1; 75–85. Oxford University Press.

Fairbairn Foundation, Esmée (2001) *Application guidelines*. London: EF.

Flood, Philip & Haines, Ella (2000) *Spitalfields Festival Education and Community Programme Evaluation Report 1999–2000*. London: Spitalfields Festival.

Franzen, Daag (1999) *Brundibar International Tour*. Brussels: Jeunesses Musicales Iinternational.

Gemini (1986) *Merseyside project report 1985–1986*. Liverpool: Merseyside Arts.

Gowrie (1996) *Striking a New Note – consultative green paper on publicly funded new music in England*. London: Arts Council of England.

Guthrie, Robin (2000) *The Good European's Dilemma*. London: New Europe Research Trust.

Hadow, Sir William Henry (1931) *Great Britain Board of Education Report of the Consultative Committee on the Primary School*. London: HMSO.

Harries, Sue & Shaw, Phyllida (1994) *Arts Education Agencies*, & (1995) *Arts Education Agencies – Progress Report*. London: Paul Hamlyn Foundation.

Haug, Toomas (1994) '125 years struggling for freedom', liner note to CD *Singing Revolution Estonia*. Erdenklang 40762.

Heaney, Seamus (1990) *New Selected Poems 1966–1987*. London & Boston: Faber & Faber.

Hedges, Alan (2001) *Arts-based projects in schools*. Leighton Buzzard: Children's Music Workshop.

Hogarth, Sylvia, Kinder, Kay and Harland, John (1997*) Arts Organisations and the Educational Programmes*. London: Arts Council of England/National Foundation for Educational Research.

Holst, Imogen (1938) 1951? *The Music of Gustav Holst*. Oxford: OUP.

Holst, Gustav (1959 rev. 1980) *Heirs and Rebels*. London: Greenwood Press.

Hoskyns, Janet (1992) 'Music Education and a European Dimension'. *BJME* 9; 97–102.

—— (1996) *Music Education and a European Dimension – A la recherche de L'Europe perdue…* D.Phil, York.

Jackson, Anthony (1995) *Anecdotes are no longer enough.* Manchester University.

Járdányi, Pál (1961) 'Folk Music in Musical Education', in Sándor, Frigyes (ed.) (1966) *Musical Education in Hungary*, 11–24. London: Barry & Rockcliffe.

Jeunesses Musicales International (2000) *Music Crossroads Southern Africa – executive summary.* Brussels: JMI.

Ketting, Knud (1987); 'Danish Music Education – A Crafts Museum' *BJME* 3; 263.

Kodály, Zoltán (1974) *Selected writings.* London: Boosey & Hawkes.

Laycock, Jolyon (1988) *Woden's Dyke,* Introductory notes. Bristol: Rainbow Foundation.

—— (1988) *Hetty Pegler's Tump,* Bristol: Rainbow Foundation.

—— (1996) *Response to 'Striking a new Note'*, Bristol: Rainbow Foundation.

—— (2002) *A Changing Role of the Composer in Society* Ph.D University of York.

LeFanu, Nicola (1997) *The Green Children.* London: Novello.

Loane, Brian (1984) 'Thinking about Children's Compositions'. *BJME* 1, 205–231.

Lowery, H. (1963) 'Music and liberal studies or challenges in Musical Education – discussion' in Colston Research Society *Music in Education' Proceedings of the 14th Symposium of the Colston Research Society,* ed. Lewis Grant, 11–21. Bristol: Butterworths.

Macdonald, Irene (1980) *Professional Arts in Schools.* London: Arts Council of Great Britain.

Martin, Anne (1985) 'Music Teaching in the 1st Years of Schooling in West Germany with particular Reference to the State of Nordheim Westfalen'. *BJME* 3, 253.

Mawby, Colin (1996) *The Torc of Gold – an opera for young people.* Dublin: National Chamber Choir.

Menuhin, Yehudi foreword to Vájdá, Cecilia (1974) *The Kodály Way to Music.* London: Boosey and Hawkes.

Nattiez, Jean-Jacques (1985) *Music and Discourse – Towards a Semiology of Music.* Princeton: University Press.

Newsom, John (1963) *Half our Future – a report of the Central Advisory Council for Education.* London: Ministry of Education.

Nyman, Michael (1999) *Experimental Music, Cage and Beyond.* Cambridge University Press.

Odam, George (1968) *Angry Arrow.* London: Chester.

—— (1972) *Tutankhamun.* London: Chester.

—— (1976) *Inca.* London: Chester.

—— (1995) *The Sounding Symbol.* London: Nelson Thornes.

—— (2000) 'Teaching composing in secondary schools – The Creative Dream' *BJME* 17:2 109–127.

Odam, George & Paterson, Anice (2000) *Composing in the Classroom – The Creative Dream.* High Wycombe, Bucks.: National Association of Music Educators.

Odie, David & Allen, Garth (1998) *Artists in Schools – a review.* London: Ofsted.

418

Okafor, Richard (1989), 'Of Ditties, Needs and Amnesia – Music & Primary School Education in Anambra State, Nigeria'. *BJME* 3; 289–305.

Orff, Carl trans. Margaret Murray (1978) 'The Schulwerk', vol. 3 of *Carl Orff Documentation, His Life and Works*. New York: Schott.

Owens, Peter (1986) 'The Contemporary Composer in the Classroom'. *BJME* 3, 341–352.

Paynter, E. & J. (1974) *The Dance and the Drum*.

Paynter, John (1982) *Music in the Secondary School Curriculum*. Cambridge University Press.

—— (1987) 'Music Education in Nordic Countries' *BJME* 3; 251–252.

—— (1992) *Sound and Structure*, Cambridge: University Press.

—— (1997a) 'Che cosa si può dire sulla musica?' *BeQuadro*, 17, 66/67, 5–33 Fiesoli: Centro di Ricercara e di Sperimentazione per la Didattica Musicale.

—— (1997b) 'The Form of Finality: a context for musical education'. *BJME* 14, 5–21.

—— (2000) 'Making Progress in Composition'. *BJME* 17:1; 8.

Paynter, John & Aston, Peter (1970) *Sound and Silence*. Cambridge: University Press.

Peggie, Andrew (1986) *Music Education Projects, Monitoring Reports*. London: Arts Council of Great Britain.

—— (1997) *Musicians go to School – Partnership in the classroom*. London: London Arts Board/Yamaha Kemble.

Penny, Fiona (2000) *The Workbook – volume 2*. London: Association of British Orchestras.

Perkins, Gillian (1990–1998) *Composer in Education evaluation reports*. London: Performing Right Society.

Pratley, David, Rhydderch, Gwyn & Stephens, John (1993) *Musicians go to School*. London Arts Board.

Renshaw, Peter (1986) 'The Conservatoire Curriculum'. *BJME* 3, 1, 79–90.

Richards, Denis (1958): *Offspring of the Vic: a History of Morley College*. London: Routledge and Kegan.

Robinson, Kenneth (1999) *All our Futures*. London: National Advisory Committee on Creative and Cultural Education.

Rogers, Rick (1997) *The Heart of the Matter – Education Research and Development Initiative* (ERDI). London: Arts Council of England.

Rogers, Rick (1998) *Developing Arts Education Agencies*. London: ACE.

Ross, Malcolm (1984) *The Aesthetic Impulse*. Oxford: Pergamon Press.

Royet, Jean-Pierre (2000) 'Emotional Responses to Pleasant and Unpleasant Olfactory, Visual, and Auditory Stimuli: a Positron Emission Tomography Study'. *The Journal of Neuroscience*, 20(20):7752–7759.

Runswick, Daryl (1995) *Blueprint II for flexible Chamber Ensemble*. London: COMA.

Russell, Barry (1997) *Symphony for Large Ensemble*. York: Music Centre.

—— (1999) *'Rituals for Orpheus'* – *report of an education project by Barry Russell and the Cornelius Cardew Ensemble in Plovdiv, Bulgaria, September 1999.* Bristol: Rainbow Foundation.

Schafer, R. Murray (1975) *The Rhinoceros in the Classroom.* London: Universal Edition.

Sharp, Caroline & Dust, Karen (1982) *Artists in Schools.* London: NFER.

Shaw, Roy (1984) *The Glory of the Garden.* London: Arts Council of Great Britain.

Short, Michael (1990) *Gustav Holst – The Man and his Music.* Oxford University Press.

Small, Christopher (1977): *Music Society Education.* Wesleyan University Press.

Spencer, A. Piers (1974) *The influence of pop on creative music in the classroom.* York: Schools Council: Music in the Secondary School.

—— (1981) *Different Drummers – The case for Afro-American Music Making.* D.Phil, York.

Stockhausen, Karlheinz (1961) 'Erfindung und Entdeckung' (Invention and Discovery). In Dieter Schnebel (ed.) *Texte zur elektonischen un instrumentalen Musik* (Texts on electronic and instrumental music) 1, 222–258. Köln: DuMont Dokumente.

Stoykov, Nikolay (1989) *Shtoorche Svirche – pieces for children's choir.* Sofia: Moozika.

Swanwick, K & Tilman, J. (1986) 'The sequence of music development'. *BJME* 3 (3), 305–309. Cambridge University Press.

Swanwick, Keith (1988) *Music Mind and Education.* London: Routledge.

Szönyi, Erszébet (1961) 'Sol Fa Teaching in Musical Education' in Sándor, Frigyes (ed.) (1966), *Musical Education in Hungary*, 25–88. London: Barry & Rockcliffe.

Terry, Roy (1985) 'Music Education in France'. *BJME* 3, 227–253.

Tippett, Michael (1941) *A Child of Our Time.* London: Schott.

—— (1980) *Music of the Angels.* London: Faber & Faber.

—— (1974) *Moving into Aquarius.* St. Albans: Granada Publishing.

Wolff, Christian (1968) *Prose Collection.* New York: Peters Edition.

Wiegold, Peter (1997) *'Rainbow over Bath' project proposal.* Bristol: Rainbow Foundation.

Winterson, Julia (1994) 'An Evaluation of the Effects of London Sinfonietta Education Projects on their Participants' *BJME* 11; 129–141.

—— (1998) *The community education work of orchestras and opera companies – principles, practice and problems.* D.Phil: University of York.

Wishart, Trevor (1975 & 1977) *Sounds Fun & Sounds Fun 2.* London: Universal.

Withers, Mark (2000) 'Composers – Are they worth it?' *The Workbook volume 2*, 12–13 London: Association of British Orchestras.

Discography

Barber, Llorenç (1998) *Glockenkonzert*. Münster, 05245.

Composers Ensemble (2000) *Composing in Education*. Rainbow over Bath.

Estonia, Combined choirs (1994) 'Mu Isamma On Minu Arm', track 2 from *Singing Revolution, Estonia – 125 years struggling for freedom*. Erdenklang 40762.

Mnaiset, Finnish women's voices (1999) 'Kuulin Äänen', track 1 from *Folk Voices – Finnish Folk Song Through the Ages*. Ondine 093429.

100 Kava bagpipes (1996) 'Bagpipe melodies', track 1 from *The Magic of Rhodopa Mountain*. Balkanton 86450.

Krasa, Hans (2000) *Brundibar – Opera Kit*. CD & CD-ROM, Brussels, JMI.

Vai Doudoulei & White, Green and Red (1998) 'Samba in 7/8', track 3 from *Folk & Jazz*. MK 3298.

Recorded musical extracts on the Rainbow Foundation website: www.rainbowtrack.co.uk

Chapter 1

Track 01 – 02'05"   51
   Extract from round with audience, David Bedford, *Timepiece*.
   Harlow Choral Society. Conductor: Sarah Tennant Flowers; 17 March 2001.

Track 02 – 01'49"   56
   Extract from Jolyon Laycock *Bladud*.
   Bathampton Primary School, 1985.

Chapter 2

Track 03 – 02'31"   93
   Extracts from improvisation led by Peter Wiegold.
   Hogeschool Alkmaar Conservatorium; December 1999.

Chapter 9

List of examples

List of photographs

Chapter 2

Chapter 5

Chapter 6

Chapter 9

Chapter 13

Index

433